Contemporary Perspectives on Religions in
Africa and the African Diaspora

Contemporary Perspectives on Religions in Africa and the African Diaspora

Edited by
*Ibigbolade S. Aderibigbe and
Carolyn M. Jones Medine*

First published 2015 by
PALGRAVE MACMILLAN

The authors have asserted their rights to be identified as the authors of this work in accordance with the Copyright, Designs and Patents Act 1988.

Palgrave Macmillan in the UK is an imprint of Macmillan Publishers Limited, registered in England, company number 785998, of Houndmills, Basingstoke, Hampshire, RG21 6XS.

Palgrave Macmillan in the US is a division of Nature America, Inc., One New York Plaza, Suite 4500, New York, NY 10004-1562.

Palgrave Macmillan is the global academic imprint of the above companies and has companies and representatives throughout the world.

Hardback ISBN: 978–1–137–50051–9
E-PUB ISBN: 978–1–137–49809–0
E-PDF ISBN: 978–1–137–49805–2
DOI: 10.1057/9781137498052

Distribution in the UK, Europe and the rest of the world is by Palgrave Macmillan®, a division of Macmillan Publishers Limited, registered in England, company number 785998, of Houndmills, Basingstoke, Hampshire RG21 6XS.

Library of Congress Cataloging-in-Publication Data

Contemporary perspectives on religions in Africa and the African diaspora / edited by Ibigbolade S. Aderibigbe and Carolyn M. Jones Medine.
    pages cm
Includes bibliographical references and index.
ISBN 978–1–137–50051–9
    1. Religions—African influences. 2. Christianity—Africa. 3. Islam—Africa. 4. Africa—Religion. I. Aderibigbe, Gbola, editor. II. Medine, Carolyn M. Jones.

BL2400.C66 2015
200.96—dc23   2015013095

A catalogue record of the book is available from the British Library.

Ibigbolade S. Aderibigbe:
To
My late parents,
Omoparusi and Folashade Aderibigbe;
My wife,
Moradeke Abimbola;
My children,
Moronkeji,
Oluwaninyo,
and Ifedolapo;
My students, past, present, and future;
And
All from whom I obtained knowledge,
to make it available to others.

Carolyn M. Jones Medine:
To my husband, Scott Medine, who is my ongoing support,
cheerleader, and partner in all I do

Contents

Tables

Introduction

Contemporary Perspectives on African and African Diaspora Religions

Carolyn M. Jones Medine and
Ibigbolade Aderibigbe

The scholarly study of African traditional and African diaspora religious traditions has generated immense interest within and outside the African continent, involving questions about the nature and scope of African and African-derived religions, as well as their relevance in a global world. In the past, African religion, as an academic discipline, often was apologetic in nature, and scholars who were interested in this field had to grapple with the problem of inadequate literature for study. They, therefore, relied on oral sources with all their attendant limitations.

With all these limitations, the pivotal efforts of early scholars—such as Bolaji Idowu, John Mbiti, Omosafe Awolalu, Geoffrey Parrinder, Asare Opoku, and Ade Dopamu, among others—have provided a platform on which modern scholarship on African religion has grown. The foundation these scholars laid opened the study of African religion to examine contemporary developments and global issues, like ecological devastation. Yet there is an ongoing need to resituate and to reexamine scholarly engagements in Africa indigenous religion.

These religious forms predate, adapt to, and survive colonial occupation and, therefore, issues of contact and competitive interactions with other world religions, both on the African continent and in the diaspora, must be accounted for, within the contexts of sociological, pedagogical, environmental, political, and existential dynamics of the evolving global religious space of the twenty-first century and beyond. The discussion includes the importance and significance of sustained discourse on the elements of the beliefs and practices of the variety of religious forms by Africans both on the continent and in the diaspora. A meaningful discourse must be aware of the existing realities of global competition for relevance, influence, and adherents—the reality that African indigenous religion shares the African continental space with other religious traditions, such as Christianity, Islam, and, in recent years, Asian-derived religions.

The religious landscape of Africa hosts all these forms in their "pure" and hybrid forms, in competitive coexistence. The ugly history of slavery also has an impact on African religions as African indigenous religious beliefs and cultures crossed the oceans, particularly to the Americas. These African-derived religions survive in various forms. Further, contemporary forms of migration have witnessed not only movement of peoples but also religions, once again, across the oceans and landscapes. Not only indigenous religions but African forms of Christianity and Islam have entered North America and become a significant part of the continent's religious space.

This book, *Contemporary Perspectives on Religions in Africa and the African Diaspora*, seeks to address some of the issues we have highlighted, examining, first, the nature of religious traditions in Africa, along with other major religious traditions on the continent; second, African-derived religions and how they shape the life of Africans outside the continent; and third, reflects on the discourse of transplantation, migration, religions, and religious identities in the United States of America across time.

We seek, though not exhaustively, of course, to identify and examine African and African diaspora religions and the impact they have in and on the diverse terrains in which they are found.

Our source and objective for this volume is our many years of research and teaching both in Africa and in the United States. The challenge of finding sources for students, and for ourselves as teachers and scholars, is a great one. This work, we hope, will make a contribution to research *and teaching*.

Chapters

In chapter 1, Ibigbolade S. Aderibigbe offers an overview of the religious traditions in Africa, arguing that African traditional religion, Christianity, and Islam are the religious heritage of the African continent and that this heritage has a deep influence on identity and community on the continent. The practice of African traditional religion can be traced to the emergence of the African peoples and their cultures, while Christianity and Islam made contact with Africa in the Common Era. Aderibigbe examines the influence of the three traditions on multiple dimensions of African life—the social, economic, and political—on a whole continent in its diversity.

In chapter 2, Rotimi Williams Omotoye examines modern efforts by scholars in the study and teaching of African religion in Africa and other parts of the world, focusing on the notion of decolonization: that is, the analysis of materials and texts from the perspective of African worldview and culture. Omotoye argues that this positionality of the scholar can address and begin to correct Eurocentric misconceptions about African religion.

In chapter 3, Francis Adewale Olajide addresses the task of mapping the philosophical relevance of African religions. Focusing on the persistence of religion in the face of secularity, Olajide turns to a philosophical examination of African religions, taking into account the potential violence of religion in a global world.

Oguntola Oye-Laguda, in chapter 4, argues that the "transparency"—in liturgy, doctrine, and social formation—of Islam and Christianity has made them potentially dominant religions on the African continent. He addresses the characterization of African religions as primitive, retrogressive, and "satanic," taking into account secrecy, as well as lack of written creed and scriptures. He suggests that, for any religious tradition to thrive on the continent, it must, at least, address and, at most, acclimate to the characteristics and features of the dominant practices.

Kevin Onogha, in chapter 5, examines the challenges for health care delivery on the African continent. These, he argues, are increasing rather than declining. Studies reveal that Africa alone carries about a quarter of the global disease burden, although it shares barely 1.3 percent of the world's health care workers. To deal with issues of health in Africa, he contends, one must take into serious account religion, the supernatural, and mystical causation, as well as traditional practices (magic, mana, and method), and a holistic worldview, that includes right relationship with the living and the dead.

In chapter 6, Rotimi Williams Omotoye examines discussions of the environment and the place of religion, as a phenomenon, in these discussions. His chapter, therefore, examines the dynamics of the African indigenous religion and Christianity within the context of ethical paradigms and the environment. Omotoye moves beyond environment to examine the issue of landscape, particularly of the religious significance of mountains in Yoruba religion.

Pius Oyeniran Abioje, in chapter 7, recognizes the impact that Christianity has had in Africa. After providing a brief history of the religion on the continent, he examines its position in the plurality of the African religious landscape and the quality of its influence, seeking to elucidate the factors that promote both the growth and the decline of Christianity in Africa. He finds that Christianity, though a majority religion, is not spread evenly throughout the continent and is not always dominant; therefore, it faces challenges in its current dominance of African spaces.

R. Ibrahim Adebayo examines, in chapter 8, the other powerful religion in Africa, Islam. Recognizing that Islam was in Africa before other continents, he explores its warm reception on the continent and its impact on literacy, governance, and healing, for example. The chapter examines cooperation and tensions between African traditional religions and Islam, as well as the positive impact of Islam on the continent. This chapter explores the use and abuse of the religion in Africa in recent times, offering suggestions to restore the glory of the religion in Africa and on other continents.

In chapter 9, M. I. Oguntoyinbo-Atere begins the discussion of diasporic African-derived religions, exported to the Americas by enslaved Africans. Oguntoyinbo-Atere seeks to examine these religions as they were, as they have survived, and as they have provided a spirituality and structure for the Africans in slavery and beyond. The influence of Christianity on African religions is a key element of this chapter.

Adeoluwa Okunade provides, in chapter 10, a general overview of music and religion in Africa as well as how these come together in African diaspora religions, particularly in Cuba and Brazil. Okunade's fieldwork in Salvador-Bahai is featured in this chapter, demonstrating to the reader the presence and importance of oral transmission and performance of African-derived religions that has created a lasting legacy of African religions in the New World.

In chapter 11, Carolyn Medine examines the contributions of and complicated place of women in the African diaspora, examining the issue of voice. After examining black women on the slave ship, this chapter concentrates on two figures, Patsey in *Twelve Years a Slave*, both slave narrative and film, and Sojourner Truth, to examine the complicated transmission of black women's experience in the diaspora, particularly in the multivocal slave narrative and "Ar'n't I a Woman?" speech of Sojourner Truth.

Melanie L. Harris turns to more contemporary women in chapter 12. Harris argues that the aim of womanist religious thought is to uncover the voices, wisdom, and critical theological reflection that emerge from the lives, moral values, and experiences of women of African descent. She turns to a powerful womanist voice—indeed, to the person who coined the term: Alice Walker. Harris explores Walker's fluid spirituality, through her essays, as a foundation for an ecojustice perspective. Harris shows us that studying Walker's nonfiction work summons us to add earth-justice to womanist religious ethical analysis.

In chapter 13, Umesh Patel turns to a theme in Medine's chapter: how the slave ship "made" slaves, but how, ironically, religious resistance began on the ships and continued, particularly in the Caribbean. Patel examines the use of masking and processes of adapation through which African-derived religions survived the Middle Passage, maintaining the essence, if not the particular form, of home away from home.

Osei A. Mensah in chapter 14, reviews some of the religious practices of devotees of Santería and Vodun in the Americas. Mensah argues that rituals and sacrifices that take place in the New World may vary, but he examines pervasive patterns of New World religions, focusing on myth, ritual, sacrifice, and methods of communication with the *orisha*. Mensah also examines how African-derived practices have influenced other migrant practices. The relationship of the individual to the spirit world is the connection, Mensah argues, between the old world and the new.

Robert Y. Owusu continues the discussion of Santería in chapter 15, in which he looks at the origin, beliefs, and rituals of Santería religion, its transmission into the United States, and contemporary forms of the religion, particularly as they have affected issues of class. Owusu argues that Santería is not syncretic but creolized, and he returns to an argument made by Oguntola Oye-Laguda, in chapter 4, that African-derived religions were viewed as evil because they involve divination, incantation, spirit possession or trance, sacrifice, and a focus on the here and now rather than a future spiritual home.

In chapter 16, Danielle N. Boaz turns to legal issues in modern practice of African diaspora religions. She focuses on ritual sacrifice, issues of health, and reception of African-derived religions as reasons that African diaspora religions have had legal difficulties in the West, particularly in the British Caribbean, South Africa, and the United States. Boaz traces legal objections from the seventeenth to the mid-twentieth century, highlighting the colonial legislative remnants in the criminalization of religion and the stereotypes, sensationalism, and misunderstanding of African derived religions.

In chapter 17, Maha Marouan analyzes the challenge of audience in teaching and speaking about African and African diaspora religions. Continuing Boaz's recognition of the negative stereotypes of such religions, Marouan recognizes that there is no neutral place from which to begin a discussion of these religions, particularly in the American South where she taught and wrote. Undoing perceptions of "the primitive" and the idea that Africa has no power on the world stage are issues that Marouan addresses. She also examines the academy's implicatedness in the negative constructions of Africa in "world religion" textbooks despite the fact that African religions are part of the remapping of the modern world.

Ibigbolade Aderibigbe's voice returns in chapter 18, in which he examines the transnational dimensions of religious identities and institutions in relation to the recent African immigrants in the United States. He describes, particularly, African-initiated Christian churches in Europe and the United States of America. The dynamics of the practices of these churches, he suggests, both conform to and differ from the identities and values of the "home" churches in Africa. Like Umesh Patel in chapter 13, he invokes the structure of home, arguing that these churches function as "homes away from home" for African immigrants in the search for integration and self-identity in a new and sometimes hostile environment.

In chapter 19, Yushua Sodiq looks at Islamic communities in the United States, thinking about issues of religion and political identity. Sodiq examines the quest for a relevant Muslim identity in the American experience. Immigrants, she contends, have brought a sense of self that undergoes constant revision and redefinition in the context of the American melting (boiling?) pot. This identity is influenced by what the immigrants bring with them as well as by their American experience, including American foreign policy in various Muslim countries. Many factors influence the reception of Muslims in America, but 9/11 has, Sodiq argues, deeply influenced how they have been received, creating what Muslims feel is a hostile American environment in which they are being held accountable for the activities of others overseas.

This volume consciously interrogates the experiences of a variety of African and African diaspora religious practices. It attempts to supply clear information about these traditions and to analyze them in multiple ways. Our contention is that multi- and interdisciplinary approaches are necessary for grappling with the complexity and plurality of African religion and African diaspora religions, neither of which is one unified belief or practice.

Chapter 1

Religious Traditions in Africa: An Overview of Origins, Basic Beliefs, and Practices

Ibigbolade S. Aderibigbe

Introduction

Africa is a massive continent with diverse religious traditions, to the extent that within the same tradition there have been variations. The three main religious traditions—African traditional religion, Christianity, and Islam—constitute the triple religious heritage of the African continent. This heritage, though contemporarily more dynamically evidenced, has a long history and influence. In the case of African traditional religion, it can be traced back to the very beginning of the emergence of African peoples. For Christianity, it is the first century AD, and maybe beyond; and for Islam the seventh century. The central place of religion that has become so evident in any meaningful understanding of African life in all its ramifications—social, economic, and political—gives credence to Mbiti's statement that African people are "notoriously religious."[1] Consequently, Africans have evolved and sustained religiously conscious communities, either as devotees of the traditional religion, or as followers of the two "converting religions"—Christianity and Islam.

It would be an impossible task to cover in this chapter the totality of all religious traditions in Africa. Consequently, the effort here can only be an exploration of the three principal religious traditions on the continent, namely: African indigenous religious beliefs and practices, which African scholarship has "christened" African traditional religion(s),[2] Christianity, and Islam. The focus, therefore, is on the African experience(s) of the religious traditions within the contexts of their origins, beliefs, doctrines, and practices as worldviews permeating and influencing various aspects of the African people's life.

In exploring the worldviews of the three religions in Africa, it is imperative to indicate certain initial operating parameters that may affect the discourse. First, African traditional religion has no sacred scriptures or clearly defined documents. Indeed, serious studies in the religion have only recently developed.[3] Even then, the studies have been largely carried out by sociologists, anthropologists, and theologians, who are "outsiders" to the religion as either "non-Africans" or Africans who are Christians, and most times have very limited knowledge of the experiences of the actual devotees of the religion. Consequently, the "authentic" source of information about the religion is embedded in oral traditions found in myths, rituals, folktales, proverbs, etcetera, and nonoral sources, such as archaeological findings, African arts of paintings, sculptures, music, and dance.

The studies of the Christian and Islamic traditions pose no difficulties with regard to sources of information. Both religions have sacred books. In addition, the founders, geographical origins, and organizational structures are well articulated and remain largely the same for the adherents, regardless of the different interpretations. However, both Christianity and Islam are regarded as "foreign" to the African continent and it peoples. For example, Christianity's advent into Africa in the first century, majorly in North Africa, was cut short by the advent of Islam in the seventh century. Its attempts in sub-Saharan religion only became successful with the involvement of the missionaries under the protection and impetus of the colonialists in the eighteenth and nineteenth centuries. Though Islam gained the control of North Africa from the seventh century, it, however, had very little impact, if any, in the sub-Saharan regions until the later part of the eighteenth century and more effectively in the eighteenth and nineteenth centuries, similar to its Christian counterpart.

However, these limitations found in varying degrees in the three principal African religious traditions until the seventeenth century, did not necessarily diminish the growing impacts of the three religions in shaping the spiritual thoughts, beliefs, and practices of Africans, and eventually blossoming and becoming the predominant religions on the continent. This is true particularly with regard to Christianity and Islam. We begin our exploration with the African traditional religion drawing substantially from the sub-Saharan Africa.

African Traditional Religion

African traditional religion(s) has no sacred books or definitive experience in creed upon which to base any organized or systematic analysis; yet, there are unique basic characteristics that clearly designate the religion as a universal religious phenomenon all over Africa. A unique characteristic of the religion is its embellishment in the heritage of the African people. This heritage, of which African religion is not just a part, is a very symbolic manifestation and is ultimately concretized in a religious belief system discernible through common components. The African heritage is rich culturally and has been sustained through a long lineage of.[4] However, many of its elements have been lost; others have undergone changes due to the dynamics of other internal modifications and expansions at contacts with influences from outside cultures. The basic or fundamental beliefs and practices have remained intact. One other important element of African heritage is its diversity—characterized by both similarities and local differences. This makes it a unique agency of a people's "world outlook" steeped in unity and diversity. Thus, the popular dictum, "Africans are in all things religious."[5] The religion actually designates the traditional worldview of Africans, manifesting both the philosophical and practical experiences developed, sustained, and passed on from one generation to the next.

The sustainability of the character and the existence of the African society are located in the traditional component of the nomenclature of the religion. This has been demonstrated in the dynamic evolution of "ancient" thoughts and practices, adapting to succeeding situations borne out of personal and communal experiences of the people, linking forefathers to their descendants. Even though these thoughts and experiences Africans were "born into" have witnessed changes, the essential distinctive elements that make African traditional religion a "living" religion have remained not only unchanged but also universally influential to Africans. These elements are laid out in the salient features of African religions located in an inclusive dynamic of beliefs and practices. These can be compressed under three headings: belief structure, functional components, and religious officials and sacred places.

Belief Structure

The belief structure of African traditional religion(s) has been presented in diverse forms by different scholars of religion. For example, P.A. Talbot propagated a four-element structure consisting of polytheism, anthropomorphism, animism, and ancestral worship.[6] For E. G. Parrinder, the structural elements are made up of Supreme Being, chief divinities, cult of divinized ancestors, and charms and amulets.[7] However, the most acceptable belief structure of the religion has been the five hierarchical structure advocated by Bolaji Idowu. These are made up of the Supreme Being, divinities, spirits, ancestors, and magic and medicine.[8]

(i) Supreme Being

The belief in the Supreme Being constitutes not just a universal belief among all Africans, but also represents the center and apex of the African religious belief system. Three forms of the dynamics of this belief have been identified among different peoples of Africa. First, there is belief without practical demonstration, such as having a cult of the Supreme Being represented by religious officials and designated locations of worship. The Yoruba people of Nigeria are a model of this kind of belief. Second, there is belief with partial worship. Here, some members of an African tribe may believe without outwardly practicing the religion while another segment of the tribe operates as a cult of worshipers of the Supreme Being. An example of such a tribe is the Ewe of Togo, where it is only in the Abomey community of the tribe that there are altars and religious officials dedicated to the Supreme Being, Plawu. The third form of belief is belief with practice. The Ashanti of Ghana are a model of this form of practice. According to P. S. Rattray, "It is hardly an exaggeration holding that every compound in Ashanti has an altar for Nyame called Nyame dua (God's tree)."[9]

Whatever the form of the religion and the demonstration of the belief, there is no doubt that against the claim of some scholars, long before the introduction of Christianity and Islam, Africans not only knew and acknowledged the existence of a supreme being, but their religious worldview was built around his being the source of all beings. Through his creative activities, humanity was believed to be inseparably bound together with all other creatures, indebted to this source of all life.[10] This perception is vividly demonstrated in various ways by African religious thoughts and practices. In most cases, the perception is captured in the names and attributes given to the Supreme Being by different African peoples. For example, in West Africa, the Yoruba people of Nigeria have many names for the Supreme Being. The most distinctive ones of these are Olorun, which means "owner of the heavens," and the ritual one Olodumare. Which means "one who owns power and authority."[11] In terms of attributes, the Yoruba describe the Supreme Being as Eleda, meaning the creator; "Oba Mimo" the Holy king; "Oba awon oba," King of kings. In addition, he is the Supreme Being, who is assisted by lesser deities called orisas. These serve as his assistants to look after his creation.[12]

In East Africa, the Akola people of Uganda call the Supreme Being "Bagyendanwa," which means "the source of all things."[13] In Southern Africa, the people of Zimbabwe call the Supreme Being "Musikawanhu," creator of humankind. This affirms that the Supreme Being is the originator of all there is.[14] Ultimately, the African belief in the Supreme Being must be understood within the context of variations, in emphasizing the local sociological complexions. Thus, while some African groups portray an anthropomorphic image of the Supreme Being, for some it is in masculine terms, some others have adopted the feminine terms; yet for others, there is no specific image.[15]

(ii) Divinities

The belief in divinities stands next in rank to the Supreme Being. Indeed, the influence and sometimes inappropriate devotion to the divinities in African traditional religion have triggered the notion that the religion is polytheistic. However, the authentic African belief about divinities totally falsifies this claim. Africans regard divinities as assistants to the Supreme Being. They are what could be regarded as "ministers" in the "theocratic government" of the Supreme Being. All over Africa, there are three identified categories of divinities. There are the primordial ones, believed to have been with the Supreme Being since the creation of the universe, and to have actually participated in the creative task. For example, the Yoruba people believe that Orisanla has been given the duty of making human bodies before Olodumare puts souls into them.[16]

There is also the category of deified divinities; these are human beings, who after their death were raised to the level of gods. A divinity that belongs to this category in Yoruba belief is Sango, the god of thunder. The third category is made up of divinities associated with natural objects such as rivers, mountains, rocks, forests, and so on.[17] The nature, number, and formation of the divinities vary from one locality to the other, and they may be either male or female. They also attract different appellations depending on the local language. For example, the Akan of Ghana call them "Bosom" whereas the Yoruba call them "Orisas." The name for the divinities among the Ewe of Togo is "Tovo" or "Trowo," whereas the Fon of Sierra Leone refer to them as "Vodu Nudu."[18]

However, these diverse tendencies in no way diminish the African common and central belief in the nature, importance, and functions of the divinities. By nature, they are not to be compared in rank to the Supreme Being. They are his subordinates, actually created at his pleasure to assist him in specific areas of responsibility. Ultimately, the divinities are regarded as intermediaries between the Supreme Being and humanity. They constitute the channels through which the Africans believe they can successfully approach the Supreme Being.

(iii) Spirits

The Africans are also conscious of the existence of nonhuman beings, which are also divinities by nature, description, and functions. These are known as spirits. The spirits usually make natural phenomenon their abodes. However, they are distinct from the material objects and are not affected by whatever happens to the objects. By nature, the spirits are immaterial beings, though some of them may possess abstract powers through which they may take both human and nonhuman forms, and assume various dimensions at will.[19] Two types of spirits are identified: nature spirits and human spirits. Nature spirits habituate trees, rivers, mountains, and other natural objects. For example, human spirits among the Yoruba are called "Iwin" or "Irunmole." They could be either benevolent or malevolent.

The malevolent types are associated with the *Abiku* (born to die) syndrome in Yoruba land. The *Abiku* spirits are accredited with the power of removing the fetus inside a pregnant woman and replacing it with one of themselves. This is why pregnant women in traditional Yoruba societies are not allowed to walk about at noontime and midnight. These are considered the periods when the *Abiku* spirits wander about looking for prey. It is also interesting to note that long-dead ancestors ultimately become spirits, roaming the spirit world, and awaiting the chance of reincarnation through family or tribal descendants. These are generally regarded as benevolent and are actually courted to be born again into the family or community.

(iv) Ancestors

The African belief in ancestors symbolizes and actually gives meaning to the immortality of humans, or life after death. It is a belief that underlines the definition of the African community of comprising both the living and the dead. It also justifies not only the practice of many African tribes burying their dead at home (to be assured of their continuous presence) but also the elaborate funeral ceremonies that are conducted as full burial rites. The full burial rites ensure that the dead are properly sent off, and received in the ancestral community in the other world. It also provides the guarantee for the ancestor to be well disposed to those still alive, and therefore look after their well-being. An inferior burial may incur the anger of the dead ancestor, and may ensure dire consequences for the living. The calamities resulting from such a situation can only be mitigated after due consultation with traditional diviners and once a proper and satisfactory burial ceremony is re-conducted.

The ancestors are called different names by different peoples of Africa. The Igbo and Yoruba of Nigeria call them "Ndichie" and "Baba-nla," respectively. The Ashanti calls them "Samanto," while the Ewe calls them "Neshuwe." Ancestors are called "Vadzium" among the Shona of Zimbabwe. The Zulu address them as "Amadhozi," while among the Zezuru they are called "Kurova Guva." The high level of significance enjoyed by the ancestral cult among Africans has led to the erroneous conception that Africans worship their ancestors. This is far from the truth. Ancestors are never objects of worship for Africans. Rather, they perform the functions of guardian spirits and consultants. Their roles are principally to be intermediaries between the living and the spiritual world. Within this context, the ancestors are venerated as a demonstration of respect for elders and forefathers. Because the ancestors exist in the spiritual world, they are regarded as more knowledgeable and not subject to the limitations of time and space. They consequently become protectors of the family. They also symbolize ideal communal existence, acting as agents of social control and communal discipline.

It should be stressed, however, that not all people who die will automatically attain the status of an ancestor. Certain qualifications must be met. These generally include, but are not limited to, dying in ripe old age, dying a good death (not death from suicide and illness such as smallpox, and others considered as moral-sanction induced). In addition, the full burial ceremonies must have been conducted. The individual must have been adjudged morally upright while alive so that he could serve as a character model for the individual, family, or community.

The ancestors are venerated in different forms and at different levels across Africa. They may be venerated by pouring of libation, offerings of food, and through elaborate ceremonies. The veneration may also be performed by individuals, family, or, as happens occasionally, on behalf of a community by religious officials. For example, among the Yoruba, the communal veneration of ancestors is annually observed in different localities in the Egungun (masquerade) festivals. The festivals are a time for visitation of the ancestors called "Ara orun" (visitors from the spiritual world). They masquerade as ancestral spirits visiting the living to bring blessings of prosperity, health, and other social benefits for the continued well-being, order, and peace within their social structure. In some, the central belief of Africans is that life would be of no value without the presence and power of the ancestors.

(v) Magic and Medicine

The belief in magic and medicine has been sometimes elevated to disproportionate status in African traditional religion. This has largely been due to the visibility of daily practical engagement in their practices by Africans. Most times, the two practices have been taken to be synonymous. For example, the Yoruba call the two phenomena "Oogun," thereby suggesting that they are one and the same. However, this is not the case in either belief or practice, though they may sometimes overlap as the agencies addressing human life situations. The distinctive natures and functionalities of magic and medicine are vividly brought out in the definitions that indicate different subject matter, attitude, and approach.[20]

For instance, magic may be defined as:

> The act of using the available resources of nature to produce therapeutic needs of man. It is the art of influencing course of events by means of supernatural control of nature and invocation of particular spirit assistance.[21]

Medicine, however, can be generally defined as:

> The traditional art and science of the prevention, and cure of diseases. It is the use of natural substances to prevent, treat, and cure diseases. It can also mean medicament used internally or externally.[22]

Magic in African belief can be used to protect or to harm. However, it is widely ascribed to the employment of spiritual powers for evil to harm. Even when it is used for protection, it is generally for the purpose of fighting evil forces. The most widely acknowledged evil forces in Africa are witches (female) and sorcerers (male). These are regarded as wicked human beings who employ their magical powers through witchcraft to intentionally kill people. It is believed that the magical powers of the witches equip them with the ability to fly at night, attend motional meetings, become invisible, and metaphysically consume human flesh and blood even when the victim is still physically alive.

Medicine in African belief is inextricably intertwined with religion. It can also be approached in two forms. The first is the simple notion of medicine. This is the healing system employed to treat minor illnesses, such as headaches, stomachache, and other forms of illnesses, curable through easily available herbs. These can be administered by anybody within the social structure. The second form is complex medicine, which deals with serious illnesses. The illnesses are treated using both physical and metaphysical components. The administration of the "medical process" here is reserved for the professionals as custodians of the traditional healing system. The intertwined relationship between religion and medicine in African belief comes from the notion that illnesses are never seen as just psychological but also spiritual. Thus, the diagnosis, prescription, and treatment must be physical and, more important, metaphysical. Thus, in Yoruba land, for example, the professional medicine man sees his profession in the realm of religion. He performs rituals, invokes spirits, and offers sacrifices for the efficacy and potency of his medicine.[23] The divinity he has to placate to ensure these outcomes is Osanyin. The diagnosing process for the Yoruba medicine man is Ifa divination, through which the cause of the illness is established. The prescription and treatment are shared between performances of necessary sacrifices followed by physical medication.

Functional Components

The devotees of African traditional religion usually express their religious beliefs in practical terms through dynamics, which are sometimes individualistic, but mostly communal. The expressions are significantly found in prayers, sacrifices, offerings, and rituals. The media of these are the family or communal festivals and ceremonies celebrated in honor of divinities, harvest periods, and significant landmarks such as birth, marriage, burial rites, and so on. The festivals and ceremonies that are agencies of these activities are manifested in rituals made up of cosmic liturgy and religious language. These manifestations are vividly expressed in music, drumming, dancing, and various forms of arts in drums dressing and other paraphernalia of liturgical celebrations. Both music and art have always had a significant and sustained cultural impact on African traditional religion. These have tremendously represented concrete means of relaying abstract themes of African religious worship. Sounds produced from songs and drumming are regarded as vehicles for articulating abstract ideas in concrete forms. This becomes very relevant in the African dependence on oral and nonoral traditions in the absence of written documents.[24]

For the African, music and religion are seen as a singular enterprise. African religious music is often rendered in a "call and response" format. This is more vividly demonstrated in the rituals of spirit possession, where singing, drumming, and dancing become a trancelike performance, invoking the direct correspondence between the divinities and the people symbolized in the possessed as the messengers of the divinities. Music for Africans and the traditional religions not only gives "live" expression to the beliefs of the people, but more importantly serves as a means of prayer, the language of communication with the divine entities, the divinities, and ultimately through them indirectly to the Supreme Being.

Art—just as music, drumming, and dancing—has always empowered African people in fulfilling various aspects of their religious obligations. For example, according to Robert Thomson, the Yoruba people regard art as avatars of "ashe" (divine energy), in ceremonial bowls, stilts, and iron sculptures. These materials are no longer regarded as ordinary works of art, but have been transferred to being sacred, by the conferment of "ashe," the divine force.[25] The undertone of the importance of arts to African religion is discernible in inscriptions found on materials used for religious ceremonies such as drums, headdresses, garments, and paraphernalia of different divinities and their devotees. Most important, African art in different forms, has given credence to the religious content of African historical heritage. Thus, temples or shrines of divinities, images of kings, and royal persons, as well as infrastructures of palaces have largely been represented in religious artifacts. Indeed, historians, anthropologists, and archaeologists have relied heavily on these to obtain a meaningful and "factual" depiction of the African people's diverse ways of life.

Religious Officials and Sacred Places

Religious officials are central to the practice of African traditional religion. This is because as religious leaders, they constitute the custodians of religious knowledge and practices. Within these contexts, the officials conduct religious rituals, and act as intermediaries between the devotees and the spiritual sphere of the divinities and Supreme Being. The religious officials can be either male or female, but they are of different kinds. There are those who are cultic officials. These are priests and priestesses who preside over activities at the shrines of the divinities. The Akan and Yoruba peoples have a sizable number of these officials. They are officially responsible for offering sacrifices, and petitioning divinities on behalf of the devotees.

Another category of religious officials is that of diviners. They are also usually of both genders. The main function of diviners is to communicate with the spirit world. This is very important to Africans because it is through such communication that they are in communion with the ancestors, divinities, and ultimately with the Supreme Being. The subject matter of the communication may be for the purpose of determining the cause of problems such as misfortunes, sicknesses, diseases, death, and other forms of calamities, as well as seeking solutions. At other times, it may be for guidance as to the course of action to be undertaken concerning, for example, the future of a newborn baby, a marriage, the building of a house, or the embarking on a journey or trade.

There are different methods of divination in different parts of Africa. Some of these include the case of wooden dice, sea shells, pieces of ivory, palm nuts, and a bowl of water. The most famous method among the Yoruba is Ifa divination, which adopts a very elaborate system of palm nuts usage. The Yoruba Ifa diviners are usually priests and priestesses of Orunmila, the Yoruba divinity of knowledge and wisdom.

One other category of traditional religious officials, and perhaps considered to be the most powerful, are the spirit mediums. These are people through whom the spirits of ancestors communicate with their descendants. Most spirit mediums are females, and they may be associated with family, tribe, or territory. Through them, Africans, at the individual, family, or communal level, discern the will of the ancestors and obtain explanations for all situations affecting them, either for good or evil. The mediums also provide solutions to problems and steps to be taken to preserve good fortunes.

Due to their office and traditional functions they perform, kings are also regarded as religious leaders. For example, the kings as community heads are responsible for the consultation of community spirits. They are also responsible for ensuring that all religious functions and observances, such as festivals, are carried out by various religious officers. Indeed for the Yoruba, the king called "Oba" is referred to as "Alase ekeji orisa"—second in command to the deity—from whom he derives his authority. Consequently, his authority is not just political but divine in source and sustenance. The Oba is therefore regarded as not only the number one religious official, but he also must partake in devotions to all divinities of his community.

Sacred places are central and vital to the practical expression and functions of religious leaders in African traditional religion. Perhaps the most prominent of these are the shrines, where the divinities may be located in family compounds or places communally dedicated to the divinities. The Ashanti of Ghana, for instance, have a familial sacred place for the Supreme Being—Nyame. This is usually in the form of a forked branch cut from a certain tree, called "Nyame dua." The Zulus of South

Africa have elevated portions of a hut called "Umsamu." This is where ancestor-related rituals are conducted. In addition, mountains, rivers, forest groves, and caves are regarded as sacred based on the notion of their being inhabited by spirits, divinities, or even the Supreme Being. These usually serve as venues of prayers, where religious officials visit. For example, in Zimbabwe, there are several such sacred places, which have become venues of prayers, particularly for petitions for rains in times of drought.

Sacred places, particularly the shrines, are very important as sources of information for African religion because they provide traditional nonoral knowledge and understanding of the African people and their religion. Artifacts of various instruments used in worship have provided archaeologists with valuable insights into not only the religious, but also the social, political, and overall cultural history as well as the worldviews of Africans.

In summary, before the advent and influence of Christianity and Islam, and particularly in precolonial Africa, the beliefs and the practices of African indigenous religion were firmly rooted in the cosmological and cosmogenial worldviews in a number of fundamental, philosophical, and theological concepts. These were based on the African people's observation of the world around them, and consequent reflections on its existence and workings. To begin with, Africans believed that the world was created and that it was created by the Supreme Being. Different myths, from different parts of Africa, portrayed diverse methods and processes through which the world came into existence. Though there may not be uniformity on these, there is the universality of looking at the world from the religious perspective and explaining it theoretically.

Africans also believe in the duality of the universe as comprising the visible (the earth) and the invisible (the heavens). However, the two are linked through the religious activities of humans linking the world to the Supreme Being. The origin, distribution, and subsequent reinstatement of this link through close relationships with the Supreme Being are narrated in many creation stories. The stories also indicate that though the universe is created, it has assumed an unending existence in terms of space and time.

Also, central to African cosmological thoughts, is the belief in the order in the universe. This order, which is inclusively morally and religiously based, depicts a mystical order responsible for governing the universe. The attempts to relate and sometimes control this order have resulted in practices such as medicine, magic, witchcraft, and other religious activities discussed earlier. The general belief is that, though the divinities and other spiritual beings may exercise mystical power, the ultimate source of the power is the Supreme Being.

Perhaps the most important cosmological belief of the African peoples is that man is the center of the universe. Indeed, the whole world is seen as existing for his sake.[26] Consequently, the world and all in it must function for the ultimate benefit of man. This may account for ascribing sacredness to even physical and natural objects in the universe. Consequently, man considers it necessary to live in harmony with nature. Though he realizes that he is not the master, but rather the beneficiary end-user, he has the obligation to preserve it and use it wisely. This is the only way that his survival can be guaranteed.[27]

Contemporary Status of African Traditional Religion

Over the centuries, African traditional religion has faced many challenges that have significantly diminished the practice and influence of the religion on the continent. These challenges are found in what could be termed internal and external factors. The internal factors, associated with the location and internal workings of the religion, have acted as barriers to its development in consonance with evolving developmental realities. External challenges arose and are still arising from the continent's contacts with the outside world, principally the Western influence through the slave trade, colonialism, and missionary activities.

The internal challenges are mainly derived from factors such as geographical expansiveness of the continent, which makes uniformity of beliefs and practices in the religion impossible. This obvious diversity has been unfortunately employed to insinuate, or even assert, that Africans have practiced different or tribal religions. Another internal factor militating against the religion is the lack of written documents in the form of a scripture as available in other religious traditions. In depending exclusively on oral sources, its claims have been usually dismissed as products of superstitious and "unintelligible" stipulations. One other internal factor, which is directly linked with lack of written documents, is the secret nature of the religion. Religious officials of different categories in African traditional religion often, for various reasons, keep to themselves vital information and knowledge pertaining to the contents, processes, and methods of the beliefs and practices of the religion. Coupled with a nonwritten tradition, these pieces of information and knowledge die with the officials and are therefore lost to present and future generations.

The external challenges faced by African traditional religion in terms of Africa's contact with the outside world substantially began with the transatlantic slave trade when significant numbers of its adherents were transported across the ocean—many of them never to return, and the few who returned after the trade, converted to other religions. This challenge was compounded by the two-dimensional and competitive evangelical "invasions" of Christianity and Islam. The propagations of the two religions have been so effective that the African continent is today split almost down the line by both religious traditions. Finally, the colonial impact became a major challenge to African traditional religion. In collaboration with the Christian missionaries, Western education and civilization were introduced. The combination of these two phenomena created an "elitist" consciousness in the followers of religions in the continent. Those who practice Christianity and Islam regard themselves as civilized and educated, while those who practice the traditional religion are regarded as largely illiterate and uncivilized.

Having said the above, it should, however, be pointed out that in spite of these challenges, African traditional religion still has a future in global religious space. This position is evidenced by a number of factors that have emerged, and are contemporarily emerging. Principal among these factors are first, the increased attention in studies and scholarships being paid to African traditional religion, not only in Africa but also all over the world. Courses in the religion are being offered in both public and private higher education institutions in all parts of the world. Numerous books have been, and are being written, on the religion. Also, conferences, symposia, and other forms of scholarly meetings deliberate on themes based on the religion.

Second, many African nations are beginning to show significant commitment to the spirit and letter of nationalism in the search for African self-identity. African traditional religion as the centerpiece and sustainer of African culture is being directly or indirectly promoted to meet this objective. Third, even with the almost total conversion of Africans to Christianity and Islam, the traditional practices of the African people continue to be relevant and observed as cultural values in their everyday engagements. Again, African traditional religion is mirrored as a basic component of the values. Fourth, through the process of acculturation, encultura- tion, and so on, African traditional religious values have become part and parcel of the practices of both Christianity and Islam on the African continent to the extent that the practices of these religions in Africa today are not in the original form in which they were introduced into the continent. As a result of the factors enumerated above, African traditional religion has become visible as a competitive religion in African and global religious spaces.

Christian Religious Tradition in Africa

As a religious tradition, it has been generally accepted that Christianity grew out of Judaism. This is evidenced and established by many studies and literatures. Foremost among these is the three-volume study of the Bible by Wilfred J. Harrington. The volume is titled *The Record of Revelation: The Bible; The Record of Promise: The Old Testament; The Record of the Fulfillment: The New Testament.*[28] Within this context, Christianity, right from its inception, has regarded itself as the direct succession of the Old Testament tradition. This claim has been vividly demonstrated in first, the origin of its name and second, the historical and theological configurations of its founder, Jesus Christ.

The word "Christ," from which Christianity is derived, comes from the Greek word "Christos." This is equivalent to the Hebrew word "Mashiah," which, when translated to English, is "Messiah." The etymological meaning of the word in the three languages is "the anointed one." It denotes someone who is given a specific mandate of undertaking a national responsibility. Second, the name Christian was first used in Antioch to describe the followers of Christ through the observation of their behaviors.

Jesus, the founder of Christianity, historically lived in Galilee in Palestine in the early first century BCE. Facts about his birth and mission come almost exclu- sively from the Christian Bible—the New Testament. His birth is claimed to be a miraculous one, since he is believed to have been conceived of the Holy Spirit and born of the Virgin Mary. He is, however, regarded as a descendant of David through lineage with Joseph his foster father to whom his mother, Mary, was betrothed. The mission of Christ, which became the foundation of Christianity, lasted about three years. During this period, Jesus traveled throughout Judea. He chose twelve men, who became his apostles. In their company, he preached about the kingdom of God.

The kingdom was distinguished from an earthly one. Though it was a Messianic kingdom foretold by the prophets, it was a heavenly one, contrary to the expectation of the Jewish people. The central message of Christ was that in this heavenly kingdom—salvation is spiritual rather than physical or political. The members would worship God as heavenly king. The worship would be spiritual in nature. The members would live by the truth and have brotherly love toward one another. Jesus, in words and actions, presented himself as the expected Messiah foretold by the prophets. His principal mission was to save the world and establish the heavenly kingdom. He was credited with many miracles—mighty works—to give credence to his messianic power. Ironically, it was the messianic claim of Jesus—the Son of God—that got him into trouble with the official Jewish establishment and eventually had him delivered to the Roman authorities and executed.

Apart from his disciples and retinues of other followers, Jesus had no organized group as such. In addition, he did not write anything down. However, his preaching and activities became perpetuated in the New Testament consisting of the Gospels, the Acts of the Apostles, and the Epistles. It is instructive that the violent death of Jesus on the cross was initially disappointing to his disciples; however, his resurrection, reappearance, and ascension reassured them of his power and truth of his promises. Finally, the events of the Pentecost—through which the apostles experienced the coming of the Holy Spirit as promised by Christ—not only emboldened them but also and more significantly "officially" constituted the first winning of souls to the movement later to be called the "Christian tradition."

The Christian Tradition

Though the mainstream doctrines of Christianity are located in the Apostles' Creed, the various interpretations they have witnessed have created controversies that have resulted in heresies and eventual schisms.[29] In spite of this situation, which has led to denominations in Christianity, the central doctrines as theological foundations of the Christian faith have remained, with the Christian Bible as the point of reference. Based on the Apostles' Creed and the scriptures, the Christian faith is presented in a number of beliefs and practices. As indicated earlier, the splitting of Christianity into denominations makes a comprehensive or universal Christian worldview very difficult, if at all achievable, and definitely not within the context and space of a single chapter. In spite of the obvious denominational challenges of the Christian faith, there are some basic beliefs and practices universally common to all Christians. These beliefs and practices are stated in the "official Christian" Apostles' Creed. They mainly consist of belief in one God, belief in the Holy Trinity, belief in Jesus, belief in the church as the kingdom of God on Earth, the concept of man, concept of worship, and concept of eschatology.

History and Influence in Africa

As a religious tradition, Christianity became part of Africa from the first century CE. There is no doubt, as noted earlier, that Christianity had to wait until the late

1800s and early 1900s to become fully established as one of the two most practiced religions on the continent. From its introduction in the first century to the
present period, Christianity has undergone different fortunes in African history.
Nevertheless, its presence, importance, and influence have always been felt significantly within African religious space. The presence and influences of Christianity
in Africa historically may be divided into three main segments. The first comprises
the earliest contacts in North Africa. The second spans the precolonial and colonial
periods consisting of Portuguese traders, and later Christian missionaries' efforts
with the support of the colonial governments. The third includes the postcolonial
and contemporary period. Within these contexts, this chapter attempts to explore
the Christian religion from the perspectives of its advent, development in different
regions, the leaders with their expansion methods, their worldviews as represented
by doctrinal peculiarities and artistic influences, as well as the contemporary facets
of the religion.

Christianity in North Africa, Ethiopia—Early Contacts in Africa

In symbolic terms, Christianity may be said to have been in early contact with
Africa in two ways. The first, according to the biblical narrative, was the taking of
the child Jesus to Egypt in order to avoid his being killed by King Herod. The second was the possibility of the infiltration of the message of Jesus into North Africa,
which at the time was part of the Roman Empire, just as was Palestine, where Jesus
carried out his ministry. However, historically as an organized religion, Christianity
came to Egypt in the first century CE. This is believed to have occurred simultaneously as Christianity was making its way into Northern Europe. According
to the church historian Eusebius, the Christian church in Egypt was founded by
Saint Mark, the writer of the fourth Gospel. The location was in Alexandria. From
Alexandria, Christianity spread to other parts of Egypt. Indeed, by the end of the
first century, the religion had penetrated into even the rural parts of Egypt and had
actually become the religion of the majority of the people. As Noel King points out,
the strong presence of Christianity in Egypt in the early history of the church is
indicated in the fact that apart from Rome, it is only Egypt that has one of the oldest
churches and also longevity of tradition and continuity in the same locality.[30] Also,
the city of Alexandria became an outstanding theological center, producing figures
such as Origen, Cyprian, Clement, and others who influenced the church for all
time through their theological writings. The spread and vibrancy of Christianity in
Egypt continued until the seventh century when it was conquered by the Muslims.
Even then, Christianity was still practiced as a minority religion.

Other parts of North Africa that had early contact with the Christian faith are
modern-day countries such as Tunisia, Morocco, and Algeria. They were known
as Roman Africa, during the period of the Roman Empire. The area had a very
strong following of Christians in the early second century. The area produced
influential theologians of early Christendom. These included Tertullian, who first

used the term Trinity to describe and explain the Godhead. There was also Saint Augustine, the Bishop of Hippo, who produced significant theological works. His theological writings were reputed for shaping Western Catholicism, as well as the Protestant Reformation. They also continued to be relevant and central to Christian thoughts of all ages.

Unfortunately, Christianity in this area did not survive the onslaught of the Islamic conquest of the seventh century, and thereafter Christianity became totally extinct in the region. Beginning from the first and through the fourth centuries, Ethiopia, which was south of Egypt and was impacted greatly by the Alexandria church, also witnessed the advent and spread of Christianity. Ethiopia's acceptance of Christianity has been accounted for in two but not necessarily exclusive fashions. The first is legendary and is reported in the Acts of the Apostles. The narrative centered on the conversion through baptism of an unnamed Ethiopian eunuch by Philip, an apostle of Jesus. The eunuch, a high official to the queen of Ethiopia, Candace, after his conversion returned to his home kingdom to propagate Christianity among the Ethiopians. The second, from independent sources and more historic ascribed the Christianization of Ethiopia to the efforts of two Syrian Greek brothers, Frumentius and Aedesius. The two were believed to have been shipwrecked off of the Eritrean coastline. They were spared and aided by the royal court of the Axumite kingdom and thereafter gained tremendous power in the kingdom. They were also so loved by the people of the Axumite kingdom of Ethiopia that Frumentius was called "revealer of light" (Kesate Birhen) and Aedesius "father of peace" (Abbeselema). The two brothers were not only able to convert King Ezna, the ruler of the kingdom, to Christianity but also persuaded him to make Christianity the official religion of the Axumite kingdom. Subsequently, Frumentius was appointed the first official bishop of the Ethiopian church by Saint Athanasius, the patriarch of Alexandria at the time.

Christianity in Sub-Saharan Africa

With all its spread and impact in North Africa and Ethiopia in the early centuries, unfortunately, there is no indication of any attempts to take Christianity into the region south of the Sahara. Consequently, the first advent of Christianity into that region, in precolonial Africa, had to wait until the fifteenth century. The principal harbingers of the religion to Africa's Eastern, Western, and Southern regions were mainly the Roman Catholic missionaries. They belonged to the Jesuit and Dominican orders, who accompanied Portuguese traders along the coastal regions of Africa. For example, by 1490, the missionaries had started to build Christian communities in the Congo and Angola. By 1560, Father Gonzalo da Silveira along with other Portuguese missionaries, had established a Christian community of about 450 persons in the empire of Mwanamtupa, today's Zimbabwe. Along the coast of West Africa, the same Portuguese missionaries brought Christianity to southern parts of today's Nigeria, of Calabar, and the Benin kingdoms. The Gold Coast, now called Ghana, also witnessed the presence of Christian missionaries and some conversions.

However, these efforts eventually proved unsuccessful for a number of reasons. Prominent among these was the issue of health. Most of the missionaries died of malaria. The death toll was so enormous that Africa came to be referred to as the "white man's grave." Also, there was the issue of the slave trade. It was ironic that the missionaries, who came to preach the Christian message of love of neighbor, were in collaboration with Portuguese traders, whose main business soon changed from seeking and transportation of gold and ivory to that of human slaves. It soon became obviously difficult, if not impossible, to sell the contradictory messages of "love" of Christianity and "cruel inhumanity" of the slave trade. In addition, there was the competition of Islam, which had actually predated Christianity into the region. Muslim trading partners of traders in these areas resisted the threat of the Portuguese traders and their trade monopoly through Portuguese missionaries. For example, Father Gonzalo da Silveira was actually executed by the emperor of Mwanamtupa, whom he had earlier converted to Christianity and baptized. This act was ascribed to pressure from Arab Muslims who were trading partners to the emperor, in order to protect their trade monopoly.[31] With the failure of these efforts, Sub-Saharan Africa had to wait until the nineteenth century and early twentieth century for Christianity to take root and grow.

The late nineteenth and early twentieth centuries actually witnessed the advent and spread of Christianity in sub-Saharan Africa. The success of this "project" is traceable to a number of favorable developments. These involved, for example, the discovery of quinine, effective against death from malaria. Also, the slave trade had ended. Thus, the moral dilemma of preaching Christian love while at the same time capturing and transporting slaves to Europe and the Americas was no longer a burden. The propagation of Christianity was then taken as a full-time campaign rather than at the part-time leisure of Portuguese traders in the coastal regions of Africa. Then, most important of all, the success was basically the product of the painstaking efforts of different Christian missionaries in Europe, who not only pioneered but also helped to sustain missionary evangelism in different parts of Africa, by making both the finance and the personnel available.

The period also coincided with the colonization of the African continent. Consequently, colonial governments contributed significantly, through various means and at different stages, to the Christianization of Africa. Moreover, freed slaves from American and European nations, who settled in different parts of Africa, particularly, in West Africa, were great catalysts in the propagation of Christianity in Africa. A combination of these dynamics took the Christian faith to the nooks and crannies of the eastern, western, and southern regions of Africa. Indeed, by the middle and definitely before African countries began to gain independence in the 1950s, the Christian religion with its counterpart, Islam, had become a dominating religion on the African continent.

Leadership, Worldviews, and Artistic Influences

From the first century through the middle centuries, Christianity in North Africa and Ethiopia became central and influential in the "evolving" and later "matured"

Christendom in terms of leadership, personnel, and doctrinal worldviews. Many leading theologians as church leaders, who shaped the doctrinal worldviews of Christianity, not only in the early and middle centuries but also for all time, were leading figures in the Alexandria church, the Ethiopian church, and Roman African churches. These were achieved through their numerous writings, establishment of schools, and propagation of doctrines.

Beginning with the Egyptian Coptic Church in Alexandria, there emerged a substantial number of church leaders from the first century to the seventh century. This crop of church leaders began with Mark—the founder of Christianity in Egypt. He was the writer of one of the four gospels. Saint Mark not only established the church but also created the catechetical school in Alexandria. The school was the oldest catechetical school in the world. The first manager of the school was Saint Justus, who later became the sixth bishop of Alexandria. Panaterious was the first teacher, and after him came many renowned church scholars such as Clement, Didymus, and Anthenagoras. The school became not only a center for theological scholarship but also mathematics, science, and humanities. However, the most well-known teacher and scholar of the school was Origen. He produced the famous Hexpla and more than 6,000 commentaries. Saint Jerome, who first translated the Bible into Latin, also visited the school in AD 600. The catechetical school has also been credited with developing a system of utilizing wood carvings as a means of reading and writing for blind students.

The Alexandria church, also in searching for authentic Christian life—devoid of all fleshy desires and serving God through a life of self-denial, prayer, and worship—introduced the first monastic movement in Christendom. The nearby caves and desert areas provided ideal locations for the ascetic pursuits.[32] The movement was introduced by Saint Macarius the great in the fourth century. The principal figures he used were Saint Pachomius the cenobite and Anthony the Great. The monasteries ended up producing prominent leaders and teachers, known as the "great fathers of Egypt desert," and their works played a significant role in shaping the characteristics for which the Coptic Orthodox Church is historically known. They also greatly influenced the formation of early and growing Christian doctrinal and practical worldviews, becoming models for Christianity in other parts of the world such as Asia Minor.

As mentioned earlier, prominent church leaders known as African church fathers, also emerged in what was then the "Roman Africa." Among these were figures such as Tertullian of Carthage and Saint Augustine of Hippo. The works of these African church fathers tremendously shaped Christian theological worldviews in their lifetimes and thereafter for centuries.

The Ethiopian Orthodox Church leaders contributed immensely to the theological issues from its inception and well into the mid-centuries. Indeed, its propagation of the "Tewahedo" doctrine, the idea that the nature of Christ is single and united, became a reference point in Christian theological development. Not only did it become a subject of controversy, it actually ultimately led to the East-West schism of 1054. The schism occurred when the Patriarchs of Alexandria, leading the Ethiopian Coptic Church, along with his counterparts in Antioch and Jerusalem, went against the historic council of Chalcedon doctrine of "two natures of Christ," and insisted on the one unified nature of Christ. Subsequently, the Orthodox Tewahedo Church and their Asian counterparts were called "Monophysite," symbolizing their adherence to the belief that Christ was of a single nature.

Interestingly, the basic beliefs of the Orthodox Ethiopian Church actually depicted some aspects of the indigenous Miaphysite beliefs. This was symbolically reflected in the general religious beliefs and practices coordinated by the local priests of the church. For instance, the belief system was founded around a belief in God, angels, and saints. The belief system definitely resonated with the indigenous religious belief in the Supreme Being, divinities, and ancestors, respectively. The role of the priests as the spokespersons for the devotees before God found commonality with functions of priests and priestesses in the indigenous religion. Another area is the practice of the priests being permitted to enter the inner sanctum of the circular church where the Ark (or Tabot) devoted to the church patron saint lies. This would find concurrence with the indigenous religious priests' functions in the shrines of the divinities and ancestors. There were also the festivities of singing, drumming, and dancing to mark special days devoted to angels and saints. Finally, the idea of a "trinate monotheist" belief would not have been too strange to the converted indigenous people with their notion of "diffused monotheism."

Christianity's advent and expansion in Africa, particularly in North Africa and Ethiopia, were phenomenal, starting from the first century and through the midcentury AD. However, beginning from the seventh century, it began a decline. Thus, by the eve of colonization, with the exception of the Coptic Church in Ethiopia, it had become almost extinct. Notwithstanding, certain legacies survived, and it was upon these that Christianity built a strong and lasting reemergence in colonial and postcolonial Africa. A significant part of these were architectural masterpieces of the Monolithic Church buildings in Ethiopia. Examples of these are the churches at Lalibala. They included two key types of artistic architecture made up of basilicas and native forms. A model of the basilica type is the Church of Our Lady of Zion in Axum. The native churches were impressively constructed with sanctuaries surrounded by a courtyard, as well as walls covered with frescos.[33]

Contemporary Trends

As stated earlier, Christianity today is one the two dominant religions in Africa. It is estimated that there are close to 390 million Christians in Africa. The religion has continued to grow at the estimated rate of 2.65 percent yearly. The phenomenal growth of Christianity, without diminishing the pioneering contributions of the missionaries, has been traced to the innovations through enculturation, which have become the hallmark of Christianity on the African continent. Consequently, the Christianity practiced in Africa today still essentially subscribes to the fundamental beliefs, doctrines, and practices of universal Christianity, and is remarkably unique and different in terms of methods and applications.

The departure from the method of propagation, application of contents, and enculturation of values actually began in the early 1920s with the establishments of African Independent Churches. These churches introduced many African cultural values and beliefs that made the belief and practice of Christianity in responding and addressing the heart of African spirituality, known to be all encompassing and spontaneous, as different from the exclusive and abstract natures of the mission of Christianity. Over the decades, indigenous African churches have expanded with the injection of the Pentecostal mode of Christianity to become the dominating Christian denominations in many parts of Africa. These denominations have become very popular because of the premium they place on existential issues of everyday Africa such as healing, poverty, witchcraft, marriage, bareness, and so on, in conjunction with spiritual concerns.

Islamic Religious Tradition in Africa

As a religious tradition, Islam postulates a worldview of an entirely monotheistic religion. This is the belief in a single indivisible God called Allah. The faith grew out of the teachings of Mohammed in Arabia in the seventh century CE. It is regarded as the third fiscal card in the monotheistic Abrahamic religions. The major themes of Islam are peace and submission. It is also a religious tradition that is named after a concept rather than a person. The unique practices required of devotees are found in the five pillars of Islam—the *Shahada* (creed), the *salat* (daily prayers), the *swam* (fasting through Ramadan), the *zakat* (giving alms), and the hajj (pilgrimage to Mecca at least once in a lifetime). The overall Islamic doctrines and practices are based on its Holy Scripture, the Qur'an, and religious traditions—the *Hadith*. The discourse on Islamic religious tradition in this section focuses on the history of the advent and spread of the religion, its distinctive African features, the influences on African indigenous religion in particular, and all aspects of African life in general.

Advent and Spread in Africa

The advent and spread of Islam in Africa can be traced to two distinct waves from the seventh century to the early nineteenth century—the eve of African colonization. There are indications that the first wave of the seventh century may have actually accommodated Islamic contact with Africa during the lifetime of Mohammed. This is reported in connection with the migration ordered by Mohammed that his followers should flee to the Christian kingdom of Abyssinia, present-day Ethiopia. The order was given so that these dedicated followers could escape the persecution of the pagan non-Muslim rulers of their homelands.

However, what has been strictly regarded as the first wave of Islam as an organized religion occurred after the death of Mohammed in CE 632. The advent and spread was through wars of conquest. By CE 640, Egypt, whose rulers were supported and influenced by the Byzantine Orthodox Church, had been overrun. The seeming ease with which the Muslims conquered Egypt has been attributed in part to the face-off between the Byzantine Orthodox Church supported by Egyptian rulers, and the majority of Egyptians who were Coptic Christians. The Coptic Christians did not accept the teachings and authority of the Orthodox Church and held the Egyptian rulers responsible for their religious oppression. They consequently welcomed the Arab rule as liberation and freedom from their Egyptian overlords.

The Islamic takeover of "Roman North Africa" was through both conquest and persuasion. First, the Christians, who were based in the towns, were defeated. Second, the Arabs gradually converted the Berbers who lived in the rural areas. This was done mostly through intermarriages. Eventually, the Berbers, Islamized and incorporated into the Arab armies, fully participated in the military campaigns for the conquests of other parts of North Africa, particularly the Maghreb.[34]

The military option employed for Islamizing most of North Africa was not adopted for Islam's advent and spread in the regions south of the Sahara. Here, Islam was propagated mainly through peaceful means. The method was essentially informal "missionary," and the missionaries were actually the Arabized Berber merchants. They traded in manufactured goods from the Mediterranean, exchanging them for raw materials, such as gum, gold, slaves, and ivory. However, wherever they went, they became proselytes of the Islamic faith. It was through this method that the West African region became Islamized. For instance, Gold Coast (now Ghana), was an already established Islamic center by 1076. This is also true of the Yoruba nation (part of present-day Nigeria). Indeed, by the fifteenth and sixteenth centuries, Islam had become the official religion of rulers and elites in many West African kingdoms. In the eastern part of Africa, Islam had been introduced by the beginning of the seventh century. This was done by the Persian and Arab merchants. While their activities were confined to the coastal trading towns, the religion also spread downward to South Africa. Its great assets of spread and popularity were intermarriages, commercial contacts, and the eventual development and adoption of the Swahili language.

The second wave of Islam in Africa can be properly located in both the Western and Eastern regions of Africa. Again, both military and missionary methods were employed. For example, in the precolonial periods of the seventeenth and eighteenth centuries, African Muslims undertook mass military movements through Jihads (Holy wars) to Islamize West Africa. A very prominent Jihad was that of Uthman dan Fodio in the area now known as Northern Nigeria. He attempted to impose religious reforms through the Jihad. The goal was to establish a more rigorous Islamic theocratic state. In the process, this became a justification for military campaigns, conquests, and political dominance.[35]

However, there were also a lot of missionary efforts at Islamizing the areas. For instance, the Sufi religious movements (Brotherhoods) were in the forefront of propagating Islam through teachings. One of these Brotherhoods, the Qadiriyya, was brought to the great Muslim center of learning in Timbuktu in the sixteenth century. The work of this group enormously impacted the efforts of Uthman Dan Fodio in carrying out his Jihad and founding the Sokoto Caliphate.[36]

Overall, the Islamic advent and spread in Africa in the first centuries witnessed diverse history of movements, and even dynasties competing for power and control of different regions of the continent. The advance moved both southward and northward, until the final years of the eleventh century when the religion became a dominant religion and political force across the continent. In terms of leadership positions, in the Islamic world, Africans did enjoy prominent status. For instance, the very first Muezzin (privileged person to lead the adhan—call to prayer), was a North African called Bilal ibn Rilah. He was of the Habasha descent. Throughout the history of Islam, numerous empires led by figures from West Africa emerged. Such empires, which had tremendous influences, included the Mali Empire, and the Songhai Empire under the leaderships of Sonni Ali and Askia Mohammed, respectively.[37] There was also the Sokoto Caliphate established by Uthman dan Fodio.

Islamic Features and Cultural Influences

Although military conquests constituted the main method of Islamizing different parts of Africa, it was more readily accepted by Africans than its main rival, Christianity, particularly in pre-colonial Africa. A number of factors have been identified for this situation. Two of these factors are distinctive. The first, and the most touted, is the accommodating nature of the Islamic beliefs and practices in relation to African indigenous beliefs and practices. Africans found Islamic beliefs and practices compatible with or at least tolerant of, their religion and cultural values and practices. For instance, religiously Islam resonated with African beliefs in ancestral veneration, magical use of objects, divinities, and spirits. Culturally, Islam also allowed polygamy, whereby a man could have more than one wife at a time, provided he could support and care equally for each wife. Circumcision, a very important practice among most African peoples, was also allowed. The Islamic religion found common ground with Africans in terms of clear gender roles for men and women. Consequently, Africans were more comfortable converting to and practicing Islam rather than Christianity. In preaching Islam, African Muslims were more committed to observing the five pillars of faith than to the elements of Sharia, which were incompatible with African social and political customs.

The second factor had to do with the Islamic civilization contributions to African cultural developments. Islam is practiced as a way of life. It affects all aspects of human endeavor, just as African religion permeates the totality of the African life. Islam also stressed community living as its followers lived as communities of believers. As the religion took root on the African soil, its emphasis on literacy and scholarship became attractive to Africans. Its Islamic law (Sharia) became the framework and model for theocratic governance, legitimizing religious leadership of rulers, and regulating the relationship between the rulers and the ruled. In addition, Islam bequeathed to Africa many great architectural models, spread across the continent. One of these was the great Ketchaoua mosque is in Algeria. This mosque is regarded as the "ancestor" of all mosques, even in Western Islamic communities. Finally, it is quite evident that Islamic civilization in Africa, as part of the global one, was highly advanced. Thus, as the religion spread across Africa, it made major impacts on Africans and their everyday lives, both in precolonial and postcolonial African settings.

Contemporary Status

In conjunction with its counterpart, Christianity—Islam, even though it is pre-dominantly practiced in the northern part of Africa, has substantial followers in sub-Saharan Africa. In 1985, the total population of Muslims in Africa was esti-mated to be 215 million. However, by 2003, the number of Muslims in sub-Saharan Africa alone was estimated to be 150–160 million. In 2004, the Muslim population in Africa was estimated to be 402 million.

Summary and Conclusion

This chapter has explored the "worlds" of the religious traditions in Africa. The dis-course centered on the three principal religious traditions—the African indigenous religion, Christianity, and Islam. The indigenous religion has been in competition with the other two religions since the time of their introduction and developmental years on the continent. Notwithstanding the challenges they have posed and are posing to it, it has struggled to withstand their strong intimidations. Consequently, it has continued to provide religious responses born out of African cultural heritage. The responses have not only defined the world views of Africans but also and, more important, have sustained the unique identity of Africans as a people vast in reli-gious values.

The advents and developments of Christianity and Islam have introduced alter-native religious dynamics into the African religious space. These have ultimately influenced the religious beliefs and practices of the African people. However, their impacts on the indigenous religion and its devotees in terms of acceptability and affiliations of the "new religions" evoked different responses. These were inadver-tently based on the approaches adopted by the two religions in practicing accommo-dation and enculturation over the centuries. Today, both religions have become the two most practiced religions in Africa and have had a huge impact with enormous influences and holds on the totality of the African life—to the extent that they have become, so to say, "African religions."

Notes

1. Mbiti, John Mbiti, *African Concept of God.* London: SMC Press, 1970, p. 1.
2. Idowu, Bolaji, Idowu, *African Traditional Religion: A Definition.* New York: Orbis, 1971, p. 3.
3. Moyo, A. (2007). "Religions of Africa" in A. Gordon and D. Gordon (Eds.) *Understanding Contemporary Africa.* London: Lynne Reiner, p. 319.
4. Mbiti, John. (1991). *Introduction to African Religion.* London: Oxford University Press, p. 3.
5. Ibid, p. 1.

6. Talbot, P.A. (1926). *The People of Southern Nigeria. Vol. 2.* London: Oxford University Press, p. 14.
7. Parrinder, E. G. (1949). *West African Religion.* London: Epworth Press, pp. 11–12.
8. Idowu, Bolaji. (1973). *African Traditional Religion: A Definition.* London: SCM Press, p. 85.
9. Aderibigbe, I. S. and Oguntola, D. (1997). *Topics in African Religion.* Lagos: Adelad Educational Publishers, p. 1.
10. Moyo, in *Understanding Contemporary Africa,* p. 319.
11. Abioye, S. O. (2001). "Introduction to African Religion" in G. Aderibigbe and D. Aiyegboyin (Eds.) *Religion Study and Practice.* Ibadan: Olu Akin Press, p. 194.
12. Awolalu, J. O. and Dopamu, P. A. (1979). *West African Religion.* Ibadan: Onibonje Press, p. 51.
13. Aderibigbe and Oguntola, *Topics in African Religion.* p. 7.
14. Moyo, in *Understanding Contemporary Africa,* p. 319.
15. Awolalu and Dopamu, *West African Religion,* p. 53.
16. Abioye, in *Religion: Study and Practice,* p. 194.
17. Bolaji Idowu. (1962). *Olodumare: God in Yoruba Belief.* Ikeja: Longman, p. 26.
18. Aderibigbe and Oguntola, *Topics in African Religion,* p. 7.
19. Abioye, in *Religion: Study and Practice,* p. 192.
20. Aderibigbe, I. S. (2006). "The Traditional Healing System among the Yoruba" in Toyin Falola and M. Heaton (eds.) *Traditional and Modern Health Systems in Nigeria.* Trenton, NJ: African World Press, p. 365.
21. Hallgreen, R. (1992). "Religion and Health among the Traditional Yoruba." *Journal of Religious Studies, ORITA* (June and December), p. 67.
22. Awolalu and Dopamu, *West African Traditional Religion,* p. 4.
23. Awolalu, J.O. (1979). *Yoruba Belief and Sacrificial Rites.* London: Longman, p. 73.
24. Ibid, p. 38.
25. Thomson, Robert. (1971). *Black Gods and Kings, Occasional Papers of the Museum and Laboratories of Ethnic Arts.* Los Angeles: University of California, pp. 1–5.
26. Mbiti, Introduction *to African Religion,* p. 43.
27. Ibid.
28. See Wilfred J. Harrington. (1962). *The Record of Revelation: The Bible; The Record of Promise: The Old Testament; The Record of the Fulfillment: The New Testament.* London: Audiobooks Publishing House, p. 230.
29. Walker, W. (1970). *A History of the Christian Church,* 3rd ed. New York: Charles Scribner's Sons, p. 61.
30. King, Noel. (1991). *Christians and Muslims in Africa.* New York: Harper and Row, p. 1.
31. Moyo, in *Understanding Contemporary Africa,* p. 329.
32. Ibid, p. 328.
33. From *Documents,* School of Alexandria, Part 1.
34. Trimingham, J. S. (1962). *A History of Islam in West Africa.* London: Oxford University Press, p. 18.
35. Mazuri, A. A. (1982). *The Africans: A Triple Heritage.* London: BBC Publication, p. 34.
36. Voll, J.O. (1981). *Islam: Continuity and Change in Modern World.* Boulder, CO: Westview Press, p. 250.
37. Davidson, Basil. (1991). *African Civilization Revisited.* Trenton, NJ: African World Press, p. 25.

Chapter 2

Modern Trends in the Teaching of African Religion in the Twenty-First Century: Conceptual Decolonization

Rotimi Williams Omotoye

Introduction

Many African scholars have held differing positions on the actual nomenclature or name to be given to African religion. According to Dopamu, "the indigenous Religion of the Africans has been inconsistently labeled African Traditional Religion (ATR), African Religions, African Indigenous Religion (AIR), African Systems of Thought, Primal Heritage . . . scholars like Parrinder and Mbiti inconsistently used African Traditional Religion and African Religion."[1] Nevertheless, we shall make use of African religion as suggested by the editors of this book. It may also be necessary to define African religion. Awolalu and Dopamu define African religion in this way:

> When we speak of African traditional religion we mean the indigenous religion of the Africans. It is the religion that has been handed down from generation to generation by the forebears of the present generation of Africans; it is not a fossil religion (a thing of the past) but a religion that Africans today have made theirs by living it and practicing it. This is a religion that has no written literature yet it is "written" everywhere for those who care to see and read. It is largely written in the peoples' myths and folktales, in their songs and dances, in their liturgies and shrines and in their proverbs and pithy sayings. It is a religion whose historical founder is neither known nor worshipped. It is a religion that has no zeal for membership drive, yet it offers persistent fascination for Africans, young or old.[2]

The above definition has given us a comprehensive summary of what African religion stands for in African society. The African religion, for a long time, was given obnoxious, derogatory and unacceptable labels by foreign explorers, missionaries, and sit-at-home research investigators. Some terms such as polytheism, juju, ancestor worship, heathenism, withdrawn god, and idolatry were used in describing African religion. These terms have been rejected by African scholars like Awolalu and Dopamu,[3] Mbiti,[4] Onibere,[5] Idowu,[6] and Kayode[7] among others.

Some foreign writers also made unacceptable statements in their analyses on African religion. For example, Emil Ludwig was quoted to have said, "How can the untutored African conceive God? How can this be? Deity is a philosophical concept which savages are incapable of framing."[8]

Another European scholar named Leo Frobenius in his book, *The Voice of Africa*, wrote:

> Before the introduction of a genuine faith and a higher standard of culture by the Arabs, the natives had no political organization, nor strictly speaking, any religion. Therefore, it is necessary in examining the pre-Muhammedan conditions of the Negro races, to confine ourselves to the description of their crude fetishism, their vulgar and repulsive idols. None but the most primitive instincts determine the lives and conduct of the Negroes, who lack every kind of ethical inspiration.[9]

The above quoted statements are just two from many uncomplimentary views of the early European scholars on African peoples' life and religion. These comments have been condemned and rejected by African scholars in their scholarly submissions.

Dr. Aderibigbe stated that "Bolaji Idowu, John Mbiti, Omosade Awolalu, Geoffrey Parrinder, Asare Opoku, and Ade Dopamu, among others, have provided a platform on which modern scholarship on African Religion could be based."[10] Many of them taught African religion in many universities and other tertiary institutions in Nigeria, West Africa, Europe, and America before their retirements or demise. The new trend, which they introduced in the twentieth century, is still subsisting in the twenty-first century. For instance, the late Professor Ade P. Dopamu brought a new scholarship and popularity to the teaching of African religion at the University of Ilorin, Ilorin, Kwara State. The curriculum, which he formulated, is still being used at the undergraduate and postgraduate levels at the Department of Religions of the university. Therefore, the decolonization of African religion is an ongoing process in the study of religion.

I first came across the term "decolonization" as an undergraduate student of Religious Studies at the University of Ife (now Obafemi Awolowo University). I took a course in the History Department at 200 levels titled "Politics and Decolonization of Africa." The course was taught by a Marxist and erudite scholar, Dr. Segun Osoba. He emphasized the importance and the need for decolonization in all areas of life of the Africans.

I also came across the concept of "decolonization" at an annual conference organized by the Nigerian Association for Biblical Studies with a theme: "Decolonization of Biblical Interpretation in Africa" at the Lagos State University; Ojo, Lagos in 2005. The discussion at the conference is quite relevant to this study. An erudite Old Testament scholar Tuesday Adamo said, "African social cultural context is a subject of interpretation. It means that an African biblical study is contextual since interpretation is always done in a particular context. Specifically, it means that analysis of the text is done from the perspective of the African world-view and culture."[11]

Further, a New Testament biblical scholar, Chris Manus, opined that "since the 1962 UN Declaration in support of the legitimate protests by colonial subjects against the dominance of the colonists, our freedom fighters and founding fathers had committed themselves irrevocably to decolonization."[12] In other words, decolonization is a way of interpreting African religion with an African eye and understanding.

The Teaching of African Religion in Nigeria

Nigeria as a country received her independence from Britain in 1960.[13] The first university in the country was established in 1948 at Ibadan, the present state capital of Oyo state. The Department of Religious Studies was one of the founding departments in the university. It was viewed as a department in which Christian theology was taught only. In such an environment, the teaching of African religion was not given a priority *ab initio*. According to Chris Manus, "the settler methods have taken possession of our hermeneutical terrain and worldview to the detriment of the flowering of indigenous methods from our native culture and ethno-philosophy that could aid us to reflect on the postmodern reality in which we live."[14] For some years, in many Nigerian universities, seminaries and Bible colleges, the teaching of African religion was forbidden or seen as a "satanic and evil" subject. In some places, African religions were taught from the Eurocentric perspective. However, the trend gradually changed after political independence. Awolalu said, "In fact, it was the inclusion of courses in African Religion that made the various governments in Africa (in the wake of national consciousness) allow the old Departments of Divinity to continue to exist but under different names and different content of teaching."[15]

Today, African religion is being taught in almost all of the Nigerian universities and colleges of education where there is a Department of Religions. At the University of Ilorin, certificates are awarded in Comparative Religious Studies at the degree, Masters, and PhD programs. The focus is on African Religion. One of the recommended literatures for university students is a book written by Awolalu and Dopamu, *West African Traditional Religion*.[16] The contents of the book include: The concept of God, the wrong nomenclature for Peoples' Religion, the True Nature of West African Traditional Religion, Features of West African Traditional Religion, Belief in God, Attributes of God in West Africa, God and the World, The Divinities, The Worship of God and the Divinities, Festivals, God and Man, Rites in Connection with Passage of Life, God and the Society, Mysterious

Powers, Women in Traditional Worship, The After Life, and the meeting of the Old and the New. Any scholar who is able to go through this book and others written by some of the African scholars will rightly come to a conclusion that the religions of Africa do indeed have the concept of God.

The Teaching of African Religion at International Levels

The teaching of African religion was not permitted or allowed at international levels for many years. The Eurocentric scholars did not see any sense, or a need for comparison of the European God with the African God. After all, the African God was seen as an "inferior and high god."

The International Association for the History of Religions—a world body for the study of religions—did not permit African scholars to present academic papers in such conferences until the XIII Congress held at Lancaster in 1975.[17] In other words, there was international discrimination and conspiracy against African religion for a long time before it was given recognition by the world body of scholars of religion. It was this initial opportunity that provided an inroad for the study and presentation of academic papers on African religion by African scholars.

In 2010, I was invited to present a paper titled "African Traditional Religion in the Age of Science and Technology" at a World Congress of the XX International Association for the History of Religions (IAHR) held at the University of Toronto, Canada. Unfortunately, I could not attend the conference; however, the paper was presented on my behalf by Professor Oyeronke Olademo. The paper has been accepted by a reputable international journal for publication. The paper highlights the importance of African religion in the face of science and technology in the twenty-first century. I concluded in the paper that African religion is still relevant in the world.

I was also invited to present another international academic paper at Chouaib Doukkhahii University, El Jadida, Morocco in September 2012 on the topic "African Traditional Religion as a Catalyst for the Emergence of Pentecostal Churches in Yorubaland, South-Western Nigeria." These international invitations are to show the acceptability of African religion as an academic discipline by scholars from all around the world.

It is now observed in the twenty-first century that there is a new trend in the teaching of African religion in many universities in America and Europe. Many Nigerian scholars in particular and African scholars in general are employed to teach African religion in prestigious universities.

At Harvard University, Cambridge, Massachusetts, there is a Centre for the Study of World Religions. According to J. O. Awolalu, who was there between 1973–74, some decades ago, "Of all the religions in the world, only African Religion is NOT studied regularly."[18] However, as a result of the new trends in the study of African religions, the situation has changed considerably. In the twenty-first century, African religion scholars are found teaching the religion in many universities all over the world. For example, Jacob Kehinde Olupona is a Professor of African Religion at Harvard University and Ibigbolade Aderibigbe teaches at the University of Georgia. It is also necessary to mention Afe Adogame of the University of Edinburgh, New College, Mound Place, Edinburgh who is an erudite and acclaimed scholar in African studies.

Problems Besetting the Study of African Religion

It is observed that in spite of all efforts being made in the study of African religions in Africa and the diaspora, there are many challenges facing these scholars.

First, there is a lack of written documents by the progenitors of the religion.[19] This is due to the fact that the majority of Africans prior to the twenty-first century were non-literate. They could not document the available information for posterity. There was also much secrecy in the attitude of the practitioners of the religion. Eventually, some of them would die without giving the necessary information to their children. Investigators are prevented from gaining access to the necessary information that is required in the course of their investigations. Most especially, women researchers are prevented from entering certain shrines and groves. There are shrines that the uninitiated are not permitted to enter; in other words, on-the-spot information may not be obtained on the needed research.

Second, Africa as a continent is too large of an area to cover for any investigator on African religion.[20] We believe that this was one of the major problems that confronted the early investigators in Africa. In Nigeria alone, there are a multitude of different languages, nationalities, and cultures. Due to the vastness of Africa, early investigators made unclaimed, unsubstantiated, and generalized conclusions about the African religion.

Third, the introduction of Christianity and Islam as two foreign and dominant religions has had a negative influence on the study of African religion.[21] The missionaries indoctrinated the African converts and caused them to lose interest in the religion of their forefathers. Many Africans who are supposed to be future priests and priestesses of African divinities are now founders of churches and pastors in the churches. They are trained to condemn African religion.

Fourth, Western education, which was a by-product of Christianity, caused the educated Africans to jettison their African religion.[22] As such, they prefer to be associated with "civilized religion." The pursuit of a higher education led educated Africans to leave their domain in pursuit of "white collar jobs" outside their region. The development of urbanization of towns and cities eventually led to the destruction of shrines in such places.

Fifth, the introduction of Western medicine has caused educated Africans to condemn African medicine.[23] As soon as Western education was introduced, Western medical facilities were provided by the Christian missionaries. Hospitals were built, and medical personnel were provided. This effort led the missionaries to condemn African medicine as noneffective and unacceptable to them. However, further study has shown that the claim of the missionaries on the ineffectiveness of traditional medicine is not correct. Research has shown that there are African herbal medicines that are prophylactic and therapeutic.

Principles to Apply for an Effective Academic Study of African Religion

Idowu, in his earlier study, has highlighted the principles and "highway" codes[24] to be observed in the academic study of African religion. These codes are still relevant in the twenty-first century.

The first to be examined is caution. It should be noted that the religion of a group of people is near and dear to them; therefore, there is a need for caution when investigating such an important topic. This is more necessary when an investigator is studying a religion which is not his own. The early European researchers made some mistakes in this regard, and those led to erroneous conclusions. Some of them had preconceived notions before they even embarked on the research, and they made use of the level of their enlightenment and civilization to judge the level of the people they were investigating. They erroneously referred to African religion as Juju, animism, mana, etc. According to Onibere, "there are always discoveries from age to age which may render past presuppositions baseless."[25] A sincere academic should be honorable, and correct earlier errors when new discoveries are made. This will guide and bring forth new findings in research and scholarship. Idowu said, "no scholar who is worth the name should create the impression that his own is the last word on the subject of religious studies."[26] If Idowu's observation is accepted, then every society and community would be given the benefit of doubt to hold and express their beliefs on their religion. The attitude of every investigator should be "Let's discover the truth." Awolalu quoted Bouquet, who said, "scholars should not study religion as if it were fossils, for such an exercise will be both meaningless and valueless."[27] In other words, we must appreciate and respectably associate with the people. If possible, we sit where they sit, if we are permitted, dance when they dance, eat what they eat, and sing along with them as best we can. To be able to get the most from the people, it may be good to spend some time learning the language of the people for a better understanding. At times, when we rely on an interpreter, some important aspect of the worship may not be understood. In fact, doing these things will give us the opportunity to gain more realistic insight about the people and their religion.

Openness

Another feature in the academic study of African religion is openness on the part of the researcher. The religion must be allowed to speak for itself. An investigator should not allow his or her own personal background to determine the conclusion of the research. Many of the early investigators were Christians and of different denominations. The interpretation some of them gave to African religion was based on their Christian tradition.

Sympathy

An investigator of other peoples' religion must be sympathetic in his research. S/he should avoid cultural and national pride. Culture is a total way of life for people; so one would not expect that the people being investigated would behave the same with an outsider. In Yorubaland, male children are expected to prostrate, and ladies are expected to kneel down when greeting elderly people, while in Igboland the situation is not similar. The difference is basically a result of culture. To cite another example, in Yorubaland, you are not expected to count the number of children in a family where an investigation is being carried out.

Reverence

African religion, like any other living religion of the people, must be handled with the reverence and utmost care it deserves. Scholars must try as much as possible to avoid generalization of ideas and distortion of historical facts on any issue. It is noted that it may be difficult, in Nigeria, for example, for a researcher to cover the whole country within a short time because of its size. Even if the resources are available, there are other challenges to be faced in the course of the research. It is also necessary to note that there are many issues that are responsible for unnecessary rivalries among the different local communities. Each community may not present the truth of a case as it may be. This calls for thorough research and patience before the final research is finally published.

The Future of African Religion in the Twenty-first Century and Beyond

It is a fact that culture and religion are inseparable. The African religion is a living religion like any other religion. It is also true that there are certain challenges, which are confronting the existence and growth of the religion in the last few centuries. In spite of the problems highlighted earlier—most especially the emergence of Christianity, Islam, Western education and Western medical facilities—African religion cannot be eroded in Africa. In the twenty-first century, some Western people have started showing interest in the worship of African divinities. For instance, the late Adunni Oloosa, also known as Sussan Wenger, was a dedicated and devoted worshipper of the Osun Osogbo deity until the date of her demise. There are students from Western countries at the Institute of African Studies, University of Ibadan who are studying about African religion. Some of them are even bearing Yoruba names.

African religion is being studied in some Western universities in the twenty-first century, and African scholars are appointed to teach in such higher education institutions. According to Awolalu, in Brazil and Cuba, some divinities have been associated with saints.[28]

In Brazil

Ogun	Saint Anthony
Sopona	Saint Lazarus
Sango	Saint Jerome
Yemoja	Lady of Conception
Oshun	Lady of Candlemas

In Cuba

Ifa	Saint Francis of Assisi
Oshun	Virgin of Cobra
Oya	Saint Teresita
Obatala	Lady of Mercy
Yemoja	Virgin of Regia
Osanyin	Saint Raphael

The Africans in Diaspora are also assisting in promoting and facilitating the worship of African divinities beyond Africa. Therefore, African religion is becoming more popular and acceptable worldwide. Locally, African names, proverbs, pithy sayings, and the teaching of Yoruba language are being encouraged in tertiary institutions.

Conclusion

African religion is the religion of our forefathers transmitted from generation unto generation; therefore, it is a living religion. As long as there is African culture, African religion will continue to be in existence. In 1977, the military government of General Olusegun Obasanjo staged what was styled "FESTAC 77" to showcase the rich culture of the African people. In Nigeria, every community is showing more interest in the celebration of annual festivals. Of recent, the Ijesa people in Osun state celebrated the Iwude festival with pomp and pageantry. The Ojude Oba festival in Ijebu-Ode, Ogun state, Eyo in Lagos, Argugu Fishing festival in Kebbi, Iro and Agbeleku festivals in Erin Ijesa/Erin Oke, Osun state, and the Ogun festival in Ondo are testimonies that it is difficult to erase the culture of the people. In fact, the Osun Osogbo annual festival has become an international festival, which has been adopted and accepted by the United Nations. Therefore, the teaching, practice and research on African culture and religion shall continue and become more acceptable in the twenty-first century.

Notes

1. Dopamu, P. (1993). "African Religion in Nigerian Society: Past, Present and the Future" in R. D. Abubakre et al. (eds)., *Studies in Religious Understanding in Nigeria*. Ilorin: Christy–David Printers, p. 239.

2. Awolalu, J. O. & Dopamu, P. A. (2005). *West African Traditional Religion*. Lagos: Macmillan Publishers, pp. 26–27.

3. Ibid, pp. 13–26.

4. Mbiti, J. S. (1982). *African Religions and Philosophy*. London: Heinemann Educational Books, p. 7.

5. Onibere, S. G. A. (1982). *Fundamentals of African Religion*. Ile-Ife: Department of Religious Studies, University of Ife, (now Obafemi Awolowo University), pp. 59–60.

6. Idowu, E. B. (1976). *African Traditional Religion: A Definition*. London: SCM Press Ltd., pp. 108–112.

7. Kayode, O. (n.d.). *Understanding African Traditional Religion*. Ile-Ife: University of Ife, (now Obafemi Awolowo University), p. 5.

8. Ibid, p. 1.

9. Awolalu, J. O. (n.d.). "African Religion as an Academic Discipline" in P. Dopamu et al. (eds.) *Dialogue Issues in Contemporary Discussion*. Lagos: Big Small Books, p. 420.

10. Aderibigbe, I. (n.d.). "Submission of Manuscripts: A book on Religions of Africa and African Diaspora" An introductory note to the writers of articles in this book project.

11. Adamo, D. T. (2005). "What is African Biblical Studies" in S. O. Abogunrin et al. (eds.) *Decolonization*. Ibadan: Alofe Publication, p. 17.

12. Manus, C. U. (2005). "Decolonizing New Testament Interpretation in Nigeria" in *Decolonization of Biblical Interpretation in Africa: A publication of the National Association for Biblical Studies*. Ibadan: Alofe Publication, pp. 281–82.

13. Crowder, M. (1978). *The Story of Nigeria*. London: Faber and Faber, p. 237.

14. Manus, pp. 281–82.

15. Awolalu, *Dialogue Issues in Contemporary Discussion*, p. 425.

16. Awolalu, J. O. and Dopamu, P. Ade. (1979). *West African Traditional Religion*. Lagos: Macmillan Nigeria Publishers.

17. Awolalu, *Dialogue Issues in Contemporary Discussion*, p. 425.

18. Ibid.

19. Jacobs, A. B. (1977). A *Textbook on West African Traditional Religion*. Ibadan: Aromolaran Publishing Company, pp. 13–14.

20. Ibid.

21. Awolalu, J. O. (1975). *Yoruba Beliefs and Sacrificial Rites*. Essex: Longman Group Limited, pp. 183–96.

22. Ibid.

23. Ibid.

24. Idowu, *African Traditional Religion: A Definition*, p. 16.

25. Onibere, *Fundamentals of African Religion*, p. 7.

26. Idowu, *African Traditional Religion: A Definition*, p. 16.

27. Ibid.

28. Awolalu, Dialogue Issues in Contemporary Discussion, p. 433.

Chapter 3

African Religion in Twenty-First Century and the Search for Philosophical Relevance

Francis Adewale Olajide

Introduction

The many faces of religions in the twenty-first century have certainly become distinctively sinister, particularly when we contemplate the rising scale of human casualties consequent upon acts of terror, religious fundamentalism, and blind fanaticism. To claim to kill for God in the defense of faith is certainly an affront on humanity.

Difficulties about religion are equally not unconnected with how best to define religion, the ambiguity of its language, and it being notoriously conservative. What is more, as Geddes MacGregor aptly observes:

> Religion sometimes appears in the guise of a highly intellectualistic enterprise, involving not only metaphysical presuppositions, hidden on affirmed, but a whole array of dogmatic utterances that raise complicated questions calling for a great deal of logical map-work.[1]

This is perhaps why our chosen task here, though difficult, is not impossible. Philosophy provides adequate tools of exploration with appropriate academic detachment and rigor. The intention is to proceed carefully and critically, as would a devil's advocate in a quest for truth as that which is coherent and consistent with what exists in the practice of religion. With particular reference to African religions, the task shall be on the available scope for the quest for philosophical relevance and its plausibility.

If the plurality of African religions is said to be in search for philosophical relevance, this is not novel; neither is the search peculiar to African religions. What afflicts African religions equally affects all other kinds and forms of religion. This affliction, with its corresponding quest for some philosophical relevance and rational justification, is consequent upon the nature of religion itself, its chosen language, and bold claims that often violate acceptable canons of meaningful discourse. A careful consideration, for example, of ecumenical clamoring and predisposition, particularly by some orthodox sects, is perhaps not unconnected with a clear intention for relevance and acceptance in a globalized world. Beyond the issue of faith, however, and if religion is not to lose its boldness, as a tool of cohesion, there is an urgent need for some cognitive relevance. The deliberate pursuit of inculturation by the Roman Catholic Church, for example, has meant for it more faithfuls and less cases of apostasy. With the of Islam, which even with her many splinter groups has continued to put in reverse a global search for peace, there is still a universal commitment to the pursuit of individual freedom and tolerance.

The quest by African religions for philosophical relevance therefore remains a necessary step. With the prevailing difficulties of acute diversity and pluralism in doctrines, practices, and the demand for justification, a strict definition and adoption of a theoretical framework on which to build a case of justification and acceptance remains imperative. Such a framework must be at least logically and epistemologically sound or, better still, it must remain incontrovertible and coherent in the adoption and use of concepts in general discourse. If religion thrives on effective communication among every adherent regardless of hierarchy or class, then boundaries that separate sense from nonsense, the intelligent from the absurd, cannot be considered arbitrary, trivial, or contingent. The mapping out of such boundaries are, by themselves, necessary in not only matters of religions but also indeed in all matters that concern man and his existence. As humans, we are after all social beings, interacting with other human beings, communicating and establishing meanings. If this is the case, then the argument according to Kwasi Weredu is this:

> Linguistic meanings are social. Social life is based on a certain community of shared ideas. To use an expression that already exists to communicate a thought, we must abide by a certain minimum of the socially recognized rules of expression, otherwise we fail to keep linguistic faith with our fellowmen.[2]

Therefore, this is, particularly if beyond the demand of an appropriate path and platform of communication, how we claim to be rational agents. This is a barefaced confirmation of the fact that we are equipped with a human brain, which enables us to think and reason. Every philosophical discourse and everything that passes for philosophy rest upon this foundation. It is what separates every sane exchange from an insane babble. It equally serves as the least ground for rationality, where by agreement,

> a rational account is broadly one which confines itself to reasons, evidence and arguments that are open to scrutiny, assessment, acceptance or rejection, on the basis of principles and facts which are available to all (humans). An optimally rational account is one in which we do not have to plug any gaps with speculation, opinion, or any other ungrounded beliefs.[3]

Religions, however, seem to shatter this cognitive prerequisite foundation with some air of arrogance that portrays them as closed, and make the charge of obscurantism most fitting. This, according to Julian Baggini, is not to say that religion is irrational. On the contrary, as he explains:

> Faith, as religion, is non-rational rather than irrational because faith is not essentially about going against the dictates of reason (although it often does) but about disregarding the usual standards of proof and evidence demanded by rationality.[4]

When we come to African religions, which some have qualified as traditional, native and/or primitive, the suggestion still is not racially demeaning as Evans-Pritchard noted:

> It is no sign of superior intelligent on my part that I attribute rain to physical causes. I did not come to this conclusion myself by observation and inference, and have in fact little knowledge of the meteorological process that lead to rain; I merely accept what everybody else in my society accepts, namely that rain is due to natural cause...Likewise, a savage who believes under suitable natural and ritual conditions that rainfall can be influenced by use of appropriate magic is not on account of this belief to be considered of interior intelligence. He and I are both thinking in patterns of thought provided for us by the societies in which we live.[5]

Notwithstanding, it is still not strange to state that religions sometimes show a rare disregard for the necessary need to provide evidence for their claims. Such a need is often considered secondary to faith with a strange conviction that the believer knows what he believes and that is that. For the philosopher, faith itself needs some justification that is sufficiently rational, if a serious intention to communicate exists. It is certainly not enough, the philosopher would insist, to consider or interpret faith as a special source of knowledge that cannot be arrived at by way of reason alone. This is because once this position is adopted as justification for every religious belief, then it is disingenuous for believers themselves to put forward argument to support their positions just as it is futile for philosophers to attack the belief if they are not genuine reasons for belief at all.

A comment still is necessary before making some specific statements regarding the status of African religions, and its search for philosophical relevance and acceptability. This concerns the language adopted by religions, and the arguments that they put up as defense and justification for some form of acceptability. I am referring here specifically to the use of metaphysical statements which by their nature are beyond being outlandish, inscrutable, and sometimes totally incomprehensible. A greater reason is provided by the Logical Positivists when they set up what is to count for meaningful discourse. According to A. J. Ayer, speaking for members of the Vienna Circle:

> No statement which refers to a reality transcending the limits of all possible sense experience can possibly have any literal significance; from which it must follow that the labors of those who have striven to describe such a reality have all been devoted to the production of nonsense.[6]

And so, the charge against metaphysicians and all those who in the name of religion make metaphysical assertions as if they are empirical, verifiable statements is that they produce sentences that fail to conform to the conditions under which alone a sentence can be literally significant, namely when the speaker:

> knows how to verify the proposition which it purports to express—that is, if he knows what observations would lead him, under certain conditions, to accept the propositions as being true, or reject it as being false.[7]

Regardless of the fact that what is said may be emotionally significant, nevertheless, it remains literally insignificant. To suggest that because the agent is privy to his own experience, and therefore that he is justified in making a cognitive claim, have little significant meaning here. If the agent is indeed serious about his intention to communicate, then it is simply necessary that s/he choose a medium through which regarding whatever is said, there are no ambiguities such that what is said can be verified and at least can be allotted one undiluted interpretation and meaning. Geddes MacGregor again provides a rather interesting example to underscore the seriousness of the point with the word for God, "Theos." According to him:

> The word 'Theos' when translated, could mean any wonder or unusual person or occurrence, such as a tornado or a man of sufficiently striking personality to cause a stir. We have a remnant of that primitive attitude in our acclamation of football "stars" and in our allusions to hurricanes as "Hilda" or "Bertha." (The result), the ambiguity of the central term in religious discourse in the West was now great enough to be capable of spawning innumerable misunderstandings.[8]

This is unacceptable among philosophers where emphasis is on precision of claims and meanings. Without such consistencies, even the issue of truth becomes remote if not totally impossible. Neither is the adoption of paradoxes and analogical statements helpful. If indeed God cannot be comprehended in any human words, or in any of the categories of our finite thought, then every assertion on "him" by whoever (say a mystic) and under any guise ceases to be a meaningful communication. At best, it is merely a soliloquy.

Some scholars have suggested that perhaps if we adopt a contextual tolerance, then metaphysical assertions may enjoy some rationality and acceptability since, after all, according to Peter Winch:

> What we may learn by studying other cultures (language processes and systems) are not merely possibilities of different ways of doing (or saying) things (or) other techniques. More importantly, we may learn different possibilities of making sense of human life, different ideas about the possible importance that the carrying out of certain activities may take on for man trying to contemplate the sense of his life as a whole.[9]

Still, we must not deny the fact that the religious, including the mystic, are rational, finite beings condemned like every other human to the imperative of sense experience as the only way of apprehending our environment and attaining knowledge.

Anything beyond this becomes a misplaced exaggeration. It is particularly misplaced, as such claims when made, not only allude to what is outside of the perceptible world about which no verifiable evidence is provided, but no reason is provided as to why there must be a universal assent to truth. This is perhaps why some philosophers claim that there is no such thing as religious knowledge.

The Case for African Religions

Strangely, some findings have revealed that afflictions that affect most orthodox religions are spared African religions such that the quest for philosophical relevance is not only feasible but also almost guaranteed. The reason for this unique characteristic is in the existential emphasis and the dynamic flavor of the religions themselves as they are all deeply rooted in the concrete affairs of everyday living. According to John Mbiti, African religions, in their pluralism, permeate all departments of life, and as such there is no distinction between

> the religious and non-religious and between the spiritual and the material areas of life. Wherever the African is, there is his religion: he carries it to the fields...He takes it with him to the beer party or to attend a funeral ceremony...chapters of African religions are written everywhere in the life of the community and in traditional society, there are no irreligious people...African peoples do not know how to exist without religion.[10]

This is no mere exaggeration until, that is, the frantic incursion of Christian and Islamic influences in their search for converts, which has since corrupted the aerated atmosphere hitherto enjoyed by Africans in their allegiance to and worship of their gods. By extension, it is necessary to state too that the belief in one God, who is supreme and is the source of all, is only a late arrival. Before the advent of Christianity and Islam, polytheism was the order of the day, and one could worship many gods as long as they met one's existential needs. As Mbiti emphasizes, while underscoring the freedom atmosphere in belief, worship, and living,

> what people do is motivated by what they believe, and what they believe, springs from what they do and experience. So the belief and action in African traditional society cannot be separated: they belong to a single whole.[11]

The existential emphasis would reflect in a religious language that is totally devoid of unintelligible and remote metaphysical propositions. There is equally no burden of theological canons, or eschatological mysteries needing the interpretations of priests. From the gods through divinities and ancestors, man enjoys a direct link albeit with supplications through these same entities. The subject knows exactly what to do to satisfy his gods, and he is most ready for his punishment, which is meted out to him on earth when he falters. There are also no metaphysical locations to visit after death. All talk about retribution is about the here and now. The focus always is on earthly matters, with man at the center. His acts of worship and turning to his gods, divinities, and ancestors, or living dead as the case may be, are essentially pragmatic and utilitarian rather than spiritual or mystical.

If African religions therefore are spared the rigors of justifying their adoption of strange languages that are devoid of meaning and sense, if they have been relieved of the burden of proof for their gods and heroes now turned ancestors, it is perhaps because of their perception of religion as essentially, a human construct whose aim chiefly is to serve man and no other. That, of course, is most familiar and well received as it serves in the moderation of community morality, trade relations, and the many issues social and political in governance. Philosophy nonetheless demands more with the emphasis on consistency and coherency of beliefs.

If African religions bear existential flavors as noted, it is certainly no excuse to parade concepts and practices within the thought system that are contradictory, thus betraying a dislocation between thought and practice, sense and nonsense. A classical example is the cult of ancestors or ancestor worship. Ancestors are dead elders from the community who are believed still to be wandering around in the world meddling in the affairs of the living. Some are said to reincarnate; others are merely contented serving as custodians of morality of the community enforcers of social norms. Some still visit as masquerades during different seasons bearing blessings like Santa Claus for farmers and barren women. These by themselves are laudable chores with attending social and moral significance. What is inherently absurd is to pour libation, offer sacrifices, and leave items of food at corners of the house for these departed beings to consume when they wander in at night. These practices, far from saluting the existential merit of African religion, suggest something short on the part of those that still uphold and defend them for whatever reasons.

Regarding the worship of ancestors, John Mbiti contends that the use of the word "worship" is mistaken and wrong regardless of the established rites of libation and food offerings. Bolaji Idowu, when examining the Yoruba traditional religions, disagrees.[12] He affirms on the contrary the correctness of choice of word and goes on to underscore its significance. It is here, in such debates that philosophy insists on proper conceptual elucidation in correspondence to prevailing existential realities. Where a belief or its practice borders on the absurd, it is no longer simply anachronistic, it is ludicrous. In the face of such contradiction and humiliation of a people, such practices should be jettisoned.

Certainly, this has absolutely nothing to do with suggesting that a people should not be proud of their beliefs whatever these are. On the contrary, what is being suggested is that where beliefs and practices portray the ludicrous, efforts to emphasize the uniqueness of cultures must be reexamined and reevaluated. It is only when this becomes a deliberate habit will the demand of philosophy for coherency, consistency, and logical correspondence of belief and practice, and the quest of African religion, particularly in the twenty-first century, for philosophical relevance will be considered serious and laudable. Not unless, of course, as Reinach suggests, that religion is nothing but an assembly of scruples impeding the free exercise of our (rational) faculties.

Notes

1. MacGregor, Geddes. (1973). *Philosophical Issues in Religious Thought*. Boston, MA: Houghton Mifflin Company, p. 12.
2. Wiredu, Kwasi. (1980). *Philosophy and an African Culture*. London: Cambridge University Press, p. 107.
3. Baggini, Julian. (2003). *Atheism: A Short Introduction*. London: Oxford University Press, p. 74.
4. Ibid., 45.
5. See, E. Ewans-Pritchard. (1934). "Levy-Bruhl's Theory of Primitive Mentality" in *Bulletin of the Faculty of Arts*, p. 32. University of Egypt.
6. Ayer, A. J. (1936). *Language, Truth and Logic*. London: Penguin Books, p. 14.
7. Ibid., 15.
8. Ibid., p. 50.
9. Winch, Peter, "Understanding A Primitive Society" in *Rationality*, Bryan R. Wilson, ed. (London: Basil Blackwell, 1979), p. 106.
10. Mbiti, J. S. (1969). *African Religions and Philosophy* (London: Heinemann), p. 2.
11. Ibid., 4.
12. See, Bolaji Idowu, *Olodumare, God in Yoruba Belief* (London: Heinemann, 1962).

Chapter 4

African Religious Movements and Pentecostalism: The Model of Ijo-Orunmila, Ato

Oguntola Oye-Laguda

Introduction

In Nigeria, Christian Pentecostals are dominating the scene, and it seems that Pentecostalism is now the strongest of religious traditions in the country. The reason for this is, primarily, that the people are still living in a religious world dominated by spiritualities, and powers that are perceived to possess capacity that can wreak havoc on humanity. The current belief is that these elements can only be challenged spiritually through prayers and, fasting, as well as vigil. The scenario posits that for any religious group to seek patronage from the people, it must pose to possess some basic characteristics that seem peculiar to Christian Pentecostals. Therefore, Pentecostalism has become the main evangelical strategy for all religious groups in Nigeria as a whole and Lagos, a cosmopolitan and commercial hub, in particular. African religious groups' response has been to reorganize its liturgy, spirituality, and sociology to conform to the situation.

In Lagos, Southwest Nigeria, we have numerous Islamic groups as well as Christian groups. The latter is akin to the scenario, which poses a danger to the continued existence of African Traditional Religious Movements (ATRM). In reaction to the situation, the ATRMs have reorganized themselves in order to face the challenges posed by the Islamic and Christian groups that now permeate the region. In this regard, groups such as Indigenous Faith of Africa, Ijo Orunmila, ChrisIslamherb, Reformed Ogboni Fraternity, and Atinga, to mention just a few, have emerged with new liturgies and doctrines "robed" in modernity, sophistication, and spirituality to attract converts and shed the garb of primitiveness, archaism, and secrecy, which, hitherto, are seen as basic characteristics of African religion. This chapter is an attempt to study the trends among practitioners of African religion to make their doctrines, rituals, and liturgy relevant to the modern and sophistications that now permeate the African religious space. This is a survival strategy adopted by the African Traditional Religious Movements as a response to the religious situation, particularly in a pluralistic society like Nigeria. In studying the trends, the researcher used the participant-observer method in the liturgy of the groups, as well as one-on-one interviews.

African Traditional Religious Movements (ATRM): A Typology

African traditional religion, the sole religion on the African continent before the importation of foreign religious traditions, has some unique characteristics. Chief among these is the fact that it has no founder and lacks written scriptures upon which its tenets and doctrines are based.[1] It relies on oral traditions—such as the Ifa corpus—and experiences for the sustenance of its doctrines and liturgies. The traditional religion has quaked under the pressure brought to bear on it by some other religious traditions that now permeate the continent. However, in spite of these observable pressures, the religion appears to persevere, although there is need for reorganization. This has made it imperative for patrons of the tradition to modernize and redefine their doctrines, liturgies, and tenets to conform to the spirituality of their environment. Hitherto, the religion has thrived on secrecy, which according to Obayemi Elemoro is to preserve the mysteries of the religion.[2]

To achieve the above objectives, the African traditional religious movements have reorganized the religion in such a way that it now conforms with modernity and sophistication expected of religion in the twenty-first century, while still retaining some, if not all, of its pristine features. This suggests that there is need for a typology and a study of the basic features of the identified groups. Allan Anderson identifies a broad category of traditional worshippers who now profess to be Christians, but still patronize the doctrine of African religion on the continent. According to him, this group offers sacrifice of chickens and other animals to the ancestors.[3] This is based on one of the five major beliefs in African religion—belief in ancestors. He identified, in particular, the Zion Christian Church in South Africa.[4] Harvey Gallagher Cox also identifies the Apostolic Church in Zimbabwe as demonstrating a commitment to the traditional religion of their forefathers. Interestingly, these groups are claiming to be Pentecostals in their orientation and commitment to spirituality. According to Cox:

> On a continent plagued by the loss of woodlands and arable land, a religiously based ecological ethics is appearing. This ethics is based on spirituality that mixes ancient African religious sensibilities with modern environmental awareness, and it is taking place within a movement that has arisen as Christian Pentecostal impulses have interacted with a throbbing universe of African primal religion.[5]

Ogbu Kalu, writing about Pentecostal Christianity among Igbo people of Nigeria, identifies some African Independence Churches as being part of this group. Although, he concludes that they cannot be called Christians because of their engagement in rituals that are congruent with African traditional religion.[6] He posits that the Aladura Church is the guiltiest of this syncretic practice. He reached this conclusion based on H. W. Turner's typology on our subject matter. He further demonstrated that this group is different from the pure traditional movements like the Brotherhood of the Cross and Star founded by Olumba Olumba Obu, in Calabar in eastern Nigeria. This pure African traditional religious movement took the garb of Pentecostalism because of its claim to the Holy Ghost, holiness of life and social ethics, as well as the mandate to evangelize. We discovered a religious movement in the Lagos area that is syncretic in nature and features. This group is known as ChrisIslamherb, and practices the tenets, doctrines, and liturgies of the three religions dominant in Nigeria today. It is situated on the outskirts of Lagos on a vast expanse of land—popularly known as Oke Tude—under the leadership of Shamsideen Saka.

Apart from the groups identified above, we also have movements or groups that are purely African traditional religion in features and characteristics. Although they still practice the religion as of the ancient form type, they have added some garb of modernity and sophistication to their tenets, doctrines, and liturgies. Under this classification, we have subgroups as the table below will show:

Cultic Groups	Healing Groups	Sociopolitical Groups	Sociocultural Groups	Evangelical Group
Ogboni Aborigine	Atinga Babalawo	Osugbo, Awo Opa	Egungun, Eyo	Indigenous faith of Africa
Reformed Ogboni Fraternity	Onisegun	Opa Amukala	Igunuko, Gelede etc	

One prevalent characteristic of these groups is the initiation rites. It has also been observed that it is possible for an individual to belong to all of the groups at the same time. In fact, in Isale-Eko—Lagos traditional settlement—the more groups you belong to, the more respect you earn in the community.

Apart from the Indigenous Faith of Africa, all other groups still swear to an oath of secrecy. Although the influence of the sociopolitical group is on the down turn, they remain the de facto kingmakers. In fact, for a king to be coroneted in Lagos traditional politics, he must be initiated into the Osugbo cult.[7] The sociocultural groups are now modernized, and they retain the garb of ancient religious practice of the Africans. They bar women from partaking in some of their activities. The cultic groups are still ancient in all ramifications, seeking spiritual powers and knowledge of the metaphysical world. In some cases, they could be diabolical. However, they also possess social, economic, and political relevance. In recent time, the healing groups are the most predominant and prominent traditional religious movement in Lagos. This is principally because of the new relevance and value that traditional medical practices have taken. In fact, in the last three decades, the federal government of Nigeria has approved the use of traditional medicament and its attendant practices as alternative to Western orthodox medicine. This has caused the Babalawo and Onisegun to gain prominence among the people. Some of them now act as catalyst to the conversion and initiation of their patrons into the cultic groups, or the evangelical groups to which they are also initiated. The evangelical group is the focus of the next section, and the doctrines, liturgies, and sociology will now engage our attention.

Indigenous Faith of Africa, Ijo Orunmila (Ato)

The Indigenous Faith of Africa, Ijo Orunmila, was founded in 1920 by the late Olorunfumi Oshiga, a native of Ijebu Ode, a town located in Southwest Nigeria. He had a vision in which Orunmila—one of the divinities in Yoruba pantheon— appeared to him. He was instructed by the deity to form a group of indigenous worshipers based on the Ifa corpus. Hitherto, Pa Oshiga was a member of Saint Judes Anglican Church, Ebute-Metta. He commenced the process of setting up a "church" where the traditional religion of the Yoruba people would be showcased.[8]

In 1932, he mobilized a substantial number of Yoruba people and built a temple where they held the first formal worship at Freeman Street, Ebute-Metta. During the same time that Oshiga was mobilizing membership for the group, another group with similar nomenclature sprang up under the leadership of Chief James Adeyemi Adeshina.[9] Adeshina was also from Ijebu Ode. He equally claimed to have had a divine call by Orunmila.[10] Interestingly, the two groups bear the same name but only differ in their cognomen—surname or family name. While the former is known as Ijo Orunmila Ato, the latter is known as Ijo Orunmila Adulawo.[11] Chief Adebola Fabunmi—the Aseda Awo and one of the registered trustees of the group—informs us that the group was to be known as Ijo Akoda (the first church) but the colonial masters rejected the name, and advised that the group's name should reflect their belief in Ifa. This is why they settled for Indigenous Faith of Africa (IFA).[12]

Membership of the group consists of all ages. It is not limited to nor restricted by sex, ethnic, tribal, or religious affiliation. According to the Oluwo, the membership strength of the group should be in the region of 2 million, both in Africa and in the diaspora. He posits that the group is an international movement that relied on the spirit of Orunmila for guidance and inspiration. The group currently has 19 branches in Lagos areas; there are also 18 parishes in Cotonou (in Benin Republic), 2 parishes in Benin (Edo State). There are also branches in New York, California, Florida, and London.[13] Although the group is exclusive, it seeks to reach out to the public through the media. In the Lagos area, they have a sponsored program, Odu Ifa on Radio Lagos.

There is also Iwure Aro on the same radio station. They also use tracts and crusades to evangelize. They initiate anyone who seeks membership based on their interest. Chief Fabunmi opines that the group is not Pentecostal, but possesses traits of a Pentecostal group since they also believe in spirits—Irumale, who are created by Olodumare.[14] He further claimed that Jesus Christ of the Christian faith might be one of the Irumale of Olodumare.[15]

The liturgy of Ijo Orunmila was formulated along the lines of the Anglican Church group in Nigeria. In fact, the group has its own creed and hymnal for worship. The group meets weekly for its service on Sundays, but this arrangement reduced patronage from members who are Christian because they have to attend Christian service on Sunday. Consequently, they opted for Saturday, a day that is not religious in Nigeria—the Muslims go for Jumat service on Friday, and the Christians meet on Sunday. During some of the worships observed by this researcher, Ifa corpus played a prominent role. The first and second lessons were taken from Ifa corpus, Yoruba oral scripture, and the sermons were based on the corpus. Moral lessons and prayers were drawn from chapters of Ifa used for the service. The group's worship service is highly organized and formal. There is a standing choir under the direction of a choirmaster, the Apena, backed by drummers. The high priest, Oluwo, is assisted by Akoda Awo, who is second in command; Aseda Awo, who is third in command; and the Abese Awo, who act as a warden. These officers attained their position in the group due to their knowledge of the Ifa corpus, and the length of their membership. For example, the Aseda Awo, Chief Fabunmi, was initiated in 1959 by his father who was also one of the pioneer members.

The worship service commences with a processional hymn that heralds the choir and the officiating ministers. This is followed by the opening prayer and the recitation of the creed. Another hymn is called to be followed by the first lesson and prayer of intercession. This is also followed by another hymn during which there will be collection of funds for missionary works. This is followed by the second lesson and the sermon. After the sermon, the Ifa symbol is brought out, and members approach the Babalawo for divination with kola nut and money. Every member present must go through the process while the choir provides lyrics and choruses to keep the "church" lively. This is known as Obi pipa—breaking the kola. In the event that there are members that want to give testimonies or thanksgiving, they are called to the altar for prayer with choruses. The service ends with closing prayer and a recessional hymn. Overall, we observe that Ijo Orunmila is a pure African Religious group. Although their worship is similar to what is obtainable at the Anglican and African churches in Nigeria, they rely on Ifa as the mouthpiece of Orunmila and Ela who is conceived as the son of Olodumare, comparable to Jesus of the Christian faith.

Its Pan-African orientation is not in doubt. Its members are sometimes syncretic. However, there are many who are dedicated to the creed of the group wholeheartedly. This former group comprises the majority of the membership. In a structured questionnaire administered at the temple, we observe that over 73.2 percent of members were once patrons of other religious traditions before joining the group. They joined the group in search of spiritual fulfillment or due to some sickness or hardship. As one of them puts it:

> I was sick for about three years, struck with a strange illness that defied [W]estern medicine; I was initiated into Ijo Orunmila, after being introduced by a friend and have since been cured. Since then, I have remained a member of the group. My life has witnessed progress and prosperity in all ramifications.

Another respondent opined that even though he still patronizes African Independent Church, he has been a member of Ijo Orunmila for over ten years. It was while he was being initiated into the group that he was directed by Ifa to his destined vocation—building engineering. Hitherto, he was into sales of insurance policies. This is a vocation that appears lucrative, but in reality brings him into debt and misfortunes. Another 26 percent of the members are born into the group, and have never gone outside it to seek spiritual succor or fulfillment. In fact, this group of worshippers believes that all other religious traditions and movements are only pretending to be the way to salvation. As one of them puts it:

> Orunmila as witness of human destiny is the one ordained by Olodumare to give spiritual guidance to people which will lead them to salvation. He (Orunmila) in alliance with Ela (omo Olodumare) is the Holy deity that deserves human reverence and loyalty, why then will I go to another group when I already know the truth.

When asked if they knew about the liturgy and doctrines of the religious traditions around them, they answered in the affirmative. They engage in crusades and itinerant evangelism. The latter is known as Iwode. During this process, they extol African people to go back to the source of things, Olodumare and Orunmila, as a solution to the problems that plague the society. Prayer sessions and vigils are often held. This is known as Iso Oru. Although members do not speak in tongues, they could be possessed by the spirit of any divinity. This situation is not visible during their regular worship, but is visible when rituals are to be performed and the spirit of the deity is invoked. This is known as Egun—spirit possession.

They also demonstrate unequivocal belief in the veneration of the ancestors. They appease these spiritual beings—divinities and ancestors—with gifts and ritual sacrifice of cow, goat or chicken. They may also take dishes of porridge, corn food, and rice among other food items. We observed that some of these features—vigil, prayer, and spirit's possession—have always been part of pristine traditional values of the religion before the adaptation and reorganization of the group.

The Indigenous Faith of Africa socializes and interacts positively in the society. The temple is situated on Freeman Street, a busy commercial street near Oyingbo market, in Lagos Mainland. In spite of the fact that most of its members are Yoruba—one of the three major tribes in Nigeria—they interact with non-Yoruba elements that make up the population of the area. They equally interact with people of other religious traditions, hoping to lure them into their own group. Furthermore, because of the belief that Olodumare (God) is the creator and source of all things, they tolerate and interact effectively in Nigeria, which is a pluralistic society.

Overall, we observe that the liturgies and doctrines of Ijo Orunmila are derived from the major beliefs of African Traditional Religion. These are beliefs in Olodumare (God), Irumale (divinities), Ancestors (Babanla) spirits, magic, and medicine (Epe, Ase, and Ogun). Emphasis is placed on Olodumare as the source of all things. This they affirm in their creed as follows:

Mo gba Olorun, Eledumare gbo
Eniti o da orun ati aye

Mo gba Orunmila gbo
Eniti nse woli Olodumare akok
I believe in God, the Almighty
Maker of heaven and earth
I believe in Orunmila
The first prophet of Olodumare...

This creed demonstrates that the people not only believe in God but they equally hold Orunmila in high esteem as the prophet of Olodumare, who must have been sent to the Yoruba people. While other divinities are not mentioned in their doctrines, they, nonetheless, patronize them at all times. The group also believes in morality, life after death, judgment day, good neighborliness, and social interaction. They promote the institution of marriage, covenant relationship based on the value and ethical principles of the Yoruba people.[16]

All of these doctrines are demonstrated in the liturgy of the group. In fact, the hymn book is replete with praises of Olodumare, Orunmila and Ela as the source, guide, and advocate respectively of humanity on earth and in the hereafter. The group is evangelical, and they seek spirituality through the agency of Ifa—the oracle—based on their beliefs earlier mentioned.

Religious Challenges Confronting Indigenous Faith of Africa, Ijo Orunmila in Nigerian Religious Space

The fad in the Nigerian religious space is Pentecostalism. This is a style of religious belief and practices that emphasizes spirit possession, signs, wonders, miracles, and spiritual gifts that comes after baptism with the Holy Spirit. These gifts include speaking in tongues and faith healing. The Pentecostals originated among Christians in the early twentieth century in the United States of America based on the Pentecost experience of early Christians as recorded in Acts chapter 2: 30. It is from this historical event that Pentecostalism as a system of belief derived its tenets, doctrines, as well as liturgy that are based on post-Christian conversion experience often referred to as "Baptism with the Holy Spirit." This baptism is expected to lead adherents to change of ethical and moral codes.

Socially, Pentecostalism encourages members to "moral rigor, ability to heal, prophesy as well as interpret speaking in tongues." The Pentecostals are not a schematic movement but puritanical in their moral and social dealings.

Encyclopedia Britannica informs that the Pentecostal "seeks to rid the Church of formalism and worldliness." This stance of the group has led to rejection and oppositions from Church leadership across the world. R. M. Anderson, in the *Encyclopedia of Religion,* informs that there are three major Pentecostal groups. First, we have the classical Pentecostals, which traced their origin to the Pentecostal revival in the United States during the nineteenth century. There are also the Charismatic whose origin is linked with non-Pentecostal Christian communities in the 1960s in United States. The third groups are those who are Pentecostal in their tenets, doctrines, and traditions but who are not acknowledged as Pentecostals by the first two groups. This is because some of their beliefs are considered heretical or non-Christian. The last group, according to R. M. Anderson, abounds in Africa, Latin America, and Asia.[17]

In Africa, there are four forms of Pentecostalism. Mission churches established by missionaries from Pentecostal denominations of Europe and North America are the first. Second, there are Charismatic movements in mainstream non-Pentecostal denominations. Third, there are independent schematic groups who are offspring of the mission churches. The last groups are the wholly indigenous movements with spirit baptism and charismata. The last group is often questioned or denied because of its patronage or toleration of beliefs and practices such as polygamy and "ancestral worship" from non-Christian traditional religion. Interestingly, all of the four forms identified above abound in Nigeria and Lagos in particular.

The Pentecostals, according to O. U. Kalu, express a belief in holiness and the power of the Holy Spirit, which acts as their guide through Jesus Christ. He informs, inter alia that:

> Pentecostals... [m]aintain that Christian experience normally finds expression in a pattern of conversion, entire sanctification as a distinct subsequent experience and a further baptism in the Holy Spirit, empowering the believers for witness and service, evidenced by the speaking in tongues. This is the born again experience.[18]

In other words, for a movement to qualify to be labeled as Pentecostal, it must demonstrate the baptism of the Holy Spirit manifesting in the ability to speak in tongues. This is the new birth phenomenon. Anderson went further to explain what he considers being a peculiar type form of Pentecostalism, when he describes African Pentecostalism as:

> Broadly to include Pentecostal Mission Churches...Independent Pentecostal Churches, founded by Africans...and Indigenous Churches who have historical theological and liturgical links with Pentecostal movement, and like Pentecostals emphasize the power and manifestation of the Holy Spirit.[19]

The interpretations given to Pentecostalism posit that it is a phenomenon in church history that emphasizes the primal role of the Holy Spirit among Christians, and spiritual gifts for those who are now "born again." Second, it points to a life of holiness and ethical principles that projects the individual or groups as having new interpretations and values for his existence based on the Bible. From the above, we may be tempted to agree that Pentecostalism is a Christian phenomenon. This may be true to some extent. R. M. Anderson thinks otherwise as mentioned above. The Nigerian experience has shown that other religious traditions have imbibed, copied, and adapted the phenomenon to their own religious beliefs and practices. They now apply the features of Pentecostalism to their tradition to enhance group spirituality and ethical values of individuals, as well as to enhance "marketability" of groups. This is the scenario with some Islamic groups observed in Southwest Nigeria.

In the same vein, traditional religious movements have laid emphasis on spirituality through the divinities as media in the attempt to reach the Supreme Being. They equally preach the "gospel" of a new birth, through initiation into the group. The admittance of the new initiates is expected to elicit a new spirituality, and ethical life that will promote social harmony and justice in the society. The Christian Pentecostal groups' experiences have witnessed increase in membership, status of Church leaders, and the wealth of the group and individuals. This has made Pentecostalism the main issue for religious groups in Nigeria and Lagos in particular. This is the situation as observed with Indigenous Faith of Africa, Ijo Orunmila. In order to promote the Pentecostal tendencies mentioned above, the group had, over the years, shed the toga of secrecy and openly professes the creed, liturgies, doctrines, and sociology of African traditional religion. It has attempted to adapt the liturgies of the mainline mission churches in Nigeria, although the adaptation may be a product of the affiliation of the founding patriarch to the Anglican Church Communion, from where the founder received his divine call from Orunmila as earlier stated. The doctrines of the group are derived solely from African traditional beliefs and philosophy—it conceives Jesus Christ as one of the divinities of Olodumare. They rather refer to Ela—a divinity in Yoruba pantheon—and claim that he is the child of Olodumare.

A member of the group, Chief Awosanmi Adeoye posits that the spiritual experience of those who have been initiated into the "truth" of the movement is akin to that of Christians who claim that they are born again. To him, the initiation process is a baptism, and a direct introduction to Orunmila who has been ordained by Olodumare to lead man to the right path through the Ifa oracle. Another member who responded to our questionnaire puts the situation this way:

> Ijo Orunmila is not a born-again church, we do not speak in tongues, but we believe in spiritual gifts as part of the spiritual development of man. Orunmila can give one the gift of vision, hallucination and healing. But to attain this level, a member should be dedicated to the cause of Olodumare through the Ifa oracle.[20]

Chief Fabunmi also posits that the group could be qualified to be called evangelicals, but we must look for an adjective to qualify Pentecostalism so that they (members of the group) will not be mistaken for people of other faiths; in his words:

> We pray, we sing, we dance, we examine the scripture (Ifa oracle), we admonish members to be morally inclined, we inform them on current situation in the nation, and we encourage them to take the message of Ifa to other members of the society. We do not discriminate but we emphasize holiness of social existence as a product of our group spirituality.[21]

From the opinion of Chief Fabunmi, the Aseda Awo of the group, we observe that the Ijo Orunmila is striving to make African traditional religion relevant to the twenty-first century spirituality in Lagos, which is attuned to Pentecostalism. This will explain the adoption of the media, crusades, tracks, itinerant preaching, and participation in several events as a means to reposition the "group" in such a way that its toga of primitiveness will wane in the face of modernity and sophistication that now characterized the practice of African traditional religious beliefs as demonstrated by the group.

Conclusion

In this chapter, we have shown that there are five forms of the emerging traditional religious movements in Africa. The groups have the peculiar characteristics of patronizing the oracle. They are also in the process of repositioning the religion of their forebearers to conform to the sociocultural demands of religion and spirituality in the society. The main trend in this regard is the claim to holiness in life occasioned by new spirituality, which is engendered by communal spirit. This is the new face of Pentecostalism in Lagos. In fact, prior to this time, Pentecostalism was limited and restricted to the Christian religious groups or those who are pretending to be Christians by liturgy, but in doctrinal matters can only be regarded as syncretic. Some of these were identified by Kalu. They include the Aladura Churches, Celestial Church of Christ, Brotherhood of Cross and Star, among others in Nigeria. These African Independent Churches (AIC) are comparable to those identified earlier by Allan Anderson in South Africa.

The Ijo Orunmila has demonstrated a new form of spirituality based on African traditional beliefs, undiluted with doctrines of other religions, but adapted to some features of Christianity to provide a basis for its continued relevance in the religious "market place." Thus, they cannot be accused of being syncretic. This is because the group still maintains pristine doctrines and liturgies of African traditional religion. However, as to the question of whether they can be aptly classified as Pentecostals, we aver that in the affirmative. This is based on the spirituality and new social value attached to the interpretation and imports of Pentecostalism in Lagos, Nigeria. Religious groups in Lagos have come to realize that the evangelical strategies of Christian Pentecostal groups are making them attractive and acceptable to the populace especially concerning spiritual healings, social ethics, and material attainments. We have also reached this conclusion due to the striking similarities in their mode of operations compared with Christian Pentecostal activities in Lagos. However, they are not "revivalists" in the sense suggested by Kalu, in the attempt to describe Christian syncretic groups, such as Brotherhood of Cross and Star, in Southeast Nigeria. This will suggest that the group demonstrates a new form of "Pentecostalism" that is not Christian in origin but in modus operandi. We may boldly refer to the group as neo-Pentecostals.

The competition is now rife among religious groups based on different traditions that abound in Lagos; the minds of Lagosian are the targets for conversion. It should be mentioned, however, that Islam and Christianity still dominate the religious landscape but traditional religious groups are now favorably situating the doctrines, liturgies, and creed of African traditional religion within the ambit of modernity in the form of "Pentecostalism." From our discussions so far, we can submit that Ijo Orunmila has provided a new direction for African religious groups with the adaptation of the Pentecostal evangelical strategies. With this development, it has become obvious that African religion can be flexible, assimilating, and compete favorably with other world religions. They can adapt the evangelical strategies of other religions and still retain the peculiarities of traditional religion of their forebearers. Here, the challenge is to "Christianize" African religion through the Pentecostal mode as a means of survival for a religion that seems to be sinking into oblivion. The adaptation of Pentecostal modus operandi is not apologetics but a real functional dimension of bringing African Religion to an acceptable standard as a religion that can be universally practiced. Further, we may submit that Pentecostalism is a fad for non-Christian groups in Lagos who now are using it as a means to an end; it could be replaced by another evangelical strategy in the future.

Notes

1. Awolalu, J. O. and Dopamu, P. A. (2005). *West African Traditional Religion.* Lagos: Macmillan Publishers, pp. 26–32.
2. Obayemi Martins Elemoro, 64, Chieftain of Awo Opa Cult Group. (Oral Interview, August, 13, 2005).
3. Anderson, A. (1993, April). "African Pentecostalism and the Ancestors: Confronting or Compromise" in *Missionalia,* Vol. 21, No 2, p. 3.
4. Ibid. p. 3.
5. Cox, H. G. (1994, November 9). "Healers and Ecologists: Pentecostalism in Africa" in *Christian Century,* p. 7.
6. Kalu, O. U. (1990). *Testing the Spirit: A Typology of Christianity in Igboland, Revisited 1890–1990.* London: International Institute of African Studies, p. 4.
7. Fadipe, M. A. (1979). *Sociology of the Yoruba.* Ibadan: University Press, p. 243.
8. A. Fabunmi, 56, Aseda Awo of Ijo Orunmila (Oral Interview, March 10, 2005).
9. Ibid.
10. A. Adesina, 64, Apena Awo (Oral Interview, March 10, 2005).
11. Ibid.
12. Fabunmi, Oral Interview.
13. Ibid.
14. Ibid.
15. Ibid.
16. Ibid.
17. Anderson, in *Missionalia,* p. 3.
18. Kalu, O. U. (1990). *The Wind of God: Evangelical Pentecostalism in Igboland.* (Unpublished Paper), p. 1.
19. Anderson, in *Missionalia,* p. 3.
20. Awosanmi, 73 (Oral Interview, March 10,2005).
21. Fabunmi, Oral Interview.

Chapter 5

African Religion and Health Care Delivery in Africa

Kelvin Onongha

Introduction

The quest for health and healing, which is basic to all cultures and people, is also a central need of the African population. This pursuit for Africans has religious implications because, as it is widely known, the Africans are notoriously religious[1] and have a holistic worldview.[2] Therefore, in order to address the health care challenges of Africans, an understanding of the religion and worldview of these people is of great importance. In the following section, an understanding of the Africans' view of sickness and health will be presented in order to comprehend the manner in which health care issues in Africa work.

African View of Illness

While modern Western medicine views sickness as a result of the invasion of germs into the human system—commonly referred to as the "germ theory"—this is not necessarily the case in the African worldview.[3] In opposition to the search for a natural cause for sickness, which appears to be the predisposition of science and Western medicine, Africans believes more on the impact of the supernatural realm on human affairs, which is seen as the major source of all illnesses.

Thus, sickness, to Africans, is attributed to the workings of spirits. The African cosmology, replete with malicious spirits, can bring untold hardship, suffering, and illness upon the unwary and unprotected person. For this reason, Africans are in constant dread of evil powers, enemies, ancestors, and witches—agencies through which illnesses can be transmitted. The foregoing discourse suggests therefore that understanding the etiological differences between the Western and African view of the origins of illnesses is of extreme importance in the discovery of viable solutions to the challenges of healthcare delivery in Africa today.

Another important dynamic in the African worldview is the issue of mystical causation. It is generally believed that in Africa nothing happens to a person without a cause—usually a spiritual one.[4] In other words, adequately to treat an ailment in a patient, it is important to identify the source/cause of the problem, then, a proper diagnosis can be considered. What this implies is, since accidents or mistakes are impossible, and are instead traceable to a person or spirit, human or ancestral, benevolent or malevolent, the most important question to ask is not "*what* is responsible?" but rather "*who* is responsible?" The import of this understanding affects how epidemics and major diseases in Africa are tackled. For instance, HIV/AIDS for a long time was considered by many in Africa, including some educated and "enlightened" persons, as being an invention of mischievous white persons or the curse of the ancestors. This view, naturally, influenced the search for a cure and the approach for treatment of the scourge that quickly attained epidemic proportions in the continent. Africa, with just about 16 percent of the world's population today, accounts for over 60 percent of the known cases of HIV/AIDS around the globe.[5]

Malaria—one of the major killers of infants responsible for the deaths of 750,000 African children annually[6]—is a disease that can be controlled only if the cooperation of the community is obtained and the mindset of the people is changed to recognize this malady for what it really is—an environmental disease.

Clearly, in order for the issue of health care delivery to be adequately addressed, the source and nature of the ailments of the diseases arising from the worldview of the local people needs clarification and resolution: Are the diseases due to natural, environmental, psychosomatic, or spiritual origins?

Traditional Approaches to Health Care Delivery

In his article "African Traditional Healing Practices," Willem Berends observes that traditional healing practices in Africa are experiencing resurgence rather than decline, in spite of the fact that these same people regularly use Western medicines.[7] Berends lists four main functions that African traditional healing practices fulfill, namely: diagnostic—through the use of divination; curative—by drinking herbal preparations or the application of potions/suppositories; preventative—which deal with natural and supernatural misfortunes; and causative—they influence the course of events in favor of the person concerned.[8] Evident in this process is the use of unscientific methods that border on the superstitious and supernatural. It is precisely for this reason that Ruby Mikulencak—a missionary and nurse who served in Africa—believes that "[o]ne of the greatest hindrances to the improvement of health and living conditions in developing African countries is the conflict between the Western scientific worldview and the African traditional worldview."[9] This conflict is explained by Paul Hiebert, an anthropologist, as being due to the flaw of the excluded middle.[10]

The Excluded Middle

Western doctors trained in the empirical school of science accept the existence of the natural world of this-worldly beings and grudgingly acknowledge the supernatural world of otherworldly beings; hence, they are limited to a two-tiered view of reality. Africans, however, have a three-tiered worldview that includes a middle zone of spirits, ancestors, ghosts, etc. Hiebert opines that prior to the seventeenth and eighteenth centuries in the West, belief in the middle level began to die out, resulting in the secularization of science and the mystification of religion.[11] Consequently, missionaries and doctors from the West, affected by the Enlightenment worldview of their age, arrived in Africa with an empirical mindset devoid of the belief in whatever could not be scientifically deduced.

Factors Influencing Wellness

A central aspect of the African worldview that has significant impact upon health care in Africa is the concept of holism. The dualistic separation of the person into spirit and body is foreign to Africans, who see life as one integral whole intricately interconnected one with the other. A common greeting in Africa is: "Are you well?" This is usually followed by inquiries concerning the state or condition of all the other members of the family or household. The question goes beyond the physiological dimension of life, probes into the emotional, socioeconomic, spiritual, and psychological condition of the family. Among the Yoruba—one of the largest ethnic groups found in the southwestern region of Nigeria—this concept of *alafia*, or wellness, is not simply a greeting but a prayer and pursuit. *Alafia* can be translated as "good health, peace of mind, and conflict-avoidance."[12]

In addition, because it is believed that health/wellness does not just result from what one takes into the body in the form of food or drugs, a number of issues that will produce this goal are important for consideration. These factors include right relationships, right living, right worship/service, and right protection.

Right Relationships

There exists in the mind of the African a mystical connection to the universe, objects seen and unseen, to persons, living and dead, and to the deities, supreme and lesser. The individual's well-being is dependent upon the harmony that exists between these various realms with which interaction is shared. The communal bonds that tie humans with the natural and spiritual worlds if broken, or dysfunctional, could result in disease, distress, or death. As a result, a primary preoccupation for many is ensuring that the ancestors, spirits, and divinities are not offended, neglected, or abandoned. Accordingly, sacrifices and libations are regularly needed to appease capricious deities and to turn away their wrath.[13]

Right Living

Another feature of the religion that has a direct influence on a person's well-being or health is how carefully one lived in order not to break a taboo and thus bring offense. Each tribe and group has its own peculiar set of taboos, which if ignored or contravened, could produce illness. As a result, moral rectitude is an important factor in maintaining optimal health conditions, whether mental, emotional, or physical. This aspect of moral rectitude highlights the psychosomatic relationship between the mind and body, between doing and being, and demonstrates the holistic view of health that Africans have.

Right Worship

Health and healing in the traditional African society is the function of the deities. Well-being, prosperity, and longevity are the gifts that the ancestors and divinities bestow upon faithful followers, while, illness, disease, or death are tokens of their displeasure. One sure indication, therefore, that not all was well regarding an individual's or a community's spiritual state was when health was lost. Evidently, the remedy to such maladies would only be obtained if the individual or community returned to the veneration of the gods of the land and paid proper observance of the rituals, festivals, and worship of the deities. Priests, who served as mediators between the people and the divinities, functioned in the place of the local health care professionals, prescribing treatment and dispensing remedies.

Agencies of Health Care Delivery

Prior to the arrival of the missionaries to Africa with their modern medical marvels, there existed agencies by which health was maintained. Primarily, these were the priests of the local cults, as well as other initiates, who specialized in herbal preparations. In this section, an examination of the roles of several agencies, which were employed in bringing healing to the community, will be considered. Among these are magic, belief in mana, methods utilized, and the men involved.

Magic

In many tribal groups in Africa, there is no clear distinction between magic and medicine. J. O. Awolalu and P. A. Dopamu in their book, *West African Traditional*

Religion, observe that among several tribes magic and medicine share the same appellation. This is true among the tribes in the northern regions of Africa, which use the same word, *magani,* both for medicine and for magic. Similarly, the Yorubas, spread across Western Nigeria and into Benin Republic, use the same word *oogun,* to denote magic and medicine. Awolalu and Dopamu further display the connections between magic and medicine—they are controlled by the same divinity, both have elements of ritual, are dependent on spiritual beliefs, involve supernatural powers, and require incantations.

Mana

The belief that certain objects and places possess special mystical powers is one of the features of the African religion. Certain rivers like the Osun, in Southwest Nigeria, are believed to possess healing virtues, even to the extent of providing cure for barrenness. Sacred trees, stones, mountains, and creatures dot the African landscape—each with their myths and legends of how powerful they are to cure, or ward off diseases or plagues. Potions are often made from portions of such objects, which may include the bones and tusks of some creatures, which when ingested or applied externally, heal from various conditions. These are besides the many herbs that have been studied, cultivated, and deployed for healing purposes over the centuries.

Methods

As with modern medicine where diagnosis precedes therapy, in traditional healing practice, the first thing done is to establish the source or cause of an ailment. While in most cases this is usually attributable to a spiritual origin, there is a process involved in establishing this conclusion which often entails the science of divination. It is acknowledged that the methodology or practice of divination differs from one tribe to another across the continent. However, in whatever place divination is involved, the help of ancestors, divinities, or spirits must be sought, not only to decipher the nature of the ailment but also to determine appropriate remedy.

Men

Perhaps the most important role in the healing process of traditional societies was played by the human agents. As Richard Gehman affirms, "In most African communities, the medicine man is the focal figure of authority. He may serve as diviner, and prophet, healer and counselor."[14] In many cases, these agents were male, although there are also several known cases where they have been female. Whatever the sex, these persons were recognized to be set apart or devoted in their service to the deities they represented. In his PhD dissertation, Leith

Mulling lists five different categories of persons involved in the task of healing in Ghana; he mentions:

> (1) herbalists who are versed in the knowledge of herbs; (2) medicine men who possess ju-ju (magic) and whose clients generally seek success; (3) Muslim healers; (4) fetish priests who divine through a particular god; (5) soothsayers who are only concerned with divination.[15]

These persons, by virtue of their perceived connection with the supernatural and their healing attributes, were regarded as powerful persons. Just as today, patients place their faith in doctors' abilities to heal them when sick, even so in these primal societies did the natives domicile their implicit trust in these powerful persons whose healing prowess were renowned.

Issues in Health Care Delivery

Optimal health care delivery in Africa will only be possible as the major players in the field of health care in the continent recognize the influential role that African traditional religion and its attendant worldview play on this sector of life. Presently, a few major issues need to be addressed before this goal can be attained. These issues include: the integration rather than segregation of traditional healers in health delivery, the need for better collaboration and cooperation between governmental and nongovernmental agencies, legal framework for traditional healers to operate, and preventive health care.

Integration

The World Health Organization reports that about 80 percent of the African populace relies on traditional healers for their primary health care needs.[16] Although the precise number of traditional healers around the continent may be impossible to determine, what is acknowledged is that the ratio of traditional healers is about 1:500 of the population, while that of Western-trained medical practitioners is 1:40,000 in Sub-Saharan Africa.[17] The UNAIDS report also explains that because pandemics such as AIDS pose such an enormous logistical challenge, other methods of healing that are alternative, available, accessible, and affordable are being marshaled in order to tackle this scourge that has in some regions wiped out an entire generation.

Consequently, rather than segregate modern and traditional methods of healing, a better approach would be an integration of both forms for effectiveness and wider coverage, considering the fact that the general population places a lot of confidence in these traditional healers. Already, in the southern and eastern regions of Africa, associations of traditional healers accredited by the government have been formed to regulate the practice and to prevent abuses by charlatans. This is in line with the WHO Alma-Ata Declaration in 1978; since then, it has organized over ten regional conferences to buttress this collaborative position.

Apart from integrating traditional healing methods as an approach to comprehensive health care delivery in the continent, another necessary factor is cooperation and collaboration with nongovernmental agencies.

Collaboration

Studies show that health institutions operated by churches provide for 40 percent of health care in Nigeria,[18] 43 percent in Tanzania, 35 percent in Malawi, and 34 percent in Ghana.[19] It is obvious that no government can provide all the infrastructural, personnel, and pharmaceutical needs to meet the health care challenge in Africa today. Partnership with nongovernmental agencies, therefore, whether religious or not, will provide a viable solution to this health care quagmire facing the countries in Africa.

Although collaboration is advocated between governmental and nongovernmental agencies, it also needs to be stated that orientation and instruction will still be vitally important if this partnership is to work. One major reason developmental efforts by donor and international agencies are stymied or fail seems to be a lack of understanding of the worldview of the people and their conceptions about sickness and health.

Legal Framework

Adherents to African traditional religion exercise more faith in traditional healers than they often do in modern health care professionals. One of the reasons advanced for this is the fact that the traditional healers "provide client-centred personalized health care that is tailored to meet the needs and expectations of their patients."[20] It is, however, important that a legal framework exist for their involvement in this venture as appears to have begun in South Africa with the drafting of the "Traditional Health Practitioners Bill."[21] Such a framework will be necessary to define the rules of engagement and will help determine culpability in the event of death. Hopefully, this would also deter frauds from a sector that so far has operated under the radar of governmental restrictions or attention.

Preventive Health

All across the world, a lot of attention is being given to the preventive aspect of health care. This is due largely to the fact that an ounce of prevention is better than a pound of cure. The major killer diseases—stroke, hypertension, heart disease, and cancer—which have been labeled lifestyle or noncommunicable diseases, are known to be preventable.

A widely practiced method of preventing sickness or disease in the African religion is through the use of charms or amulets. These may be worn visibly or invisibly, carried in pockets or tied around the arms or waist, tied on the doors, or buried in the ground. Also, they may be eaten with roots or leaves, rubbed on the body, or bathed with as soap.[22] These charms are used to guard against witches and evil spirits, small pox, accidents and general misfortune, and even against venereal and any infectious diseases.[23]

Another important aspect of preventive and primary health care that needs to be mentioned is the attitude towards filth. While modern health care establishes a strong connection between cleanliness and health, this idea does not resonate with the African worldview, which rather attributes sickness and ill health to spiritual factors. Consequently, the environment and its vectors for the transmission of diseases that plague the continent, in the absence of proper education and enlightenment, largely go unattended. Among the diseases that afflict the region that could be controlled by environmental education programs are malaria, typhoid, and tuberculosis.

In order adequately to respond to the health care challenges found in the continent, a number of factors need to be addressed. This final section will deal with recommendations that should help bridge the gap between the traditional view of health and the modern Western approach, which ultimately will produce better health services for the populace.

Recommendations

1. Personnel involved in health care service delivery should receive instruction on the worldviews and belief systems of those they are ministering to. They should patiently strive to understand what the people believe to be the causes for their conditions, and seek to in turn give education on the pathology of environmental disease using culture-specific aids and illustrations.
2. Better, intentional, governmental participation is needed to structure the legal framework for licensing, accrediting, and organizing associations of traditional healers. In rural and suburban areas where belief in the powers of these persons seem stronger than in trained medical personnel, this aspect of governmental involvement is needed rather than the present situation of neglect, pretense, or unconcern witnessed in some regions.
3. While it is widely accepted that Western medical science can explain *how* illness or diseases work, it really does not satisfactorily answer *why* they come. This knowledge should lead to a cooperative relationship between the scientific and the spiritual dimensions of health care that will encourage referral.

Notes

1. Mbiti, John S. (1969). *African Religions and Philosophy*. Nairobi, Kenya: East African Educational Publ., p. 1.
2. Turaki, Yusufu. (2001). *Foundation of African Traditional Religions and Worldview*. Nairobi, Kenya: International Bible Society Africa, p. 39.

3. Mikulencak, Ruby. (1987). Science and Magic Collide in African Medicine. *Evangelical Missions Quarterly* (23) 4, p. 358.

4. Imasogie, Osadolor. (1983). *Guidelines for Christian Theology in Africa*. Achimota, Ghana: African Christian Theology in Africa, p. 60.

5. Barbiero, Victor K. (n.d.). "Africa Health Trends: A 21st Century Imperative," in *Global Health Initiative: Policy Brief* Woodrow Wilson International Center for Scholars. http://www.wilsoncenter. org/topics/pubs/PolicyBrief.pdf (accessed July 28, 2010).

6. Ibid.

7. Berends, Willem. (1993). African Traditional Healing Practices and the Christian Community. *Missiology: An International Review*, Vol 21, No 3, p. 276.

8. Ibid, pp. 278–281.

9. Mikulencak, p. 358.

10. Hiebert, Paul G. (1999). "The Flaw of the Excluded Middle," In Ralph D. Winter and Steven C. Hawthorne (eds.) *Perspectives: On the World Christian Movement*, pp. 414–21. Pasadena, CA: William Carey Library.

11. Ibid, p. 418.

12. Toyin Falola, "The Social and Cultural Paradigms of Human Dignity and Health Care in Africa." Paper presented at the Human Dignity and Health Care Conference, Baylor University, Waco, Texas, October 30, 2010.

13. Mbiti, John. (1969). *African Religions and Philosophy*. London, UK: Heinemann, p. 9.

14. Gehman, Richard. (1989). *African Traditional Religion in Biblical Perspective*. Nairobi, Kenya: East African Educational Publishers, p. 103.

15. Mikulencak, p. 36.

16. Anderson, Sandra and Kaleeba, Noerine, "Ancient Remedies, New Disease: Involving Traditional Healers in Increasing Access to AIDS Care and Prevention in East Africa," *UNAIDS Case Study* (Geneva, Switzerland: Joint United Nations Programme on HIV AIDS, June 2002), p. 7. Marlise Richter, "Traditional Medicines and Traditional Healers in South Africa," *Treatment Action Campaign and AIDS Law Project*, (27 November, 2003), p. 10.

17. Richter, p. 10.

18. Aja, Godwin N., Modeste, Naomi N., Lee, Jerry W, Montogomery, Susanne, Belliard, Juan C.. "Perceived Importance of Church-Based Assets to HIV/AIDS Prevention and Control in a Nigerian City. *International Quarterly of Community Health Education*. Ed George P. Cernada Vol 29: 2; (2008–2009).

19. Green, A., Shaw, J., Dimmock, F., and Conn, Cath. (2002). "A Shared Mission? Changing Relationships Between Government and Church Health Services in Africa." *International Journal on Health Planning and Management* 17: pp. 333–53.

20. Anderson and Kaleeba, p. 7.

21. Richter, p. 11.

22. Rinne, Eva-Marita. (2001). "Water and Healing Experiences from the Traditional Healers in Ile-Ife, Nigeria." *Nordic Journal of African Studies* 10:1, p. 50.

23. Rinne, p. 51.

Chapter 6

Religion and the Environment: Some Ethical Reflections on African Indigenous Religion and Christianity

Rotimi Williams Omotoye

Introduction

In 1992, the World Development report focused on the theme: Development and the Environment.[1] Many issues of concern were considered in the report. In realizing the importance of religion and the environment, the National Association for the Study of Religions and Education (NASRED)[2] in her twelfth annual conference held in 1999 at Adeyemi College of Education, Ondo, examined the theme: "Religion and the Environment." A book of readings from the conference was published in the year 2000.

The same issue was addressed at the conference organized by the National Association for Biblical Studies (NABIS), Western zone at the Evangelical Church Winning All (EWCA) Theological Seminary held in Igbaja, Nigeria in 2008. This shows the concern of the Association for the role of religion in environmental issues. Adherents of every religion, no matter the level of civilization and enlightenment are found and located in a particular environment.

The concept of environment has been defined by S. O. Oyewole in various ways. As a social scientist, he defines the term as the area of land inhabited by a people, including all that the land supports—plants and animal lives, water bodies both running and stagnant, and the atmosphere overcasting that land—constitutes the environment of that people.[3]

Oyewole further stated that to a natural scientist the environment is much more complex, much more inclusive than the definition of a social scientist. According to him, the environment is both "physical and non physical"; it

consists of both the biotic—the life forms— flora, fauna, and microorganisms—
which can be seen as both internal and external.[4] Moreover, from an ecological
perspective, it is all these features together with the interaction between and
among them that affect the life and behavior of the inhabitants, not just as individuals but also as community of individuals.[5] All the above three definitions of
environment are relevant to our understanding of religion and environment as
presented herein.

Thus, it is important to highlight the significance attached to mountains
and hills, among other environmental issues, as it affects traditional religion and
Christianity in Yorubaland of Southwestern Nigeria. It is also our considered view
that man be encouraged to learn how to respect and care for natural creatures of
God, such as mountains and hills, which have been devastated to give way for the
provision of other social facilities like roads and buildings. The terms "mountains"
and "hills" will be used interchangeably in this chapter. Our scope of study will be
limited to Christianity and African traditional religion in Yorubaland.

The concept of mountain is found in both the Old and New Testament.
Many important events are recorded and associated with it. Ojebode also emphasized the importance of the mountains in the Old and New Testament books.[6]
According to him, the Jewish people used to worship Yahweh on the mountain.
For example, in Exodus 19 and Deuteronomy 12, the two passages emphasize the
importance of mountains in the worship of God. Moses—one of the respected
leaders and the appointed deliverer of Israel from Egyptian slavery—collected
the Ten Commandments on Mount Sinai. "Then Moses brought the people out
of the camp to meet God; and they took their stand at the foot of the mountain"
(Exodus 19:17).

Mountains also serve as geographical boundaries among states (Joshua 15:8–11).
The power of God is also demonstrated over nature in the scriptures. For example,
Psalm 97:5 says, "The Mountain melt like wax before the Lord, of all the earth."
The Psalmists in Psalm 99:2 further say, "That Lord is great in Zion and He is high
above all the people."

In the New Testament, two of the temptations of Jesus Christ took place on
the mountain (Matthew 4:5–10). He also delivered his masterpiece sermon on
the mountain, popularly known as "sermon on the mount" (Matthew 5). It is also
important to know that the transfiguration of Jesus Christ took place on a mountain (Matthew 17:1–3).

The Importance of Mountains in the History of Christianity in Yorubaland

It is necessary at this juncture to correct some wrongly held notions by some earlier writers that mountain sites are peculiar to African Independent Churches in
Yorubaland. For instance, Ayodele said, "[T]his is common with some African
Independent Churches."[7] However, it is true that visits to sacred sites like mountains,
hills, river banks, etc. is a common feature in African Independent Churches.[8]

We shall not emphasize the geographical areas occupied by the Yoruba people, as this has been done several times in our earlier works on Christian Missionary Enterprise in Yorubaland.[9] However, when the early European Christian Missionaries came to Yorubaland in the second half of the nineteenth century, most of them settled on mountains and hills.

The buildings in which they lived were located far from their targeted converts. For example, David and Anna Hinderer in Ibadan lived at Kudeti.[10] According to Oduyoye, "[T]hey established the mission house away from the noise of the city at Kudeti."[11] Other missions were later opened at Oke-Ogunpa and Oke-Aremo in 1857.[12] The Roman Catholic Church established her station in Ibadan at Oke-Parde, Oke-Ofa, Oke-Ado and Oke-Are.[13] In Epe, Lagos State, the early Missionaries settled at Oke-Oyinbo,[14] while in Osogbo the early Catholic Missionaries were stationed on a hill top.[15] The Roman Catholics used to go on annual pilgrimage to Oke Maria in Otan Ayegbaju, Osun State.

In Ado-Ekiti, the Anglican Missionaries located their station on a mountain top.[16] Oduyoye is of the opinion that they behaved in such a way "to create a new community."[17] This attitude displayed by the early Christian missionaries was probably to live in a cool and serene environment, separated from the indigenous people. We believe that the action was counter-productive in the propagation of the gospel because they abandoned their major assignment by living remotely from the people.

This attitude was contrary to the action of the Muslim preachers in Yorubaland. The latter lived among the aborigines. In fact, it was one of the factors that led to the early spread of Islam in Yorubaland. According to Gbadamosi, "[I]t lived more closely than Christianity with the pagans, whom it cleverly sought to convert."[18] In other words, the environment is an important strategy in mission work. For a missionary work to be highly successful, the missionaries must take into consideration their level of interaction with the converts seriously. They must live where they live and share some common everyday things with them. This is what Idowu refers to as "participatory observation."[19]

The idea of isolation or segregation living was alien to the Yoruba people. They were used to the *Agbo-ile* system[20] of living. The family solidarity was a common feature in Yorubaland in the past. However, the idea of living on the mountain satisfied the aspirations and yearnings of the white missionaries.

"Mountain Experience" in the Aladura Churches

One of the characteristics of the Aladura Churches in Yorubaland is a visit to sacred sites or location of churches on mountains or hills. In our earlier works, emphasis has been laid on the Aladura churches generally, especially the features of the churches.[21] In this piece, we agree with Oshitelu that the *Aladura* churches believe in *Ori oke* (Mountain). According to him, most of the Christ Apostolic Church branches are to have a prefix "Oke" before the name of the church, such as, Oke Sioni (Mount Zion) and Oke-Igbala (mount of salvation). This is not surprising, because of the place where the 1930 revival of Apostle Ayo Babalola took place at

Oke-Oye[22] Ilesa, Osun State. The Christ Apostolic Church in Erin-Ijesa was named Christ Apostolic Church, Oke Isegun. In Ilorin, the first Christ Apostolic Church was named Oke-Isegun. The Church of the Lord (*Aladura*) performs the annual Ori-Oke (Mount Taborah) Festival.[23]

According to Omoyajowo, the hill top is regarded as a secret place in Cherubim and Seraphim. "To be at a sacred place...means to participate in life eternal; it is the place where an imperishable life force has been available."[24] The members of the church are encouraged to go on hill/mountain tops for prayers, because the place is the point of contact with God or with infinite power; the place itself takes the quality of holiness or sacredness.

Edward Smith, quoted by Omoyajowo, said, "Mountains themselves are frequently taken to be living places of God." He further said, "They go out to Hills in Holy weeks and at all Hallows to fast and pray for children."[25] Some of the important hills and mountains in Yorubaland are: Olorunkole hill, Oke-Erinmo (hill), Oke Igbala at Ondo, Oke Calvary (Ikare), and Okejigbo (Abeokuta).[26] Others are: Ori-Oke Taborah in Ilorin, Ori-Oke Ikoyi, Ori-Oke Akinkemi Okesasa, Oke-aanu, Oke Irapada Oluwa, Oke-Atunyan all in Ibadan; Ori Oke pele in Ondo; Ori-Oke Maria in Ikare; and Ori-Oke Abiye in Ede, Osun State.

The Cherubim and Seraphim members go to the mountain in imitation of Jesus Christ who often prayed on Mount Olivet and was crucified on Mount Calvary.[27] Ayodele, in an interview conducted among some priests in the Aladura churches, responded that mountains are usually located in the outskirts of the town and are visited only on special occasions for special services.[28] According to him, the General Overseer of the United Spiritual Gospel Church explained that they were usually set seven days apart every year during which time they go to a particular mountain for serious prayer and study in order to receive guidance for the church in the upcoming year.[29]

Mountains/Hills in African Traditional Religion

Traditional religion has been defined by Awolalu and Dopamu as the indigenous religion of the African; it is the religion that has been handed down through generations by forebears of the present generation of Africans.[30] Mountains and hills are part of the monuments inherited from the forebears and are regarded as creatures of *Oldunmare* (God).

The history of African communities is intricately associated with some natural formations, such as hills, mountains, rivers, and lakes.[31] Such formations are so revered that in certain cases, they may be deified and celebrated on an annual basis to honor them. Examples are the Oke-Ibadan (Ibadan), Orosun (Oke Idanre), and Osun (Osogbo) festival.[32] The Orosun and Oke-Ibadan festivals are in honor of hills in both places and are both associated with crop harvest.

There are spiritual blessing when prayers are made on such mountains. Women that suffer from infertility received answer to their prayers on mountains. Such children received are named after mountains like *Okebunmi, Okeseyi, Okedele, and Olokede.*[33]

It is important to note that geology is an important factor in the location of human settlement. In Yorubaland, topography was of great importance to the historical determination of human abode, especially during the period of civil and religious wars.[34] During these times, people did settle on hilly and rugged areas, so as to take refuge from the attacks of more powerful groups. Such areas included Idanre, Ikare, Ado-Awaye, Igbeti, and Igbajo.[35] Indeed, the establishment of Igbajo during the Kiriji war in Yorubaland could not be in doubt. The town situated within the hills was founded by the cooperation effort—and the name of the town implies a sort of cooperative of the Oyo and Ijesa people. According to Olusegun, still today, the people of Igbajo and Otan-Ayegbaju speak the Oyo and Ijesa dialects.[36]

The establishment of Ibadan on a hill during the period of Yoruba wars should also be noted. Ibadan served primarily as a collection center for refugees and subsequently became militarily so important during the nineteenth century that its influence reached its climax because of the victory during the Ijaye war.[37] Indeed, the establishment of some settlements on hills was so impressive that T. J.Bowen, writing about such sites, asserted that nothing but the terror of war could have planted such settlement in such places as they were found.[38]

The end of the Yoruba warfare also witnessed the abandonment of some settlements by the original inhabitants for new places they founded. Most of the locations in this category were mainly those situated on the hills. The abandonment of such places in the western part of Yorubaland has been well documented by Gleave. According to him, it appears that most of the hill settlers moved downhill primarily as a result of the restoration of peace.[39] It is also known that such hill settlement could no longer satisfy the yearnings of the inhabitants with regard to expansion and farming activities.

The example of Ado-Awaye could be given. From available evidence, it is clear that Ado-Awaye started to move immediately after the Kiriji/Ekitiparapo peace treaty.[40] Other towns that moved after the war were Oke-ho, Eruwa, Igbeti, and Idanre. It is observed that the new settlement was better planned than the abandoned ones. During the Ekitiparapo War in Yorubaland, the mountains were used to study the movements and point of station of the enemies. It was a good strategy for winning a war against an enemy. In other words, mountains and hills are useful for political advantages.

Mountains and hills are also good sources of water for the people. For example, the waterfalls resort center at Erin-Ijesa, Osun State takes its source from the Yoruba hills that surrounds the town. The waterfall is supplying uninterrupted water to the town and its surrounding communities.[41] Another example is Oyo Alafin water works reservoir, which is situated on Soro Hills.[42]

Comparatively, mountains and hills are useful and are regarded as sacred phenomena in Christian and African traditional religion. They were created for the use of man by God. The Christian and adherents of traditional religion in Yorubaland make adequate use of mountains to achieve their religious satisfaction. Olumide once said, "[T]hose who settle near a high mountain, hill or rock will feel the urge to worship the spiritual powers believed to be inherent in such phenomena."[43]

Conclusion

God, in demonstration of His omnipotent power, created mountains and hills to show His attributes of greatness. Man, as his creature, adequately makes use of these for his/her religious, political, and socioeconomic well-being. In other words, the environment created by God for man will not be adequate without mountains and hills. It is, therefore, necessary for man to maintain it properly and adequately.

We conclude this chapter by quoting Mbiti: "God is omnipresent, and is reachable at any time and at any place people worship Him where and whenever the need arises."[44] In other words, God can be worshipped on a mountain, hill, church, synagogue, river bank, crossroads, or thresholds of their homes. Jesus Christ, the founder of Christianity, told the Samaritan woman in the gospel of John that "a time will come, however, indeed it is already here, when the true (genuine) worshippers will worship the father in spirit and in truth (reality), for the Father is seeking just such people as these as His worshippers" (Amplified Bible; John 4:23).

Notes

1. O. J. Olaniyan, (2003). "Environmental Management from the Perspective of Culture" In P. Ade Dopamu et al. (eds.) *African Culture, Modern Science and Religious Thought.* Ilorin: African Centre for Religions and the Sciences (ACRS), p. 577.
2. The National Association for the Study of Religions and Education (NASRED) organized a conference at Adeyemi College of Education, Ondo in 1999 and published the conference papers in 2000 with a title *Religion and the Environment.*
3. Oyewole, S. O. (2003). "African Cultural Response to Ecological and Environmental Concerns." In P. Ade Dopamu et al. (eds.). *African Culture, Modern Science and Religious Thought.* Ilorin, African Centre for Religions and the Sciences (ACRS), p. 368.
4. Ibid, p. 369.
5. Ibid.
6. Ojebode, P. A. (2000). "The Mountainous Environment in the Bible: Its Implications for the Development of Christianity and Humanity." In Gbola Aderibigbe and Deji Ayegboyin (eds.). *Religion and the Environment.* Ibadan: Olu-Akin Publishers, pp. 131–32.
7. Ayodele, A. A. (2000). "Environmental Influence on Christian Worship: A Survey of African Independent Churches Experience." In Gbola Aderibigbe and Deji Ayegboyin (eds.). *Religion and the Environment.* Ibadan: Olu-Akin publishers, p. 126.
8. Oshitelu, G. A. (2007). *History of the Aladura (Independent) Churches 1918–1940: An Interpretation.* Ibadan: Hope Publications, p. 107.
9. Omotoye, Rotimi. "An Examination of the Attitude of Traditional Rulers to the Introduction of Christianity in the Pre-Colonial Era of Christianity in Yorubaland." In *Centre Point: A Journal of Intellectual, Scientific and Cultural Interest.* University of Ilorin, Humanities Edition, vol.11, no. 1, p. 1. See also, Rotimi Omotoye, "The Concept of God and Its Understanding by the Christian Missionaries in Yorubaland." In E. Ade Odumuyiwa et al. (eds.). *God: The Contemporary Discussion.* Ilorin: Decency Printers, 2005, p. 101. See also, Rotimi Omotoye, "Historical

Perspective of the Decolonization of the Church in Yorubaland (1842–1960)." In S. O Abogunrin (ed.). *Decolonization of Biblical Interpretation in Africa.* Ibadan: M. Alofe Publishers, 2005, p. 395.

10. Kalu, O. U. (ed). (1978). *Christianity in West Africa: The Nigerian Story.* Ibadan: Daystar Press, p. 269.

11. Ibid.

12. Ibid, p. 272.

13. O'Neill, Patrick. (1981). *The Catholic Faith in Ibadan Diocese 1884–1974.* Ibadan: Daystar Press, pp. 7–28. See also, A. O. Makozi and G. J. Afolabi Ojo. (1982). *The History of the Catholic Church in Nigeria.* Ibadan: Macmillan, p. 21.

14. The Researcher was in Epe, Lagos State on July 15, 2007, on research assignment. A visit was made to Oke-Oyinbo.

15. The researcher equally visited Osogbo on July 20, 2007.

16. The site at Ado-Ekiti was visited on April 26, 2006.

17. Kalu, *Christianity in West Africa: The Nigerian Story,* p. 248.

18. Gbadamosi, T. G. O. (1978). *The Growth of Islam Among the Yoruba, 1841–1908.* London: Longman Group Limited, p. 144.

19. Idowu, E. B. (1973). *African Traditional Religion: A Definition.* Ibadan: Longman, pp. 15–17. See also, Olumide Kayode. (1980). *Understanding African Traditional Religion,* Department of Religious Studies, University of Ife, Ile-Ife, pp. 111–113.

20. Fadipe, N. A. (1970). *Sociology of the Yoruba.* Ibadan: Ibadan University Press, pp. 65–77.

21. Omotoye, Rotimi. (1999). "Aladura Churches and Cultural Revival in Yorubaland." Olu Obafeni et al. (eds.). *An Intellectual Journal of African Studies,* vol. 3, no. 1, pp. 72–77.

22. Oshitelu, G. A. (2007). *History of the Aladura (Independent) Churches 1918–1940: An Interpretation.* Ibadan: Hope Publications, pp. 102–10.

23. Ayegboyin, Deji, and and A. Ademola Ishola (eds.). (1989). *African Indigenous Churches: An Historical Perspective.* Lagos: Greater Heights Publication, p. 73.

24. Omoyajowo, J. Akinyele. (1982). *Cherubim and Seraphim: The History of an African Independent Church.* New York: Nok Publishers, p. 160.

25. Ibid, p. 161.

26. Ibid.

27. Ibid.

28. Ayodele, *Religion and the Environment,* p. 128.

29. Ibid, p. 129.

30. Awolalu, J. O., and P. Ade Dopamu. (1979). *West African Traditional Religion.* Ibadan: Onibonoje, p. 26.

31. Oyewole, "African Cultural Response to Ecological and Environmental Concerns" In P. Ade Dopamu et al. (eds) *African Culture, Modern Science and Religious Thought,* p. 371.

32. Ibid.

33. Ayodele, *Religion and the Environment,* p. 133.

34. Ekanade, Olusegun, and Oluwole Aloba. (1998). "19th Century Yoruba: The Geographer's Viewpoint." In Adeagbo Akinjogin (ed.). *War and Peace in Yorubaland 1793–1893.* Ibadan: Heinemann Educational Books, p. 24.

35. Ibid.

36. Ibid, p. 27.

37. Ibid.

38. Ibid.

39. Ibid.

40. Ibid.
41. The Researcher grew up in the community.
42. Ojebode, in *Religion and the Environment*, p. 134.
43. Kayode, Olumide. (1980). *Understanding African Traditional Religion*. Department of Religious Studies, University of Ife, Ile-Ife, p. 10.
44. Mbiti, J. S. (1969). *African Religions and Philosophy*. London: Heinemann, p. 74.

Chapter 7

Christianity in Contemporary African Religious Space

Pius Oyeniran Abioje

Introduction

This chapter is comparative in the sense that it tries to situate Christianity within the religious plurality of Africa in order to determine its spread and the quality of its influence. It is done from the perspective of a systematic doctrinal theologian, but history features prominently, wherever it is considered necessary for illumination and clarification.

A Brief History of Christianity in Africa

Historically, Christianity did not originate in Africa, but its long existence in the continent is well known. Elizabeth Isichei notes, for instance, that:

> By 600 C.E., there were flourishing Christian churches in North Africa, Egypt, Nubia, and in Aksum, near the Red Sea, in northern Ethiopia. The North African and Egyptian churches, in particular, had sustained a brilliant intellectual life, and their debates had helped shape the core beliefs of Christendom. The churches of North Africa and Nubia came to an end at different points in time after the Arab invasions. Much has been written on why some churches survived and others did not, but the answer is to a large extent, a mystery.[1]

Beyond the "mystery," some of the reasons for the loss of Christianity in North Africa are said to include the fact that the religion had not blended well with the local culture[2] and the division that tugged at Christendom in those days.[3]

Another point that requires some explanation in the above quotation from Isichei concerns her observation on the intellectual contribution of the ancient church in North Africa to shaping "the core beliefs of Christendom." That no doubt refers especially to Saint Augustine of Hippo. Garver notes that "basic theological dogmas of Christendom" were shaped by "ecumenical councils," which preceded the divisions within Christendom.[4] In the words of Placher:

> More than anyone else, Augustine shaped Western theology, and made it different from the traditions of the East. For the [W]estern half of the church throughout the Middle Ages his authority stood second only to that of Scripture. Historians have with some justice described the reformation as a struggle between two sides of Augustine: Protestantism began with his doctrine of grace, and the Roman Catholic response grew out of his doctoring of the church.[5]

Unfortunately, Augustine is not known to have contributed toward a symbiotic integration of the Christian doctrine and message with African culture. Indeed, he is said to have been foreign in his orientation.[6] That notwithstanding, he is widely acknowledged as the most profound ancient theologian who helped to define and/ or prop up the essential content of the teaching of Christianity in its Western mode. What is more, the commonest form of Christianity in Africa is the Western type. The Orthodox Church of Ethiopia and the Coptic Church of Egypt remain small minorities.[7] And so, indirectly, Saint Augustine remains prominent in his contribution to the form of Christianity that is predominant in Africa by way of principal doctrines, such as those regarding the Holy Trinity and matrimony.

In the final analysis, the ancient glory of Christianity in North Africa started to decimate from 640 Common Era (CE), with the defeat of Egypt by the Muslim Arabs in that year. As Kenny notes in respect to Saudi Arabia, Egypt constituted the gateway to the rest of Africa.[8] With the Arab invasions, all of the churches disappeared, except as Isichei notes: "[T]he Coptic Church of Egypt has survived as the faith of small minority in an overwhelming Muslim nation, [and] the Ethiopian Church also survives, and was for many centuries central to national identity."[9] According to Raymond Hickey, Christianity survived in the two lands because it had been indigenized, while, as he notes with respect to the rest of North Africa: "Within two hundred years of the Arab invasion the last surviving pockets of Christians had disappeared and the new Muslim city of Tunis had replaced Christian Carthage as the centre of North African civilization."[10] That constituted the end of an era of Christianity in ancient Africa. All of the efforts that were made to regain North Africa for Christianity, through the new Mendicant Orders, in personalities, such as Saint Francis of Assisi, Saint Louis of France, and Raymond Lull, achieved very limited success. According to Hickey, "It was Cardinal Lavigerie (1825–92), founder of the Society of Missionaries of Africa and Archbishop of Algiers, who worked hardest for the rebirth of the church in North Africa." His priests were called "White fathers" because they wore the flowing robe of the Muslim population. Hickey quotes a report to the effect that

> There were indeed hopeful signs for many years: a renaissance of desert monasticism which was inspired by the saintly Charles de Foucauld, who was killed in his desert

hermitage in 1916: the conversion of a small number of members to Christianity; and a largely urban "settler" population of over a million in Algeria. But the essential for an incarnate church, an indigenous Christian population, was missing.[11]

This report was reconfirmed to this writer at a study workshop held in Dakar, Senegal, August 4–29, 2008, by three young Algerian scholars who attended it: Bouabdellah Kacemi, Boumohart Belk Heir, and Mustapha Radji. They said the Christian population of Algeria contained an insignificant number of indigenous Algerians, but the Christians were free to practice their religion.

From 1450–1750, some fairly remarkable Portuguese missionary activities took place in Africa, but without much enduring success. Hildebrandt suggests that the failure was most probably because the principal interests of the Portuguese were trade and wealth. In his words: "They encouraged missionary work, but if they needed more slaves and the missionaries stood in the way, they would abandon the missionary effort in order to increase trade."[12] Similarly, but much more elaborately, Hickey notes that the Portuguese missionary endeavor had no permanent result because of:

> The difficulty in communication which made sustained efforts impossible; the lack of quinie and of medication for the coastal fevers; the scourge of the slave trade which seemed to dominate all dealings between Europe and West Africa; and the rivalry between the Portuguese and other European missionaries.[13]

Principal among the factors that are said to aid missionary activities later in Africa, as from the mid-nineteen century are: the suppression and termination of the slave trade and the resettlement of many freed slaves in several places along the West African coast. Of particular interest are the three countries that became the havens for many freed slaves, namely, Liberia—"land of the free"—which was established by America in 1822; Sierra Leone, whose capital, Freetown, was established by the English in 1787; and Gabon, which was established by the French in 1849, with the capital Libreville, which also means Freetown in French language. Hickey notes that:

> The new communities of slaves on the West African coast were all Christians, and they cried out for priests and missionaries. Anglican and Methodist missionaries were first in the field, and they established the nuclei of strong local churches around the West African coast. The evangelical Anglican Church missionary society, established in 1799, was particularly active, and together with the London Missionary society (1795) led to a nation-wide crusade to bring the light of the Gospel to Africa.[14]

Thus, a new, and hopefully everlasting, Christian life began in Africa. Hickey balances the Protestant picture by stating, inter alia, that the Roman Catholic Church's "first missionary expedition sailed for West Africa in 1842." The sky almost became the limit, so to say, for diverse missionary work in different parts of Africa.

Types of Christianity in Africa Today

Three stages of Christianity in Africa are identifiable. The first dates back to the life and times of Jesus himself. It began with "the flight to Egypt." As Isichei notes, "Both Egypt's Christians and Muslims believe that the Holy Family stayed there for some time."[15] She refers to the ancient tradition that claims that Saint Mark was the first person who brought Christianity to Alexandria—a seaport in North Egypt—but as she further notes, "We have no way of knowing whether this is true, most scholars regard it as a legend." What has not been disproved, as she notes later on, is that a catechetical school flourished at Alexandria at about 150–215 CE, headed by Clement of Alexandria.

Much has been said on the glory, the fall, and even the disappearance of ancient Christianity in North Africa. The account notes the Coptic version of Christianity, which dates back to the first century and is still surviving as a minority religion in Egypt, as well as the Orthodox version, which is a majority religion in Ethiopia and dates back to the fourth century CE

Heretofore, little note has been made of the second stage of Christianity in Africa—about 1500–1800—which consisted mainly in the Portuguese trade adventure and missionary activities. The latter had no lasting effect, according to the factors that were listed above. Then came the third stage of the postslave trade era, which ushered in a new, extensive, and hopefully permanent implantation of Christianity in Africa in the nineteenth century. In the twentieth century, Christianity became a very big tree. As Carpenter notes:

> In 1900, there were only about 9 million Christians in all of Africa. By 1945, however, this number had more than tripled to 30 million. By 1970, this number had more than tripled again to more than 115 million. Today, there are an estimated 380 million Christians in Africa.[16]

He obtained the figures from Barret and Johnson.[17] The figures are rightly called estimates. But there are countries, such as Uganda, the Democratic Republic of Congo, Kenya, Tanzania, Nigeria, Ghana, Ivory Coast, and so on, with large Christian populations and with churches springing-up like mushrooms in virgin lands. Carpenter notes that:

> African influence on the world Christian scene is growing, and it is becoming much more common to see Africans leading Christian agencies and shaping Christian thought. The newly elected executive of the World Council of Churches is Samuel Kobia, a Kenyan. A Chief Officer for the Alliance of Reformed Churches is Setri Nyomi, a Ghanaian. The presenter of the prestigious Stone Lectures at Princeton Theological Seminary in 2003 was Kwame Bediako, also a Ghanaian.[18]

Carpenter concludes, that without doubt, "Africa is fast becoming a heartland of world Christianity." Of course, it is arguable that Africa is not just "becoming a heartland of world Christianity," it has been so for at least more than a century in many respects, but Carpenter is talking with specific reference to leadership of universal Christian bodies. In that light, Koschorke also notes that:

> In August 2003, the Kenyan Methodist Samuel Kobia was elected General Secretary of the World Council of Churches. The Lutheran World Federation is led by Ishmail Noko from Zimbabwe, and the General Secretary of the World Alliance of Reformed Churches, Setri Nyomi, comes from Ghana. So at the beginning of the 21st century, the three major Protestant ecumenical institutions are headed by Africans. Today most Anglicans live in Africa, thus turning the former "Church of England" by numerical majority into an African church.[19]

There seems to be no greater evidence that Christianity has regained, and to a large extent, expanded its foothold in Africa.

Many Christian historians have identified four categories of Christianity in Africa, apart from the Egyptian Coptic version and the Ethiopian Orthodoxy. These include: the historic/established churches, the independent African churches, the Zionist/Aladura churches, and the new Fundamentalist-Pentecostal churches. As Engelbert Beyer notes, the historic/established churches include the Roman Catholic Church, the Anglican, Methodist, and Lutheran, Presbyterian, Baptist, as well as the long-existing Ethiopian Orthodox Church and the Coptic Church of Egypt. Among the groups that separated from one or the other of these churches are the Seventh Day Adventists, the Jehovah's Witnesses, and the Mormons.[20]

The second branch of churches is the independent African churches, which are in four categories. In the first category are the churches that separated from the historic churches because they wanted their own indigenous leadership, and they maintain some affinity with the doctrines and forms of worship of their former historic churches.[21]

The second type of African church is called "Zionist" in South and East Africa, while they are called "Aladura" (praying) churches in Nigeria, with specific reference to Yorubaland. Universally, they are referred to as Spiritual, Healing, or Pentecostal. Beyer notes about their characterization that:

> They emphasize healing by faith and prayer. They demand radical rejection of paganism, charms, fetishes, etc. They call for a radical faith in Jesus Christ as the only Saviour. They believe in the continuous guidance of the Holy Spirit in prophecies, visions and dreams. They have a very elaborate hierarchy, use local cultural elements in their services and have many external observances, partly from the Old Testament.[22]

Those, basically, are the characteristics of most of the early Pentecostalism movements in Africa. They no doubt share some of the traits with corresponding ones around the world.

The third type of African independent church is described as "messianic," and said to be fewer in number compared to the other brands. They are said to include "Manuel Antonio's Naparamas in Mozambique, whose main objective is initially of political military type" (Meeting for African Collaboration).[23] As Beyer notes, in the Messianic Church movement, "the prophet becomes the 'new Moses' or 'Black Messiah.'"[24] It sounds all good though Africa remains largely "The Shackled Continent."[25]

The fourth type of church in Africa is the new "Fundamentalist-Pentecostal churches of mainly American origin; among these, some like the Potter's House, Chrisco, and the Rhema churches could almost be described as new denominations, but most are independent and autonomous fellowships."[26] On clarification of terms, one reads that the word "Fundamentalist" was "first used of that segment of Christianity which began in the United States of America" in the early part of the twentieth century. It is said to have emerged as a reaction to developments in the mainline traditional churches, with particular reference to the tendency of the latter to accept the historical approach to the study of the Bible and be socially involved. As Meeting for African Collaboration (MAC) notes, "Fundamentalists regarded both these developments as destructive of true Christianity."[27] It is stated further:

> This segment of Christianity has come to be distinguished by a cluster of characteristics: insistence on biblical inerrancy; the identification of Christianity with the fundamentalist version of it; a negative evaluation of the modern world; a militant attitude towards movements like liberalism, modernism, and secular Humanism; and a call to some form of separation from non-believers—in some cases even from mainline Christians.[28]

The new Fundamentalist-Pentecostal churches are also identified with emphasis on charismatic gifts of the Holy Spirit and the accomplishment of miracle feats in the life of believers. As MacArthur, Jr. notes, charismatic historians trace the movement's modern origins to a small Bible college in Topeka, Kansas, run by Charles Fox Parham, who was a member of the Holiness movement. The movement teaches that an entire sanctification—spiritual state amounting to sinless perfection in this life—is obtainable by Christians through a "second blessing," a dramatic postsalvation experience of transformation.[29] Parham is personally said to be an enthusiastic advocate of faith healing, based on "an experience in which he says he was healed of 'heart disease in its worst form,'" and upon that, "he discarded all his medicine, canceled his insurance, and refused every form of medical treatment for the rest of his life." Characteristically, all in the Charismatic-Pentecostal movement and churches believe that God, through the Holy Sprit, provides all the needs of a believer, medically, economically, professionally, and otherwise in miraculous ways, through group and personal prayers, in ways that are peculiar to those in the movement.

Basically, these are the churches and Christian movements that are found in Africa. One has tried to minimize mentioning of names of persons and institutions, as much as possible, to concentrate on categorization and typology, generically speaking.

The Spread of Christianity in Africa

The expansion of Christianity in Africa is hampered, to a great extent, by both external and internal factors. One or the other of the external factors has been discussed, with particular reference to Islam which, together with Christianity, forms the dominant religion in most countries of Africa. Beyond that, MAC[30] notes that "there are Eastern imports like the Baha'is, Eckankar, and various forms of the New Age Movement." This section offers some discussion on the challenges posed to the expansion of Christianity in Africa by Islam, African traditional religion (ATR), many minor religions, vicious cults, and social clubs. The principal challenge to the spread of Christianity in Africa is Islam. Of course, Islam also considers Christianity to be an obstacle to its advancement in many parts of Africa, except that here, Christianity is the cynosure. The strength of ATR is also critical in this study.

Available statistics may not be accurate; they nevertheless give a high approximation of the actual figures. According to a compilation accessed by Hildebrandt,[31] the 1995 estimates are:

Table 7.1 Christians Population in Africa

Country	Population estimate	Christian population	Muslim population	ATR population	Year of compilation
1. Egypt	60,470,000	14.2%	85.4%	-	1995
2. Libya	5, 445,000	3%	96%	-	1995
3. Tunisia	9,019,000	0.25%	99.5%	-	1995
4. Morocco	29,116,000	0.16%	99.8%	-	1995
5. Algeria	29,306,000	0.40%	99.4%	-	1995
6. Liberia	3,005,000	37%	13.3%	49.4%	1995
7. Ivory coast	15,315,000	31%	38.7%	30.3%	1995
8. Ghana	17,543,000	64%	16%	20%	1995
9. Togo	4,038,000	43%	21%	36%	1995
10. Bemin	5,573,000	28.2%	17%	54.8%	1995
11. Nigeria	100,580,000	50%	40%	10%	1995
12. Niger	8,313,000	0.38%	90.5%	9%	1995
13. Burkina Faso	10,382,000	19%	48%	33%	1995
14. Mali	10,878,000	3.8%	86%	11.2%	1995
15. Guinea	7,807,000	4.5%	83.1%	12.4%	1995
16. Gambia	983,000	3.7%	95.4%	0.3%	1995
17. Senegal	8,448,000	5.6%	90.8%	3.6%	1995
18. Sierra Leone	4,726,000	8.9%	43.1%	48%	1995
19. Guinea-Bissau	1,105,000	7.9%	44%	48.1%	1995
20. Mauritania	2,329,000	0.26%	99.7%	-	1995
21. Cameroon	12,875,000	63.2%	24%	12%	1995
22. Chad	6, 447,000	35.1%	45.5%	19.1%	1995
23. Gabon	1,380,000	87.1%	4.25	7.7%	1995
24. Congo	2,289,000	85.4%	1.3%	10.2%	1993
25. DRC (Zaire)	41,813,000	95.9%	1.4%	2.7%	1995
26. Rwanda	8,582,000	80%	10%	9.%	1995

Continued

Table 7.1 Continued

Country	Population estimate	Christian population	Muslim population	ATR population	Year of compilation
27. Burundi	6,299,000	91.8%	1%	7.1%	1995
28. Equatorial Guinea	497,000	93%	0.5%	5.1%	1995
29. Central African Republic	3,306,000	83%	3.3%	12.3%	1995
30. Sudan	29,116,000	19%	70%	9.9%	1995
31. Ethiopia & Eritrea	52,569,000	58%	35%	6%	1995
33. Kenya	30,844,000	82.1%	6%	10%	1995
34. Uganda	22,012,000	83.4%	8%	5.9%	1995
35. Tanzania	32,892,000	51%	35%	13.2%	1995
36. Djibouti	473,000	4.8%	94.6%	-	1995
37. Angola	11,531,000	84.6%	-	13.9%	1995
38. Namibia	2,191,000	91%	0.01%	5%	1995
39. South Africa	39,189,000	72.6%	1.25%	17.7%	1995
40. Lesotho	2,020,000	93%	-	6%	1995
41. Swaziland	938,000	80.2%	0.8%	17.6%	1995
42. Botswana	1,528,000	62%	0.2%	37%	1995
43. Zimbabwe	11,352,000	61.7%	1.6%	32.6%	1995
44. Mozambique	17,913,000	42%	13%	40%	1995
45. Malawi	9,950,000	81.1%	14.5%	4.2%	1995
56. Zambia	10,174,000	75%	1%	23%	1995

An alternative survey of religious allegiance in Africa in 1980, which Hickey[32] quotes, goes thus:

Table 7.2 Northeast Africa

Country	Population	Muslim percentage	Christian percentage
1. Egypt	42,144,000	90%	10%
2. Sudan	19,191,000	72%	9%
3. Ethiopia	32,522,000	38%	57%
4. Djibouti	119,000	95%	5%
5. Somalia	3,650,000	99%	-
TOTAL	**97,626,000**		

Table 7.3 North Africa

1. Libya	2,980,000	98%	-
2. Tunisia	6,365,000	98%	-
3. Algeria	18,594,000	98%	-
4. Morocco	20,391,000	98%	-
5. Mauretania	1,630,000	98%	-
6. Chad	C 1,000,000	100%	
TOTAL	**50,958,000**		

Table 7.4 West Africa

1. Cape Verde	325,000	-	99%
2. Senegal	5,660,000	85%	6%
3. Gambia	600,000	88%	3%
4.Guinea-Bissau	570,000	38%	10%
5. Guinea	5,010,000	68%	1%
6. Sierra Leone	3,470,000	40%	9%
7. Liberia	1,937,000	20%	35%
8. Ivory Coast	7,970,000	24%	32%
9. Ghana	11,450,000	16%	63%
10. Togo	2,699,000	13%	37%
11. Benin	3,570,000	15%	23%
12. Upper Volta	6,910,000	30%	12%
13. Mali	6,530,000	75%	2%
14. Niger	5,320,000	90%	0.5%
15. Nigeria	c.90,000,000	46%	43%
TOTAL	**152,021,000**		

Table 7.5 Central Africa

1.Chad	c. 3,520,000	32%	46%
2. Central Africa Republic	2,238,000	4%	84%
3. Cameroon	8,500,000	23%	56%
4. Equatorial Guinea	363,000	-	89%
5. Sao Tome	85,000	-	98%
6. Gabon	550,000	1%	96%
7. Congo	1,540,000	-	93%
8. Zaire	28,290,000	1%	95%
9. Angola	7,181,000	-	90%
10. Zambia	5,830,000	1%	72%
TOTAL	**58,097,000**		

Table 7.6   East Africa

1. Kenya	16,400,000	7%	73%
2. Uganda	13,675,000	7%	78%
3. Tanzania	18,519,000	32%	44%
4. Rwanda	5,046,000	2%	73%
5. Burundi	4,510,000	2%	86%
6. Malawi	5,970,000	15%	65%
7. Mozambique	10,470,000	15%	39%
TOTAL	**74,590,000**		

Table 7.7   Southern Africa

1. South Africa	29,290,000	2%	79%
2. Lesotho	1,340,000	-	93%
3. Swaziland	550,000	-	77%
4. Namibia	1,022,000	-	96%
5. Botswana	819,000	-	50%
6. Zimbabwe	7,495,000	-	58%
TOTAL	**40,516,000**		

Table 7.8   Indo-Malagasy Island

1. Madagascar	8,740,000	12%	51%
2. Comoros Islands	300,000	100%	-
3. Mayotte	49,000	80%	65%
4. Mauritius	969,000	16%	35%
5. Reunion	548,000	2%	98%
6. Seychelles	66,000	-	98%
TOTAL	**10,672d**		
Total for Africa 484,480,000			

Survey of Religious Allegiance (1980)

Hildebrandt explains that the figures he has quoted represent the estimated percentage of the total number who are claimed to be Christian, Muslim, and adherents of ATR.[33] The year of compilation and the actual total populations are considered not to be as significant as the fact that the figures offer a fair idea of the spread of the religions.

The table from Hildebrandt indicates that Christianity has the majority percentage of membership in 25 countries, Islam in 17, and ATR in 4 countries. Islam and Christianity are close in percentage in Nigeria and Chad; Christianity is close to ATR in percentage in Togo, while the three religions are close in percentage in the Ivory Coast. The Patrick Johnstone's statistics adopted by Hildebrandt simply puts the Muslim population of Chad at 45.5 percent, and the Christian population at 35.1 percent,[34] but the Barret alternative statistics adopted by Hickey separately puts the Muslim population of North Chad at 100 percent, while Chad-Ndjamena is said to have 32 percent Muslims and 46 percent Christians.[35]

One can also note a dispute over the percentage of Muslim and Christian populations in Nigeria. Hickey is of the opinion that Barret presents fairly acceptable statistics of the population of Christians and Muslims in Africa in the World Christian Encyclopedia (1981), "with just a few exceptions."[36] One of the exceptions happens to be that he would rather put the Muslim population in Nigeria at 49 percent, instead of the 46 percent given by Barret. But he raises no objection to the 43 percent given to Christians, with the implication that he believes that the Muslims are underrated in population. It should be noted that the version adopted by Hildebrandt (above), in contrast with both Barret and Hickey, assigns a higher percentage to Christians. Onaiyekan notes that:

> We have always insisted that Christians are in the majority in this country. Unfortunately, there are no hard figures to confirm this. We had an opportunity to clarify this during our last census but the chance was denied us. We do believe it is necessary at some point that we have a good and reliable census. Meanwhile, we continue to speculate and insist that Christians are at least a big number in this country.[37]

Indeed, it became the talk of the town in 2006 when Muslim leaders threatened to boycott the census, with one of the conditions being that religion must not appear on the identity list. Christian population seems to be higher in Nigeria, when one considers that Christians appear to be in overwhelming majority in most parts of the South, in many parts of the Middle-belt, and toward the North, leaving only a few states in the far North as a real stronghold of Islam. Apart from Onaiyekan (above), some other observers also note that lack of insufficient data notwithstanding, Christianity is larger in population than Islam in Nigeria. In the words of Gaya:

> The church has grown in northern Nigeria. Its growth in the farther north is phenomenal, perhaps giving Muslims much concern. The destruction of some of these churches in this area is an indication of the restiveness that Christian growth has caused.[38]

It is equally noteworthy the observation that it is in the northern stronghold of Muslims that Christianity suffers severe persecution, with loss of lives and property.[39] Growing conversion and efforts at converting Church buildings into mosques are also reported.[40] But, as Kukah notes, although the Muslim population in the Southwest Nigeria is fairly large in some areas, Muslim militarism is stiffly resisted. Some "weak" Christians in Nigeria, for example, are known to have converted to Islam for job, business, and other benefits.[41] But there seems to be some other Africans also who prefer the Islamic doctrine and practice, for whatever reasons. Ayandele,[42] among some other scholars, notes that "in many ways Islam integrated and assimilated, preserving vital indigenous and social units like polygamy, slavery and the family" whereas, "Christian missionaries, fired by idealism of a faith to which they ascribed, rightly or wrongly, the enlightenment, progress and techno-logical achievements of their countries, perceived no wisdom in compromising with indigenous customs and institutions." This means, in the context of this study, that although very many Africans seem to be proud Christians, some of them are con-verting to Islam from either ATR or Christianity, as applicable to any religion.

The second religion that constitutes a fairly serious challenge to the spread of Christianity in Africa is ATR. Apart from the fact that it is shown to have majority population percentages in four countries, as seen in Table 1 above, it is also said to be a very resilient religion that continues to constitute various forms of attraction to many Africans, including many Christians and Muslims. As scholars, such as Joseph Gbenda note, Africanized forms of Christianity "tend to provide solutions to existential problems such as health problems, fear of witches, spiritual problems, fulfillment of ambitions and hopes."[43] But that has not completely satisfied the longing of many Africans for the original ATR-related oath-taking when the truth must be known,[44] festivals such as Olojo in Ile-Ife and Osun Osogbo in Yorubaland, Nigeria,[45] or the belief that African divinities are powerful[46] and that the divinities can bless the faithful and supplicants with gifts, such as fruits of the womb, sound health, prosperity, long life, etc.

Beyond the foregoing, indications are emerging that some adherents of ATR are trying to modernize. The endeavor can be seen in uniformed choir and printed programs of funeral, outing, and marriage ceremonies, by some ATR organizations. Assimeng notes that:

> Another example of this cultural re-appraisal is the inauguration in Accra on December 19, 1975, of "the National Association of Priests of African Religion (NAPAR)." This Association aims at reviving indigenous African beliefs and forms of worship...to unite all traditional priests and priestesses with a view to initiating policies which will correct the wrong impressions created about traditional culture, beliefs and forms of worship.[47]

Thus, in spite of the effort made by both Islam and Christianity, from the very beginning until now to exterminate ATR, the religion tends to survive, suffering both losses and gains like its counterparts. Michael Umudu[48] reports how some groups of Christians went on a rampage in Igboland, in the Amaekwulu com-munity of Eastern Nigeria, burning shrines and emblems of ATR, so as to exter-minate the religion from the community entirely. Christian presence was said to be so massive that the unprovoked rage met no resistance. But the reporter quotes an Igbo Chief, from a nearby community, Chibe Uzzimba, who was a medical doctor, as regretting that while ATR was a delight in some communities overseas ("America, the Caribbean and other parts of the world"), it was "neglected at home." Uzzimba is quoted as adding that "[t]hose that destroy shrines thinking they have destroyed the gods, what they don't know is that the gods are spirits and cannot be seen, just as the Almighty God (Olisabuluwa) cannot be seen...the gods are somewhere watching them." He blamed African traditional practitioners for thwarting the cause of ATR.

The reporter quotes another Igbo Chief, Emmanuel Ugochukwu, as berating Christian leaders who misguided the youth that committed the crime. He is quoted as emphasizing that burning shrines and images was not the solution to the problems of impoverization, unemployment, poverty, and frustration that are perpetrated by much contemporary leadership in Africa. Moreover, Adiele notes that:

> It is impossible for the rich African culture and religion to be completely wiped out even by modern changes...Every religion has its own limitations and it would be wrong for anyone to stretch African Traditional Religion beyond its limitations.[49]

It would thus appear that while ATR may seem to be highly disadvantaged in many societies and communities in Africa, it has its own strongholds, visible or invisible, and it certainly constitutes some serious challenges to the spread and space of Christianity in the continent. In my own experience in Nigeria, many young people still participate in ATR festivals in many communities and in different parts of the country. In Yorubaland where I come from, many young people still pray and curse in the name of Yoruba traditional divinities. No religion seems to have monopoly of knowledge, virtue, and vice.

The Impact of Minority Religions on Christianity in Africa

Reference has been made to the issue of minority religions in Africa. This section delves into the general picture of how some of the minority religions constitute a challenge to the spread of Christianity in Africa, with particular regard to some Eastern-based religions that are said to hold their own in the religious space of Africa. Nihin/ola and Olaniyan[50] list some of those found in Nigeria, which may be found elsewhere in the continent as: Eckankar, the Bahai faith, and Hare Krishna. Within that same section, they mention the Grail Movement, a local variant of the Eastern religious tradition that is called Guru Maharaj Ji. From an American perspective, O'Connor notes what seems to reflect a universal outlook:

> In the past decade alone, more than 2,500 "new" religious cults have appeared in the United States. They have promised happiness, contentment, and purpose in life to the hundreds of thousands of young people they have attracted...the mystically inclined are attracted to those cults which offer guru-style meditation.[51]

Meanwhile, there may be no statistics to support an estimate of the number of religious cults in Africa. Yet, cultism is said to be thriving. LeBar[52] explains that "the cults are a problem in modern society" because of the "ambiguity and confusion" surrounding them. He notes how "the destructive, pseudo-religious cults" deprive a person of "freedom: freedom of thought, freedom of worship, freedom of choice," and what is worse, "these same groups add deception, manipulation and control to an excessive degree." The trend really seems to be universal. For instance, secret cults are a menace in many universities in Nigeria.

There are African scholars, such as Bernard Joinet[53] who attribute deviant behaviors, such as described by LeBar to the problem that is associated with unemployment, joblessness, and poverty. How then does one explain the situation in America? At any rate, one's concern here is the religious cults and social clubs that are mushrooming in many parts of Africa that tend to shrink the religious space (Christianity included), even though sometimes, one gets the hint that the same people patronize churches or mosques or ATR, as well as their clubs and/or secret cults.

Closely related to the issue of cults is what is said to be a rising level of atheism. Probably because it is generally believed that Africans are highly religious,[54] the word atheism rarely surfaces in the index of books on religion in Africa. Among the limited exemptions is Assimeng who notes that:

> Although enough research is yet to be conducted into the incidence and spread of agnostic and atheistic dispositions in West Africa, it might well be that there are now some people who are noted to show open skepticism about religious explanations of the physical world.[55]

Thus, if Africa was ever an atheistically free society, that can no longer be said to be the case in an absolute sense.

Around the world today, there seem to be many people who make no categorical denial of God, but obviously do not put religion as a priority, except probably when it is convenient or inescapable. Principal among such people are those who tend to have made football a form of consuming passion. Assimeng notes about "competitive sports, especially soccer" that:

> Sports have become, in contemporary West Africa, what Wilkerson and Dodder have noted concerning sports elsewhere: "theatrical liturgy through which mankind can be recast in a legitimate heroic image."[56]

Indeed, football in particular has become a weird deity to which human sacrifice is made, either by a form of suicide by some few individuals who take their own lives because a predicted team lost a match unexpectedly or homicide arising from arguments, betting, and quarrel over which team wins or loses. Thus, football also reduces the religious space in Africa, including Christianity.

The Future of Christianity in Africa

Apart from the foregoing external factors that are limiting the space of Christianity in Africa, there are some internal ones regarding doctrines, official policies, attitudes, and behaviors that may scare some members and prospective members. Richard McBrien[57] notes how the Second Vatican Council of the Roman Catholic Church (held 1962–1965) "acknowledged that the failure of believers to live up to their beliefs is one of the chief causes of unbelief." With regard to the official level, Fuller also notes that:

> Many people have rejected the gospel because it was presented to them in the form of bad news, for example, that if they become Christians they must no longer drink beer and will be allowed only one wife. Since beer is the foundation of their social life and polygamy the foundation of their economy, this does not look attractive at all.[58]

The point seems germane in respect to the prevalent situation in Africa, but some Christian leaders might argue that Christianity is about "the truth" and not about being "attractive." That is the case with policy, attitude, and behavior, in a nutshell.

In reference to sociopolitical and economic influences that focus on morality concerns, many scholars feel that both Christianity and Islam have not made much fundamental difference in the life of Africa, generally speaking. As many scholars have noted, "religion naturally evokes positive sentiments of goodness, kindness, love, rectitude, peace with God, with oneself, and with fellow men, but the ideal is still hard to attain."[59] Iyekolo notes that religion can be the foundation of moral value and ethical principles, but it can promote both good and evil, such as human solidarity and division.[60] With specific reference to Christianity, Mbefo notes that:

> Questions have arisen about the salvific claims of Christianity. After nearly two thousand years of its history, the world has remained unchanged, unredeemed. People still behave and react to situations exactly as ancient human documents narrate it since the dawn of written literature and as far as oral tradition can remember. There have always been good and bad guys.[61]

That seems unassailable by any historical consideration. Assimeng[62] quotes an editorial of the *Ghanaian Times,* which notes that "[a] lot of our discredited former politicians were and are now known to be closely associated with the Churches," and "[t]hese churches were obviously proud of them as shown in their readiness to offer them front seats at functions during the old regime." The editorial notes further that "[i]nstead of encouraging thrift among its followers, the Churches today have become places of ostentation," where "[m]emorial services have become near-fashion shows where the best and latest dresses are displayed." What is more, "[a] lot of ardent believers brought up by the church have not shown exemplary character worthy of emulation," but "on the contrary, they have been involved in scandals and shady deals which could be classified as being unworthy of followers of Christ." That seems to be consistent with the experience in some other countries in Africa where Christianity has a substantial presence.

Moreover, some bizarre reports are sometimes found in the daily newspapers, for instance in Nigeria, the home base of this writer, concerning how some Pentecostal/ posterity gospel pastors were involved in homicidal moneymaking rituals. For example, the *Sunday Vanguard* of June 1, 2008 has the caption and report of how "pastor confesses: we use human heads to prepare prosperity rituals for church members." Asked how he and his wife came by human heads, the pastor responded that they bought them through one John who was working in a cemetery to prepare charms for fighting witches and attaining prosperity.

Another problem that is experienced in Nigeria from some Pentecostal pastors is that in an attempt to demonstrate mystical powers, some of the pastors allege that some girls are possessed of witchcraft, which they say is responsible for the socioeconomic misfortune of the families concerned. Unfortunately, some credulous families believe and so reject their own children. Chukwudi Akasike[63] reports how the National Agency for Prohibition of Traffic in Persons (NAPTIP) and other related matters raised the alarm over the increasing rate of child rejection in Akwa Ibom State in South Nigeria, based on the allegation by the concerned Pentecostal pastors. Akasike quotes Carol Ndaguba, the executive secretary of NAPTIP as saying, "It is very disheartening that the institutions of the family and the church, which are meant to protect the child and to dispel retrogressive beliefs and practices are the ones fuelling the practice—a practice reminiscent of the Dark Age's witch-hunting in Europe."

That is the level to which Christianity seems to have degenerated in Africa, but that is not to say the whole sky is black. Historically, Christianity was known for its role in supporting, and later opposing and helping in the abolition of the transatlantic slave trade and any form of slave dealings.[64] It can also be said that Christianity supported apartheid in South Africa but also contributed to its dismantlement, through such Christian leaders as Archbishop Desmond Tutu.[65]

Moreover some Christian missionaries, such as Mary Slessor, worked for human rights, with particular reference to women and children.[66] Political enlightenment, is also said to have been imparted by some missionaries.[67] Sociopolitically speaking in contemporary times, Christianity in Africa is said to radiate positive influence through such international figures as the former general secretary of the United Nations Organization Boutros Boutros-Ghali (1992–1997), who was a member of the Coptic Church of Egypt, and his immediate successor, Kofi Annan, who is said to be a Christian from Ghana.[68] But, on the whole, it does not seem that many African Christian leaders are found to be as politically influential in a progressive way as Archbishop Desmond Tutu of South Africa.[69] Many scholars, such as Assimeng, quote an editorial of *Ghanaian Times* as saying it is "debatable whether the churches' claim to molding the character of the Ghanaian youth over the years has made any headway."[70] Ayandele also notes that:

> Christian missions were to a certain extent disappointed in their schools, which could not fulfill completely the moral and spiritual purpose they expected of them...Manifestations they did not bargain for were the results of the education they gave. Sexual immorality in Nigeria began earlier among the so-called Christians than

among the "pagans" and was common among the African staff. The mission pupils became arrogant, disrespectful and dishonest.[71]

The fact that both Christianity and Islam have failed Africa, morally, to a great extent, is found in the observation that most African societies are corrupt and brimming with mass exploitation and poverty.[72]

Above all, one would say that the Christian space in Africa is indeterminate, to some extent, in spite of the figures given in the tables above. As Assimeng notes:

> Although huge religious assemblages are still visible in the urban communities of West Africa, especially on Fridays, Sundays, and other festive days, the reasons for such religious assemblages should now be perhaps sought in other than purely spiritual spheres. Much of what is done now is done on grounds of rationally calculated utility, pleasure, and practical need.[73]

With specific reference to Christianity, Gbenda[74] notes that many Christian missionaries, through their approach to evangelization, split the African personality between Christian and ATR practices, and inevitably, lip service tends to make Christianity in Africa quantitative rather than qualitative. In other words, it has become difficult to know in practical terms, who is a Christian, and who is not. All the foregoing has some lessons to teach on the future of Christianity in Africa. As Aylward Shorter notes:

> Two writers foretell the possible death of the church in Africa. It is the opinion Nyerere that the church will surely die if she continues to be identified with injustice in the world. For Nwasaru, the church is doomed to die if she retains structures and symbols that are alien to the African tradition.[75]

The two persons quoted by Shorter have been hypothetical in their remarks. Tai Solarin,[76] however, asserts that Nigeria is not, in any real way, Christian, but "a nation of make-belief," which in the course of time "will not only stop looking towards Canterbury or the Vatican or Mecca, but will turn more into themselves for the salvation of themselves." That may appear to sound doom, but it seems possible that Christianity in Africa will go the way it went in Europe and America, when the totality of the discoveries of this study is put into consideration, unless the pieces of advice quoted by Shorter are hearkened to.

Arguably, Tai Solarin is an unbeliever, but a Catholic priest Anthony Ekwunife,[77] among some other scholars, for example, Gbenda,[78] expresses the conviction "that modern Christianity in Africa and Nigeria in particular is still floating in the air." Of course, Christianity is not likely to disappear in the course of time, but the optimism about Africa becoming the center of Christianity may not be as feasible as some outsiders and some apparently wishful-thinking insiders may want us to believe, unless a form of revolution occurs. Besides, one would guess that no amount of African Christians will remove the headquarters and final authority of Anglicanism from Canterbury or that of Roman Catholicism from the Vatican City, even if an African were to become the pope.

Conclusion

Christianity is a majority religion in Africa, but it is not evenly spread and not always dominant. Its population is said to be somehow indeterminate, even though there are estimates. The uncertainty surrounding the Christian population in Africa, as in most other continents, possibly, is due to problems that are associated with census-taking and the fact that the Christian faith of many, though not all, Africans is doubtful or debatable.

The religion faces both internal and external challenges, both of which are sometimes insurmountable. The internal challenges are said to derive from the moral laxity of many of the leaders and their followers, as well as from doctrines, policies, principles, and practices that are said to be incompatible with African worldviews.

The external challenges, however, refer to other religions, the principal among which are Islam and ATR. Islam, in particular, is said to be highly antagonistic and militant in opposition to the Christian existence in some of its major areas.

Some of the findings also indicate some Christian hostility against non-Christians in some of its strongholds. On the whole, there seems to be no reason to suggest that the Christian space in Africa will expand tremendously in the long run. Indeed, it appears much more likely that the space will shrink, as happened in Europe and America, unless a revolution occurs. Generally speaking, a level of irreligiosity also is perceived to be growing in Africa.

Notes

1. Isichei, Elizabeth. (2004). *The Religious Traditions of Africa: A History*. London: Praeger Publishers, p. 15.
2. Hickey, Raymond. (1987). *Two Thousand Years of African Christianity*. Ibadan: Daystar Press, p. 10.
3. Kenny, Joseph. (2000). *The Spread of Islam through North to West Africa 7th to 19th Century: A Historical Survey with Relevant Arab Documents*. Lagos: Dominican Publishers, p. 3ff.
4. Garver, Stuart. (1973). *Watch Your Teaching: A Comparative Study of Roman Catholic and Protestant Teaching Since Vatican II*. San Diego: Mission to Catholic International Inc., p. 9.
5. Placher, William. (1983). *A History of Christian Theology: An Introduction*. Philadelphia, PA: Westminster Press, p. 108.
6. Hickey, *Two Thousand Years of African Christianity*, p. 10ff.
7. Isichei, *The Religious Traditions of Africa*, p. 15.
8. Kenny, *The Spread of Islam Through North to West Africa*, p. 15.
9. Isichei, *The Religious Traditions of Africa*, p. 15.
10. Hickey, *Two Thousand Years of African Christianity*, p. 11.
11. Ibid, p. 13.
12. Hildebrandt, Jonathan. (1996). *History of the Church in Africa: A Survey*. Achimota: African Christian Press, p. 68.

13. Hickey, *Two Thousand Years of African Christianity*, p. 24.

14. Ibid, p. 25.

15. Isichei, *The Religious Traditions of Africa*, p. 17.

16. Carpenter, Joel. (2005). "Preface." In Sanneh, Lamin and Carpenter (eds.) *The Changing Face of Christianity: Africa, the West and the World*. Oxford: University Press, p. vii.

17. Barrett, David, and Johnson, Todd. (2004). "Annual Statistical Table on Global Mission: 2004." *International Bulletin of Missionary Research*, January 28, p. 25.

18. Carpenter, *The Changing Face of Christianity*, p. viiff.

19. Koschorke, Klaus. (2005). "Introduction." In Koschorke and Schjorring (eds.) *African Identities and World Christianity in the Twentieth Century*. WI: Harrassowitz Verlag, p. 10.

20. Beyer, Engelbert. (1998). *New Christian Movements in West Africa*. Ibadan: Sefer, p. 1.

21. Ibid, p. 1.

22. Ibid, p. 2.

23. Meeting for African Collaboration of the Symposium of the Episcopal Conferences of Africa and Madagascar-SECAM (MAC) *New Christian Movements in Africa and Madagascar* (Roma: Tipografia S.G.S., 1992).

24. Beyer, *New Christian Movements in West Africa*, p. 2.

25. Guest, Robbert. (2004). *The Shackled Continent: Africa's Past, Present and Future*. London: Pan Books, Title Page.

26. Meeting for African Collaboration, *New Christian Movements in Africa and Madagascar*, p. 6.

27. Ibid, p. 7.

28. Ibid, p. 7.

29. MacArthur Jr., John. (1992). *Charismatic Chaos: Signs and Wonders, Speaking in Tongues, Health, Wealth and Property, Charismatic Televangelism, Does God Still Speak Today?* Michigan: Oasis Ltd., p. 32ff.

30. Meeting for African Collaboration, *New Christian Movements in Africa and Madagascar*, p. 6.

31. Hildebrandt, *History of the Church in Africa*, pp. 247–281.

32. Hickey, *Two Thousand Years of African Christianity*, p. 49ff.

33. Hildebrandt, *History of the Church in Africa*, p. 247.

34. Ibid, p. 262.

35. Hickey, *Two Thousand Years of African Christianity*, p. 49ff.

36. Ibid, p. 47.

37. Onaiyekan, J. O. (1984). "Religion and Peace: Ideals versus Realities." In Mala and Oseni (eds.) *Religion, Peace and Unity in Nigeria*. Ibadan: NASR, p. 25..

38. Gaya, Musa. (2004). "Further Reflections on Christianity in Northern Nigeria: 1975–2000." In Crampton, E. P. T. (ed.). *Christianity in Northern Nigeria*, London: Geoffrey Chapman, p. 268.

39. Alemika, Etannbi. (2004). "Foreward." In Gofwen, R. (ed.) *Religious Conflicts in Northern Nigeria and National Building: The Throes of Two Decades*. Kaduna: Human Right Monitor, p. vii..

40. Gofwen (ed.), *Religious Conflicts in Northern Nigeria and National Building*, p. 68ff.

41. Kukah, M. H. (2003). *Religion, Politics and Power in Northern Nigeria*. Ibadan: Spectrum Books, p. 169.

42. Ayandele, E. A. (1991). *The Missionary Impact on Modern Nigeria 1842–1914: A Political and Social Analysis*. London: Longman Group Ltd., p. 4.

43. Gbenda, Joseph. (2001). *The Africanization of Christianity*. Nsukka: Chuka Educational publishers, p. 17.

44. Fuller, Lois. *Going to the Missions: An Introduction to Cross-Cultural.* Bukuru: Nigeria Evangelical Missionary Institute and African Christian Textbooks, p. 41ff.
45. Awolalu, J. O., and P. A. Dopamu. (2005). *West African Traditional Religion.* Lagos: Macmillan Nigeria Publishers Ltd., p. 88.
46. Fuller, *Going to the Missions*, p. 42.
47. Assimeng, Max. (1989). *Religion and Social Change in West Africa.* Accra: Ghana University Press, p. 206.
48. Umudu, Michael. "Slaughter of the gods" in *Nation on Sunday* (September 21, 2008), 17ff.
49. Adiele, S. N. "Religious Co-operation in Eastern Nigeria." In *Religion, Peace and Unity in Nigeria*, p. 191.
50. Nihinlola, E., and Olaniyan, M. (eds.). *Discovering the Other Side: Challenges of other Religion.* Ibadan: Flourish Books Ltd., p. 68–94.
51. O'Connor, John. (1989). "Preface." In LeBar, J. (ed.) *Cult, Sects and the New Age,* Huntington, Indiana: Our Sunday Visitor Inc., p. 7.
52. LeBar, *Cult, Sects and the New Age,* p. 18.
53. Joinet, Bernard. (2000). *The Challenge of Modernity in Africa.* Nairobi: Daughters of St. Paul, p. 30.
54. Idowu, Bolaji. (1996). *Olodumare God in Yoruba Belief.* Lagos: Longman Nigeria, p. 5.
55. Assimeng, *Religion and Social Change in West Africa,* p. 129.
56. Ibid, p. 129.
57. McBrien, Richard. (1994). *Catholicism.* San Francisco, CA: Harper, p. 224.
58. Fuller, *Going to the Missions,* p. 114.
59. Onaiyekan, *Religion, Peace and Unity in Nigeria,* p. 124.
60. Iyekolo, E. B. (2006). *The Peoples of Okunland.* Lagos: Concept Publication Ltd., p. 105.
61. Mbefo, L. M. (1997). *The Liturgical Year in Action.* Nsukka: Spritan Publications, p. 9.
62. Assimeng, *Religion and Social Change in West Africa,* 220ff.
63. Akasike, Chukwudi. (2008). "NAPTIP worried over child rejection in A'Ibom." In *The Punch.* June 11, p. 12.
64. Isichei, *The Religious Traditions of Africa,* 144ff.
65. Ramsay, William. (1986). *Four Modern Prophets: Walter Rauschenbusch, Martin Luther King Jr., Gustavo Gutierrez and Rosemary Ruther.* Louisville, KY: John Knox Press, p. 77.
66. Fajana, A. (1973). *Nigeria and Her Neighbours Book Two.* Lagos: African Christian University Press, pp. 27–29.
67. Crane, Paul. (1973). "Preface." In T. Agostoni, *Every Citizen's Handbook,* Dublin: C. J. Fallon Ltd., p. i.
68. Kosechorke, "Introduction." In *African Identities and World in the Twentieth Century,* pp. 9–17.
69. Ramsay, *Four Modern Prophets,* p. 77.
70. Assimeng, *Religion and Social Change in West,* p. 220.
71. Ayandele, *The Missionary Impact on Modern Nigeria 1842–1914,* 291ff.
72. Turaki, Yusufu. (1997). *Tribal Gods of Africa: Ethnicity, Racism, Tribalism, and the Gospel of Christ.* Nairobi: Ethics, Peace and Justice Commission of the Association of Evangelicals in Africa, p. 3.
73. Assimeng, *Religion and Social Change in West,* p. 125.
74. Gbenda, Joseph. (2001). *The Africanization of Christianity.* Nsukka: Chuka Educational Publishers, p. vi.

75. Shorter, Aylward. (1978). *African Christian Spirituality.* New York: Orbis Book, p. 20.
76. Solarin, Tai. (1976). "The God of Nigeria is not Christian" In Onibonje, Omotosho and Lawal (eds.) *The Indigenous for National Development: Essay on Social, Political, Educational, Economic and Cultural Issues.* Ibadan: Onibonoje Press and Books (Nig) Ltd., p. 34, 42.
77. Ekwunife, Anthony. (1995). *Spiritual Expressions: Reflections on Christian Lives and Practices in Nigeriant Context.* Nsukka: Chuka Educational Publishers, p. vii.
78. Gbenda, *The Africanization of Christianity,* p. 12.

Chapter 8

Islam in the Contemporary African Society

R. Ibrahim Adebayo

Introduction

The word *Ifriqiya* has featured prominently in some Muslim history books, although it does not connote the contemporary continent of Africa. The name has been given various interpretations by different scholars. It is believed by Leo Africanus to have been derived from an Arabic word *Faraqa*, which means to divide—an indication of the division of Africa from Europe and Asia by the Mediterranean and the Nile respectively.[1] According to Al-Masudi, the name is also said to have been taken from Ifriqos bin Qais bin Saifi, one of the kings of Yemen. Some other historians hold that it came from the name of Ifriq, son of Quatura, the second wife of the patriarch.[2] Whatever the case may be, the continent of Africa has remained one of the seven continents of the world and has been known to the Arabs and non-Arabs to include North Africa (including the Maghrib), East Africa, West Africa, Central Africa, and South Africa.[3]

The initial contact of Islam with the African community is dated back to the time of Prophet Muhammad in the year 615 CE. The maltreatment and persecution of the early Muslims by the Makkans caused the Prophet to suggest to the Muslims to migrate to Abyssinia, which he described as a place "where a king rules without injustice and a land of truthfulness."[4] The first batch of Muslim immigrants to Abyssinia, numbering 16—12 men and 4 women—was led by Uthman ibn Affan and his wife Ruqayah, the daughter of Prophet Muhammad. Soon afterward, the second batch consisting of 83 men and 11 women joined them. The warm reception accorded the Muslims in the land of Africa, and the denial of king Negus to hand over the Muslims to the Makkans who made a move for their expatriation back to Makkah, confirmed the foresightedness of the Prophet to have suggested the place.

It also substantiated the generosity and justice of the headship of the Abyssinian Negus who refused to "concur in the judgement of his patriarch until he had had a chance to hear the refugees plead their own case."[5] This episode further substantiated the supporting hand that the early Muslims had from a Christian ruler, regardless of their differences in faith. The acceptance of Africans to accommodate the early Muslims in their land laid the groundwork for Islam to prosper during its trial period, as many of these Muslims stayed for a long period, leaving only later after the Prophet had migrated to Madinah.

With the migration of the Prophet to Madinah, Ja'afar bin Abu Talib was said to have led the returnees from Abyssinia to Madinah and to have left with a 70-man Abyssinian delegation to the Prophet. A demonstration of the delegates' commitments to the message brought by the Prophet was confirmed when the Prophet read a portion of *Surat-Yasin* to them, and they burst into tears. The recognition of this high-level dedication by the Abyssinians was said to have led to the revelation of two verses of chapter 28 of the Qur'an.[6]

A clear demonstration of the stand of Africans on what they believed in was made by an Abyssinian slave, Bilal—whose master made him face the burning sun and laid a heavy stone on his chest just because he had accepted Islam. He rather preferred to die than to renounce his new faith, until he was rescued by Abu Bakr, who bought him from his master and set him free.[7] The recognition of his commitment to Islam manifested when he was chosen as one of the four notable personalities to enter the Ka'abah on the day of the conquest of Makkah.[8] Apart from this, he became the first *muazzin* (caller to prayers) in Islam, and he was credited with the addition of the expression: *As-salat khayrun mina nnawm*—prayer is better than sleeping—into the early morning call to prayer, to which the Prophet raised no objection. This has been regarded as a great honor done to Africa by the Prophet.[9]

It is observed that the Prophet maintained the cordial relationship he had with Africa by sending delegates to them and writing letters to various rulers informing them of his message of Islam. This hand of fellowship was recognized by the Coptic ruler of Egypt called Jurai bin Minahey. Although did not accept Islam, he sent among other properties, five slaves among whom was Mariyatu el-Qibtiyat, who later became one of the wives of the Prophet and mother of his male son Ibrahim. The Prophet was also said to have sent two letters to King Negus of Abyssinia requesting him to accept Islam and used the cordial relationship between them to ask him to conduct a marriage on his behalf between him and Ramlah (Ummu Habibah), the daughter of Abu Sufyan, who was residing in Abyssinia at the time. The king was said to have paid her dowry on behalf of the Prophet before she later joined the Prophet at Madinah.[10]

The above clearly shows the relationship between Africans and the Prophet of Islam, as well as the interaction of Islam with Africans right from the inception of the religion. It will, therefore, not be an overstatement to say that the flavor of Islam had been tasted by Africans right from the time of the Prophet and before his emigration to Madinah. His movement to Madinah must have hampered the spread of the religion in Africa, as the Muslims who were residing in Abyssinia then had to move down to Madinah in order for them to receive more knowledge of the new religion from the Prophet.

The Spread of Islam in Africa

It was easier for the Arab Muslims to penetrate North Africa due to the political situation between the popes in whose jurisdiction was the African Church and the government from Constantinople. In the same vein, the religious persecution to which the native Coptics of Egypt had been subjected by the official Melkite Church paved the way for the rapid expansion of Islam in the land. It was in 639 CE that the Muslim volunteer force, led by Amr bin al-As, merged against Egypt, and the latter sued for peace by signing the first treaty of peace with the Muslims. Some steps were therefore taken by Amr to consolidate Muslim hegemony in the area, among which were the building of a new capital, which he named Fustat (old Cairo), and the erection of a simple mosque there in 641 CE, which happened to be the first to be built in Egypt. He also opened a direct waterway to the Holy cities of Arabia by clearing the ancient Phraonic Canal, and named it *Khalij Amir al-Muminin,* the Canal of the Caliph. Soon afterward, Egypt became an important Islamic center consequent upon the establishment of a number of mosques and Islamic schools (*madrasa*).[11]

The occupation of Egypt by the Arab Muslims facilitated easy penetration of Islam into other provinces in the region. Barqah was captured by the Muslims, while the Berber tribes of Tripoli equally surrendered to them. Abdullah, who succeeded Amr as the leader of the Muslim army during the third caliph, Uthman ibn Affan, made a historic landmark by capturing part of Ifriqiyyah and making the Nubians enter into a treaty with the Muslims.

The history of Islam in Africa would remain incomplete if Uqba bin Nafi' is not mentioned. He was credited with the launching of Islam throughout the African continent by planting a permanent camp at Kairawan (Qayrawan) in 670 CE, and thus he encroached the Byzantines and the Berbers. He was said to have taken Islam to the north of the Awras, Tangier, and Morocco. He went as far as to the Atlantic before he was died in 683 CE near Biskara and close to Algeria.[12] During the tenure of Muawiyyah, Hassan bin Nu'man, who was sent to Africa, also did his best by suppressing the uprisings of the Byzantine authority. The routes followed by the early Muslims to spread Islam in Africa have been documented by Bely, and referred to by both Abdullah and Adua. The Muslims who first migrated to Abyssinia went across the Red Sea through Habasah, Ethiopia. Other routes include:

(i)   through the Red Sea upward to North Africa (i.e., Egypt; then Libya, Tunisia, Algeria and Morocco);

(ii) through the course of the Nile from Egypt to the Nubian land and the Sudan. From there to the Sahara Desert; then Lake Chad to Bornu and Hausa lands;

(iii) through North Africa, particularly Morocco and Libya across Sahara to West Africa of Mali, Songhay, Ghana, the Yoruba land, etc.;

(iv) through the Indian Ocean from Yemen to Somalia, from Oman and Albahrain to the Island of Zanzibar and Tanganyika, now Tanzania, then penetrated into Southeast Africa to Uganda, Malawi, Kenya, Madagascar, and Comoro Islands.[13]

The establishment of Islam in North Africa facilitated its introduction to West Africa as far back as the eighth century. The trade link between the two geographical areas assisted in the spread of Islam in West Africa. The trade and economic activities also led to the introduction of literacy there.

Islamic Impact on Africa

One major impact of Islam on Africa is the spread of literacy in the continent. Although the art of reading and writing was not new to the people of North Africa, the opportunity to spread it to the West African people was facilitated by Islam, which could not be practiced conscientiously without having knowledge of Arabic. It is an undeniable fact that apart from elementary and traditional Qur'anic schools that spread all over the places to where Islam spread, the early universities of the Muslims were established in Africa. This is true of Al-Azhar University in Cairo, Egypt, the University of Az-Zaytun founded in Tunisia by Hassan ibn An-Numan, and the University of al-Qairawan in Fez (Morocco) founded by Sayyidah Fatima, sister of Maryam, the daughter of Muhammad ibn Abdullah al-Fahr al-Quairawan.[14] Particular reference was made to this by Kwame Nkrumah of Ghana while inaugurating the University of Ghana in 1961. Nkrumah eulogized the West African centers of Islamic scholarship—Timbuktu and Walata—and lamented the effects of the destruction of the University of Sankore, saying that the academic and cultural history of Africa might have been different from what it is today ifthe university had not been destroyed and had survived the ravages of foreign invasions.[15]

Apart from the above, a sort of international relation was established with other continents, as some kings employed Muslim interpreters who also doubled as a secretary keeping records for them. A great service to the continent by Islam is that it has assisted Africa to obtain a true knowledge of its past. Findings from researches into the Arabic legacy in Nigeria and the entire Africa West Atlantic revealed different patterns of government; some established political and economic systems were identified as surviving over a period of ten centuries. To explicate this, there were official correspondences in Arabic between the Bornu court and Al-Azhar in Egypt, and later the British government; the Sokoto jihadists and the Bornu scholars; and between the Sultan of Sokoto and the Iwo community of the present Osun State in Nigeria. A corroboration of this could be inferred from the submission of a renowned professor of History and former Vice-Chancellor of the University of Ibadan Professor K. O. Dike, who wrote:

> As an historian myself, I have taken the keenest interest in this development, for it is through the aid of these Arabic documents and those written in African language in the Arabic script, that the scholar will be aided in his task of unlocking the secrets of the African past. It has been a revelation to the whole world of scholarship to realize for the first time that Africa before the European penetration, so far from being a dark continent, was in fact a continent where the light of scholarship shone brightly, as the

Arabic works now being discovered bear testimony... The Arabic scholars of the present, drawing upon the writings of the Arabic scholars of the past, will be able to bring before us the events and happenings of the past ages of Nigeria and so help to write a history we may rightly call our own.[16]

By means of digression, though relevant to this piece, writings on Africa by Western writers have been grossly biased and sentimental to justify the British colonialism as a "messianic, redemptive and noble civilising mission undertaken to bring light to the poor creatures of the Dark Continent."[17] Substantiating this, Kukah could not afford quoting copiously from *How to Write about Africa* of one Binyavanga Wainnaina Granta, who gave some conditions for an author to be acceptable to the Western mind. Among such conditions is the description of Africans and painting them as miserable and filthy characters like "corrupt politicians, inept polygamous travel guides and prostitutes... A fat man who steals and works in the visa office, refusing to give work permits to qualified Westerners who really care about Africa."[18]

Still, regarding literacy, it is interesting to note that Africans have gone so far as domesticating Arabic to suit their local taste by using Arabic letters for their local language. This method is referred to as *Ajami*. Bobboyi, who undertook a study of the intellectual legacy of the Sokoto Caliphate in Nigeria, observed that many of the writings of the Sokoto jihadist leaders were in Arabic and that most of them were in local languages of Fulfulde and Hausa but written in the Arabic scripts, the contents of which covered poems on the social ills of the Hausa society, admonition, *fiqh, tawhid, sirah,* and politics.[19] In his own finding, Hassane posited that the African *Ajami* scripts cut across all fields of scholarly activity. He particularly mentioned such areas being covered to have included:

(i)   *al-tib al-mahali*—the description and traditional treatment of various illnesses;

(ii) *al-saudala*—the properties of plants and ways of using them;

(iii) *'ilm al-Asrar*—texts dealing with the field of the occult sciences;

(iv) translations of works and texts from Arabic into African languages; and

(v)   numerous texts on administrative and diplomatic matters (correspondence between sultans or provincial rulers and between literate people).[20]

Closely related to this is the fact that many languages have borrowed from Arabic.

The Arabic alphabet was adapted, with some modifications, to such diverse languages as the Slavic tongues, Spanish, Persian, Urdu, Turkish, Hebrew, Berber, Swahili, Malay, Sudanese, and others.[21]

In Nigeria, Arabic has donated some words to many languages. For instance, the Hausas would refer to scissors and thumb as *Almakashi* and *ibhami,* respectively; the equivalent words of these are *Al-Miqass* and *Ibham* in Arabic. In Yorubaland, *Laluuri* and *Riba* are two words that connote necessity and usury, respectively. They have their origin in *Daruri* and *Riba* in Arabic.[22] Adamu stresses further on the contribution of Islam to advancement of, and influence of Arabic on the language in Africa. With particular reference to the Swahili in East Africa, he submits:

> Under Arab influence, Swahili originated as a lingua franca used by several closely related Bantu-speaking tribal groups. In the early 19th century, the spread of Swahili inland received a great impetus from its being the language of the Arab ivory and slave caravans, which penetrated as far north as Uganda and as far west as Zaire. Swahili was later adopted by European colonialists, especially the Germans, who used it extensively as the language of administration in Tanganyika, thus laying the foundation for its adoption as the national language of independent Tanzania.[23]

Africanization of Islam

Even before the coming of Islam to Africa, Africans had their culture, which was greatly influenced by Islam. With the adoption of Islam, a sort of cross-fertilization of culture arose, as some African practices influenced the practice of Islam in Africa. One of the African ethical values is respect to elders, which is explicated among the Sufis in the elevation of their leaders. Sufism has been a strong instrument for the spread and consolidation of Islam in Africa. The accommodation of the Sufi brotherhood in Islam has facilitated introduction of certain ideologies and practices that are considered alien to it. This happened, according to Doi, because of keen competitions and jealousy of one another among the brotherhoods.[24] The affection and veneration to a Shaykh, or spiritual mentor, later developed into the worshiping of saints. Visitations (ziyarah) are paid to these saints, and their tombs become centers of attraction where the muridis flock to offer prayers. In Algeria, the tomb of Abu Madyan Shuayb b. al-Husayn—popularly called "Sidi Boumediene" in the village of al-Eubbad of the periphery of Tlemcen—has become a shrine people visit during religious holidays. However, the reactions of some Muslim reformers to this development have been generating tension among Muslims. The reformers point accusing fingers to the Sufis of encouraging the worship of the dead. Such a reaction has led to civil war in Algeria where the *Muqaddim* of the Shrine of Sidi Boumediene was handled roughly and people were denied access to the shrine. Relating this to the Nigeria situation, Doi equally cited cases of religious syncretism in Yorubaland. This includes the Bilqis Sungbo of Ijebu who was identified as the Queen of Sheba and whose tomb has become a tourist attraction where people flocked for spiritual blessings and healing.[25] There is also the case of Muhammad Jimoh, the Mahdi of Ijebu-Ode, who mixed African traditional religion, Christianity, and Islam together.[26]

Another area where Africans have domesticated Islam is in the use of the Qur'an for healing. Numerous sources are being relied upon by scholars to substantiate the miraculous healing qualities of the Qur'an. Some texts have therefore been written by scholars to prove this. In Nigeria, for instance, Shaykh Ya'qub Abdullah al-Iluri published the *'Awnul-'Ulama'*, while Ustadh Abdul-Azeez Balogun wrote *Du'a Ghayatil-Maqsudatil-Kubra*. The books contain prescription of the usage of some

Qur'anic chapters and verses to cure certain ailments or solve certain problems. A cursory look at these books shows that some Qur'anic chapters written out in those books are closely followed by *khutbah,* which contains spurious invocation of jinn and other names not known by the majority of scholars. Apart from textbooks written for this purpose, Qur'anic chapters or verses are also written on wooden black slate *(walaa)* with ink called *tadaa* and washed with clean water. This is called hantu in Yorubaland, and it is given to the client to drink with some ingredients added to it. Opeloye and Jimoh demonstrated how a Yoruba *Mallam* made use of the Qur'anic chapter to treat madness of chemogenic origin by writing *Suratu'l-Kafirun* on a wooden slate in large numbers and washing with water. Then the feces of a sheep is dried and ground as ingredients for the written exorcism. This mixture is presented to the patient to drink continuously until he is completely cured of the ailment.[27]

Some well-known festivals in Islam are the *'idil-Fitr* and *'idil kabir* celebrated at the ninth and twelfth month of the Hijrah calendar. However, in some countries in Africa, most especially in Ghana and Nigeria, the celebration of the birthday of Prophet Muhammad called *Maulud Nabiyy* has been added. Also, the first of *Muharram* is now being celebrated to mark the beginning of the Muslim Hijrah year. The Maulud Nabiyy is celebrated with a great deal of pomp and pageantry around the Emir's palaces in Hausaland. In Yorubaland, the Qur'anic and Arabic schools mark it with processions parading through the streets of their towns, singing praise-songs about the Prophet.[28]

Muslims and Government Policies

Most African nations do not adopt a religion as the state religion, though tactfully, they tend to support one religion over the other. However, some policies of some countries are considered unfavorable to the Muslims, hence instances of misunderstanding between the government policy and the Muslim community. Tanzania could be taken as an example. In August 2003, the government decided to use the Ilala Muslim graveyard near Dar es Salaam city center for a mayoral office school. There, about 1,400 corpses were to be excavated by the municipal authority to be reburied at Segera by the relatives at a cost of 60,000 shillings. This step was considered a gross disrespect to the dead and an attempt to slight the Muslim community.[29]

In Ethiopia, the massive Muslim demonstration of April 1974 against the popular opposition of the Imperial Government with a 13-point demand seemed to have marked the serious agitation of the Muslims to fight for their rights in the country. Among such demands according to Ostebo, were "recognition of Muslim festivals as public holidays, financial support for the construction of mosques and permission to establish a national Islamic council."[30] The demonstrators also demanded the change in the official description of the country's Muslim population from *Muslim living in Ethiopia* to *Ethiopian Muslims.* The consequence of this demonstration was the establishment of the Ethiopian Islamic Affairs Supreme Council (EIASC), which was the first Muslim organization in the country.

The policies of the Ethiopian People's Democratic Revolutionary Front (EPDRF) were beneficial to the Ethiopian Muslims, as bans were lifted on some religious activities in the country. For instance, restrictions on construction of mosques were removed; while Islamic organizations, newspapers, and magazines were allowed to operate. This culminated in a proliferation of mosques, Islamic organizations, and active involvement of Muslims in public life. This was confirmed by the findings of Ostebo in 2005 where he discovered two international Islamic NGOs and 45 local Islamic NGOs, which registered with the government. That notwithstanding, the EIASC could not sustain itself for long due to internal rancor and misunderstanding from within the body. Its freedom was therefore curtailed by government intervention in the affairs of the body.[31] The February 1995 violent clash between police and worshippers around the Anwar mosque in Addis Ababa, which recorded about nine casualties, as well as the assassination attempt on Hosni Mubarak in Addis Ababa in June 1996, caused the government to take drastic measures to cut down the wing of the Muslims in the country. This was done in the form of arrests of prominent Muslim leaders and banning some Islamic organizations from operating.[32]

The situation of the introduction of *Shari'ah* in Sudan is aptly recorded by Awet, when he wrote:

> As part of political religious strategy of the Islamic Movement in Sudan in the mid-1970s, Hassan al-Turabi, the leader of the National Islamic Front (NIF) took advantage of Numeiri's military regime and obtained important posts in the administrative and education systems for some of its members. Thus, they further increased their influence, which led to the introduction of the Shari'a in September 1983.[33]

The introduction of *Shari'ah* in Sudan was considered a breach of the peaceful coexistence between adherents of different religions in the country, as Sudan is a country of "a multi-religious, multi-cultural and ethnic diversity with different ethical values, ways of governance and life experiences that should be mutually respected."[34] This consequently led to the political separation of the Sudan North and Sudan South.

In Nigeria, the introduction of *Shari'ah* in Zamfara State by Governor Sani Yerima on October 27, 1999 marked the beginning of the step in the northern part of the country. The highly publicized and well-celebrated launching of *Shari'ah* in the State drew representatives from some African countries like Chad, Niger, Sudan, and Egypt and faraway countries like Saudi Arabia, Iran, and Pakistan. Consequently, some other Muslim-dominated northern states also followed suit, such as Kano, Kebbi, Sokoto, Borno, Niger, and Yobe.[35] From time immemorial, the *Shari'ah* has become part and parcel of the culture of the Hausa. Ibn Battuta was said to have confirmed its practice as far back as the fourteenth century, while Henry Barth, an explorer, was not allowed to bring alcohol and the Bible to Northern Nigeria.[36] It was the advent of the British in 1900 that restricted the *Shari'ah* to civil life of the people. The Zamfara State experiment of the *Shari'ah* further triggered the establishment of the Supreme Council for Shari'ah in Nigeria under which the Independent Shari'ah Panel in Lagos State operates. The recent establishment of the Independent *Shari'ah* panel in some southwestern states of Nigeria confirms the

Muslims' consciousness of the need and aspiration to imbibe the teachings of their religion, which they were used to prior to the advent of colonialism in the country.[37] In states where the panel operates, successes are being recorded, as Muslims voluntarily take their cases to it for adjudication. Cases like dissolutions of marriage at the insistence of the wife on grounds of cruelty, lack of insufficient support by the husband, and others and voluntary confession of *zina*, as well as requesting the panel to perform the role of *waliyy* in case of the absence of agnatic relation to give the hands of his relation in marriage have been performed by the panel in Lagos State.[38]

Interreligious Crises

It has been established by scholars that many religious crises in Africa are ethnically motivated, as a particular religion is commonly attached to a particular ethnic group. Take for instance, in Nigeria, the Hausa ethnic group practices Islam, while in Igboland, Christianity is commonly professed. This is not to say that there are no Christians among the Hausa and no Muslims among the Igbo, but they are in the minority, respectively. Consequently, any ethnic clash between the two is taken to be a religious clash. That notwithstanding, there have been many religious clashes in Africa during which lives and properties were lost. Instances of this abound in Nigeria. The 2006 mayhem in Maiduguri led to the death of many Igbo, while the Hausa communities in Enugu, Abia, Anambra, and Delta states, had their own share of Igbo retaliation where many Hausa Muslims were killed and mosques were destroyed and burnt. In the Kafanchan riot of March 1987, in addition to some mosques and churches that were burnt, about 25 people were killed, and several others hospitalized.[39] Lateju and Adebayo cited a case in which the Muslims were worshipping on a Friday in Jos and so sealed off a popular street. This was not taken lightly by a woman who decided to pass through the barricade. In the midst of the conflict that came after this, she felt assaulted, and so she went to invite a group of young men who engaged the worshipper in a brawl, which consequently ended up in a serious battle that claimed lives.[40] A similar happening was recorded in Kamise (Wollo), Ethiopia where the procession of Christians celebrating Epiphany led to a clash, because the Muslims claimed that the procession was too close to the mosque where they were preparing for prayer.[41]

Apart from the above, the enormous casualty of the Maitatsine uprising of Bullum-Kuttu of October 26–29, 1982, the Jimeta Maitatsine crisis of February 26–March 5, 1984, and the Gombe Maitatsine disturbance of April 26–28, 1985—all in Nigeria—have been adequately documented by scholars. It was observed that not less than 400 lives were lost in the Bullum-Kuttu uprising; 1,004 lives were lost, with 5,913 families displaced in the Jimeta crisis; and over 100 lives were lost in the Gombe disturbance. These crises led to destruction and looting of properties worth millions of Naira.[42]

One instance of a Muslim/Christian clash was recorded in Tanzania on February 1998 when a priest at Mburahati Parish accused a Muslim cleric of misinterpreting the Holy Bible and ridiculing Jesus Christ during his open-air public lectures, which attracted an audience of thousands of Muslims, Christians, and others who did not belong to the two. The intervention of the police consequently led to the killing of four people and the arrest of the Mwembechai leadership. The leaders were later released by the court for lack of evidence. However, in the opinion of Masudi and Mwaskabana, the event was "related to the occupation of the Kwa Mtoro Mosque by some radical young Muslim clerics than the "open-air" religious lecture.[43]

In Ethiopia, there were instances of Muslim/Christian clashes. An example could be cited of the controversies that surrounded the Muslims' request for permission to construct a mosque in the ancient town of Axum, but which was vehemently opposed by the Christians who upheld that the town was a sacred place. Lalibela is another town considered holy by the Christians, and so, no mosque was allowed to be constructed there.[44] There was another demonstration in Addis Ababa in 2006 when a mosque that was believed to have been illegally built was demolished.

It has been identified by Masudi and Mwakabana that religious tensions in other parts of the world, at times, stirred up religious sentiments in Africa.[45] In other words, some religious zealots with possible foreign influence often lead to confrontation and even conflict as a mark of demonstration of solidarity. Narrating the influence of such on Tanzania, they cited as an example, the bombing of the American Embassy in Dar es Salaam on August 7, 1998 by a group of Al-Qaeda terrorists where 11 people were killed and more than 80 were wounded. They claimed that this happened simultaneously with the bomb explosion near the US Embassy in Nairobi, which killed about 250 people and wounded 4,000 others.[46]

In Nigeria, similar reaction trailed the movement of the allied forces at the height of the war against Iraq. The *Daily Times* offices in Nigeria, and copies of *Fun Times* were set ablaze probably because the anti-Western Shiite Muslims in Nigeria felt offended with the way the case was reported or were motivated by the idea of universal Muslim brotherhood. They, therefore, attacked the newspaper office because of the belief that "any aggression against a fellow Muslim at the hands of an opponent is considered to be an attack on the community as a whole."[47] In the same vein, the caricatures of Prophet Muhammad published by a Danish newspaper in February 2006 elicited different reactions from Muslims in various parts of the world. In some parts of Nigeria, particularly Kano and Lagos, peaceful demonstrations were staged to express their displeasure, describing the cartoon as a deliberate attempt to drag Islam through the mud. However, that was not the case in Maiduguri, where it assumed a violent dimension, and many Igbo Christians residing in the area were killed and their property looted. The wave of the crisis in Maiduguri later spread to other parts of northern states. The tension was aggravated when the Igbo saw the corpses of their beloved ones being brought home on February 20, 2006. They, in turn, descended on the Hausa communities in such areas as Enugu, Abia, Anambra, and Delta states, killing many of them and burning down many mosques in the areas.[48] This type of negative solidarity of Muslims and Christians express the multiple identities of Africans and raised a critical question from Mbillah, who wrote:

The critical question for Christians and Muslims to ask themselves is whether Christians in Africa regard themselves as African Christians or Christian Africans?

In the same vein, do Muslims in Africa see themselves as African Muslims or Muslim Africans?...Though there are deep theological considerations on this, we still have to consider whether we are Africans who happen to be Christians and Muslims, or Christians and Muslims who happen to be Africans. In a broader sense, we have to ask the question whether we are Christians and Muslims who happen to be human beings, or human beings who happen to be Christians and Muslims. The way in which we answer these questions will definitely assist us to consider what we have in common as we seek to talk, live, and promote peace with one another and with the wider society.[49]

Still, in relation to Nigeria, the recent outbreak of the menace of the *Boko Haram* deserves to be mentioned. The *Boko Haram* has been described as a group of Muslim fanatics, who, out of hatred for anything that comes from the West, declared the Western education—which in Hausa is referred to as Boko—as unlawful *(haram)*. The activity of the body took a serious dimension when cases of suicide bombings happening in some public places like the police headquarters, and the United Nations' building in the Federal Capital Territory, Abuja, were attributed to them. The religious color with which the occurrences were painted may not be taken with all seriousness, in view of the fact that some mosques had been involved in the bombing. About six pupils of an Arabic school were said to have died due to a bomb explosion in the school in Sapele, Delta State on December 28, 2011. This could, however, be a retaliatory step on the Muslims for the bombing of the Saint Theresa Catholic Church in Madalla, Niger State on Christmas day, where about 30 worshippers were said to have lost their lives. The incessant bomb explosion in some parts of Northern Nigeria has caused the government to declare a state of emergency in some parts of Northern Nigeria.

African Countries and Membership of the OIC

The Organization of Islamic Conference (OIC) could be said to have established off in Rabat in 1969 with some African countries as members. Such countries include the Republic of Benin, Cameroon, Chad, Burkina Faso, Egypt, Sudan, Niger, and Nigeria. The Charter of the Organization outlines its objectives to have included, among others:

i. to consolidate co-operation among member states in the economic, social, cultural, scientific and other vital fields of activities and to carry out consultations among member states in international organizations;
ii. to endeavour to eliminate racial segregation, discrimination, and to eradicate colonialism in all its forms;
iii. to take necessary measures to support international peace and security founded on justice;
iv. to create a suitable atmosphere for the promotion of cooperation and understanding among member states and countries.[50]

Our interest in highlighting part of the charters of the organization is to discuss the views of some people on the focus of the body. The OIC has been presumed to mean a forum for Islamizing member countries and is also considered the master-mind behind the upsurge of religious militancy in some countries. In the view of Umejesi, the incessant religious crises in the northern part of Nigeria are a result of the country's membership of the organization.[51] Umejesi identified another orga-nization called the Islam in Africa Organization (IAO), which aims at eradicating "in all its forms and manifestations all non-Muslim religions in member nations" and ensuring "the declaration of Nigeria (the 24th African and 40th world member of the OIC), a Federal Islamic Sultanate at a convenient date, any time from 28th March 1990, with the Sultan of Sokoto enthroned the Sultan and the Supreme Sovereign of Nigeria."[52]

In our own view, the above submission could be said to have lacked credibil-ity, due to the fact that he refused to divulge where precisely this information was obtained. His failure to identify other member countries of the IAO, the head-quarters, and the officials of the organization makes his submission unreliable and a deliberate means of arousing unnecessary tension amongst the Muslims and Christians in Nigeria. The fact that such African countries like Gabon, Cameroon, Benin, Sierra Leone, and others are members of the OIC, and none of them has transformed into an Islamic country by virtue of being a member of the organiza-tion, renders the wild cacophony, which surrounded the membership of Nigeria in this body, unacceptable. In the view of Oloyede, the Nigeria's membership in this body, which qualifies her to borrow money from the Islamic Development Bank in Jeddah, Kingdom of Saudi Arabia without interest, might inform the decision of the London and Paris Clubs of creditors to cancel part of the accumulated debt of Nigeria from their extortionate interest.[53]

Muslim Organizations

It is important to mention that many Muslim organizations have been put in place to see to the affairs of Muslims in different African countries. The Supreme Muslim Council of Tanzania (BAKWATA) is the principal representative of Muslims' interests in the country, though there exists other smaller organizations. In Ghana, the Gold Coast Muslims' Association had been founded as far back as 1932. It was established to see to the interests of immigrant Muslims who had formed the vast majority of the Muslim community in the country. However, for political reasons, the Muslim youth decided to break away from the Gold Coast Muslims' Association to form the Muslim Youth Congress (MYC), which was a strong supporter of Nkrumah's party and government. There was also the Supreme Council for Islamic Affairs, which was later replaced with the Ghana Muslims' Representative Council formed by the National Redemption Council (NRC)/ Supreme Military Council of Acheampong.

In Nigeria, the Supreme Council for Islamic Affairs, under the leadership of the Sultan of Sokoto, is being put in place. The National Council of Muslim Youth

Organizations (NACOMYO) serves as an umbrella body of all Muslim youth organizations in the country. Apart from the early Islamic organizations like the Ahmadiyyah Movement, the Ansarud-Deen Society, the Nawairu-deen and others, a new dawn in the history of Islamic organizations came, with the establishment of different *Asalatu* groups, the first of which is the Nasrullah-Fatih Society of Nigeria (NASFAT) established in March 1995. As of now, the society has more than 130 branches in Nigeria and 10 abroad. These *Asalatu* groups have programs that are designed for spiritual development of its members. With particular reference to NASFAT, it has *Asalatu* sessions held every Sunday morning from 8:30 a.m. to 12:30 p.m., *Tahajjud* session is observed on the night of every first and third Friday of the month (12:00 a.m. until *Subh*), and Ramadan programs are carried out throughout the holy month including the celebration of the *Laylatul-Qadr*.[54] The *Asalatu* groups are so popular in Nigeria that virtually every *Ratibi* (compound) mosque in some southwestern cities of the country hosts one or the other. However, NASFAT has made giant strides by establishing the Fountain University in Osogbo, the Osun State capital, in addition to a number of nursery, primary, and postprimary institutions established in some towns.

Muslim/Christian Healthy Rivalry and Collaborations

Education has been considered an essential commodity that must be obtained by every citizen of a country. From all indications, governments alone could not meet the educational needs of all citizens of the country. Religious bodies and individuals have therefore come to the aid of government by establishing schools, colleges, and universities. The efforts toward establishing private universities were made first by Christian bodies and individuals in Nigeria. As far back as 1999, the Babcock University, Ilishan-Remo, had been established by the Seventh-day Adventist Mission. In 2001, the Baptist Mission in Nigeria equally established the Bowen University, Iwo. The Church of God Mission International and the Living Faith Mission followed by establishing the Benson Idahosa University, Benin City, and Covenant University, Ota in 2002, respectively. The Muslims also joined them in the task of establishing universities in 2005 when Al-Hikmah University Ilorin was established by Alhaji Abdur-Raheem Oladimeji, a renowned Muslim philanthropist. In the same year, the Katsina State Muslim community established the Katsina University, while Crescent University, Abeokuta was established by Prince Bola Ajibola of the Islamic Movement for Africa. The NASFAT association also established Fountain University, Osogbo in 2007.[55] It is interesting to note that the majority of private universities in Nigeria are established by religious bodies. However, the Muslims have not been able to match their Christian counterparts; out of the 45 private universities in Nigeria, only four could be said to have been established by Muslim groups or individuals. It needs to be mentioned as well that Ghana has an Islamic university, while Uganda hosts an International Islamic University (IUIU), which was founded by the OIC. The IUIU admits students from neighboring countries such as Kenya, Tanzania, Malawi, South

Africa, Rwanda, Burundi, Eritrea, Somalia, Ethiopia, Sudan, Cameroon, Nigeria, Ghana, Sierra Leone, and Mali, among others.

In the health sphere, history has made it clear that Islam had played a significant role in the healing and liberating of some Yoruba towns of their ailments and sickness. Many people embraced the new religion by virtue of the efficacy of their prayers and spiritual assistance rendered to some towns. This is true of Ede, Osogbo, and Ikire in Osun State in Nigeria. Apart from spiritual assistance rendered by religionists to solve personal and national problems, the Christians have come to establish health centers to take care of people. Through these mission hospitals, diseases which proved to be stubborn to the traditional healers, like yaws, hernia, small pox, and leprosy, were not only treated but were also prevented.[56] However, the feeling that most of the hospitals established by Christian bodies do discriminate against Muslims caused some Muslim bodies to establish their own hospitals.[57] The Muslim Hospital of Shaki was consequently established in 1974; however, it only became operational in 1987. The Ansar-ud-Deen Society also has a clinic in Lagos, and one hospital in Oyo. However, the Muslim Hospital of Shaki has been going through a series of crises, one of which is unavailability of enough Muslim doctors to manage the hospital. The situation was so terrible that at one point, a Christian had to be employed as the medical director for the hospital.[58]

It needs to be mentioned that there are instances of clashes between Muslims and Christians in some African countries. Efforts at settling and checking such crises led to the formation of bodies, membership of which includes representatives of the two faiths. Such includes the joint Christian and Muslim Commission for Development and Unity called *Tume ya Wakristo no Waislamu ya Maendeleo na Umoja Tanzania* established in 1995, and the *Jitihada za Viongozi wa Dini Kudumisha Amani*—religious leaders efforts to promote peace—established in 2004, both in Tanzania.[59] The Nigeria Inter-Religious Council (NIREC) started in the year 1999, at the initiative of the National Executive Committee of the Christian Association of Nigeria (CAN). Worried by the incessant clashes between the Muslims and Christians, a meeting was held with the leadership of the Supreme Council for Islamic Affairs, and the two bodies agreed to come together under the name NIREC. The body was formally inaugurated by the then President Olusegun Obasanjo on September 29, 1999.[60]

Another collaborative effort at ensuring peaceful coexistence between the Muslims and Christians is the establishment of the Programme for Christian-Muslim Relations in Africa (PROCMURA), which is a Pan-African Christian organization dedicated to Christian constructive engagement with Muslims for peace in the society and peaceful coexistence between Christians and Muslims. A remarkable achievement has been made by this organization in the advocacy for cessation of hostilities among warring parties in Liberia. The collaboration alliance between the Liberian Council of Churches and National Muslim Council of Liberia later metamorphosed to the establishment of the Inter-Faith Mediation Committee (IFMC), the activities of which contributed to the Liberia election in 1997. The IFMC was later modified to the Inter-Religious Council of Liberia (IRCL). Another process was initiated by the religious leaders to consolidate the peace in both Liberia and neighboring countries of the Mano River Union. This assisted greatly in the success of the 2005 elections, which brought the first democratically elected female president in Africa, Ellen Johnson Sirleaf, to power.[61] It needs to be mentioned that this development was possible because there was peace among the two religious groups at the time. The violent confrontations between Muslims and Christians in Ghana in the late 1990s made it impossible for the Christian Council of Ghana and the Ghana Muslim Representative Councils to intervene in the simmering conflict in the country between the then ruling party of former President Jerry John Rawlings and the then opposition party led by the immediate past President John Agyekum Kufuor. The attempt of the Muslim and Christian councils to broker peace between the feuding political factions was laid to rest by the opening remarks of the then President John Rawlings, when he urged the religious leaders to remove the bundle of wood from their eyes before removing the pegs from the eyes of the political figures, as it was difficult for those whose houses were not in order to restore peace among political actors.[62]

Conclusion

Islam made its first contact with Africa right from the time of its Prophet. The relationship of the religion with Africa then was cordial, as Africa was able to gain extensively from Islam, though some African cultural values were also internalized imbibed by Africans who professed the religion. A sort of Islamization of Africa and Africanization of Islam therefore was experienced. In the contemporary period, Islam is competing with a lot of forces. The competition for membership and for space, coupled with fear of marginalization, prompted the Muslims to downplay the moral and ethical values of the religion in order for them to achieve their goals. The move for recognition has led Muslims to involve themselves in partisan politics, hence the usage and abuse of Islam by politicians for their partisan political ends. Candidates now become favorites of the electorates not by virtue of their competences but rather due to their religious affiliation. The failure of such candidates to demonstrate or put into practical use the teaching of Islam in their respective office leads one to conclude that Islam has not impacted positively in the life of those who profess it. This, however, is not the fault of the religion but that of its adherents; perhaps because of the environment, which, under the pretext of secularism, is not made conducive for practicing such values.

The attachment of Islam to terrorism and suicide bombing has been considered by some scholars as a way of calling a dog a bad name so as to hang it and a planned conspiracy to paint the religion dark so as to make it unattractive to people. That notwithstanding, Muslims too need to be cautious of their actions and attitudes toward their neighbours and adherents of other religions so that their actions speak better than their utterances. Contemporary Muslims in Africa, therefore, should back to the drawing board to plan how to continue the good works of their predecessors and make Islam more attractive to people. We strongly suggest that Islamic institutions organize an annual conference on Islam in Africa, where the legacy of Islam to the continent would be academically showcased and scrutinized and the new course for development would be channelled. Such a conference would also assist in formulating an integrative and demand-driven curriculum for Imams and Muslim leaders to become informed of modern approaches to Islamic propagation. Additionally, Muslims in Africa should interact with other international Islamic organizations, as well as seek approval of their respective countries to establish purely Islamic radio and television stations where pure Islamic teaching would be broadcast and the beauty of the religion can be publicized.

Notes

1. Doi, A. R. I. (1984). *Islam in Nigeria.* Zaria: Gaskiya Corporation Limited, p. 3.
2. Ibid.
3. Abdullah, U. Y. (1998). *Sharia in Africa.* Ijebu-Ode: Shebiotimo Publications, p. 1.
4. Haykal, M. H. (1982). *The Life of Muhammad,* n.p, North American Trust Publications, p. 97.
5. Ibid, p. 98.
6. The verses read: "Now have We caused the word to reach them themselves in order that they may receive admonition. Those to whom We sent the book before this—they do believe in this (revelation). And when it is recited to them, they say: We believe therein, for it is the truth from our Lord: Indeed we have been Muslims (bowing to God's will) before this. Twice will they be given their reward, for that they have persevered, that they avert evil with good, and that they spend (in charity) out of what We have given them. And when they hear vain talk, they turn away therefrom and say "To us our deeds and to you yours; peace be to you, we seek not the ignorant."
7. Haykal, *The Life of Muhammad,* p. 91.
8. The four notable personalities were the Prophet; Uthman ibn Talha, who was keeping the keys; Ussama ibn Yazid; and Bilal ibn Rabiah, who was an African.
9. Adua, S. S. (2005). "Africa and Africans in the History of Islam." *Journal of Human Studies,* (4)1, pp. 70–71.
10. Abdullah, *Sharia in Africa,* pp. 5–6.
11. Doi, *Islam in Nigeria,* p. 6.
12. Ibid, p. 7.
13. Abdullah, *Sharia in Africa,* p. 11.
14. Adua, "Africa and Africans in the History of Islam," pp. 69–70.
15. Cleaveland, T. (2008). "Timbuktu and Walata: Lineages and Higher Education" In S. Jeppie and S. B. Diagne (eds). *The Meaning of Timbuktu.* Cape Town: HSRC Press, p. 77.
16. See O. A. Bamiro's forward to J.O. Hunwick's *Islam Arabic into Western Nigeria,* 14th Exchange Lecture Series, University of Ibadan, 2008, p. v.
17. Kukah, M. H. (2007). *Religion, Culture and the Politics of Development.* Lagos: Centre for Black and African Arts and Civilisation, p. 3.
18. Ibid, pp. 4–5.
19. Bobboyi, H. "Ajami Literature and the Study of the Sokoto Caliphate" In S. Jeppie and S.B. Diagne (eds) *The Meaning of Timbuktu,* pp. 125–32.
20. Hassane, M. (2008). "Ajami in Africa: The Use of Arabic Script in the Transcription of African Languages." In S. Jeppie and S. B. Diagne (eds), *The Meaning of Timbuktu,* p. 115. Cape Town: HSRC Press.

21. Adamu, A. U. (2009). "Ajamization of Knowledge: Challenges and Prospects of an Educational Strategy," *Al-Ijtihad, the Journal of Islamization of Knowledge and Contemporary Issues,* (1)2, p. 7.
22. Oloyede, I. O. (2010). "Religious Experiences in a Multi-Religious State: The Nigeria Example." A Keynote Address delivered at the 1st National Conference of the Department of Religious Studies, Kwara State University, Malete, on 19 October, 2010, p. 5.
23. Adamu, "Ajamization of Knowledge", p. 13.
24. Doi, *Islam in Nigeria*, p. 217.
25. Ibid, pp. 264–78.
26. Ibid.
27. Opeloye, M. O. and Jimoh, S. L. (2004). "The Yoruba Muslims of Nigeria and the Glorious Qur'an," *NATAIS Journal of the Nigeria Association of Teachers of Arabic and Islamic Studies,* vol. 7, pp. 79–80.
28. Doi, *Islam in Nigeria*, pp. 151–152.
29. Masudi, A. and Mwakabana, H. (2008). "Governance and Interfaith Relations in Tanzania" In A. N. Kubai and T. Adebo (eds.). *Striving in Faith Christians and Muslims in Africa*.Sweden: Life and Peace Institute, p. 60.
30. Otsebo, T. (2008). "Christian-Muslim Relations in Ethiopia." In A. N. Kubai and T. Adebo (eds.). *Striving in Faith Christians and Muslims in Africa,*Sweden: Life and Peace Institute, p. 79.
31. Ibid, p. 80
32. Ibid.
33. Awet, M. (2008). "Religion as an Expression of Shared Ethical Values of the State." In A. N. Kubai and T. Adebo (eds.). *Striving in Faith Christians and Muslims in Africa*.Sweden: Life and Peace Institute, p. 28.
34. Ibid.
35. Okene, A. A. (2011). "The Demand for Shari'ah Implementation in a Democratic Setting: A Historical Background and the Zamfara State Experience" In H. Salihi, B. A. Umar, and H. A. Suleiman (eds.). *Shari'ah, Democracy and Governance in Islam,* pp. 47–48. Kano: International Institute of Islamic Thought, Nigeria office.
36. Ayandele, E. A. (1979). *Nigerian Historical Studies.* London: Frank Cass & Co., p. 148.
37. A recent Doctoral thesis of Department of Arabic and Islamic Studies, University of Ibadan, confirms this. See A. K. Makinde, (2007). "The Institution of Shari'ah in Oyo and Osun States, Nigeria, 1890–2005" (Unpublished Ph.D thesis), Department of Arabic and Islamic Studies, University of Ibadan.
38. Lagos State Chapter of Supreme Council for Shari'ah in Nigeria, *Selected Judgements of the Lagos State Independent Shari'ah Panel,* vol. 1, pp. i-ii.
39. Lateju, F., and Adebayo, R. I. (2008). "On Community Relations: Christians and Muslims in Nigeria" In A. N. Kubai and T. Adebo (eds.). *Striving in Faith Christians and Muslims in Africa*Sweden: Life and Peace Institute, p. 102.
40. Ibid, p. 101.
41. Ostebo, "Christian-Muslim Relations in Ethiopia," p. 84.
42. Adebayo, R. I. (2010). "Strategising Peace through Islamic Ethical Values" In I. O. Albert and I. O. Oloyede (eds.)., *Dynamics of Peace Process.*Ilorin: Centre for Peace and Strategic Studies, University of Ilorin, p. 28.
43. Masudi and Mwakabana, "Governance and Interfaith Relations in Tanzania," p. 60.
44. Ostebo, "Christian-Muslim Relations in Ethiopia," pp. 83–84.
45. Masudi and Mwakabana, "Governance and Interfaith Relations in Tanzania," p. 62.
46. Ibid.

47. Lateju and Adebayo, "On Community Relations: Christians and Muslims in Nigeria," pp. 100–101.
48. Ibid, p. 103.
49. Mbillah, J. (2009). "Keynote Address Outlining Conference Focus." A Keynote address to the Programme for Christian-Muslim Relations in Africa (PROCMURA) on Religion and Conflict Prevention/Management, Peace building and Reconciliation in West Africa held in Accra, Ghana between 20–24 July 2009, p. 4.
50. Umejesi, I. O. (2010). "Religion and Politics in Africa: The OIC Membership and Implications for Member States—Nigeria as a Case Study" In C. O. Isiramen et Al. (eds.). *Issues in Religious Studies and Philosophy*Ibadan: En-Joy Press and Books, p. 331..
51. Ibid, p. 333.
52. Ibid.
53. Oloyede, "Religious Experiences in a Multi-Religious State: The Nigeria Example," p. 6.
54. Imam, Y.O. (2008). "Healing in Islam: A Case Study of the Spiritual Effects of NASFAT among Nigerian Muslims" In Z. I. Oseni (ed), *Fluorescence of Arabic and Islamic Studies in Nigeria*. Ibadan: HEBN Publishers Plc, p. 83.
55. Adebayo, R. I. (2010). "Prospects and Challenges of Private Universities in Nigeria: Focus on Islamic Missions' Universities." In J. Okojie, I. O. Oloyede, and P. Obanya (eds), *50 Years of University Education in Nigeria: Evolution, Achievements and Future Directions*, pp. 191–97. Ilorin: University of Ilorin & National Universities Commission.
56. Oloyede, "Religious Experiences in a Multi-Religious State: The Nigeria Example," p. 8.
57. Abdul Fattah, pp. 235–237.
58. Jimoh, S.L. (2004). "Health Care Services and Hospital Management in Islam: Policies and Distinctive Features." *Al-Ijtihad Journal of Islamization of Knowledge and Contemporary Issues,* (5)1, pp. 48–50.
59. Masudi & Mwakabana, "Governance and Interfaith Relations in Tanzania," p. 61.
60. Onaiyekan, J. (2011). *Dividends of Religion in Nigeria*. Ilorin: Department of Religions, University of Ilorin, pp. 15–16.
61. Lartey, B.D. (2009). "Presentation on Liberia." A presentation at the West Africa Christian and Muslim Leaders Consolidation on Religion and Conflict Prevention, Peace building and Reconciliation held in Accra, Ghana by PROCMURA/PRICA, July 20–24, 2009. pp. 4–5.
62. Mbillah, "Keynote Address Outlining Conference Focus," p. 8.

Chapter 9

African-Derived Religions in Diaspora: An Overview

M. I. Oguntoyinbo-Atere

Introduction

African-derived religions (ADRs) are used to identify the religions that were transplanted to the Americas with the enslavement of Africans. The term is used to cover the Afro-Caribbean and Afro-Brazilian religions whose traditions have survived until today, and they continue to be sources of spirituality to the people.[1]

These religious have been grouped into types by George Simpson: the neo-African religions—Santería in Cuba, the Dominican Republic, and Puerto Rico; Vodun in Haiti; Shango in Trinidad and Grenada; and Candoblé in Brazil. The second type includes Cumina and the convince cult in Jamaica, the Big Drum Dance of Carriacou (Grenada), and Kele in St. Lucia. Another type include religions that emphasize divination, healing, and spirit mediumship like Umbanda in Brazil, the María Lionza cult in Venezuela, and Espiritismo in Puerto Rico.[2]

Santería, which is practiced in Cuba and in many parts of the United States, is perhaps the most well-known of the African-derived religions.[3] There is also a reference to the Shango religion, practiced in Trinidad and Grenada, which started in 1849, when some African laborers who were brought in from Ijesha[4] in Nigeria began to practice Yoruba beliefs.

However, our focus is on Afro-Brazilian religious symbiosis. Afro-Brazilian religions refer to the religious traditional practices in Brazil. Candomblé and Umbada are very strong Afro-Brazilian religions.[5] In these religions, there are close interactions, interrelatedness, and interdependent relationships. These have helped them in their survival.

Origin

In colonial times (1500–1822), and during the years of the Brazilian Empire (1822–1889), Roman Catholicism, with a special link to the throne of Portugal, held the status of the official religionin Brazil. However, as a result of the colonization process, as in many other places in Latin America, the indigenous people were soon reduced to a small minority of the population with immigrants from Europe (now in the majority), African slaves, and mulattoes making up the bulk of the population.

All of these brought their religions, and Brazil moved from "Catholic Monopoly" to contemporary religious diversity.[6] Candomblé, Umbanda, Xango, Tambor de Mina, Tambor de Nagô, Tereco, Pajelança, Catimbó, Batuque, and Macumba are some of the names given to Afro-Brazilian religions in various regions of the nation.[7] These were mostly products of the nineteenth-century slave societies, who were Africans, along with their descendants. These black slaves had to look for a way of defending their humanity in the face of hopelessness. While some religions originated from slave settlements, some out of the celebration of saints' days. Whenever these African slaves were given a respite to stay away from work for the celebration of the holy days, they gathered in the small homes and rented rooms by African religious leaders in order to worship and to receive healing.

It is worthy of note that Afro-Brazilian religions exhibit some distinctions and similarities in their traditions. Part of what they have in common are emphasis on ritual and medical healing, intimate relationships with spiritual entities, mutual aids, "concept of obligation and reciprocity between human beings and the ancestral/spiritual energies who are gods, saints, orixas, nkisis, voduns, caboclos."[8] Spirit possession is also common to them. They also share in different degrees, a combination of influences from Western and Central African traditions, native Amerindian cultural and religious practice, and popular Catholicism.

Their religions have unique features derived from the combination of the elements of their rituals, orientations, and meanings based on the historical, geographical, and cultural context. For example, Candomblé[9] developed with strong elements of Yoruba and Ewe-Fon ritual organizations language and mythology.[10] Umbanda[11] relies heavily on Candomblé, Spiritism, Catholicism, and persistent black and Indian folk representations in popular culture.

Xango has a history that is similar to Candombléand is found mostly in Recife, in the state of Pernambuco. Tambor de Mina[12] has Dahomean influence, while Tambor de Nagô is influenced by Yoruba traditions. Tambor de Mata[13] has additional Cabindam ritual elements.

Transportation

When the Portuguese occupied Brazil, they realized that there were no mineral resources there. Therefore, they resorted to agriculture. However, the population of Portugal was insufficient to accomplish their aim, and they resorted to the import of African slaves.[14] From the middle of the sixth to the middle of the nineteenth centuries, millions of slaves were exported from Africa to the Americas. Brazil was said to have received the biggest share of about 4 million slaves.[15] African slaves were used in sugar plantations. As the importance of sugar grew, so did the importation of slaves.[16]

Slave trade was a huge business, which involved hundreds of ships and thousands of people transported from the coast of Africa to the regional dealers in Brazil. Half of the 30 richest merchants of Rio de Janeiro were slave traders; their purses were extremely fat as they made huge profits. Prisoners of war were kidnapped in Africa by fellow Africans, who were also merchants, and sold to Portuguese slave traders.[17]

Several of the blacks died between the area of capture and the African coast; some died on the ships traveling between Africa and Brazil.[18] Less than half of the Africans captured for this purpose died before delivery to their future masters in Brazil.[19]

Religious Practices

Candomblé and Umbanda have many followers, and they are open to all; however blacks are a majority in Umbanda and a minority in Candomblé. Both have their concentration in urban centers like Salvador de Bahia, Recife, Rio de Janeiro, Porto Alegre, Brasilia, Sao Luis. In practice, Candomblé is closer to the original West African religions, while Umbanda blends Catholicism, Spiritism, and African beliefs. These African slaves would summon their gods called *orixas*[20] with chants and dances they had brought from Africa. Candomblé activities are more hidden from general view except in famous festivals such as the *Iemanja* festival and the waters of *Oxala*. Each African god is called an *orixa* and has a saint counterpart except for *Oxala*, who is equated with Jesus Christ.[21] Priesthood was taken over by the women because three female former slaves founded a center for Candomblé in Salvador, Bahia in 1830.[22] Some of these female African slaves were also mistresses to the Portuguese masters. The influence of Candomblé was spread evenly regardless of social economic position.[23]

Candomblé holds dearly to the belief that healing of the soul is of utmost importance. The candomble ritual begins with an offering or invocation to Exu, the messenger through which they communicate with the orixas, and builds into what they believe to be their patron *orixa*.[24]

Umbanda, which is the second most popular of the Afro–Brazilian religions, was founded in 1904 and uses the names of Catholic saints instead of the African names for the *orixas*.[25] It is said that though practitioners of Umbanda fear that direct contact with the gods would kill or harm a mortal, they believe in consultation through mediums; Exu is consulted and asked for protection against evil in the beginning of the Umbanda ritual. The priest or priestess goes into a trance and becomes possessed by spirits, which are usually Native American or African ancestors.[26]

Syncretic Beliefs

Though Brazil has no official or state religion, Roman Catholic is the religion of the majority of the inhabitants of Brazil. However, the Brazilian Roman Catholicism is different from any other form because of the way in which Brazilians have incorporated famous religious figures from Brazil in their worship. This popular Catholicism includes elements of African religiosity originally brought by slaves. This blending of Christian elements with African religiosity was originally repressed by the Catholic Church and civil authorities; yet, excluded from the Roman Catholic Church, it developed independently.[27] A revealing phrase commonly used in contemporary Brazil is "Brazilian style Catholicism."[28]

The 2000 census reveals that there are relatively low percentages of followers of other religions, like the Afro–Brazilian religions. This was possibly due to the phenomenon of double affiliation, a mixing of religion as discussed above in popular Brazilian Catholicism, an invisible syncretism not publicly admitted by those who practice it and who opted to declare themselves Catholic despite all adopting practices of other creeds.[29] In 2000, the statistics available showed the population was 169.4 million. Christians—152.3 million or 90 percent; Roman Catholics—125 million, or 73.8 percent; Evangelicals/Protestants—26 million, or 15.45 percent; marginal Christians—1.3 million, or 0.75 percent; other religionists—5 million, or 3 percent; nonreligious—12 million, or 7 percent.[30]

Candomblé is Brazil's most influential Afro–Brazilian religion. It mixes Catholicism and Yoruba traditional religion from the Yoruba tribe of Nigeria. This religion is characterized by the gods and goddesses called *orishas*. These Yoruba slaves took their religion to Brazil as they did in Cuba.[31]

In Brazil, these *orishas* are divided into seven divinities with defined functions. Some are represented as saints of Catholic religion or a natural element, and each has a symbolic color. They are: (a) *Oxala* is the supreme authority of Candomblé represented in the form of Jesus Christ or the sun, and his color is white. This must be a reference to Orisanla[32] in Yoruba religion. (b) *Ogum* is seen as the lord of war, who overcomes obstacles and difficulties. He is represented in the form of Saint George on his horse. He is also represented by himself. The colors are red, white, and green. (c) *Xango* is the *orisha* of justice. Myth has it that he had three wives—Oxum, Yansa, and Oba. He is represented in the form of Moses, holding the Ten Commandments, and his color is brown. A few changes occur in the names of gods and goddesses from the way they are originally in Yoruba language. In the Cuban case, Sango became Chango; Oshun became Ochun; Yemoja became Yemeja. We have observed some changes in names of these *orishas* in Brazil too. Cladenogenesis takes place.[33] (d) *Yemanja* is the most well-known *orisha*. She is viewed as the queen of the seas and the oceans and is represented in the form of a young woman with long, black hair in a flowing blue dress. Her colors are blue and white. (e) *Yansa* is a god of thunder and lightning. She has the posture of a fighting god. Her color is golden yellow, and she is represented in the form of Saint Barbara. (f) *Oxum* is the goddess of the rivers, calm in appearance, and her colors are purple and dark blue.[34] (g) *Oxossy* is the *orisha* known as the god of victory, a representative of the forest and all animals; he is associated with the color green.[35]

Conclusion

The Africans transported to Brazil belong to two major groups: the West African and the Bantu people. The study of Afro–Brazilian religions has revealed that these religions originate mostly from the Yoruba tribe of Nigeria. The Yoruba sold into slavery took along their *orishas* and their religious beliefs, as well as others from Ibo land (Nigeria), some from Ghana, Benin Republic, Guinea Bissau, Angola, Zimbabwe, and Mozambique. No doubt, the Catholic religion and these African-based religions have rubbed off on one another greatly. None of these religions, as practiced in Brazil, can be said to have retained all of their original features.

Notes

1. Bongmba, Elias. (2005). *Religion: African Diaspora*. Farmington Hills, MI: The Gale Group, Inc.
2. Ibid.
3. It is also called Regla de Ocha or Regla Lucumi.
4. Ijesha covers Ilesa and all the villages surrounding it. Ilesa is one of the major cities in Osun State of Nigeria. It is a part of the Yoruba tribe.
5. An interview with Dr. Da Silva, a Brazilian, on the of September 16, 2011.
6. Marcelo Timotheo Da Costa, (2010). "Brazil." In Daniel Patte (ed.). *The Cambridge Dictionary of Christianity*. Cambridge University Press, p. 141.
7. Afro-Brazilian Religions, http://library.thinkquest.org/C005537/religions.html
8. Ibid.
9. Ibid.
10. Ibid. *See also* Awolalu, J. O. and P. A. Dopamu. (1979). *West African Traditional Religion*. Ibadan: Onibonoje Press and Books Industries (Nig.) Ltd., pp. 54–57.
11. Umbanda is a more recent phenomenon dating from the 1920s.
12. This was organized in the nineteenth century by blacks who worked in the coastal economy in the state of Maranhao.
13. Tambo de mate is also called Tereco.
14. Maria Graham, *Journal of a Voyage to Brazil*, and resident there, during part of the years 1821, 1822, 1823. London: Longman.
15. Ibid.
16. Braun, Theodore A. (1999). *Perspectives on Cuba and its People*. New York: Friendship Press. National Council of Churches.
17. Graham, *Journal of a Voyage to Brazil*.
18. Ibid.
19. Ibid.

20. In Yoruba land, they are known as *orishas*. *See also* Idowu, E. B. (1962). *Olodumare: God in Yoruba Belief.* Longman: London, p. 1184. *See also* Dopamu, Abiola T. (2007). "Religious Pluralism in Nigeria: The Example of the Yoruba." In Ade P. Dopamu et al. (eds.). *Dialogue: Issues in Contemporary Discussion.* Lagos: Small Books.

21. The Religions of Brazil, http:/library,thinkquest.org/C005537/religions.html. *See also* Awolalu and Dopamu, *West African Traditional Religion,* pp. 54–57.

22. Three female former slaves that founded the center for Candomblé are known as: Iya Deta, Iya Kala, and Iya Nasso.

23. The Religions of Brazil, http:/library.thinkquest.org/c00537/religions.html

24. Ibid. *See also* Dopamu, P. Ade. (1986, 2000). *Esu the Invisible Foe of Man: A Comparative Study of Satan in Christianity, Islam and Yoruba Religion.* Ijebu Ode: Shebiotimo Publications, pp. 20–26.

25. Ibid.

26. The Religions of Brazil, http:/library,thinkquest.org/C005537/religions.html

27. Da Costa, "Brazil." In Daniel Patte (ed.). *The Cambridge Dictionary of Christianity,* p. 141.

28. Ibid, p. 141.

29. Ibid.

30. Ibid, p. 148.

31. Oguntoyinbo-Atere, Martina. (2001). "An Exhibition of Yoruba Religion, Arts and Culture among the Cubans: A Visitation." In *Papers in Honour of Tekena N. Tamuno. Professor Emeritus at 70.* Egbe Ifie (ed.). Ibadan: Oputoru Books, pp. 103–109.

32. Awolalu and Dopamu, *West African Traditional Religion,* pp. 54–57.

33. Cladenogenesis is the process of branching out into newer species having lost communication with their origin, changes are accumulated in phonology, syntax, and semantics. *See* Yusuf Noah and Andy Olagbemi. (1988). "Language, Society and Culture." In *Communication, Language & Culture in Society.* Lagos: Bolaji & Associates.

34. For more information on Oshun, *see* M. I. Oguntoyinbo-Atere, "Women, Religion and Culture: An Appraisal of the Position of Women in Yoruba land (Nigeria)." *Africa: Our Times and Culture,* Vol. 1, part two, pp. 215–223. *See also* Diedre L. Badejo (1991). "Oral Literature of the Yoruba Goddess Osun." In Jacob K. Olupona and Toyin Falola (eds.). *Religion and Society in Nigeria. Historical and Sociological Perspectives.* Ibadan: Spectrum Books Limited, pp. 81–96.

35. Religion in Brazil, http://en.wikipedia.org/wiki/ReligioninBrazil

Chapter 10

Arts and Music in African Derived Diaspora Religions

Adeoluwa Okunade

Introduction

The Europeans and other colonial masters in Africa used religion as one of its strategies to enslave Africans both mentally and physically, which eventually led to highest degree of mental castration. The colonial masters were not clever enough to discern that no culture is superior to others; as long as the culture of the people's lives are with them, then, such culture becomes authentic. Music and religion in the African setting form a greater part of the cultural lives of the peoples. One of the gravest errors that the colonial masters committed was to first pronounce that Africans had no music, and since the continent was perceived as a "musicless" world space, religions that were part of the bedrock of African music ultimately became ostracized. However, the soul of the two sister arts—music and religion— refused to die; rather, they were transplanted through their reincarnation strength and moved with the slave merchants outside Africa, and became entrenched into the lives of the survivors of the enslavement trade.

This chapter focuses on the presence of musical activities within the spheres of African-derived diaspora religions, with special reference to Cuba and Brazil. The history of arts and music in the African-derived diaspora religions is a history of forced movements and of events that are associated with these movements.

The major migration event is that of the enslavement of Africans and racial discrimination that followed their freedom. Religion and music have been omnipresent in the lives of Africans, and these two are integrated to the extent that an average African is a practitioner not through written words but through digestion via activities of worship, festival, play, and other communal ceremonies. The implication of this is that the traditional African knows what to do, when, and how to do it when it comes to issues of religion. He does not need a written document to serve as the liturgy or compilation of pieces that forms the repertoire. It is part of the inner-most being that could not be destroyed. The two religions being discussed here are Santería and Candomblé in Cuba and Brazil, respectively; both of which were trans-planted from Africa. The origins of Santería are found within the traditional reli-gion of the Yorùbá people of Southwest Nigeria in West Africa, while Candomblé is a mixture of traditional religious beliefs of the Yorùbá, Fon, and Bantu people. In addition to bibliographical evidences, the author had opportunity of attending the worship session of the Candomble in Salvador-Bahia. However, there were restric-tions on use of recording materials, audio and visual; however, few of the devotees and enthusiasts volunteered limited facts and information on the religion. The inti-macies about the religion are exposed only to the initiates.

To give this chapter wider coverage, therefore, it is pertinent to spread its ten-tacles to a survey of the African diaspora. If details would cannot be given of the dispersion of Africans, mention must be made at least, of the Atlantic slave trade. Records show that there was a viable market in African slaves around the mid-four-teenth century in Southern Europe. The instrument used in dehumanizing Africans surfaced through the Atlantic slave trade effectively in 1441 on the Western Sahara coast. The Portuguese mariners floundered the West African coast toward the gold resources after failing in 1415 to capture the gold trade by occupying Ceuta on the Moroccan coast.[1] The business of enslavement increased through the break-through in sugar production across Europe, which also found its way through the Mediterranean to Atlantic islands, and ultimately to the Americas.[2] Though the direct exportation of enslaved Africans to the Americas began in 1532, by the late sixteenth century, about 80 percent of these slaves from West Africa were already taken to the Americas, especially Brazil, which had a strong base in sugar planta-tions. Lliff, in his study on the Atlantic slave trade, put estimates of slaves that reached the Americas between 1451—1870 at 9,391,100, with the possible range between 8,000,000 and 10,500,000.[3] Babawale reported that another researcher had raised the figure slightly to 11,863,000 slaves exported from Africa, signifying that between 9,600,000 and 10,800,000 reached the Americas, with the caveat that further study may increase the figure.[4]

Inikori, in his own study, submitted that no fewer than 25 million people were exported out of Africa, south of the Sahara.[5] Babawale summarized all of these sub-missions by concluding with an approximate figure of no fewer than 10,000 Africans who were exported as slaves each year to Brazil, the British colony of Barbados, and the French Caribbean Islands of Martinique and Guadeloupe.[6] Most of the slaves who survived this harrowing period could not go back to their places of origin. They remained in the land of the oppressed but retained their distinctiveness; some in their religion, and most in their artistic sensibilities, remained intact. It should be mentioned that these "freed slaves" also were enmeshed into the slave masters' communities across the world. This contributed to the spread of African arts and culture all over the world. The beauty found in African arts is so unfathomable that the "tenants" found it so convenient through forceful means to take it away from the "landlords." The slave trade, therefore, can rightly be pointed to as the origin of the diaspora. Not only musical consciousness of the slaves were taken along, but other art works and artifacts were taken along, and some were forcibly taken by the imperialists to the nations of the slave masters. Oba of Benin (Nigeria) Omo N'oba Erediauwa, in his introductory note in "Benin Kings and Rituals: Court Arts from Nigeria" asserted that:

> The exhibition is showcasing some of the works that made Benin (Nigeria) famous. It once again, reminds the world of a civilization truncated by the imperial forces of the colonialists. The works on show at this exhibition is some of the 3,000-odd pieces of bronze and ivory works forcibly removed from my great grand-father's palace by some Britons who invaded Benin in 1897.[7]

Historical Background of Santería and Candomblé

The origins of Santería are found among the Yoruba people of West Africa, of whose religion is based upon a hierarchical, pantheistic system of thought that stretches from God Almighty in the most rarified heaven down to man on earth. During the Atlantic slave trade, the enslaved Africans carried along with them their various religious practices and beliefs. Part of these practices today is what has come to stay in Cuba as Santería, dominant of which is the worship of some Yoruba deities. Olorun is regarded as "The Almighty," whose presence no man can withstand, and for this reason, man must go through other deities to reach him. The believers then send their petition through the deities, *orisha* to the almighty. The Yoruba believe that each of these *orisha* has powers over specific aspects of the earth. For each of the *orisha* to be worshipped, music and other types of communication are used appropriately. It is then believed that when the *orisha* has been praised through music and other oral praise means, the *orisha* is happy and in turn takes the practitioners' messages to the almighty. The belief in these *orisha,* as transported by the enslaved Africans to both Cuba and Brazil, became their spiritual strength. At some point, as recorded by Amira and Cornelius, the Catholic Church demanded some rights for the slaves, and through this demand, the enslaved Africans were allowed to form their own social and religious organizations.[8] Amira and Cornelius added that:

> Rather than try to destroy traditional beliefs, the church embraced a stance whereby within the Negro *cabildos* (social clubs), the traditional religion would be allowed to continue and gradually become influenced by Christian teachings. Membership within the *cabildos* followed regional African groupings called *naciones*, and members shared common ethnic and linguistic origins. Each cabildo was associated with a specific Catholic saint.[9]

This opportunity gave the Africans room to equate the strength, role, and function of the *orisha* with those of the Catholic saints, and they began to merge the concepts. In essence, the Africans placed the Catholic saints on the surface to make their masters happy but religiously practiced their African traditional beliefs underneath. These *orisha* have several avatars, which are regarded as "roads" by the practitioners, who are referred to as santeros. It is observed that the spelling of some of the names of the *orisha* are quite different from the original Yoruba spellings, however, the attributes are not too distant from each other, both at "home and abroad." Listed below are some these *orishas,* their attributes, and their equivalent Catholic saints.

Osain—This is a god that has herbs and healing in his custody. He is, therefore, revered as god of the forest, who is physically disabled with only one arm, one leg, and one eye.

Ogun—This is god of iron associated with wars and warriors. Santeros associate this god with Saint Peter.

Eleggua—*Elegbara* in Yorubaland—This god is seen as a trickster and also a warrior. He is associated with Catholic Saint Roque.

Ochosi—*Ososi* in Yorubaland—He is the seen as the god of the hunt and another powerful warrior. He is an equivalent of the Catholic Saint Nobert.

Babaluaye—*Obaluaye* in Yorubaland—this is seen as a god in charge of diseases like smallpox and leprosy. He is viewed as a hot dangerous god who must always be placated with water. Hence, his musicians are always seen pouring water on the floor before performing his praise poetry.

Similar to its sister religion, Santería, Candomblé is a religion of a people who were forcefully moved from their origins through the enslavement. It is today viewed as an African-Brazilian religion. It is a mixture of traditional Yoruba, Fon, and Bantu beliefs, which originated from different regions of Africa with the added flavor of Catholicism over time. The author's interaction with some of the devotees in Salvador-Bahia (Brazil) revealed that the elements of Catholicism were incorporated when the slaves were not allowed to worship in their original ways. As such, they needed to satisfy their slave masters by worshipping in the introduced Catholic faith, and later or secretly did their indigenous worship. Over time, elements of Catholicism came to remain as part of their mode of worship. One finds cross symbols, images of saints, and that of Virgin Mary in the Candomblé temple. The worship session of Candomble truly reflects the musical arts concept of Africa. Candomblé itself means music and dance in honor of gods. Music, dance, drama, costume, and hairdo are the full ingredients of what constitutes music in Africa, which are exhibited in Candomblé worship. From the beginning of slave trade period, many Christian slave owners believed that it was part of their religious obligation to convert the slaves into their own faith and make them forget their past. This effort did not totally succeed, as is evident in the Candomblé religion. Outwardly, most of the slaves became what their masters wanted, but secretly they went back to pray to their gods or ancestral spirits. The adherents of Candomblé equally saw the similarity between of the worship of saints in Catholicism with their own deities, which caused most of the devotees to conceal symbols of their deities inside their corresponding Catholic saints. It was not easy for the Candomblé devotees to gather and worship in Brazil. The origin of the religion was still disgusting to generations of the slave masters to the extent that any gatherings of Candomblé settings would attract the wrath of the government. It was not until the 1970s, when the government scrapped a law requiring police permission to hold public ceremonies, that the Candomblé religion became free from being an underground religion.

To many of the adherents or devotees, Candomblé was not just a mere religion, but an avenue to connect to their cultural roots for the satisfaction of their psyche and soul, of which slave trade had stripped them. The devotees believe in one almighty God who can only be approached through lesser deities, which they call *orixas*. The *orixas* are the African ancestors who have been deified and are believed to have become a link between the spiritual world and the world of humans. It is believed that each human being has his or her own *orixa* that controls his destiny, or serves as the protector.

Musical Structure and Instrumental Ensemble

The overwhelming conception in musical performance of most traditional African religions is a unique combination of music and dance, or stylistic movement of some sort. However, there are a few cases where some ceremonies will emphasize music only. Such may have to do with initiation or some important rites. In Santería religion, there are two public music ceremonies. One is named after the popular Yoruba drum called *Bembé*, which is performed on conga drums. The second public ceremony is called *guemilere*, which is performed on Batá drums. The Bembé is combined with iron bells, while the guemilere is combined with rattles. These public ceremonies are held in honor of one *orisha* or the other. As recorded by Amira and Cornelius, who worked extensively among the santeros of Cuba, the public music ceremonies have various distinct sections.[10] For instance, if Batá drums are used, the first section is called *orul del igbodu*, which literally means "ceremony in the *orisha* room." This takes place before the general social activities of the *guemilere*. This performance is always staged in a secluded place meant for a few people who probably belong to the leadership class of the religion. The second section called *oru del eya aranla*, which literally means "ceremony in the main room," is performed by a lead singer who uses call-and-response style in the rendition. The attendees at the ceremony assume the part of the chorus. This is open to all, and the main room referred to here is a usually a large room. While the *oru del igbodu* is performed in honor of all the *orisha*, the *oru del eya aranla*, in addition to honoring the *orisha*, each Santero is equally honored and comes out to dance when his own *orisha* is being praised. The rhythmic pattern of Batá drums here is slightly different from that of *oru del igbodu*.

The ceremony from *oru del eya aranla* moves without a break to the next section, which is *iban balo*, which literally means "patio." The *iban balo* is freer in terms of rhythmic structure compared to the preceding sections. The free rhythm can be best described as a hot rhythm, because here there is spirit possession of the devotees, which is propelled by the hot rhythm of the ensemble. This section leads to the final one, which is of the bembé called *cierre*, or literally "closing." This section is dedicated to honoring the ancestral spirits called *egun*, by the santeros, and the *orisha*—*Oya, Babaluaye, Osain, Yeggua, Eleggua, Yemaya*, and *Olokun*. The *cierre* is similar to the *oru del igbodu*; both are instrumental performance and are in recognition of the *orisha*. The Batá drum ensemble used in Santería religion consists of three sets, each playing a specified role. These are *okonkolo, itotele*, and *iya*. From the role each of these plays, it is deduced that the equivalent of the drums' names in Yoruba Batá ensemble are "omele, *atele,* and iya." The *okokonlo* keeps the pause, which serves as the bedrock for others, with short cycles without opportunities for improvization. The *itotele* builds on the *okokolo* rhythmic pattern with longer cycles and fills the gap within the metric pulses. The *iya,* which is the "mother," plays the motherly role of exhibition of improvization and embellishment. The creativity of the instruments are well handled and exposed on the *Iya* through the player. The *Iya* drummer is seen as the master drummer of the ensemble.

As in the Santería religion, music, drumming, and dancing are key elements of worship in the Candomblé religion. Drums known as *atabaque* are major instruments of the Candomblé religion; these are barrel-shaped drums similar in look to congas. The drums are played with both hands and appropriate sticks. The author witnessed that the elderly members of the devotees are masters in the art of playing the drums, but they have given room to the younger ones to improve on the instruments. Intermittently, the elders may decide to take over one or two of the instruments either to get to the peak of the art of drumming to project the worshippers into the appropriate realm of worship or to relieve any of the younger ones on the instrument. There are three different sizes of the drum, which are *le, rumpi,* and *rum.* In addition to these are the *agogo*—bells, which keep the timeline, and the *xekere*—gourd rattle.

The worship session begins with drumming alone, followed by the procession of devotees before the arrival of the priestess who is highly revered in worship. The music produced graduates from simple to complex rhythms so as to propel members into spirit possession, which leads them into trance sessions. The *rum* plays the role of the master drum, giving directives to the *le* and the *rumpi.* Amy Cunningham observed that the heavy percussive session and the ritualistic ceremonies of the Candomblé worship have distinctly shaped the musical sound space of Brazil, influencing many contemporary styles of samba and bossa nova.[11] This reminds one of the influence of church music in the Yoruba Juju music of Nigeria, where most of the popular musicians began their musical experience from the church choir. The heavy presence of drumming and songs in the worship is also used to appease the *orixas.*

The devotees do not take the music lightly; neither do they view the drummers as mere men during the worship session. They consider the musicians closer to the deities who in turn inspire them to be able give appropriate music. There is a large repertoire of Candomblé music, which is connected with rituals and in accompanying or honoring of different rhythms. Some of these deities are *Ojo ibi, Exu, Ogun, Oxosi, Omolu, Iroko, Oxumare, Nana, Oxun, Ewa, Iansa, Yemoja, Xango, Ramunha, Oxala, and Sarewa.* All of the instruments mentioned earlier are employed during celebration of any of these deities. During worship or special festivals, all of the deities are honored with appropriate music meant for each. Songs are not shared among the deities. While this music remains an integral part of the Candomblé worship, it has also found its way into the popular music space of Brazil. Cunningham reports that:

> Popularizing the sacred sounds are the *afoxe* groups, a carnival-type fraternal organization who followed in the footsteps of the *irmandades,* a Catholic lay group, formed in Salvador in the seventeenth century in avocation for African traditions... due to the

1964 coup resulting in various governmental restrictions, *afoxe* groups and the public performing of Candomble music had severely declined. A decade later, renowned musician Gilberto Gil played a significant role in the resurgence of *afoxe* ideology... Also, ground breaking was Gil's introduction of the well-known Candomble *Ijexa* rhythm that today is a distinct feature of unique styles like the samba and bossa-nova.[12]

Today, Candomblé music is heard not only in the temples but at carnival centers throughout Brazil; the religion itself has already spread to Italy, Germany, and Spain.

Integrating the Arts in Santería and Candomblé Religion

Existence of the total art or holistic approach that gives African music its peculiarities are expressly exhibited in the Santería and Candomblé worship sessions. If all arts are considered in the worship sessions as one unit, which indeed they are, the term "musical arts" is the appropriate term for the music presentations in these religions. Musical arts signifies a combination of the performance disciplines of music, dance, drama, and costume art. These arts are prevalent in the indigenous African musical presentation.

Meki Nzewi described these arts as creative inspiration, or a musical theme, which is a taproot fed by cultural and cosmic ideas of which the artistic branches are expressed and perceived simultaneously, separately, or sequentially. These are reflected through structured sound from sonic objects which is the music; the aesthetic/poetic stylization of body, which is the dance; the measured stylization of spoken language, which is the poetry and lyrics; the metaphorical reflection of life and cosmos displayed in action, which is the drama; and symbolized text and décor embodied in material objects, which is the costume and scenery.[13] All of these form part of the music worship session, especially in the Candomblé religion.

Elsewhere, Okunade subscribed that the best adjective to use in qualifying music-making in Africa is play.[14] This is because of the aforementioned art and artistic activities that are embedded in the presentation. Any African stage presentation that does not incorporate these arts is novel to the artistic sensibilities of the African people. These arts are an integral part of the presentation at the worship session of the Santería and Candomblé. The integration of these arts in the Candomblé religion has a subtle feature of formality. The fact that all of these arts are an integral part of the musical presentation does not allow room for an unorganized presentation. The presentation, ultimately, constitutes specialized modes of action and communication that have an impact in the lives of the devotees in a supernatural way.

Conclusion

Arts and music in African-derived diaspora religions is a history of forced movements of the African people from their roots to several parts of the world. The intention of the slave masters culminated to an attitude of "use and dump," which means their interest was to only get the best from the enslaved people and make them look inferior before their masters. However, the spirit of the two sister arts—music and religion—surpasses any other force in the Africans' mind. This spirit refused to die. It was like killing the body, but the soul remains intact. Africans who were dehumanized in the land of the slave masters had their religious spirit rejuvenated against all odds. They gathered themselves in bits and pieces and reconstructed their history using religion and other embedded arts to drive their spirit-mind home. Today, some of these arts and religions have become part and parcel of the society that hosted the enslaved Africans. A good example of this is the popular Cumbia music in the Latin America societies. The Cumbia music was exported through the captives of the slave merchant from Nigeria and Cameroon. This chapter has therefore used two religions, Santería and Candomblé, as good examples of the remains of the African legacies in the diaspora.

Notes

1. Lliffe, John. (1995). *Africans the History of a Continent*. United Kingdom: Cambridge University Press, p. 127.
2. Babawale, Tunde. (2008). "Africa and African Diaspora Relations: Challenges, Opportunities and Prospects" In *CBAAC Occasional Monograph, No 10*. Lagos: Malthouse Press Ltd., p. 11.
3. Lliffe, *Africans the History of a Continent*, p. 127.
4. Babawale, "African and African Diaspora Relations: Challenges, Opportunities and Properties" p. 11.
5. Inkori, J. E. (1978). "The Origin of the Diaspora: The Slave Trade from Africa" In TARIKH, Vol. 5, No 4.
6. Babawale, "African and African Diaspora Relations: Challenges, Opportunities and Properties," p. 11.
7. Erediauwa, Omo N'oba. (2008). "Introductory Note." In Plankensteiner B. (ed.). *Benin Kings and Rituals, Court Arts from Nigeria*, p. 13. Belgium: Snoeck Publishers.
8. Amira, J. & Cornelious, S. (1992). *The Music of Santeria*. New York: White Cliffs Media Company, p. 7.
9. Ibid, p. 6.
10. Ibid, p.. 7.
11. A. Cunningham (2011), retrieved from www.soundsandcolors.com
12. Ibid.
13. Nzewi, M. (2003). "Acquiring Knowledge of the Musical Arts in Traditional society." In Anri Herbst (ed.). *Musical Arts in Africa*. South Africa: Unisa Press.
14. Okunade, A. A. (2001). "Play: A Synonymous Moniker for Music in Africa." In *Book of Proceedings*. Kular Lumpur: International Society for Music.

Chapter 11

Women in the African Diaspora: Sojourner Truth, Hybrid Identity, and Multi-vocal Text

Carolyn M. Jones Medine

Introduction: the Slave Ship and Roles of Women

Marcus Rediker, in *The Slave Ship: A Human History*, focuses less on the technical elements of the Triangle Trade and more fully on the relationships onboard slave ships—the formation and deformation of identity. The success of a voyage depended on the captain and crew, who could not have "'dainty fingers nor dainty noses,'" because "theirs was a filthy business in almost every conceivable sense."[1] The captain, who had to control both his crew and slaves, oversaw the relationship between the sailors and slaves, which included intense brutality, which, for women, involved beating and rape.

While we cannot generalize about the slave ship, on some ships, African women, who were kept separate from men, were allowed some movement, being supplied with beads with which to work.[2] There usually were far less women than men aboard a ship, at least early in the slave system, because plantations needed physical laborers.[3] Since there were few women and slavers assumed that they could overpower them, women, at times, were able to use their relative freedom to advantage. Rediker writes of "Sarah," who, onboard the slaver *Hudibras*, enjoyed "highest esteem" and freedom from the captain. When the enslaved men revolted, it became clear that Sarah and her mother had been involved in fomenting the insurrection. Sarah was passing information to the male slaves in her movements around the ship, making the revolt possible.[4]

Any freedoms, however, were probably made possible by and offset by the white slavers' "unrestricted access" to black women's bodies. Reverend John Newton, in

Thoughts Upon the African Slave Trade (1788), writes of the terrified women being brought onboard ships, naked, and "exposed to the wanton rudeness of white savages." While the women could not understand the language, "the looks and manners of the speakers are sufficiently intelligible."[5] Rediker speculates that many sailors signed on to slave ships to gain this sexual access to black women's bodies, though merchants denied that this was true; perhaps they were unable to have such liberty with white women, unless they were poor. Newton spoke of some captains who denied sexual license, but, overall, "Anyone who did his work and 'did it properly' might, in other respects, do what they pleased."[6]

Rediker is clear that the slave ships "made" slaves, and sexual violence was part of that (de)formation. A combination of war machine, prison, and factory, it produced modernity even as it leveled categories of difference among African tribes, producing the racial category of blackness (in tension with whiteness) and slaves.

It also "made" new kinship relationships. Rediker cites Dr. Thomas Winterbottom's understanding of the term "shipmate" among enslaved Africans. This term suggested a link made on the ships that "is almost equivalent to brother or sister."[7] This persisted, Rediker argues, in the Atlantic colonies. In the Dutch colonies, like that in which Sojourner Truth lived, those who came together called each other "*sibbi* or *sippi*." In the Portuguese colonies, the word was "*mulango*."[8] New families, therefore, were made on shipboard, which we take as another form of resistance that "gave birth to defiant, resilient, life-affirming African-American and Pan-African cultures."[9]

Slavery in America is usually defined by plantation slavery. Deborah Gray White's now classic, *Ar'n't I a Woman: Female Slaves in the Plantation South*, offers a major corrective to works on slavery that had come before, focusing on women in the system. Beginning with two stereotypes, Jezebel and Mammy, White examines the sexual exploitation of slave women and its effect on white and black families. The Jezebel is coded as the sexually promiscuous black woman in the white fantastical hegemonic imagination, as Emilie Townes calls it in *Womanist Ethics and the Cultural Production of Evil*. Townes, using Gramsci, thinks about the interplay of history and memory and how the imagination of the metanarrative spawns caricatures and stereotypes, "controlling the world in its own image."[10]

White exposes the positions of black and white women in the triangulated relationships of white men with both. Black women were forced into sexual roles. Cast as Jezebel, black women had no choice in these relationships, and white women found themselves powerless—except for the cruelty they could mete out—in the face of them.[11] In contrast, the opposing mothering role, the Mammy was the desexualized mother who took care of the whole household. We might speculate that Nell I. Painter's critique of Sojourner Truth as a symbol is connected to her being stereotyped as a potential Mammy figure.

Neither woman is safe. To parallel black women with white prostitues as casually done by William Harper,[12] reveals the violence of the lives black slave women led and denies the reality that black women's children were "product" for profit.[13] The exploitation of women's bodies also bound them—women's pregnancies and childrearing also kept them bound more tightly to slave situations and underrepresented in the fugitive slave population.[14]

Mammy provided the "facade," as Emilie Townes tells, that the sexual exploitation of black women by white men was not taking place: the "confirmation."[15] If such a figure existed in plantation households, it, as we see in Frederick Douglass' grandmother's fate, offered no protection. Older slaves often ended up cast off when they were of no more use. Douglass writes of his grandmother's multiple roles in the household: "She had served my old master faithfully from youth to old age. She had been the source of all his wealth; she had peopled his plantation with slaves; she had become a great grandmother in his service. She had rocked him in infancy, attended him in childhood, served him through life, and at his death wiped from his icy brow the cold death-sweat, and closed his eyes forever."[16] Still, when she is no longer useful, she is abandoned:

And, to cap the climax of their base ingratitude and fiendish barbarity, my grandmother, who was now very old, having outlived my old master and all his children, having seen the beginning and end of all of them, and her present owners finding she was of but little value, her frame already racked with the pains of old age, and complete helplessness fast stealing over her once active limbs, they took her to the woods, built her a little hut, put up a little mud-chimney, and then made her welcome to the privilege of supporting herself there in perfect loneliness; thus virtually turning her out to die![17]

Women were not confined to the household as slavery developed. The figure of Patsey in Steve McQueen's 2013 film, *Twelve Years a Slave*, so captured the imaginations of moviegoers that the actress who portrayed the part, Lupita Nyong'o, received an Academy Award. Patsey is a key figure in Northup's narrative, both noble and pitiable. She is the best at picking cotton on the plantation, picking 512 pounds. She is, as her owner Epps says in the screenplay, a "Damned Queen. Born and bred to the field. A nigger among niggers."[18] She is also Epps' victim, repeatedly and violently raped. In his narrative, Northup says that, in addition to sexual violence, she suffered extreme punishment; she "had been literally excoriated," flayed, despite being "queen of the field."[19] As Gray White suggests, Epps' wife hates Patsey and uses any opportunity to have her punished.

While women did not escape sexual violence,[20] they might, if in more urban settings, find independence through their work, even in the South. For example, Lizzetta Lefalle-Collins suggests that women could sell independently farmed produce in urban markets even in Charleston and New Orleans. Slaveholders had to "recognize and concede, on a limited basis, to the 'laws of the market' that followed the dictates of property and price rather than those of deference and duty. Slave women, by these means, could assert their own property rights and gain a degree of autonomy and self-control."[21] Women, by and large, were the beneficiaries of such systems. In cities, women could work in commercial establishments, with the permission of their masters, and could pass on, as Frederick Douglass did, geographical knowledge to their children.

If "the enactment of subjugation and the constitution of the subject" are bound in slavery, as Saidiya V. Hartman in *Scenes of Subjection* and Jasmine Nicole Cobb in her review of the film *Twelve Years a Slave*, suggest, how did black women survive and become agents of change?[22] For women, Rediker emphasizes, were a key part of adaptation, resistance, and survival. Bernice Johnson Reagon uses the term "cultural workers" to describe black women who forged paths of "continuance and transformation" in a "new space for a new people in a new time."[23] Reagon calls these transformational processes "mothering" and "nurturing," but not in the biological sense. These were women of powerful voices: articulating the African American condition. These women were and are cultural mothers, making a future for the next generation. One such mother was Sojourner Truth.

Sojourner Truth: "Ar'n't I A Woman?" and Conversion Narrative:African American Identity and Multi-vocal Text

Sojourner Truth (1797–1883), born Isabella Bomfree, is a key figure in American history.[24] She left us a narrative of Dutch New York slavery, which, otherwise, would remain shrouded in mystery, and she was a major force in abolition, women's rights, and freedman's rights after the Civil War. In addition, her travels intersected with major new religious movements of her time, from the Kingdom of Matthias to revivalist camp meetings, to the Second Advent Doctrines of William Miller. She is a widely celebrated figure. There is a Sojourner Truth Institute in Battle Creek, Michigan, where Truth lived late in her life, and a statue in Florence, MA, where she lived from 1843–1856, as well as a bust, the first of an African American woman, in the US Capitol building. One can follow the Trail of Sojourner Truth in Ulster County, New York, where she was a slave and claimed her freedom, walking away from her master; that location also houses a library.

Truth emerges as a key figure in African American thought, but her most famous texts, her *Narrative* and her "Ar'n't I a Woman?" speech, because she was unable to read or write, are collaboratively written, seeming to give over her agency to other, white women writers. Indeed, her *Narrative* is in two parts—the narrative proper, written with Olive Gilbert, and a *Book of Life*, assembled by Frances Titus, a collection of letters to and articles about Sojourner Truth, as well as her autograph book.

While we might worry that Truth's identity may be misrepresented, at least, and appropriated, at best—her voice is so determined that we never can find a "real" Sojourner Truth. I want to suggest that the choral, collaborative, and multi-vocal voice serves the purpose of integrating the singular voice into community—and, for Truth, those communities were multiple—and preserving voices that would be otherwise lost, as we see in the opposite example of W. E. B. DuBois' *The Souls of Black Folk*. If DuBois is the controlling narrative voice, Truth seems to be the controlled narrative voice. While some of her biographers suggest that this means that the "real" Sojourner Truth, finally, was erased in the service of others, I want to suggest that she emerges as a curious, moving center, an outsider—a true sojourner—whose call elicited and still elicits creative response. To examine this positionality, we will look at two key pieces of Sojourner Truth's life: her "Ar'n't I a Woman?" speech and her conversion from the *Narrative*.

"Ar'n't I a Woman?"

Sojourner Truth's "Ar'n't I a Woman" speech has a complex transmission history. Truth is said to have given the speech at the Akron Women's Conference in 1852, but Frances Gage first recorded it in an article in the *Anti-Slavery Standard* in 1863. The speech was reprinted in Truth's *Book of Life*, the addition to her *Narrative*, in 1875 and again in 1881 in Elizabeth Cady Stanton, Susan B. Anthony, and Matilda Joslyn Gage's 1881 *History of Women's Suffrage*. The text, then, seems to have struck a powerful note in both women's suffrage and abolitionist circles.[25] Sojourner Truth historians, however, have questioned the authenticity of the speech, noting Truth's illiteracy, and going so far as to argue that Truth never gave it.

Nell Irvin Painter, in her autobiography of Truth, *Sojourner Truth: A Life, A Symbol*, and in an earlier article, "Sojourner Truth in Life and Memory: Writing the Biography of An American Exotic," argues that though Truth was in Akron, Ohio, she may not have spoken at the conference.[26] She writes that Frances Gage, who chaired the meeting, wrote out the speech 20-years after the meeting, and Painter suggests that what Sojourner Truth said can never be known and that Gage, essentially, invented the speech.

Painter reads Truth's image and the speech through the lens of Harriet Beecher Stowe's *Atlantic Monthly* article, "The Libyan Sibyl." This article, also reprinted in the *Book of Life* gave Truth, Painter argues, national attention. Stowe paints a picture of Truth as "a singular character" who gave an "amusing performance," playing "a part reminiscent of one of P. T. Barnum's antebellum performers, Joice Heth, who claimed to be a 161-year-old slave who had nursed George Washington."[27] Performing for white people, she spices up a dull evening for Stowe's prominent guests. Painter argues that Truth appears "first and foremost as an exotic...far outside the cultured mainstream."[28] Painter's point is that the "naïve," rather than the educated, black woman—like Maria Stewart—"seems to have better facilitated black women's entry into American memory."[29]

Painter, in later works, argues that Truth's image moves from being this "exotic" other into the mainstream after the Civil War and into the twentieth century. When Truth went to Washington, DC and discovered the "pressing needs" of the Southern refugees there, her speeches, which had been general, "took on a pointed edge."[30] Her "coverage" grew serious, and, Painter argues, after her retirement, her currency rose again. And, by the late twentieth century, Painter argues, Truth is an "admirable figure who is not at all to be patronized or dismissed." This is because her words are available without her problematic presence, which "played into the hands of romantic racists," allowing her to be distilled into one who has "an ability to delve to the heart of a controversial matter with a few, well-chosen words"[31]— the intellectual mammy, as I would put it. Painter does not go as far as Carleton Mabee in his biography, *Sojourner Truth: Slave, Prophet, Legend,* who argues that the speech is "folklore."[32] Instead, Painter argues that Truth's memory, because of her illiteracy, meant that she left few documents other than her narrative, which has been "stylized and sanitized" to make a "figurative"[33] epistemological image of the poor, deeply religious, uneducated, rural, raced female, who is nonetheless wise and resistant to authority, that fills a cultural need, both for nineteenth-, twentieth-, and twenty-first-century Americans.[34] Her "Ar'n't I a Woman?" speech then is a construction that serves the needs of others.

In *Sojourner Truth's America*, Margaret Washington reevaluates Painter's interpretation of this key speech. Her biography of Truth tracks down new documentation of the event. Washington writes that a few newspapers did not mention Truth's being at the conference for two reasons. First, some newspapers probably saw her as beneath mention as a black woman in Ohio at that time, and, second, one of the powerful organizers, Jane Swisshelm, who wanted to fight for women's rights without considerations of race, did not want Truth acknowledged. Overwhelmed by Swisshelm's influence, some newspapers did not even report Truth's presence at the meeting.

Other newspapers, however, did. Washington accesses sources, reports by Marius Robinson in the *Bugle,* reports in the *New York Tribune,* and an eyewitness report by Hannah Cutler, that do record Truth's presence and words. According to these reports, Truth did challenge the conference, particularly the clerics there. While she did not speak formally in Akron, she did so at a later meeting in New Marlborough, a Quaker village nearby,[35] saying some of what would, later, be the "Ar'n't I A Woman" speech, as Hannah Cutler, an eyewitness, wrote:

> At the New Marlborough meeting, Cutler wrote, "I recall Mrs. Swissehelm as insisting that woman should claim her right to be helped over bad roads and to be fed whether she worked or not." Cutler also recalled, "But Sojourner Truth replied that she never found any man ready to carry her over mud puddles." Although Cutler did not say so, Truth could easily have added "And ar'n't I a woman?"[36]

Frances Gage was present at both the Akron and New Marlborough meetings. Gage's reconstruction of Truth's speech, in Washington's reading, comes from two separate meetings. Parts of the speech—particularly the parts in which Truth spoke about the intellect of women—are, the newspapers report, what Sojourner said at the two meetings. Therefore, the *content* is what she said, though not in the *form*. It seems that Gage later created the "speech," bringing together several of Truth's statements in the two meetings, shaping them into a single speech.

As Washington points out, Gage wrote her piece in imitation of Stowe's work. In both, looking at the language of the "Ar'n't I A Woman" speech, some of which I will quote here, we see Sojourner Truth speaking in what a white audience would expect from a Southern slave:

> "Wall, chilern, whar dar is so much racket dar must be somethin' out o' kilter. I tink dat'twixt de nigger of de Souf and de womin at de Norf, all talkin' 'bout rights, de white men will be in a fix pretty soon. But what's all dis here talkin' 'bout?
>
> "Dat man ober dar say dat womin needs to be helped into carriages, and lifted ober ditches, and to hab de best place everywhar. Nobody eber halps me into carriages, or ober mudpuddles, or gibs me any best place!"
>
> And raising herself to her full height, and her voice to a pitch like rolling thunder, she asked, "And ar'n't I a woman? Look at me! Look at my arm! [And here she bared her right arm to the shoulder, showing her tremendous muscular power] "I have

ploughed, and planted, and gathered into barns, and no man could head me! And ar'n't I a woman? I could work as much and eat as much as a man—when I could get it—and bear de lash as well! And ar'n't' I a woman? I have borne thirteen chilern, and seen 'em mos' all sold off the slavery, and when I cried out with my mother's grief, none but Jesus heard me! And ar'n't I a woman?[37]

Gage and Stowe have Truth use the pejorative "nigger," which Truth never used and to which she objected, and both gave her a thick Southern accent, though Truth, who never lived in the South and whose first language was Dutch, probably had an accent more like a present day Afrikaner. Newspaper accounts do confirm that Truth spoke of herself as a woman—one paper reporting that she did not ask a question but said, "I am a woman"—thereby confirming that she intervened in the discussion, adding the connection between race and gender. Washington concludes: "Gage assuming control of Sojourner Truth's discourse and minstrelizing her language seems more significant than whether or not she said, 'Ar'n't I a woman?'"[38]

The conversion narrative, in *The Narrative of Sojourner Truth*, in contrast, is as close to Truth's voice as we can come—though, in her *Narrative,* it is interspersed with that of her amanuensis, Olive Gilbert.[39] Truth told the story of her conversion many times—as to Harriet Beecher Stowe—and in many speeches, and the details remain the same in each telling. The conversion narrative, however, is documented: for Truth, it was so important that she dictated it to Gilbert, had it written down, and carried it with her at all times, as she sold the *Narrative* in her public speaking events. Gilbert renders Truth's voice in Standard American English, as we shall see in our analysis of the conversion narrative.

The conversion narrative is particularly located. Isabella has left the home of her owner, John Dumont. During the Pinkster holiday, Pentecost, Dutch-owned slaves were given free time, and families were reunited. Isabella, who was lonely, looked back to the Dumont household where her children lived, and longed for home. She was tempted back into slavery. Dumont, who may have fathered some of her children, was a key figure in Isabella's life; in one of the last chapters of the *Narrative,* she visits him, and her daughter (and perhaps his) Diana is living with him. When she was tempted to return to him at Pinkster, just as she walked to Dumont's wagon, however, she was seized by, confronted by, God.

Isabella was afraid: "A dire dread of annihilation now seized her." She said, 'Oh, God. I did not know you were so big."[40] She felt the need for someone to intercede on her behalf with this powerful God, to intervene for her, and that "Friend" appeared, a Friend she recognizes as Jesus.

> 'Who are you' was the cry of her heart, and her whole soul was in one deep prayer that this heavenly personage might be revealed to her. When she said, 'I know you,' the subject of the vision remained distinct and quiet. When she said, 'I don't know you,' it moved restlessly about, like agitated waters.[41]

Suddenly, Isabella realizes, "it is *Jesus.*"[42] When she names Him, He appears "to her mental vision as so mild, so good, and so every way lovely, and he loved her so much!"[43] He brings about reconciliation: between God and Sojourner, and Sojourner and God, and propels her to freedom. This moment fills her with joy.

This moment of conversion, of inwardness, is a result of teachings from Isabella's mother, Mau-Mau Bett who taught her that there is a God of whom "'you must ask help...and he will always hear and help you.'"[44] From Mau-Mau's teaching, Isabella has a deep relationship with God, even before her conversion: "She would sometimes repeat, 'Our Father in heaven,' in her Low Dutch, as taught her by her mother...She related to God, in minute detail, all of her troubles and sufferings, inquiring, as she proceeded, 'Do you think that's right, God?' and closed by begging to be delivered from the evil, whatever it might be."[45] Second Great Awakening revivalism and her owners' Dutch pietism, which Isabella would have absorbed while working in the Ardinburgh household, also influenced her spirituality:

> The Dutch Pietists believed that the heart was central: That the heart had to receive God. They listened to the "inner spirit," the voice of the Holy Spirit, to find God. The Dutch embraced, James W. Van Hoevven in World and Word: Reformed Theology in America "That only in the lives of Christian can Christian truth be found, and that communities of Christian people cannot rely on the state for their establishment." It was not a missionary kind of religion; it is more focused inward.[46]

The question she directs to God, "Who are you?" is linked, intimately, to the questions "Who am I?" After her conversion, Isabella feels fully human, a spiritual being, not just a black slave woman. She really *feels* for the first time, a coming out of the numbness of being a slave. This is literally a new life in Christ.

The fruit of Isabella's conversion, however, takes time to grow. Isabella, after her time in the Matthias movement,[47] finally leaves the city. As she makes this Exodus, she, called by the Spirit, changes her name:

> she informed Mrs. Whiting, the woman of the house where she was stopping, that her name was no longer Isabella, but SOJOURNER; and that she was going east. And to her inquiry, "What are you going east for?" hers was, "The Spirit calls me there, and I must go."[48]

So begins her life as an itinerant preacher and activist.

Multi-Vocal Text

The two contrasting examples of Truth's voice suggest that the real Sojourner Truth seems both clearly defined and difficult to locate. On one of her photographs is written, "I sell the shadow to support the substance."[49] While she means, on the surface, that the photograph as a shadow, we can see that Truth was, in many ways, a shadow whose substance those she encountered filled in according to their own needs. Harriet Beecher Stowe made Truth into a black minstrel; Gage made her into a feminist; and Painter argues that we make Sojourner Truth, like so many historical persons from whom we do not have direct speeches, like Chief Joseph, whatever we need them to be.[50]

I am fascinated by how Truth's voice, shaped by how others shape her language, was simultaneously deeply needed and resisted in the American culture of her time. Truth was a "sojourner," a pilgrim, and traveler, who seems to have had a habit of just showing up at key meetings, sitting down in a corner or on some steps, and deciding when she wanted to speak—and being unstoppable. She travelled dangerous territory, like Indiana and Missouri before Emancipation, in a buggy, seemingly without fear. She is said to have said to Frederick Douglass, "'with startling effect'" when he wanted to abandon peaceful means for freedom, "Is God gone?"[51] As powerfully as she presents, still, it is sometimes difficult to see the substance for the shadows. Is she a "multivocal, boundary-blurring subaltern"[52] or an example of a true American hybrid thinker? A mammy who entertains like a minstrel or a precursor of black power?

Sojourner Truth seems to me, however constructed, to be a woman who took as much agency as a black woman in her circumstances and her time could have taken, and more. I refuse to call her "illiterate." Nel Painter contrasts Sojourner Truth with the journalist and writer Maria Stewart. Valerie C. Cooper's recent book, *Word Like Fire: Maria Stewart, the Bible, and the Rights of African Americans*, masterfully analyzes Cooper's thought.[53] For Stewart, in an Enlightenment mode, literacy was a sign of humanity, and her theology created a counternarrative—as Cooper puts it, manipulating "the words themselves" and "their "semiotic webs."[54] Though Stewart was a published writer and journalist and Truth a woman of oral culture, their goals and powers seem, to me, to move toward similar goals from opposite ends.

Truth was uneducated, in the conventional sense—she never learned to read or write—but she was highly literate, and spent a great deal of time with some of the finest intellects and important thinkers of her day and influenced them, and she was both wise and perspicacious: "She did not need to read in order to know."[55]

One way to assess voice in Truth's *Narrative* and the "Ar'n't I a Woman" speech is to parallel these with W. E. B. DuBois' *Souls of Black Folk* to think through the narrator and the narrated.[56] In *Souls*, DuBois' voice is a filter, controlling his multivocal autobiography, and DuBois brings together voices that constitute his and the variety of late nineteenth and early twentieth-century black identity, preserving in his work voices from the famous, like Alexander Crummell to those lost to history without this book.

Truth's *Narrative* is the opposite: her voice is constructed, through Olive Gilbert's—although Truth clearly authorized this biography—as well as in the putting together of pieces and fragments in the *Book of Life*. These include letters—for a woman who could not read, she got a lot of letters—articles about her, autographs, etcetera that give us a picture of who she was, narrated by many people—from intimate friends and abolitionist collaborators to President Lincoln—from multiple angles. Yet, we see in her insistence on—for example, in the narrative of her conversion—the right record of her thoughts and words, which she claimed as authentically her own, even as she sees her image, certainly without her permission, to be utilized in multiple ways.[57] And, surely, no other African American woman of her time was so often photographed. There is even a mocked-up image of her with Abraham Lincoln.[58] Whatever the difficulties of reading her, we cannot forget that Sojourner Truth was self-named and, as the narrative was dictated in the company of a group of women friends, self-narrated. She controlled her voice as much as she could.

Multi-vocality provides a clue to understanding Truth's unique position. Margaret C. Rodman's "Empowering Place: Multilocality and Multivocality," offers an insight that is helpful to this discussion. Multi-vocality, she argues, offers a decentered analysis, able to speak from multiple non-Western as well as Eurocentric viewpoints.[59] The polyphonic, multiply located voice occupies a unique position in America thought.

Both W. E. B. DuBois and Sojourner Truth are simultaneously insiders and outsiders: border people. As insiders, they participated in some of the great events of our time—DuBois from Reconstruction to Civil Rights and Truth in abolition, emancipation, and the beginnings of what became a failed Reconstruction. R. Laurence Moore argues that the discourse of insider and outsider is a powerful one for analyzing American thought. For historians, that construction is "about how power and status have been distributed in American life, and how values have been created and disseminated in a plural society."[60] Moore is concerned about both groups, like Roman Catholics, and individuals, like Eugene V. Debs, as he argues that various historians' narratives—radical and progressive—read these figures as either heroes or victims, or a combination of both, who bear a "counterimage of the American mainstream," "agitating" egalitarian principles when mainstream narratives are problematic.[61] To be an outsider strategically, "can really mean, both objectively and figuratively, to stand at the center of American experience."[62] I would see such figures generating sites of tension around them, spaces, in which narrative ambiguities[63] can be acknowledged, explored, and negotiated. As Moore puts it:

> Insider/outsider discourse works because the contests themselves were typically American, rather than necessarily the values that one side or the other proclaimed. Historical analysis of the contests is a means to open up, not settle prematurely, a multitude of questions about what were typical or dominant values in America's past. Such analysis must examine the social costs and benefits that attached to insider and outsider identifications on a case by case basis.[64]

Outsiders unsettle authority through charisma.[65] Sojourner Truth gains her authentic voice through divine contact, and as a black, nonliterate but powerfully charismatic speaker, singer, and presence, her outsider status allows her to "agitate" the basic ideals of the democratic order through her words and image, by her very presence. We cannot know, finally, how she felt about manipulations of her voice. What we can see is how she composed herself in photographs—always neatly dressed and fully covered, wearing a head covering or bonnet and shawl, and usually holding some work in her lap and/or carrying her purse and, later, a cane. Her image neither suggests a mammy nor a radical—except for the drawings of the younger Isabella—but a composed woman who seems clear about who and what she is. We might conclude that, at times, she allowed herself to be and, at other times, was exploited as a useful symbol, always as Painter recognizes, under threat of "domestication."[66] What we can admire about Truth is that her endless self-invention and her courage, her contest, and relationship with insiders, as Moore put it, was a means by which what it means to be American, in all its hybridity and with all its voices, was and does continue to be debated. As for Truth herself—along with the brave women, like Sarah, on the slave ships and even the brutalized slave, like Patsey, who works to maintain her dignity in the face of terror—she paves a way for future "culture workers" and toward a meaning of the human not defined or confined by social situation. As she said, "I am not going to die, I'm going home like a shooting star."

Notes

1. Rediker, Marcus. (2007). *The Slave Ship: A Human History.* New York: Viking Press, p. 6.
2. Ibid, p. 31.
3. White, Deborah Gray. (1985). *Ar'n't I a Woman?: Female Slaves in the Plantation South.* New York: W. W. Norton, p. 64ff.
4. Ibid, pp. 19–20.
5. Ibid, p. 241.
6. Ibid, p. 242.
7. Ibid, p. 305.
8. Ibid, p. 306.
9. Ibid, p. 307.
10. Townes, Emilie. (2006). *Womanist Ethics and the Cultural Production of Evil.* New York: Palgrave-Macmillan, pp. 7, 21.
11. See, for example, Thavolia Glymph, *Out of the House of Bondage: The Transformation of the Plantation Household* (Cambridge University Press, 2008). Glymph argues that the plantation household was a workplace, hence, it was not fully "private," but was a space in which practices of domination were exercised daily (2). White women, then, "wielded the power of slave ownership. They owned slaves and managed households in which they held the power of life and death...far from being victims of the slave system, they dominated slaves" (4). They beat, scarred, and otherwise dominated the women who worked in their households.
12. White, *Ar'n't I a Woman?* p. 36.
13. Ibid, p. 68.
14. Ibid, p. 70.
15. Townes, *Womanist Ethics and the Cultural Production of Evil,* p. 32.
16. Douglass, Frederick. (1986). *Narrative of the Life of Frederick Douglass: An American Slave.* New York: Penguin Books, p. 92.
17. Ibid.
18. Ridley, John. *Twelve Years a Slave,* p. 92. Simply Scripts, http://d97a3ad6c1b09e180027-5c35be6f174b10f62347680d094e609a.r46.cf2.rackcdn.com/film_scripts/12YAS_SCRIPT_BK_COVER_PAGES_FINAL.pdf. Accessed December 29, 2014.
19. Northup, Solomon. *Twelve Years a Slave,* http://docsouth.unc.edu/fpn/northup/northup.html#northup176. Accessed December 29, 2014.
20. See, for example, Melton McLaurin's historical parallel to Toni Morrison's (1991). *Beloved: Celia, A Slave.* Athens, GA: University of Georgia Press. Celia murdered the master who victimized her.
21. Lefalle-Collins, Lizzetta. (2000) "Slavery in the USA." In *Encyclopedia of Feminist Theories* Oxfordshire, UK: Taylor and Francis, Ltd., pp. 449–450.

22. Hartman, Saidiya V. (1997). *Scenes of Subjection: Terror, Slavery and Self-Making in Nineteenth-Century America*. New York: Oxford University Press. Jasmine Nichole Cobb, "Directed by Himself: Steve McQueen's *12 Years a Slave*," *American Literary History* 26:2 (Summer 2014). Project Muse, http://muse.jhu.edu.proxy-remote.galib.uga.edu/journals/american_literary_history/v026/26.2.cobb.html?#b6 Accessed December 29, 2014.

23. Johnson Reagon, Bernice. "American Diaspora Women: The Making of Cultural Workers," *Feminist Studies* 12:1 (Spring 1986), p. 89.

24. I will call her "Isabella" before her conversion and name change and "Sojourner" after.

25. Washington, Margaret. (2009). *Sojourner Truth's America*. Urbana: University of Illinois Press, p. 224.

26. Painter, Nell Irvin. (1997). *Sojourner Truth: A Life, A Symbol*. New York: W.W. Norton and Co. and "Sojourner Truth in Life and Memory: Writing the Biography of An American Exotic," *Gender and History* 2:1 (Spring 1990): pp. 1–16.

27. Painter, "Sojourner Truth in Life and Memory," p. 9.

28. Ibid.

29. Ibid, p. 11.

30. Ibid.

31. Ibid, p. 13.

32. Mabee, Carleton. (1995). *Sojourner Truth: Slave, Prophet, Legend*. New York: New York University Press.

33. Painter, Nell Irvin. "Representing Truth: Sojourner Truth's Knowing and Becoming Known," *The Journal of American History* (81)2 (September 1994), pp. 461–492; 465.

34. Ibid, p. 465.

35. Painter, *A Life*, p. 227.

36. Ibid, pp. 227–228.

37. Truth, Sojourner. "Ain't I A Woman," Sojourner Truth Institute, http://www.sojournertruth.org/Library/Speeches/AintIAWoman.htm. Accessed March 5, 2015. Sojourner Truth, *Narrative of Sojourner Truth* (New York: Penguin Books, 1998), p. 92.

38. Painter, *A Life*, p. 228.

39. Gilbert, like Truth, was a woman who lived on her own resources. She and Sojourner Truth nursed Gilbert's sister, Sarah Benson, while Benson was dying of breast cancer. It was in the Benson house that the narrative was dictated. Therefore, as Mary Helen Washington speculates, both Sarah Benson, who knew Truth well, and Gilbert, as well as a group of committed women who were in and out of the household, probably shaped the story. These women regarded Truth as "a woman and an equal sister" in contrast to her former life as a housekeeper and cook. Gilbert and Truth did not have much association after this narrative. After 1850, each went her way. Gilbert was a teacher and thinker; Truth was an activist and organizer.

40. Truth, *Narrative*, p. 45.

41. Ibid.

42. Ibid.

43. Ibid, p. 37.

44. Ibid, p. 12.

45. Ibid, p. 41.

46. Beardslee III, John W. (1986). "Orthodoxy and Piety: Two Styles of Faith in the Colonial Period." In James W. Van Hoeven (ed.) *World and Word: Reformed Theology in America*, p. 14. Grand Rapids, MI: William B. Eerdmans Publishing Co.

47. The most comprehensive work on the Matthias movement is Paul E. Johnson and Sean Wilentz, *The Kingdom of Matthias: A Story of Sex and Salvation in 19th Century America*

(New York: Oxford University Press, 2012). Isabella was involved with Matthias through an employer, Elijah Pearson. When Pearson died a suspicious death, Isabella was accused, as the only black person in the movement, of her murder. With her characteristic sense of justice, Isabella went to the press. Gilbert G. Vale recorded her version of the story in *Fanaticism: Its Source and Influence. Illustrated by the Simple Narrative of Isabella, in the Case of Matthias* (available at: http://docsouth.unc.edu/neh/vale/vale.html).

48. Truth, *Narrative*, p. 68. The last name Truth, she explains, came right after. Mrs. White asked "Sojourner what?" and pondering that, Truth says in "A Memorial Chapter" in the *Book of Life*: "And in my wretchedness I said, 'O God, give me a name with a handle to it.'…And it came to me in that moment, dear child, like a voice, just as true as God is true, Sojourner *Truth*." This name mirrors God as truth.

49. See, for example, the photograph at: http://metmuseum.org/exhibitions/view?exhibitionId={9400f95d-89a4-4920-a05e-46ee3cedc9c0}&oid=301989.

50. Painter, "Representing Truth," p. 479.

51. Quoted in Washington, *Sojourner Truth's America*, p. 243.

52. A wonderful phrase from James Christmann, "Raising Voices, Lifting Shadows: Competing Voice-Paradigms in Frances E. W. Harper's Iola Leroy." The Free Library. 2000. African American Review 05 Mar. 2015. http://www.thefreelibrary.com/Raising+Voices%2c+Lifting+Shadows%3a+Competing+Voice-Paradigms+in+Frances...-a062258903.

53. Cooper, Valerie C. (2011). *Word Like Fire: Maria Stewart, the Bible, and the Rights of African Americans*. Carter G. Woodson Institute Series. Charlottesville and London: University of Virginia Press.

54. Ibid, p. 96.

55. Ibid, p. 466.

56. DuBois, W. E. B. (1996). *The Souls of Black Folk*. New York: Penguin Books.

57. Thanks to Raleigh Heth for this formulation.

58. This image is on many sites, including: http://potus-geeks.livejournal.com/239782.html.

59. Rodman, Margaret C. "Empowering Place: Multilocality and Multivocality. *American Anthropologist* 94:3 (September 1992), p. 647.

60. Moore, R. Laurence. (1998). "Insiders and Outsiders in American Historical Narrative and American History." In Jon Butler and Harry S. Stout, *Religion in American History: A Reader*, p. 200. New York: Oxford University Press.

61. Ibid, p. 201.

62. Ibid, p. 207.

63. Ibid, p. 214.

64. Ibid, p. 215.

65. I am thankful to Patricia O'Connell Killen for this formulation.

66. Moore, "Insiders and Outsiders in American Historical Narrative and American History," p. 211.

Chapter 12

Womanist Spirituality: Legacies of Freedom

Melanie L. Harris

Introduction

This chapter will focus on Alice Walker's fluid spirituality and show how it serves as a foundation for the grounding of an eco-justice perspective. Examination of Walker's nonfiction essays about eco-womanist spirituality reveals an important ethical imperative for womanist ethical analysis—earth justice. In addition to race, class, gender, and heterosexist analysis, I argue that studying Walker's nonfiction work summons us to add earth-justice to womanist religious ethical analysis. Eco-womanist spirituality, and its focus on the interconnections between the oppressions faced by women of African descent and the unjust treatment of the earth, becomes a new aspect of theo-ethical discourse whereby we are moved to heal our own bodies and communities in connection with healing the body of the Earth. Studying Alice Walker's spirituality helps us chart our course.

Alice Walker's Fluid Spirituality

> I'm probably tri-spiritual. I was raised as a Christian. Now, I love Buddhism, and I love earth religion.—Alice Walker, *Moved To Speak*[1]

The fluid spirituality that Alice Walker embodies features a number of aspects from a variety of religious traditions that shape her perspective, aid in expanding her sense of community, and grounds her connection to and with the earth. In an interview with Scott Winn, "Walker: Moved to Speak," she identifies herself as a "pagan Buddhist who was brought up as a Christian."[2] Noting how all of these traditions show up in her writings and interviews regarding her spirituality, author, Karla Simcikova writes about Alice Walker's fluid spirituality in her book, *To Live Fully, Here and Now: The Healing Vision in the Works of Alice Walker.*[3] The book dives into the intriguing work of attempting to "fully understand Walker's complex and multilayered concept of spirituality that developed in the mid-1980s and that has continued to evolve."[4]

Walker's fluid and evolving spirituality can be best understood by first presenting her concept of spiritual plateaus. Rather than one's spiritual development moving along a linear progression, the metaphor of the plateau suggests that a "multilayered spiral, a process that incorporates the wisdom or lessons learned from the past or prior plateaus, in which the 'truths' embedded...become a part of the irreducible core of...(an) existing belief system, a foundation in which a new spiritual impetus may take root."[5] Instead of one's spiritual development being measured linearly, spiritual plateau's suggests that one's spiritual practice is seen as a process, or journey of becoming aware; knowing the self, the community, the divine realm, nature, and the earth in deeper tones.

It is this sense of Walker's spiritual fluidity that serves as base from which to understand the premise and shifts of thought evident in her work. According to Simcikova, there are at least three major shifts in Walker's thought that mark significant changes and approaches in her writings. These shifts of thought coincide with the shifts in Walker's spiritual becoming. Beginning with her own racial and cultural identity as an African American woman, and as an African American Southern writer who often raised critiques of the Christianity that her parents' ardently believed, Simcikova claims that the inquisitive nature found in the term *womanist*, as well as books like *In Search of Our Mothers' Gardens: Womanist Prose* rightly fit the initial phase of Walker's writing identity. However, as Walker embraced her own Native American identity as part of her "tri-racial"[6] self, and welcomed Native American spiritual practices into her own fluid spirituality, her writings began to reflect this consciousness, and revealed a deeper and more global reach. Simcikova claims that it was this shift that places Walker, "beyond womanism."

> Beyond the womanist model to include, incorporate, and/or accommodate all influences that have had a significant impact on Walker's way of seeing and participating in the world, particularly her interest in Native American spirituality...Walker's preoccupation is no longer only with the survival of her people, but also, and perhaps more importantly, with the survival of the whole planet.[7]

While acknowledging that the womanist consciousness grounds much of Walker's work and initial identity—made so clear in works such as *In Search of Our Mothers' Gardens: Womanist Prose* and *The Color Purple*—Simcikova claims that womanism was only the first phase of Walker's literary identity. In her second collection of nonfiction essays, *Living By The Word,*[8] Simcikova suggests that Walker's embrace of her own self-identity as Native American (Cherokee) produces a great shift not only in her writing focus but also in her own spirituality and self-awareness. This shift to another spiritual plateau breaks Walker from her womanist identity, and gives her a new global and earth consciousness that eventually leads to a third shift in her spiritual identity, one toward pagan, goddess, and earth-based spirituality.[9]

I respectfully disagree with Simcikova's argument that Walker is "beyond womanism." While the explanation of the spiritual plateau metaphor is extremely helpful in understanding Walker's fluid spirituality, I believe Simcikova incorrectly assumes that a womanist spirituality is concrete and unbending. Simcikova seems to relegate womanist spirituality to be focused solely on African American culture and life and embedded within a specific tradition of Christianity, instead of being the fluid creation that it is. She mentions the work and movement of Womanist Theology and Ethics, the writings of such Christian womanists as Delores S. Williams, Katie G. Cannon, and Jacquelyn Grant, however, her own reading of these works negates a deep presence of the deep diversity of perspectives, varied tones, shifts of thought, spirit, and movement alive in womanist spirituality today. Many womanists—Christian, Islamic, Yoruba, and Pagan[10]—have described womanist spirituality as encompassing a number of religious traditions, rites, and rituals that are life affirming to African American women and point out that it also speaks to an awareness of spiritual fluidity and religious plurality. All of this carries an emphasis on justice for the wholeness of humanity and creation. Perhaps, one of the best descriptions of womanist spirituality comes from womanist ethicist, Emilie M. Townes, in her work, *A Blaze of Glory: Womanist Spirituality As Social Witness*. Here, she offers, "womanist spirituality is embodied, personal, communal" and explains that it:

> Grows out of these roots. This spirituality is a social witness…grounded (in)…the deep kneading of humanity and divinity into one breath, one hope, one vision. Womanist spirituality is not only a way of living, it is a style of witness that seeks to cross the yawning chasm of hatreds and prejudices and oppressions into a deeper and richer love…Womanist spirituality is the working out of what it means for each of us to seek compassion, justice, worship, and devotion in our witness. This understanding of spirituality seeks to grow into wholeness of spirit and body, mind and heart.[11]

Since womanist spirituality embraces a number of varied religious practices, and religions, and at the same time acknowledges the fluid nature of African-descended peoples' spirituality that has flowed for centuries, Walker's fluid spirituality is at home in this concept of womanist spirituality.[12] For this reason, I would argue that Walker's spirituality, and her writings indicate that she has not moved "beyond womanism" but rather deeper into it as womanism itself grows deeper.

Simcikova's notation of the shifts in Walker's fluid spirituality are extremely helpful; however, it is equally important to see what Walker has said about the fluid nature of her own spirituality. She does so in her essay, "The Only Reason You Want to Go to Heaven is that You Have Been Driven Out of Your Mind (Off Your Land and Out of Your Lover's Arms) Clear Seeing Inherited Religion and Reclaiming the Pagan Self."[13]

The Only Reason You Want to Go to Heaven...

Walker's pivotal essay, "The Only Reason You Want to Go to Heaven is that You
Have Been Driven Out of Your Mind, (Off Your Land and Out of Your Lover's
Arms) Clear Seeing Inherited Religion and Reclaiming the Pagan Self,"[14] is a detailed
account of her spiritual journey. Presented to an audience at Auburn Seminary in
New York in 1995, Walker engages a theological audience, giving account of the
shifts in her thought, and claiming her own spiritual path as earth-honoring. The
essay begins with her earlier memories of feeling sheltered and experiencing the deep
love of community offered by her own family and the religious, Christian family
of believers who worshipped along with her and her family in the black-segregated
Christian Methodist church community of her youth in rural Georgia.

Naming the important values of community and love for humanity and creation
as central aspects to her fluid spirituality, Walker comments in the essay that these
values emerged from her parents and, at least initially, from the religious community that welcomed her into life. However, she also expresses her deep convictions
that Christianity and its roots in patriarchal doctrines were not for her. Recalling
moments at both three years old, and again at seven years of age, when she questioned the sexism embedded in her parents' Christianity, Walker writes that she
disagreed with several doctrines of the church, including the doctrine of original
sin. "I had a problem with this doctrine at a very early age: I could not see how my
parents had sinned...I did not see that they were evil, that they should be cursed
because they were black, because my mother was a woman. They were as innocent
as trees, I felt."[15] Instead of accepting the God whom her parents' worshipped, "a
picture of a blond, blue-eyed Jesus Christ...son of God...his father: an older version of him,[16]" Walker provides a detailed account about how she began to concep-
tualize an image of God as Nature at a young age. In a poem entitled, "Baptism,"
she recalls the moment of her baptism in the murky waters of a rural Georgia
creek. She remembers neither the doctrine of salvation, nor the teachings of the
repentance of sin, but rather the feel of the soggy earth around her feet, welcoming
her into the family of creation. She recalls being lifted from the "brooklet" covered
in "bullfrog spoores gluing up my face" feeling as if she had truly encountered the
love of God, through the touch and feel of Mother Nature. Walker goes on to not
only articulate her nuanced understanding of God as Nature in the essay but also
problematizes such doctrines as the doctrine of sin and the idea of a faraway heaven.
Noting her early dismissal of the idea of such a place, she claims that paradise is in
the here and now.

Perhaps, one of Walker's strongest critiques of Christianity is the inherent sexism and violence embedded in the scriptural texts. Patriarchal interpretations of the
Bible that viewed women as vessels of evil (Eve), pieces of property to be exploited
(Tamar), and human persons mostly valued for their ability to give birth to sons,
strongly shaped the sexist ideology that undergirded the theology practiced in
the black church of Walker's childhood. False interpretations of the Bible, and a
general devaluing of women by church leaders, meant that even contributions of

redesigning the pulpit area by women like Mrs. Walker was not valued. According to Walker, women's voices in their church community seemed to have been considered less important than men's.

> One reason why they [mother and other women] were not permitted to speak [was that] They might have demanded that the men of the church notice Earth. Which always leads to revolution... For the other, more immediate and basic, reason my mother and the other women were not permitted to speak in church was that the Bible forbade it. And it is forbidden in the Bible because, in the Bible men alone are sanctioned to own property, in this case, Earth itself. And woman herself *is* property, along with the asses, the oxen, and the sheep.[17]

Questioning the nature of God is a primary theme in this essay as Walker wrestles with the notion of a *loving* God who would "curse women," and sanction the murder of women and children. By analyzing the sexism in the Bible—which served to legitimate the sexist practices of the black church in which she was raised—Walker not only critiques the sexist and patriarchal structure of the church but the sexism innate within Christianity itself.[18]

Walker's belief in Christian doctrine waned and faded during her high school and college years,[19] just as her belief in activism, humanity, and her connection to the earth was strengthened. During her involvement in social associations like the Civil Rights Movement, the Feminist Movement, the Black Women's Literary Movement, the Anti-Nuclear War Movement, and the Peace movement, Walker began to embrace a spirituality that honored the multiplicity of religious paths, remained open to wisdom born of experience, celebrated women's stories, and offered reverence to earth.

Attention to Walker's fluid spirituality and journey reveals a voyage within itself beginning with the sharing of human community, and acknowledgment of the earth, even as she was born into the Christian faith of her parents, and enjoyed the singing tradition alive in the black Southern Methodist church of her childhood.[20] Walker's fiction writings also shed light on the shaping of her own path, especially through the spiritual awakening of Celie and the liberating theology of Shug Avery in *The Color Purple*. Here, Walker's writings show how the Christianity of her parents provided more questions than answers. Placing important emphasis on her identity and perspective as a feminist writer, scholar, and activis, and on the role and voices of women in her work, Walker would come to heavily critique the sexism embedded in many traditional forms of religion including Christianity and Rastafarianism.[21] Recalling how she wrestled to maintain certain aspects of her parents' faith while maintaining her commitment to feminist thought, Walker's writings reveal a shift in her concepts of the divine, show how she first became interested in Native American spirituality, and suggests that Walker believes there are several different ways, paths, and perspectives to having a healthy relationship with the divine in and as the earth.

One of these reflections that captures a glimpse into Walker's spiritual shifts and the tensions she felt in trying to maintain, reject, altar, and transform certain aspects of the faith that she learned from her parents is captured in the essay, "Coretta King: Revisited." Here, she recalls the utter pain and grief of losing an unborn child, just days after suffering the deep pain and sorrow following the assassination of Martin Luther King Jr. Remembering a moment in which seeing Mrs. Coretta Scott King on television three weeks after the four-mile funeral march for her husband, Walker writes, "[U]nlike Coretta, I had wandered very far, I think, from my belief in God if not from my faith in humanity but she pulled me to my feet, as her husband had done in a different way, and forced me to acknowledge the debt I owed, not only to her husband's memory but also to the living continuation of is work."[22] From this quote, one can sense Walker's belief in hope, a true base for her spirituality, which includes a belief in nature as sacred and a deep abiding hope in humanity. This basic root of her spirituality comes from her definition of activism, "My activism—cultural, political, spiritual—is rooted in my love of nature and my delight in human beings."[23] Though maintaining a sense of the divine, and especially a hope in humanity, her writings record a clear movement from the Christian faith of her parents to pagan, or earth-based, spirituality. She writes,

> In day-to-day life, I worship the Earth as God—representing everything—and Nature as its spirit... "Pagan" means "of the land, country dweller, peasant"... It also means a person whose primary spiritual relationship is with Nature and the Earth.[24]

This statement recorded in Alice Walker's essay, "The Only Reason You Want to Go to Heaven Is That You Have Been Driven Out of Your Mind (Off Your Land and Out of Your Lover's Arms) Clear Seeing Inherited Religion and Reclaiming The Pagan Self" summarizes Walker's earth-reverencing spirituality. A spiritual path grounded in respect, worship, and honor of the Earth as divine, Walker's earth orientation is infused with aspects of Native American spirituality, an interconnectedness of all beings, and emphasizes the feminine—as in "Earth as Mother." It also celebrates women's experience and the interconnected relationship between humans and the earth. In connecting the basic roots of Walker's fluid spirituality with the term "womanism"—and the uniqueness fluidity described in the heart of the term—it becomes clear why it is so important for womanist religious thought to explore the deep theological connections between monotheistic and polytheistic belief systems, and the syncretism that can occur between the theologies of some African ingenious religious traditions, such as Santería and Candomblé with Christianity and other mainline religious traditions.[25]

Religious Fluidity in Womanist Spirituality

Celebrating the work of first-wave womanist religious scholars and building upon the methodologies articulated by the second-wave, one of the primary hallmarks of third-wave womanist scholarship is the expansion of comparative religious and interreligious dialogue featuring the religiously pluralistic perspectives embodied by women of African descent across the globe.[26] Across the diaspora, women of African heritage find their religious traditions and spiritual practices affirming who they are and complimenting how women refer to themselves as womanists.

Scholars including, Tracey Hucks, Dianne Stewart, Carole Dufrene, Debra Mubashshir Majeed, Arisika Rasak, Linda A. Thomas, and Monica A. Coleman,[27] have written extensively about the ways in which womanism honors and at the same time reaches beyond the traditional Christian landscape of womanist theological inquiry. Their works, as well as other voices in the field signal a shift in the discourse that invites special consideration of the diasporic connection alive in most womanist, African, and African American religious reflection.[28]

One example of this is Emilie M. Townes who points out the theoretical, practical, constructive, and imaginative elements in womanist religious thought by offering the image of the "womanist dancing mind" in her book, *Womanist Ethics and the Cultural Production of Evil*.[29] Here, she writes that scholars are taking a new direction to identify all kinds of intersections between African diasporic life and religion. Bringing together such disciplines as critical race theory, social justice, art, religion, literature, ethics, sociology, and culture, Townes suggests that the practice of African diasporic religion is varied and diverse and that womanist study ought to honor this fluidity. She writes,

> The womanist dancing mind—the one that weaves in and out of Africa, the Caribbean, Brazil, the United States (South, North, East, and West); the Christian, the Jewish, the Muslim, the Candomble, the Santeria, the Vodun, the Native American, the caste of color, the sexuality, the sexual orientation, the socioeconomic class, the age, the body image, the environment, the pedagogies, the academy—has before it an enormous intracommunal task. One in which we are trying to understand the assortments of African American life.[30]

It is from this challenge and the work of womanist scholars pushing for comparative religious and interreligious inquiry that the third-wave finds its grounding to investigate, and become more inclusive of various religious perspectives held by women of African descent across the globe.

Third-wave womanist approaches also examine ways in which many women of African descent combine aspects of a variety of religions to shape a spiritual path that empowers them to overcome oppressions. As we have seen, one of these paths, that of Alice Walker, is helpful to look at for the construction of an eco-womanist perspective. It is from interviews with her, and other major literary and activist African American figures, that author Akasha Hull comes to recognize an emergence of "a new spirituality" being practiced among women of African descent in the twenty-first century. Hull explains that this new spirituality involves combining, layering, or mixing and mashing elements of multiple religious traditions together in order to form one's spiritual path, help guide one's spiritual journey, and create a sense of wholeness in life. She writes,

> (a) new spirituality…is taking shape among many progressive African-American women at this turning of the twenty-first century. Arising around 1980…this

spiritual expression builds on firm cultural foundation and traditional Christian religions, but also freely incorporates...(other religious) elements. [31]

The "new" phenomenon of fluid spirituality that Hull presumes in her book, *Soul Talk: The New Spirituality of African American Women* may not be as novel as one might think. The concept and reality of religious hybridity or spiritual fluidity, wherein multiple forms of religion are fused together, or merged to provide a life orientation that honors the multiplicity of identities, dimensions, connections to community, the spirit realm, and the earth has existed long before the twenty-first century; especially in African American religious history and culture. I would contend that Hull's observation signals a deeper acceptance and uncovering of the historically underground or "hidden" practice of fluid spirituality among African Americans and people of African descent rather than a new event in and of itself.[32] According to Gayraud S. Wilmore, multiple forms of religion, especially those with an African base, were fused together and practiced by slaves who were carried from Africa to the new world beginning in 1607. As a way of orienting themselves to a new world in which they were forced into the slavery and perceived as less than human, and in an attempt to give meaning to their lives, slaves maintained elements of their own African religious base in order to survive.

> Well into the nineteenth century the slaves relied upon the most elemental presuppositions of a religious way of life to give consolation and meaning to their suffering. Whatever specific beliefs may have been salvaged from Africa, or from the breaking-in period in the Caribbean, they came under the most vigorous assault by the North American missionaries and plantation preachers. The polytheistic aspect of traditional African religion had to be surrendered under great duress despite the fact that the idea of a Supreme Being was not foreign to Africans. Yet the spirits of the ancestral gods, disembodied and depersonalized, invaded the interstices of the objective world and impregnated the imagination with an interminable variety.[33]

Describing the fluidity and fusing between African-based religious rites and traditions and slave's embrace of Christianity, Wilmore explains:

> It was from within an African religious framework that the slaves made adjustments to Christianity after hearing the gospel. The influences of the African religious past extended into their new life, first in the Caribbean and later in the United States and, far from being completely obliterated, were reshaped by the circumstances of enslavement...African elements were enhanced and strengthened in the subterranean vaults of the unconscious from when they arose—time and time again during moments of greatest adversity and repression.[34]

As important as Akasha Hull's *Soul Talk* is in uncovering the spiritualities, values, and voices of present-day African American women writers, artists, spiritualists, religious practitioners, and activists, including Alice Walker, the assumption that hybrid or fluid practices of religion among African American women hardly takes into account the varied religious beliefs and practices of African slaves who journeyed to America in chains, or religious figures of the nineteenth and twentieth centuries such as Rebecca Jackson and Zora Neale Hurston. Both of these figures hold great significance for the uncovering of Alice Walker's own spiritual fluidity and leanings toward environmental justice. The fluid spiritual paths of Rebecca Jackson and Zora Neale Hurston served as topics of interest and road maps for Alice Walker. This, I believe, is indicated in Walker's essays about both women found in *In Search of Our Mothers' Gardens: Womanist Prose*.[35]

Rebecca Jackson

Born Rebecca Cox in 1795 to free parents in Philadelphia, her writings tell her story of being a black woman living through the emotional upheaval of being called to preach the gospel by the Spirit of God in a Christian community that silenced women—as a result of embedded sexism—and prevented her—a free black woman—from the freedom to preach and live fully into her own life and calling. The sexism that enveloped her African Methodist Episcopal Church also found its way into her home, as both her brother, Joseph Cox, and her husband, Samuel Jackson, served as elders and leaders in the church. Deeply involved with the church and sincere believers in the role of education to liberate black peoples, ironically neither Rebecca's brother nor husband assisted her in learning how to read or write. In one story, Jackson writes about the loss she feels when her brother, rushing her to dictate a letter that he is writing, impatiently attempted to write the letter for her, in his own words, instead of waiting for her to come to voice.

> So I went to get my brother to write my letters and to read them. So he was writing a letter in answer to one he had just read. I told him what to put in. Then I asked him to read. He did. I said, "Thee has put in more than I told thee…I don't want thee to *word* my letter. I only want thee to *write* it!" Then he said, "Sister, thee is the hardest one I ever wrote for!" These words, together with the manner that he had wrote my letter, pierced my soul like a sword…I could not keep from crying. And these words were spoken in my heart, "Be faithful, and the time shall come when you can write." These words were spoken in my heart as though a tender father spoke them. My tears were gone in a moment.[36]

Later, Jackson recounts that the Spirit of God taught her to read and that miraculously she also picked up the talent to write. Before long, she began spreading the gospel through various churches in her community but was hindered by church leaders in the A. M. E church who were intimidated by her abilities and charged her with "chopping up the churches" because she refused to join one particular church community. Called a heretic by many, and receiving threats upon her life for following her inner spirit voice, Jackson eventually left her husband, home, and community to follow her call—preach and start her life. According to biographer

Jean McMahon Humez, Jackson joined a Shaker religious community in early 1841 that welcomed her spiritual gifts and gender wholeheartedly. Struggling to find a balance between having full autonomy and control over her own being and life and also needing a spiritual community, Humez writes that "her life in the predominantly white Shaker sisterhood at Watervliet, New York was to clarify her ideas about community... (and) provide a feminist theology, useful when she came to the decision to create and lead her own, predominantly black, Shaker sisterhood in Philadelphia."[37]

It is this feminist theology, alive in the Shaker Eldress tradition that Alice Walker finds most interesting about Rebecca Jackson, not only because of its woman-affirming doctrine but also because of the fluid ways it mixed both traditional Christian ideas with what Walker alludes to as, goddess, "magic" and African spiritualist traditions. Walker asks:

> What... are we to make of Rebecca Jackson's obviously gnostic beliefs (that the "resurrection" occurs in life, not after death; that the spirit of "Christ" is manifested through the "mind" in visions and dreams and not through the bureaucracy of the church) a hundred years before the Nag Hammadi "Gnostic Gospels, The Secret Teachings of Christ" was found? What are we to make of her discovery that she had not only a divine Father but also a divine Mother—which is consistent with pre-Western Indian and African religious belief?[38]

The three questions that Walker presents—the first referring to a Gnostic reading of the doctrinal understanding of the "resurrection," the second about the nature of Christ (Christology) and the power of revelation through visions and dreams, and the third concerning the presence of the divine as feminine—suggests that, like the African descendants of slavery before her, Rebecca Jackson's spiritual journey involved the engagement and fusing of several different religions. Moreover, for Jackson, each of the religious communities that she was a part of, though different, influenced and informed the Spirit-led woman she became. In a similar vein, the various religious communities that Alice Walker has been a part of during her spiritual journey have indeed influenced her own sense of fluid spirituality. While the concept of plateaus may not be appropriate to explain Jackson's spiritual journey, it is easy to see how her spiritual journey might have been of special interest to Walker and may have provided Walker with a model of a woman's spiritual path that embraces a fluid process of becoming rather than a linear course of development.[39]

Zora Neale Hurston

Immediately following Walker's account of the strength and power of Rebecca Jackson's spiritual life in *In Search of Our Mothers' Gardens: Womanist Prose* is an often-cited essay on the life of Zora Neale Hurston. In this essay, "Zora Neale Hurston: A Cautionary Tale and a Partisan View,"[40] Walker discusses the profound influence that Hurston's literary writings and work as an anthropologist had on Walker's own writing style. She also writes about the significant role that Hurston plays as a key figure in the Black Women's Literary Movement. Of special interest to the discourse about spiritual fluidity is Walker's complimentary attention to Huston's free and fluid spirituality, placing her in a genre of spiritually in tune with black women artists like Billie Holiday and Bessie Smith who each charted their own course in life.

> In my mind, Zora Neale Hurston, Billie Holiday, and Bessie Smith form a sort of unholy trinity. Zora *belongs* in the tradition of black woman singers, rather than among "the literati," at least to me. There were the extreme highs and lows of her life, her undaunted pursuit of adventure, passionate emotional and sexual experience, and her love of freedom. Like Billie and Bessie she followed her own road, believed in her own gods, pursued her own dreams and refused to separate herself from "common" people.[41]

Walker's attention to Hurston's self-knowledge, autonomy, and power to "believe in her own gods" is an interesting and important observation especially because it was Hurston's interest and research on Voodoo across the South and throughout the African diaspora that reveals the initial connection between Hurston and Walker. In this essay as well as, "Saving the Life That Is Your Own: The Importance of Models in the Artist Life,"[42] Walker talks about how she first found the name of Zora Neale Hurston in 1970 as she was "writing a story that required accurate material on voodoo practices among rural Southern blacks of the thirties."[43] Upon investigating the voices of the popular white scholars on the subject, and unsatisfied with their results, Walker explains that she began to wonder, "Where are the black collectors of folklore? Where is the black anthropologist? Where is the black person who took the time to travel the back roads of the South and collect the information I need."[44] Zora Neale Hurston's name first appeared to Alice Walker as a footnote "to the white voices of authority"[45] in a book on black folklore. Finding Hurston's *Mules and Men*, she writes, "I was delighted. Here was the perfect book."[46] Not only did the book offer her the resources she needed concerning Voodoo rituals, rites and traditions, the work also gave Walker insight into the anthropological method that Hurston used to accurately report on the traditions of Voodoo, and provided information as to how and why Hurston became an initiate of Voodoo religious practice. It was not just Hurston's solid work and thorough research that Walker found impressive. The discovery of Hurston was extremely rewarding for Walker because it uncovered a model of a black woman literary artist whose spiritual and life path provided an example for Walker, from which she could learn and become the kind of artist, activist, and writer that she wanted to be.

Beyond Hurston's rich work on Voodoo, including the record she kept as she became a Voodun initiate—in order to follow the "participate-observer" anthropological method that she developed—Walker's own sense of fluid spirituality may also have been inspired by Hurston's own experience of Christianity, and her later creative and literary use of biblical imagery, Christ-like figures, and

criticism of the religion that her father followed and preached. In a section entitled, "Religion" in Hurston's autobiography *Dust Tracks on a Road*,[47] an additional
layer (plateau) of Hurston's fluid spirituality is found. Naming the Christianity
of her preacher father as the root religion that she was introduced into as a child,
Hurston admits that she began questioning the doctrines of the religion early on,
"You wouldn't think that a person who was born with God in the house would
ever have any questions to ask on the subject."[48] Similar to Alice Walker's own
questioning of the doctrine of original sin early in her own life,[49] Hurston too
asked questions about how it could be believed that "people were so prone to sin,
that they sinned with every breath they drew."[50] Shocked and concerned that
"You couldn't even breathe without sinning!" and that the Christian life required
certain perfectionism she felt was unattainable, Hurston gives up on Christian
religion by the end of the reflection. Slighting past actually denouncing the existence of God, she seems to refer to God as just another entity existing to give
people hope and to help shoulder some of the responsibility that they are unwilling to carry themselves.

> I do not pretend to read God's mind. If He has a plan of the universe worked out to
> the smallest detail, it would be folly for me to presume to get down on my knees and
> attempt to revise it...So I do not pray. I accept the means at my disposal for working
> out my destiny. It seems to me that I have been given a mind and will-power for that
> very purpose. I do not expect God to single me out and grant me advantages over my
> fellow men. Prayer is for those who need it. Prayer seems to me a cry of weakness, and
> an attempt to avoid, by trickery, the rules of the game as laid down. I do not choose to
> admit weakness. I accept the challenge of responsibility.[51]

Some scholars claim that Hurston's acceptance of human "responsibility" for societal, personal, and communal ills identifies her as an agnostic or a humanist.[52]
However, I believe that Hurston's inclusion of the person or character of God in
the passage signals that she does not in fact discount God, but rather philosophi-
cally and intrinsically disagrees with some of the doctrines of Christianity that
she understands as hampering people's sense of self-reliance. At the same time,
there is a tone in the passage the connotes that Hurston fully understands that
some people "need" prayer in order to help them create lives that are productive
in spite of the brutal realities of racism in the South. What is certain about this
passage is that it indicates a different plateau of religious belief—or nonbelief as
the case may be—than the one of her youth and even suggests a different religious orientation than the religion she conducts so much research on, Voodoo as
recorded in *Mules and Men*.[53] Hurston's example of movement through a variety
of religious traditions including Christianity, Voodoo, and a possible form of
humanism indicate that she too, like Rebecca Jackson followed a spiritual path
that was fluid in nature and hybrid in the sense that she combined a number of
religious beliefs, rites, and traditions to frame her own orientation to life and to
the world.

Both the eclectic spiritual lives of Zora Neale Hurston and Rebecca Jackson serve
as important historical models of African American women who practiced fluid

spirituality. They can also be seen as important and influential figures upon the spiritual life journey of Alice Walker in that they practiced the same kind of fluid spirituality that gives life to her "tri-spiritual" identity in which earth religion is a practice, and earth justice is a moral imperative.

Notes

1. Walker, Alice. *Moved to Speak* interview by Scott Winn on November 15, 2000 found on http://www.realchangenews.org/2000/2000_11_15/features/walker_moved_to.html
2. *See* footnote citing an interview with Scott Winn in Karla Simcikova's *To Live Fully, Here and Now: The Healing Vision in the Works of Alice Walker* (New York: Lexington Books, 2007), p. 20.
3. Simcikova, Karla. (2006). *To Live Fully, Here and Now: The Healing Vision in the Works of Alice Walker*. NewYork: Lexington Books.
4. Ibid, p. 4.
5. Ibid, p. 10.
6. Ibid, p. 24–25.
7. Ibid, p. 4.
8. Walker, Alice. (1988). *Living by the Word: Selected Writings 1973–1987*. New York: Harcourt Brace Jovanovich.
9. Simcikova, *To Live Fully, Here and Now*, pp. 9–26.
10. Coleman, Monica A. (2006). "Must I Be a Womanist?" *Journal of Feminist Studies in Religion*, vol. 22, no. 1, pp. 85–96. *See also*, Hucks, Tracey E. & Stewart, Dianne M. (2003). "Authenticity and Authority in the Shaping of theTrinidad Orisha Identity: Toward an African-derived Religious Theory" *Western Journal of Black Studies*, volume 27.
11. Townes, Emilie M. (1995). *In a Blaze of Glory: Womanist Spirituality as Social Witness*. Nashville, TN: Abingdon Press, pp. 11–13. Just as the thought and spirituality of Alice Walker can be seen as fluid, so too can the thought and spirituality of womanists scholars, including Townes. While in her 1995 book, quoted above, she gives reference to God and Jesus as important aspects of her womanist spirituality, just over a decade later, in her landmark essay, "The Womanist Dancing Mind: Speaking to the Expansiveness of Womanist Discourse." In Stacey Floyd-Thomas (ed.). *Deeper Shades of Purple: Womanism in Religion and Society*. New York: New York University Press, pp. 236–24. Townes uncovers a shifting in her own thought based on the fact that she does not often see Christianity truly being lived out in a way that promotes social witness. She writes, "for many years, I have been a somewhat reluctant Christian. From childhood, I listened to and took seriously what the older folks told me about what being a Christian meant and I watched with equal care as almost no one ever came close to being one. It was for me, as a child, a strange disconnect and in many ways I thought (and continue to think) that Christianity is a wonderful religion but hardly anyone is actually doing it. What I found far too often, however, is a Christianity that sanctions oppression as holy or a religiosity that separates spirituality and social witness...The dilemma is one of being—not so much in the dense ontological sense, but in a more mundane one. What is the difference for me when I say "I am a Christian" and "being Christian?" This is more than rhetorical ruffles and flourishes for me because as a womanist Christian ethicist, I am deeply concerned about the ways in which our actions and

values line up or not" (p. 239). Townes' more extensive analysis on the importance of expanding womanist discourse appears in her groundbreaking work, *Womanist Ethics and the Cultural Production of Evil* (New York: Palgrave MacMillan, 2006) wherein she argues that womanist scholarship must expand its focus and expand its study into the multiplicity of religious understandings and belief systems held by peoples of various faiths across the African Diaspora.

12. More information on how the womanist spirituality has developed in the work of third-wave womanist religious scholars will be discussed more fully in chapter six.

13. Walker, *The Only Reason You Want to Go to Heaven*, pp. 3–27.

14. Ibid.

15. Ibid, p. 19.

16. Ibid, p. 9.

17. Ibid, pp. 14–15.

18. Walker's critiques of Christianity in this essay shed much light on her own understanding of Christian theology, the nature of God and humanity, soteriology, as well as her deconstruction of Christian concepts of sin, Satan, and evil. Examining this particular essay for Walker's critique and reworking of Christian categories and concepts is an important project; however, that focus lays outside of the scope of this chapter.

19. She writes, "As a college student I came to reject the Christianity of my parents, and it took me years to realize that though they had been force-fed a white man's palliative, in the form of religion, they had made it into something at once simple and noble" in "The Black Writer and the Southern Experience." In *In Search of Our Mothers' Gardens: Womanist Prose.* (New York: Harcourt Brace Jovanovich, 1983), pp. 17–18.

20. Walker refers to the sense of community and song being important joys and aspects of her childhood in, "The Only Reason You Want to Go to Heaven." In *Anything We Love Can Be Saved: A Writer's Activism* (New York: Ballantine Books, 2007), p. 11.

21. Walker, Alice. (1998). "Journey to Nine Miles." In *Living By the Word*. New York: Harcourt Brace Jovanovich, p. 114.

22. Walker, Alice. (1983). "Coretta King: Revisited." In *In Search of Our Mothers' Gardens: Womanist Prose*. New York: Harcourt Brace Jovanovich Publishers, p. 148.

23. Walker, Alice. (1997). "Introduction" In *Anything We Love Can Be Saved: A Writer's Activism*. New York: Ballantine Books, p. xxii.

24. Walker, *The Only Reason You Want to Go to Heaven*, pp. 9–17.

25. For more on each of these traditions, *see* Margarite Fernandez Olmos and Lizabeth Paravisini-Gebert, *Creole Religions of the Caribbean: An Introduction from Vodou and Santeria to Obeah and Espiritismo* (New York: New York University Press, 2003) and Rachel Harding, *A Refuge in Thunder: Candomble and Alternative Spaces of Blackness* (Indiana University Press, 2000); and Carole Christ, *She Who Changes: Re-Imagining the Divine in the World* (Palgrave McMillian, 2003).

26. For more on distinctions between the waves in womanist thought *see*, Melanie L. Harris' (2010). *Gifts of Virtue, Alice Walker, and Womanist Ethics*. New York: Palgrave McMillian.

27. Harding, Rachel E. (2000). *Candomble and Alternative Spaces of Blackness*. Indiana: Indiana University Press; Tracey Hucks, "I Smoothed the Way, I Opened Doors Women in the Yoruba-Orisha Tradition of Trinidad." In *Women and Religion in the African Diaspora: Knowledge, Power and Performance*. Ruth Marie Griffith and Barbara Dianne Savage(ed.). (Baltimore, Maryland: John Hopkins University Press, 2006), pp. 19–36; Dianne Stewart. (2005). *Three Eyes for the Journey: African Dimensions of the Jamaican Religious Experience*. New York: Oxford University Press;

Carol B. Duncan, "From 'Force-Ripe'" to "Womanish/ist": Black Girlhood and African Diasporan Feminist Consciousness." In *Deeper Shades of Purple: Womanism in Religion and Society.* Stacey Floyd-Thomas (ed.). (New York: New York University Press, 2006), pp. 29–27; Debra Mubashshir Majeed, "Womanism Encounters Islam: A Muslim Scholar Considers the Efficacy of a Method Rooted in the Academy and the Church." In *Deeper Shades of Purple: Womanism in Religion and Society.* Stacy Floyd-Thomas (ed.). (New York: NYU Press, 2006), pp. 38–53; Arisika Rasak, "Her Blue Body: A Pagan Reading of Alice Walker Womanism." Paper presented at the annual meeting of the American Academy of Religion, San Diego, California, November, 2007; and Linda A. Thomas. (1999). *Under the Canopy: Ritual Process and Spiritual Resilience in South Africa* (Columbia: University of South Carolina Press.[27] Thomas, *Under the Canopy: Ritual Process and Spiritual Resilience in South Africa.* For example, in noting the importance of both Western forms of Protestant Christianity and forms of African indigenous religion among congregations in a South African context, Thomas writes, "The signs, symbols, and practices used in rituals build a bridge between African religion and western Protestant Christianity. While Christian symbols may seem more dominant, indigenous meaning systems are also present. Cultural signs and symbols of blended African cosmologies are evident" (p. 5).

28. Ibid, p. 5.
29. Townes, Emilie M. (2006). *Womanist Ethics and the Cultural Production of Evil.* New York: Palgrave Macmillan.
30. Ibid, p. 2.
31. Hull, Akasha. (2001). *Soul Talk: The New Spirituality of African American Women.* Rochester, VT: Inner Traditions, pp. 1–2.
32. In other words, I think Hull's notice of a shift in African American women's spirituality that often departs from the base religion of Christianity, is an important one, however, it is a phase within a larger movement. The shift that Hull notes happening during and after the 1980s is another phase of African American fluid spirituality that has been practiced since the times of slavery. As Gayraud S. Wilmore, Charles H. Long, and others offer, certain elements of African religious tradition, rites and rituals were maintained through the era of slavery and fused with the Christianity and other traditional religions that slaves were introduced to. In the same way that an African religious base was fused with Christianity by slaves attempting to create meaning to their lives, and re-establish their own sense of humanity, so too have some of the descendants of slaves borrowed from this same Christianity developed by slaves (fused with elements of African religiosity) and chosen to expand "spiritual expression... (building from a) firm cultural foundation and traditional Christian religions." Thus, the hybrid spirituality that Hull witnesses in the lives of twenty-first century African American women is another phase of African American fluid spirituality and religiosity.
33. Wilmore, Gayraud S. (1973). *Black Religion and Black Radicalism: An Interpretation of the Religious History of Afro-American People, 2nd Edition.* New York: Orbis Books, p. 11.
34. Ibid, p. 27. Historian Charles H. Long's argument about the significance of the African religious base for the study of African American Religion also provides invaluable insights. *See* Charles H. Long, (1995) "Perspective for a Study of Afro-American Religion in the United States." In *Significations: Signs, Symbols, and Images in the Interpretation of Religion,* pp. 187–98. Aurora, CO: The Davies Group Publishers.
35. Both these women's religious lives and spiritualities are particularly important for any study of Alice Walker's spirituality because Walker herself studied the spiritual

journeys of both these women, the essays on each fall beside each other in the volume, *In Search of Our Mothers' Gardens*. This placement I believe is no accident but rather speaks to the significance that the spiritual lives, journeys, and Gnostic and religiously pluralistic beliefs of both women who influenced Alice Walker. I believe these and other women whose spiritual journey fused different aspects of various religious traditions influenced Walker's own fluid spirituality prompting her initially in high school and college to leave behind the Christianity of her parents in search of an inner spirit that was in keeping with women and life-affirming principles. *See* Alice Walker, (1983) "Gifts of Power: The Writings of Rebecca Jackson" In *In Search of Our Mothers' Gardens: Womanist Prose*, pp. 71–82. New York: Harcourt Brace Jovanovich Publishers; *See also* "Zora Neale Hurston: A Cautionary Tale and a Partisan View" In *In Search of Our Mothers' Gardens: Womanist Prose*, pp. 83–92. For more on the life and spiritual path and journey of Zora Neale Hurston see, *Dust Tracks on a Road* (Philadelphia: J.B. Lippincott Company, 1942, 1971). A section engaging her own personal thoughts on religion shows both her critiques of the Christianity that her own father preached and reveals her indebtedness to the rich culture, metaphors, stories and images of the black southern church tradition.

36. McMahon Humez, Jean. (1981). *Gifts of Power: The Writings of Rebecca Jackson, Black Visionary, Shaker Eldress*. The University of Massachusetts Press, p. 19.

37. Ibid, p. 24.

38. Walker, *Gifts of Power*.

39. For more on Walker's concept of spiritual development see, Karla Simcikova, *To Live Fully, Here and Now*, pp. 10–11.

40. Alice Walker, "Zora Neale Hurston: A Cautionary Tale and A Partisan View" in *In Search of Our Mothers' Gardens: Womanist Prose* (New York: Harcourt Brace Jovanovich, 1983), 83 – 92.

41. Ibid., 91.

42. Walker, Alice. (1983). "Saving the Life That is Your Own: The Importance of Models in the Artist Life" in *In Search of Our Mothers' Gardens: Womanist Prose*, pp. 3–14. New York: Harcourt Brace Jovanovich.

43. Ibid, p. 83.

44. Ibid, p. 11.

45. Ibid. In light of the fact that at least one of the white male authors whom Walker read also implied that black peoples lacked human intelligence, trust became a central factor in how Walker determined whether her sources were trustworthy for her books and stories. As a theme, accuracy, like in the work of Ida B. Wells shows up here as well as an important mark of the black women's literary tradition in that it solidifies and validates the actual experiences of black peoples.

46. Walker, "Zora Neale Hurston: A Cautionary Tale and A Partisan View," p. 84.

47. Hurston, Zora Neale. (1942, 1971). *Dust Tracks on a Road*. Philadelphia: J.B. Lippincott Company.

48. Ibid, p. 193.

49. In Walker's "The Only Reason You Want to Go to Heaven..." in *Anything We Love Can Be Saved: A Writers' Activism* Walker writes, "I had a problem with this doctrine at a very early age: I could not see how my parents had sinned...I did not see that they were evil, that they should be cursed because they were black, because my mother was a woman. They were as innocent as tress, I felt. And, at heart, generous and sweet. I resented the minister and the book he read from that implied they could be "saved" only by confessing their sin and accepting suffering and degradation as they due, just because

a very long time ago, a snake had given a white woman an apple and she had eaten it and generously given a bite to her craven-hearted husband. This was insulting to the most drowsy intelligence, I thought...But what could I do? I was three years old" (p. 19).

50. Ibid, p. 194.

51. Ibid, p. 202.

52. Pinn, Anthony B. (2001). *By These Hands: A Documentary History of African American Humanism*. New York University Press, pp. 171–82.

53. Hurston, Zora Neale. *Mules and Men*. (Philadelphia: J. B. Lippincott, 1935. Reprinted, New York: Negro Universities Press, 1969. Reprinted, with an introduction by Darwin Turner, New York: Harper and Row, 1970.)

Chapter 13

Finding Home in a Foreign Land: Initiation and Possession in Santería, Candomblé, and Voudou

Umesh Patel

Introduction

In the forming of new syncretic religions, the slaves had to adjust certain rituals to accommodate new surroundings. However, the traditional belief systems are far from obsolete. As George Eaton Simpson writes:

> The religious behavior of these persons of African descent in the Caribbean sector of the diaspora has been part of their attempt to identify with forces in the universe greater than themselves, to express themselves, to escape—at least temporarily and imaginatively—from rejection, discrimination, and exploitation, and, in some cases, to change their life situations.[1]

To survive the constant influence of the dominant regional religions, adaptations had to be made to conform to the social conditions of specific locations. Although the slave trade was successful in upsetting the African social structure, threats and the thought of isolation have failed to hinder derived religions from thriving. In many cases, the religion of the Africans was draped in the belief system of the dominating whites; if religion could not be practiced publicly, it would be done so secretly. In the following pages, we will explore the growing interest in initiation, possession, and the healing processes of Cuban Santería, Brazilian Candomblé, and Haitian Vodou in an attempt to uncover why many seek the essence of home away from home.

At the dawn of creation, there was a pure cosmic energy known as *ashé*.[2] Through the workings of the ultimate creator, Olodumare, everything that our eyes can see, and everything that we cannot, came into existence. Throughout human history, He has been called Allah, Yahweh, and God, all of which are different guises for the same entity, but Olodumare cannot be captured in any image conceivable to mankind; he is without beginning and without end. His force exists in the air we breathe, the food we eat, the world we see, and the wind we feel. His energy fuels the life force of reality, transcending all things beyond human perception. *Ashé* is unlimited. In his infinite ability, Olodumare created entities to rule over aspects of existence in his stead. Known as *orishas*, these secondary gods serve as intermediaries between Olodumare and his creations. It is impossible to separate mankind from these entities so that wherever the individual lives, the spirit world follows.

The Santería Experience

Through the slave trade and the dispersion of many Africans to Cuba, traditional elements of the Yoruba religion seemed to die away as families were torn apart in the New World. Marked by slavery, the Yoruba felt no reason to seek salvation in the white face of Jesus. Although they were outwardly prevented from worshipping traditional figures, no form of oppression could prevent them from draping their *orishas* with the clothing of Catholicism. Thus, Santería emerged as the neo-African religion of the oppressed people.[3] While many of the practices were secretive in the beginning, the confines of slavery could not effectively eliminate the elements of the Yoruba tradition that dwells within the individual. Under constant criticism by slave owners, those who began to practice Santería continued to do so in every action and with every decision they made. It became more than a religion but a way of life. Having been uprooted from their native Yoruba lands, however, practitioners of this new religion sought new ways of communicating with the divine entities they were forced to leave behind. In turn, new initiates to Santería inevitably reestablished their ontology in a suitable way to accompany the complex understanding of *ashé*. With initiation comes the shaping force of illnesses, and the healing practices associated therein. As we seek to understand the terms "illness" and "healing," we must allow ourselves to synthesize this as a "transformation of the self in which the ill person begins to experience the world in new ways."[4] The process allows the initiate to sift through the impurities of life, and ultimately emerge in a purer state of existence.

For the initiate, the sign of an illness marks the liminal state of existence in which new realms of cosmology and ontology begin to open. Within the framework of Santería, illnesses are not seen as being caused by viruses, but as the result of various acts of sorcery brought about by strained social relationships. When one is dealing with such an illness, pharmaceutical medications will not suffice. In order to manage an illness caused by forms of magic, one must approach a healer skilled in developing relations with divine elements beyond the physical realm of existence. According to Johan Wedel, "the world is ruled by divine forces. Illness is prevented and healing is achieved by creating and maintaining relations with these divine beings and spirits."[5] With such a wide array of potential causes, inflicted individuals likely begin the healing process by consulting a medium known as an *espiritismo*, a person skilled in Spiritism. Because of the slave trade, the traditional understanding of ancestor worship ended in the diaspora because of the destruction of a strong family unit. In the Yorubaland, families consider the spirits of the deceased as members of the "living-dead" and "ancestral spirits" through which connections to the divinities are made. In Cuba, however, these specialists are responsible for forming and maintaining this important connection with the living-dead. Therefore, during a personal consultation between a spiritist and the inflicted, the former will assume the role of the desired spirit for the inflicted individual. Through this process, the once lost living-dead can speak through the mouth of the spiritist to advise those present about their weakened condition. Although this may sound like a very outdated way of dealing with problems,

> Today in Cuba one can find in the home of a spiritist a boveda, a table covered with a white cloth. On top of it there are usually photographs of departed family members, a crucifix, dolls, and glasses of water. The dolls represent spiritual guides, and each glass represents a particular muerto, often a deceased family member.[6]

It is important to note here that the elements described therein are an amalgamation of traditions incorporated into Santería by priests from different parts of the Yorubaland. The desire, therefore, is to attract a member of the living-dead through at least one of the objects presented on the spiritist's table. If successful, the spirit of the deceased will aid the inflicted by pointing the individual in the direction of the root problem.

Within Santería, illnesses are explained using sorcery as a framework for understanding. For example, if one member of the community has been blessed with new child and the mother or child falls ill, it can often be assumed that the barren neighbor holds some responsibility. In polygamous societies, if the youngest of wives falls ill, one assumes that jealousy among the other wives has played a role in the ailment. Therefore, illnesses caused by strained relationships within a community or family unit are often explained as acts of sorcery. In such a situation, the healing process described above will come into play. However, a simple end to the pain and suffering of the individual is not the only goal. As we have discussed, the healing process and the various rituals involved seeks to open one's mind to new dimensions of cosmology and ontology. In the example of the youngest wife, for instance, the healing process will encourage this woman to broaden her scope of those around her and to scrutinize her actions carefully. In the end, her pain will cease, and she will have developed a better relationship with the women in her company. As one can imagine, by associating personal health problems with the larger society, an individual is forced to see his or her life in a new light in order to solve that problem. After all, since Santería originated as the religion of the oppressed, these individuals cannot afford to oppress others within their own communities on smaller scales. In order to ensure the safety and security of those within African societies in the diaspora, various rituals are performed for the sake of those involved.

Most important throughout the Santería tradition is the role of drumming and dance in the *bembé* festivals. Originating through Yoruba tradition, these festivals "are generally given to honor, thank, supplicate, or repay an *orisha*. The rhythm of the drums invites the *orishas* to come and possess the dancers, bridging the gap between the physical and spiritual worlds."[7] Because of the diaspora, this festival and the ensuing possession allows the participant to experience the unique connection to the spirit world that was once common in their native land. When the possession takes place in the appropriate conditions, the possessed individual will transcend the limits of time and space into the liminal space. Through this process, the possessed will ultimately reestablish (in the closest way possible) the connection to the African traditional religion, while expanding upon Santería's ontological views.

As we have seen through the initiation process, members of the religion seek to blend mind and body in order to establish a greater connection to a world that transcends the physical. In the modern Western mindset, a stomach ache rarely gives way to a new outlook on the world—Santería proposes the opposite. However, the relationship between the self and other *physical* objects must be considered when discussing acts of sorcery. According to Wedel, "when sorcery is performed in order to cause a mental or bodily illness, the intended victim's name and his nails, hair, blood, semen, sweat, and urine are often used."[8] Evidently, a person's life force still exists in the fluids and other things that have since left the body. Therefore, it is common practice to dispose of such material in order to protect oneself from harm. As a point of comparison, it must be stressed that illnesses result from the material world while healing delves into spiritual world, emphasizing the need for reestablished views of ontology. When the practice of divination fails to guide the inflicted toward greater insight, one must resort to the controversial practice of animal sacrifice for help.

With the understanding that illnesses are often carried throughout the body by one's own blood, the ideal solution would be to replace it in much the same way that one would replace a broken light bulb with a new one. In Santería, animal blood is often rubbed on the body of the ailing individual, symbolically replacing the diseased life force of one with the cleaner life force of the other. Since the animal has already been slaughtered, it is understood that it has died for the sake of the human.[9] While this ritual often causes tension to those unfamiliar with such practices, it must be noted that Olodumare created these animals with the same life force as he created mankind. With this in mind, mankind was the last of the Supreme Being's creations and thus everything created before is for human use. Although many may argue that the blood of an animal is unfit for the human body, we must stress that the blood is not being replaced but rather the same God-given life force. Even though the very idea seems incomprehensible in a world of modern medicine, this "life force transfusion" ultimately allows the patient to cast aside old worldviews in favor of fresh perceptions.

As we have seen in this short assessment of Santería practices, the roles of illness and healing are not simply *a part* of the religion, but rather the *foundation* of the religion. With each of these rituals, we begin to understand that there are forces in nature that are beyond human comprehension at work in the world. Using various herbs, plants, and objects from the human body utilized in sorcery and healing, one recognizes that *everything* encompasses elements of the divine and should not be overlooked. Each breath one takes is consumption of the divine. Each blade of grass or drop of rain serves a purpose for the individuals who walk the earth. When one understands the importance of nature and allows oneself to be carried to another plane through trance and possession, one begins to see the world in a new, ever evolving way.

The Candomblé Experience

Standing on the Brazilian coastline, one hears the ebb and flow of the waters inching closer and closer towards the feet of a passerby. Closing your eyes, you are engulfed by the deafening rhythm of nature and are lulled into relaxation and are momentarily lifted to a new realm of existence never before appreciated until that singular moment. This is the spirit of Candomblé. Among the religions that derived as a result of the slave trade, Candomblé has become one of the most widely recognized African religions outside of the continent. Originating as a form of protest during the period of slavery, this religion forced its way onto the global scene in an attempt to establish a sense of meaning for those torn apart from Africa. As we have seen with Santería, this religion is largely defined by ritual dance, spiritual healing, divination, possession, and sacrificial offerings. Following the lines of the Yoruba tradition, these elements are not simply a part of the religion, but are at its very core. Although many elements of "traditional" practices inevitably fade as families are scattered throughout Brazil, the human condition remains "a product of interrelations with the spirit world."[10] This connection is not a part of one's life, it is the foundation of one's life.

Before exploring the complex elements associated with the Candomblé concept of spiritism and healing, we should consider the following as a foundation of our study:

> Olorun, the Supreme Being, decided to create the universe that we see today. Having set the plan in motion, he gave the orders to a male Orisha who plotted his journey to scatter the contents that Olorun had given him. Having become intoxicated by palm wine, the male Orisha fell asleep and his wife continued the task set out by the Supreme Being. When the sleeping Orisha awoke, a world resembling the Kingdom of Olorun had been created. After confessing his negligence to the Supreme Being, the male Orisha was ordered to conclude the task and create human beings to populate the earth that was already created.[11]

Through this adaptation of a Yoruba creation myth, we see that the Supreme Being created the universe and its inhabitants before ordering the *Orishas* to put everything in the proper positions. What this implies is that everything found on the earth is created from the same ethereal substance as human beings—mankind shares the same vital life force as every other living thing on Earth. Furthermore, it reveals, "that the material and spiritual worlds are exact duplicates, parallel expressions of the same reality."[12] Therefore, everything that happens to mankind in the natural world inevitably has a connection to the spiritual world.

With this understanding in mind, it comes as no surprise that accidents occurring in one's life are attributed to a higher spiritual cause. Nothing "just happens" to someone. According to Nathan Samuel Murrell, "in the African cosmology, a direct relationship exists between most human tragedies and the ability of mortals to live in concord with the immortal world. That is, few human misfortunes happen by chance."[13] Much like the belief structure of Santería, a connection with the spiritual world is essential for a peaceful existence. In the secular Western mindset, one often places religion in a "box" separated from other aspects of human life. Within the system of Candomblé, this separation causes an unbalance, a disequilibrium, in the workings of day to day activity which can lead to illness, financial ruin, marital feuds, or simply the smallest accident. In order to reestablish the spiritual connection necessary for a steady balance, a small ceremony or an elaborate process may be required.

As a branch of the African worldview, these rituals not only seek to forge a balance in one's world, but they also serve the purpose of reaffirming or strengthening one's ontological views of the world around them. This is where the concept of *ashé* comes into play in the Candomblé tradition. As we established in our discussion of Santeria, *ashé* is the life-force provided by an *orisha* to humans, plants, and animals. To take this concept a step further, *ashé* supplies the "power, energy, and strength necessary to deal with life's problems"[14] that are *always* present in some capacity in the human body. When one loses the vital life-force and problems arise, it becomes imperative that a diviner be consulted to determine the best path to a cure.

When approached, the diviner will determine whether or not it is necessary for the client to undergo the initiation process to reestablish a connection with the divinities. If the elaborate process is required, the initiate will experience a spiritual death and rebirth that seeks to reform the individual's ontological views. Much like the prophets Moses, Jesus, and Muhammad in the Western traditions, initiates go through a liminal period of isolation and seclusion in order to find what is necessary in the spiritual realm of existence. One can imagine the experience of being alone for the sake of "soul searching," free of distractions and confined to one's own mind. Although no one but the individual can truly express what the process was like, every person's account would vary because of his or her unique connection to the spiritual world. In solitude, one has time to reflect on the life that she left in the profane world and to search for something she may not have been looking for. With *orishas* circling the sojourner, the deepest aspects of that person's life will attract the appropriate spirits from above. After spending some time alone, the initiate and the diviner work together to forge a connection between the spirit world and the human world to call forth the *orishas* with the strongest ties to the initiate. When successful, "a medium gives his or her body as a conduit for the [Orishas'] manifestation and cognitive communication to the community. Upon possession, the medium speaks with authority and can allegedly diagnose mysterious evils and afflictions, find lost objects, give advice on or predict future events, and resolve puzzling enigmas or problems."[15] Furthermore, while this possession is particularly important for the initiate, others in attendance reaffirm their faith by witnessing the manifested connection between the human world and the spirit world. By hearing the potential path of the future, those hearing the prophecy are granted the opportunity to make necessary changes to his or her life in order to avoid the ill fate of the community. Again, we see that this process seeks to maintain strong societal relationships in the diaspora communities.

In addition to this aspect of possession, the initiate participates in numerous rituals designed to infuse the soul with *ashé*. For example, "the neck of a white dove or pigeon chosen for the sacrifice is wrung and the head of the initiate is anointed with the blood."[16] By having the blood rubbed over the head, the epicenter of religious thought, the initiate is primed to become the embodiment of an *orisha*. During this particular period of time, the initiate's only sense of comfort comes through possession, while other members of the community dance and chant to the rhythm of a drum to keep the spirit within the profane world. Having originated through the confines of slavery, Candomblé is not simply a "religion" in the common sense of the word, but rather a way to gain honor, self-esteem, and solid grounding in a foreign land. Therefore, it is through this initiation process that one joins the family system of Candomblé to live in harmony with fellow initiates. As Joseph M. Murphy states, "[T]o enter the Candomblé is to make Africa present, either by returning to Africa or bringing Africa to Brazil."[17] Unfortunately, even if an individual is initiated, s/he is still responsible for doing what s/he can in the profane world to maintain this balance and harmony.

When one loses sight of the purpose of one's life, *ashé*-damaging illnesses are likely to overcome the human body. While this can take the form of pain and suffering characteristic of "illness" in the common sense of the word, our definition here can be expanded to include selfish attitudes, habitual arguments, and a general disturbance of the social structure. As we have been exploring, the likely cause of these illnesses belong to the lack of *ashé* in the individual's body. Although this individual was directly infused with *ashé* from the *Orisha* during the initiation process, regeneration of this spiritual life-force must now come from other sources. Luckily, all aspects of creation, including plants and animals, contain an abundance of *ashé* for the individual to use. According to Murrell, "medicine may come in the form of drinking potions, inhaling substances, or rubbing the body with special herbs [...] The [cleansing bath], done along with animal sacrifice, rids the body of negative fluids and energy."[18] With the assumption that the cause of the illness is a result of the natural and spiritual world, it only seems appropriate to utilize natural and spiritual substances to neutralize the illness and to restore the afflicted individual to a harmonious state with the world.

Although the use of herbal medicines can seem far-fetched in world full of pharmaceutical drugs, we must understand that there is a second (and more important) function of these medicines. For a group of people who have been separated from the traditional elements of African religion, it becomes extraordinarily important for the participants to grasp a strong understanding of ontology and cosmology. Having a lineage tracing back to a religion based largely on oral tradition, the connection with the divine realm not only keeps tradition alive, but it reforms the ties to the ancestral cults common in African traditional religions. Unfortunately, however, onlookers misinterpret the practices of Candomblé as a form of devil worship when, in fact, their practices resemble elements of mysticism in the world's largest religions. Continuing along these lines, it becomes clear that the point of Candomblé is to worship nothing other than the Supreme Being and to build a direct connection to the spirit world where individuals can turn to for answers.

Despite the misunderstandings that arise in the study of Candomblé, one cannot deny that this African-derived religion provides what all religions do: a sense of hope to promote survival, community, and love for the ones around us. Although the role of spirits and possession challenge the notions set forth by the dominating religions of the world, the individuals involved find great meaning in the practices nevertheless. While scriptures in Western traditions seek to validate a particular ontology, the experience and elements within Candomblé do much the same thing.

The Vodou Experience

Turning to the oldest of the African-derived religions, Vodou's combination of music, dance, prayer, and ritual is the most famous, and most misunderstood of the religions strengthened in the diaspora. Unlike our understandings of Santería and Candomblé, one does not become a member of this religion but rather a servant of the *lwa*—the equivalent of the *orishas*. Using language associated with servitude, it should come as no surprises that Vodou practices involve a great deal of action to sustain the connection to the divine. Before focusing on elements of divination, possession, and healing, we must first understand that "the lwa depend on the rites for their sustenance; without these rites, the lwa would wither and die. So the living community hold the responsibility for the definition and maintenance of the divine."[19] Through this brief description, we begin to expand the idea of the individual ontological growth explored in Santería and Candomblé to include the well-being and growth of the entire Vodou community. Through the various rites and activities, the spirit is ultimately brought into focus, and is open to communication with the human world in an unlimited capacity.

On the surface, the understanding of the spirit world is that of a "cloud" of spirits without specific identities. However, through the rituals and ceremonies performed in Vodou circles, this "spiritual cloud" begins to rain down the many individual identities that originate in the African motherland. According to Murphy, "to understand the spirit of vodou, then, is to see that it is an orientation to a historical memory and to a living reality."[20] Therefore, by concentrating on the lwa, practitioners bring elements of Africa to Haiti while the spirits form a mental bridge from Haiti back to Africa. For those living in diaspora, the desire to be an active participant in this living history requires a great deal of preparation, and the understanding that much is going to change from that point onward. Generally speaking, "through divination or luck or, most usually, critical misfortune, a lwa reveals itself as the master of one's head."[21] As we explored in our discussion of Santería and Candomblé, initiation into this religion demands a great deal from those who wish to undergo the process.

Since initiation is intended to help build a bridge from the past to the present, the initiate must be willing to participate in a series of difficult rituals. For those who are mentally capable of the mystical experience, they will ultimately form a direct contact with the divine world and will have a lwa bestowed upon him as a personal protector, combating misfortune, and the various illnesses caused by spiritual turbulence. In much the same ways that were mentioned in the other derived religions, any illness is typically attributed to some form of supernatural causation. Therefore, in order for one to be "called" to initiation, a priest will diagnose and prescribe the ceremony as a form of apology for the lwa that the initiate may have unknowingly offended. As we continue to approach the process of initiation, it is important to note that it is "both a death and resurrection. It gives those who undergo it the chance of rising from the profane state to a new life in which they will be dependent upon—but also in the good graces of—the [lwa]."[22] While this seems to match much of what has been discussed in the previous sections, the biggest difference is that the lwa may even suggest that initiation take place through various signs, like a dream perhaps. If such an event were to take place, the individual should not consider it his or her choice to answer the call that the lwa has made—it is now an obligation. However, the initiation process is approached the initiate becomes the ultimate benefactor.

At its core, the initiation process, in addition to all of the mystical elements and ontological understandings that become prominent in the initiate's life, brings that individual luck.[23] With this understanding of Vodou initiation, it seems natural that the members of the community at large would desire to be a part of the process for themselves. Although initiation is typically brought on by signs of illnesses, a person is allowed to devote a considerable amount of time and money to learn all that needs to be learned to go through the process for himself. In this situation, however, the initiates become responsible for presenting themselves in ways that appeal to the lwa that they are hoping to be mounted by. In order for this to happen, the prospective initiate must learn the precise dance steps, songs, chants, and mannerisms to attract a member of the spirit world. Once all of the preparations are in order—a process that may take weeks, months, or even years—the "putting-to-bed"[24] ceremony begins. During this rite of passage, the initiates are withdrawn from the community and enter into the liminal phase of the existence. Although much of what occurs during this period of time vary from person to person, one can assume that a greater appreciation for the natural world and the creator of that world begins to amplify. At this moment, the ontological understanding of the reality begins to collapse and rebuild from the ground up. Furthermore, during this period, the initiates are ritually cleansed with herbs and naturally derived substances. With our understanding of *ashé* from Santería and Candomblé, one can see the importance of having "life-force" infuse the body through every pore in the skin. It must be noted that "what goes on behind the locked doors is a secret which initiates may not reveal."[25] However, whatever goes on during this retreat definitely contributes to the new world view and mentality of the initiates that emerge at the end of the ceremony.

While the ceremonies are far more elaborate than what has been explained thus far, it is important to note that the end of the initiation process begins with a ritual "baptism" in which the initiate is cleansed again. Until the final rites of passage that all initiates experience, the initiate still remains vulnerable to supernatural dangers but can now use his newfound intellect to help him ward off such dangers. Similar to the concepts of *Karma* and *Samsara* in Hinduism and Buddhism, this interim period leading up to the final ceremonies allows the individual to learn from past mistakes so that he may avoid making them again. Since the individual has been approached by the lwa at this time, the initiate should have discovered a new knowledge of himself that has strengthened his relationship with the divinities, the community, and with his own soul. According to Murphy, "the lwa makes the person whole."[26] Furthermore, this interim period acts as a test for the initiate to use his newfound knowledge in the profane world that he originally came from. After avoiding the ever-present dangers of the world, the "decent of the necklaces" ceremony commences, and the initiate gives the "reins of his life" over to the lwa to control from that point forward.

While the initiation process is extraordinarily beneficial for the initiate in particular, the ritual dancing involved in the communal ceremonies play a significant role to all of those in attendance. As we have seen throughout this discussion, music and dance are seen as ways of attracting the spirits. In Vodou, in particular, the incorporation of ritual music and dance are used to entice the "cloud" of spirits to assume their individual identities. For those involved in the motions of Vodou dance, intercourse between the visible and the invisible world becomes possible through possession trances. When possession occurs, it becomes obvious to all of those present in that the dances become more exaggerated and frenzied. Although possession in Santería and Candomblé last for short periods of time, Vodou has seen possession last for considerable expanses, emphasizing the importance placed on the spirits' desire to connect the possessed to the origins of Africa. When the possession ends, however, the possessed no longer remembers the experience. In fact, "for a person to admit that he remembers what he has said or done as a god, is to admit that he was not genuinely possessed—it being impossible to be oneself and a lwa at the same time."[27] After an individual is officially initiated into the Vodou religion, participation in magic and sorcery becomes a very realistic possibility.

Based on common Hollywood depictions, the image that comes to mind when "magic" and "Vodou" are presented together is often quite negative, and for that reason, magic should be seen as having two forms: black and white. This distinction, however, does not discount the popular conception of the Vodou doll. In fact:

> The sorcerer, by means of incantation, tries to lure the person he is required to kill into a bucket of water. When he sees the image of his victim reflected in the water, he stabs it. If successful the water immediately reddens. Naturally a person can be killed if certain rites are carried out on objects which have belonged to him. [Therefore, deaths cause by] suicide [are] not regarded as truly voluntary act[s], but as the consequence of a state of mental alienation brought about by a sorcerer.[28]

To combat these acts of black magic, divination is seen as a form of white magic used to locate the cause of a problem. Although the belief is that the lwa will protect the initiate from harm, this does not mean that the practitioners will never encounter the presence of evil in the world ever again. While human may never attack human, lwa can still attack lwa. Therefore, through this new ontological understanding and with the connection to the divine realm of existence, the clearest and most effective way to attack forms of black magic is through the spirit world.

It is through the spirit world that these African-derived religions maintain their connections to the traditional Yoruba traditions. As we have seen through Santería, Candomblé, and Vodou, the belief in Olodumare is the underlying element that unites these religions in the diaspora. Among the Yoruba people, "the existence of the Supreme Being is taken as a matter of course. It is rare, if not impossible, to come across a Yoruba who will doubt the existence of the Supreme Being or claim to be an atheist."[29] As noted before, the traditional religions of Africa cannot be entered into easily since one is typically born with a particular religion in his or her heart. Therefore, wherever a practitioner lands, the religion follows closely. Even though adjustments have to be made for assimilative purposes, the strongest elements persist in every derivation. For example, "the Yoruba hold the belief that as the Supreme Being created heaven and earth and all the inhabitants, so also did He bring into being the divinities and spirits [...] to serve His theocratic world."[30] While these divinities and spirits assume different names and forms in various parts of the world, they nevertheless continue to assist mankind in achieving goals and maintaining a relationship with the Supreme Being.

While it is absurd to assume that specific prayers and rituals have remained unchanged in the diaspora, the importance of music and dancing has grown in the derived religions. For the Yoruba people, song and dance are apart of one's daily life, and easily makes its way into religious ritual. With the understanding that the divinities are a central part of the Yoruba life, it comes as no surprise that much of the music is dedicated toward particular divinities. Furthermore, "dancing is no less prominent during worship than songs. The dances take definite forms, depending on the divinities to which their offerings are made. These ritual dances are not mere emotional responses to the rhythm of music. They are symbolic, often reenactments of something sacred."[31] Although these elements of music and dance seem very similar to the rituals performed in Santería, Candomblé, and Vodou, we must note the connection that the practitioners have with the divinities being honored. For the Yoruba people, the relationship with the divinities is quite strong, and the song and dance are used as modes of celebrating their presence. For those in the African-derived religions, however, the incorporation of song and dance into religious practice is of greater importance. The purpose in the diaspora is to *form* a connection with the spirit world. Through the songs and the carefully learned dances, initiates are initially opened to a greater ontological understanding of the world. These elements, in a way, allows the initiate to be spiritually lifted back to the Yorubaland where their ancestors come from.

In much the same way as song and dance, divination plays as great a role in traditional religions as it does in the diaspora. Although initiates in Santería, Candomblé, and Vodou turn to divination to begin the initiation process, the Yoruba see it as always being "associated with a situation which, from the point of view of the client or investigator, calls for a decision upon important plans or vital actions to be taken on important occasions."[32] With the understanding that community and religion are inseparable, divination is not only intended to help the individual but the larger community as well. Since African religions, whether traditional or derived, place great emphasis on ancestors, the process of divination assures that the history of a lineage is involved in every major decision in a person's life. For those dispersed as a result of the slave trade, divination has not only been used as a way to reconnect individuals to the heart of the religious tradition, but has reestablished a sense of "family" in spirit, if not in form.

Finally, in conjunction with the belief in divinities and the process of divination, sacrifice has played a key role within the Yoruba and derived traditions across the world. Although claims have been made in the studies of Santería, Candomblé, and Vodou as to the purpose of sacrifices, agreeing on a single answer in the traditional sense is far more difficult to determine. According to Awolalu:

> the various theories propounded by the different scholars attempt to spell out the purposes of sacrifice, but we do not consider it necessary to regard one theory alone as correct; each theory has an element of truth in it. When we examine sacrificial practices among the Yoruba, we discover that we cannot speak of one purpose of sacrifice—the purposes are multiple.[33]

Looking at the derived religions, however, we can be sure of one thing: if initiates are going to effectively maintain a relationship with the divinities, the divinities must be pleased by means of sacrificial offerings. Beyond the scope of initiation, sacrifices can be made for countless reasons specific to the practitioner. Despite the variations, each act of sacrifice, whether in the Yorubaland or in the diaspora, assures continued support and comfort from the spiritual world in daily life. It reaffirms the notion that there can be a home away from home.

Therefore, although the transatlantic slave trade effectively tore countless Africans out of Africa, elements of Africa can never be fully separated from the African. In countries like Brazil, Cuba, and Haiti, adjustments have been made but the traditional elements live on. As generations pass and the influence of Christianity and Islam spread, the rituals discussed above become of greater importance for the survival of the Yoruba tradition. It is through these rituals that practitioners remain connected with their religious foundations and their historical heritage. To allow oneself to be separated from a religious and familial heritage, both physically and spiritually is to lose a sense of home; to be a nomad in the world forever.

Notes

1. Simpson, George Eaton. (1978). *Black Religions in the New World*. New York: Columbia University Press, p. 171.
2. De La Torre, Miguel A. (2004). *Santería: The Beliefs and Rituals of a Growing Religion in America*. Grand Rapids, MI: William B. Eerdmans Publishing Company, p. 12.
3. Mercedes Cros Sandoval. (2006). *Worldview, The Orichas, and Santería: Africa to Cuba and Beyond*. University Press of Florida, pp. 50–52.
4. Wedel, Johan. (2004). *Santería Healing: A Journey into the Afro-Cuban World of Divinities, Spirits, and Sorcery*. University of Florida Press, p. 5.
5. Ibid, p. 47.
6. Wedel, *Santería Healing*, pp. 52–53.
7. De La Torre, *Santería: The Beliefs and Rituals of a Growing Religion in America*, p. 119.

8. Wedel, *Santería Healing*, p. 111.
9. Cros Sandoval, Mercedes. *Worldview, The Orichas, and Santería: Africa to Cuba and Beyond*, pp. 112–115.
10. Voeks, Robert A. (1997). *Sacred Leaves of Candomblé*. Austin, TX: University of Texas Press, p. 69.
11. Anderson, David A. (1991). *The Origin of Life on Earth: An African Creation Myth*. Mt. Airy, MD: Sights Productions, p. 31.
12. Voeks, *Sacred Leaves of Candomblé*, p. 71.
13. Murrell, Nathaniel S. (2010). *Afro-Caribbean Religions*. Philadelphia, PA: Temple University Press, p. 180.
14. Ibid, p. 180.
15. Ibid, p. 176.
16. Ibid, p. 178.
17. Murphy, Joseph M. (1994). *Working the Spirit: Ceremonies of the African Diaspora*. Boston: Beacon Press, p. 75.
18. Murrell, *Afro-Caribbean Religions*, p. 181.
19. Murphy, *Working the Spirit*, p. 37.
20. Ibid, p. 38.
21. Ibid, p. 40.
22. Metraux, Alfred. (1959). *Voodoo in Haiti*. London: Andre Deutsch Limited, p. 193.
23. Ibid.
24. Ibid, p. 195.
25. Ibid, p. 199.
26. Murphy, *Working the Spirit*, p. 41.
27. Metraux, *Voodoo in Haiti*, p. 140.
28. Ibid, pp. 272–73.
29. Awolalu, J. Omosade. (1979). *Yorùbá Beliefs and Sacrificial Rites*. London: Longman Group Limited, p. 3.
30. Ibid, p. 20.
31. Ibid, p. 107.
32. Ibid, p. 120.
33. Ibid, p. 138.

Chapter 14

Mythology of Rituals and Sacrifices in African-Derived Diaspora Religions

Osei A. Mensah

Introduction

In this chapter, an attempt is made to review some of the religious practices of Santería's and Vodun's (also spelled Vodoun, Vaudun, or Voodoo) devotees. Although rituals and sacrifices that take place in Atlanta will vary greatly from those that take place in Miami, New Orleans, Newark, or Havana, we will try to focus on the aspects that are basic to all of them. These rituals and sacrifices embody their relationship with the Divine. According to De la Torre, in the absence of central creed, Santería has to be understood in terms of rituals because it is a religion based on orthopraxis, as opposed to orthodoxy. He argues that the emphasis on rituals show that the religion is more than simply an abstract set of beliefs and teachings, it ties believers to a particular social order, giving meaning and purpose to their lives, as well as justifying the overall faith community, and its role within the society at large.[1]

African-Derived Religions

The term "African-derived religions" (ADR) is used to denote various religions transplanted to the Americas following the enslavement of Africans. For convenience, ADR will be used in this discourse to identify Afro-Caribbean and Afro-Brazilian religions and those in the Americas. These traditions survived cultural and ideological assault, and continued to provide spiritual resources for a civilization rooted in African cosmologies. Although Mary Curry asserts that notable ritual differences between African American houses and other Santería houses do not exist, nationalistic tendencies and race-based issues shape theology and ritual activities.[2] A case in point is that African Americans and Caribbeans call the tradition "Yoruba religion" or "*Orisha* religion" instead of Santería. For them, their own term provides a much wanted and much stronger link to an "African past" and allows for attention to race-based issues. In many of these cases, there is a concern with ritual and theological orthodoxy using Nigerian practice as the standard.

George Simpson (1978)[3] groups these religions into five types. First is the neo-African religions: Santería in Cuba, the Dominican Republic, and Puerto Rico; Vodun in Haiti; Shango in Trinidad and Grenada; and Candomblé in Brazil borrowed practices from Catholicism that reminded them of African realities. The second type are religions influenced by Protestant missionary activity in the region: Cumina and the Convince cult in Jamaica, The Big Drum Dance of Carriacou (Grenada), and Kele in St. Lucia. Third were groups influenced by Pentecostal groups from the United States. Religions that emphasize divination, healing, and spirit mediumship were the fourth type: Umbanda in Brazil, the Maria Lionza cult in Venezuela, and Espiritismo in Puerto Rico. The fifth type was Rastafarianism, a twentieth-century religion with a sociopolitical agenda.[4]

Mythology

The term "mythology" can refer to either the study of myths or to a body of myths. Read one way, myths are tales of gods and demons, exaggerated humans, improbable animals, impossible places, and unbelievable events—engaging, to be sure, but at face value simply untrue. Yet read another way, myths are absolutely true: not as fact but as metaphor. Mythology is interested in the timeless questions of humanity. Some of these questions are: What is the relationship of human life to the great mystery of being behind all life? How are we to understand our relationship to the earth we inhabit and to the cosmos in which we find ourselves? How am I to pass through the stages of my life? And how is my life coordinated with the life of the society I live in? Answers to the above questions will tell you that mythology was traditionally a means of healing self and society by helping people bring the circumstances of their lives into harmony with these larger more abiding concerns.

In most African myths, there is an attempt to make moral sense of lived experience, and especially to account for suffering. Isichei continues that not all myths do this. For example, an Igbo myth, which is part of a worldwide genre, explains the origins of agriculture: when Nri, the founder of ritual community that bears his name, sacrificed his son and buried him, yams then grew from the body. The Nuer has a myth that attributes their political fragmentation to disputes over cattle.[5]

Myth, like ritual, is in a process of constant change. New myths evolve in novel situations. Thus, some are a response to the vast disparity in wealth and power between colonial Europeans and Africans. Myths draw on new sources of ideas, such as biblical episodes, which are often transformed in the narration. Not all Africans have a rich store of mythology.[6]

There is an intricate and varying relationship between myth, ritual, and sacred roles. According to legends, most of the rituals and sacrifices were once part of Yoruba religion. That is why to the Santería practitioners, religious mythology plays a major role in adding logic and depth to the symbolic nature of their practices. Understanding the myths and legends of each god or goddess is essential in determining what animals or foods are offered, what colors are associated with the deities, what ceremonies are conducted on particular days of the week, the specific dances performed, and a host of other details pertinent to the religion. It is important to point out that these myths and legends are real and meaningful to the members of this religion. For example, the ultimate authority in Santería, the Ooni is the spiritual head of the Yoruba in Nigeria. Legend has it that historically Ooni was a linear descendant of one of the original families responsible for founding the Yoruba nation.

Ritual

According to Freud, ritual serves to discharge repressed sexual feelings, and again ritual, or religion, generally, serves to effect the illusory belief that human beings are one with the world and thus secure in it.[7] Turner suggests, to the contrary, that ritual simply expresses the belief, which, moreover, stems from humans' actual experience of unity with the world:

> to my mind it seems just as feasible to argue that "the wish to gain control of the sensory world" may proceed from something else—a deep intuition of a real and spiritual unity in all things. It may be a wish to overcome arbitrary and man-made divisions, to overcome for a moment...the material conditions that disunite men and set them at odds with nature.[8]

Turner is not saying that the belief in unity with the world is true, but that its function is irreducibly religious rather than psychological. The Drums of Affliction focuses on Ndembu rituals of affliction, rituals performed on behalf of persons whose illnesses or misfortunes are believed to be the work of ancestors or witches. Symptoms of affliction, including backache, fever, boils, and difficulties in childbirth are an indication that either some forces are working against that person, or the person might have inadvertently offended these spirits. Consequently, the needed ritual is meant to placate the spirits that are responsible. Unlike rites of passage and other life-crisis rituals, which occur at regular times in the lives of individuals or of society, rituals of affliction are performed only in times of individual or social stress.

On the one hand, Turner says that ritual serves to alleviate social turmoil: "Ndembu ritual...may be regarded as a magnificent instrument for expressing, maintaining, and periodically cleansing a secular order of society without strong political centralization and all too full of social conflict."[9] On the other hand, he says that ritual also serves to alleviate intellectual turmoil. One of Turner's favorite phrases of ritual is "social drama": This notion of drama is crucial to the understanding of ritual. Both in its plot and in its symbolism, a ritual is "an epitome of the wider and spontaneous social process in which it is embodied and which ideally it controls."

As preoccupied as Turner is with what ritual says, he fails to explain how it does so. How ritual releases emotion he may partly explain, but how it conveys meaning he does not. Turner also fails to justify his nonreductionist stance.

Sacrifices

Sacrifice forms an essential part of most religions. Sacrifice is primarily a means of contact or communion between human beings and spiritual powers. It is human being's best way of maintaining an established relationship between himself and one's object of worship. What is offered, and how it is offered depends on the nature of the particular cult, as well as the occasion of the sacrifice.

Theories of Sacrifice

Ubruhe asserts that three main theories have been advanced about sacrifice.[10] These include the communion, gift, and expiation. The communion theory was popularized by Robertson Smith in his lectures on the *Religion of the Semites* in 1889. He argued that primitive sacrifice, and especially early Semitic sacrifice, was a feast in which both the god and his worshippers ate together. He viewed the feast as a communion or act of social fellowship.[11] Such sacrifice was neither a covenant nor expiation. It was not even propitiation. He saw these ideas as secondary if they were at all present. The sacrificial victim, he argued, was inherently sacred. He claimed that this sacred beast was the totem of the clan, which had the same blood as the people who slew and ate it. He contended further that the totem was the god and ancestor of the clan. There was, therefore, kinship relationship between the totemic victim and his worshippers. Through the sacramental eating of their god, the worshippers acquired spiritual strength. This theory cited sacrifices of ancient Arabs who attached much importance to blood-ties and Israelite sacrifice as a more highly developed form of the same concept.[12] This theory is no longer fashionable because it has been discovered that totem is not a regular phenomenon especially among the Arabs and Israelites. Even where totems are eaten, it is not with the purpose of uniting themselves with their deities. In sacrifice, it is the life of the victim that is made sacred by the consecration and not the flesh that the sacrifices eat.[13] Among the Ashanti of Ghana, the totems are never killed and eaten.[14] The gift theory was propounded by Renan in his book *Histoire d'Israel*. It was supported by anthropological writers like Sir Edward Tylor and Herbert Spencer. The theory viewed sacrifice as a gift to a malevolent or a selfish deity. Renan argued that primitive man of whatever race thought of the means of securing the favor of their gods as they also did with men by offering the gods something. The gods, according to the primitive man, were malevolent and selfish. This theory viewed man as the liege of Deities.[15] On the one hand, to Tylor, sacrifices were gifts made to a deity as if it were a chief. On the other hand, Spencer traced the origin of sacrifice to the placing of offerings on the graves of the dead to please their ghosts.

The third theory deals with union with a god through the immolation of a victim representing man. Its emphasis was on the immolation and shedding of the victim's blood. By placing his hand on the victim, man transferred his sins and life principle to the animal. The animal became a substitute for the sacrificer. The killing of the animal meant symbolic death, or carrying away of the sacrificer's sins. The victim's blood that was shed incorporated its life-principle and that of the sacrificer. When the blood was poured or sprinkled on something representing the deity, the blood brought the life of the sacrificer into contact with the deity.

The theories propounded are not valid because they do not demonstrate the religious significance of sacrifice. In a way, they discuss an unhealthy relationship between God and humanity, but the main purpose in the conception of sacrifice is that it brings people together.

Mythology in African-Derived Religions

The Yoruba in West Africa, from which the slaves were taken, were religious people. They believed in a Supreme Being, Olodumare, who was the creator and sustainer of the universe, although far removed from everyday mundane or human affairs. The social structure of the Africans demanded that, like their king, contact could only be made with the Supreme Being with the aid of divine intermediaries. These intermediaries, known as, *orishas*, became central in Yoruba religion and have featured prominently in ADR. Although Olodumare, the high God, is considered as the ultimate reality in the African cosmology, it is *orisha* who form the major focus of the adherents' beliefs and practices. Every ritual involves the invocation of one or more *orisha*. Each *orisha* is considered to "rule" a particular part of human life.[16] Every prayer and every offering is offered to a specific *orisha*. Yoruba mythology suggests that there are an infinite number of *orisha*, but devotees in the diaspora recognize about 16 major *orisha*. The adherents discover the *orisha* from their personal interactions with these sacred beings through their stories. These stories have never been written down but passed on to devotees by their elders, as part of a divination session, as an explanation about why things are the way they are, or why things are done in a particular way.[17]

Colors are used to reiterate and argue the colors used to represent and differentiate the *orisha* presences in rituals or ceremonies. Clothing worn by initiates, priests and priestesses, objects, stones, and bracelets used in a ceremony reflect the colors associated with the *orishas*. The following is a description of the most popular *orishas* in ADR in the Americas.

Eleggua—also known as Echu, is the guardian of the crossroads. All rituals are first begun by invoking Eleggua. He is known to punish those who do not respect him. He is a restless god, and for his own amusement causes much annoyance to mortals. It seems that even among the other deities, he is a bit of a practical joker, though at times not very funny. The colors of Eleggua are red and black. His numbers are three and twenty-one.

Obatala—is considered the creator of the world. The father of all the *Orishas* and the god of peace. His color is white, and the numbers are eight and sixteen.

Yemaya—queen of the seas and goddess of motherhood. She is depicted as a virtuous mother, prudent, intelligent, and at the same time warm, human, and happy. Her colors are blue and white, and the number is seven.

Oshun—goddess of love and lust. She is depicted as being sensuous, witty, and wicked. She is also the goddess of rivers, lagoons, and gold. Oshun represents all things sweet, beautiful, and voluptuous. Her colors are yellow and gold, and the number is five.

Chango—god of virility and strength, and of thunder and lightning. Above all, he is representative of unbridled sexuality. There is no deity more vehement or energetic. His color is red and white, and the numbers are four and six.

Oggun—the god of all things made of iron and mineral. A warlike god. He is symbolized by machetes, picks, shovels, hammers, and any object made of steel or iron. His colors are green and black, and the number is seven.

Babaluaye—god of illnesses and seer who can look into the future. His colors are purple and brown or purple and yellow, and the number is 17.

Ochosi—is the god of hunters and spell casters. He is also known as a god of justice. He is frequently associated with the police, the jails, and the legal system. His color is brown and beige, and the number is three.

Rituals in African-Derived Religions

In African religion, rituals are concrete expression of belief and religiously meaningful acts that people perform in appropriate circumstances, usually following strictly prescribed patterns.[18] Believers feel that they have to show their belief in some way. They do this by worshipping the Supreme Being, by doing reverence to superhuman beings, and paying respect to their fellow human beings.

Prayer, music, and dancing enhance the effectiveness of ritual acts. Sacrifices and offerings help to confirm the relationship between the Supreme Being, super humanity, and humanity. Like any other religion, ritual is at the core of all ADR. The majority of ADR are wonderfully ceremonial-based. Ceremonies and rituals play a large part in the practice of Voodoo and Santería. Some can include the following: prayer, dance, music, animal and blood sacrifice, and spell work.

Religious Functionaries

In the native African systems, women are as likely as men to be priests. The tradition of women leadership in African religion and culture has significantly influenced women's dominance in ADR particularly Afro-Caribbean. In the Western "creolized" version of the religions, there are differences. In Brazil, all of the major Candomblé houses are led by women. Cuba tends more toward *machismo*, so there are more male leaders in Santería. In Haitian Vodun, there are more women priests, but leaders who are associated with temples tend to be men. This is probably due to disparities in income more than anything else, because temples tend to be expensive to maintain.

Vodun priests can be male (*hungan* houngan), or female (*mambo*). A Vodun temple is called a *hounfour* (or *humfort*). At its center is a *poteau-mitan*—a pole where the God and spirits communicate with the people. An altar will be elaborately decorated with candles, pictures of Christian saints, symbolic items related to the loa (or lwa, Vodun spirits), etc. Not only do women often fill the role of primary caretaker, and thus take its responsibilities, but they must also serve the spirits who possess them in order to keep the lwa satisfied and potentially helpful with daily issues. Lwa come from a place called Gine, which looks a lot like Haiti. Serving the spirits requires more of woman than just their time and energy. It requires them to stop serving men. As a result, many mambo become lonely. Although they are said to marry their spirit, the relationship between a male lwa and his female host does not completely mirror a marriage between a human man and woman. It is clear that women possess important leadership roles in the Vodun religion. A priestess, also called a *mambo*, can serve as a spiritual leader, healer, diviner, musician, and psychologist for her community. A priest, or *houngan,* can act in similar roles in his community. *Mambos* and *houngan*s have authority over their temples. They can also initiate people into their tradition. A major role of the *mambos* and *houngans* is to act as intermediaries between humans and the *loas*. They can summon *loas* into this world, and then help them depart.

Rituals are held to celebrate lucky events, to attempt to escape a run of bad fortune, to concrete expression of belief, participate in a seasonal day of celebration associated with a Loa, for healing, at birth, marriage, and death. Rituals in Vodun consist of some of the following components: before the main ceremony; creation of a *veve*, a pattern of flour or cornmeal on the floor, which is unique to the loa for whom the ritual is to be conducted; shaking a rattle and beating drums that have been cleansed and purified; chanting; dancing by the *houngan* and/or *mambo* and the *hounsis* (students studying Vodun). The dancing will typically build in intensity until one of the dancers (usually a *hounsis*) becomes possessed by a loa and falls. His or her *ti bon ange* has left their body, and the spirit has taken control. The possessed dancer will behave as the loa, and is treated with respect and ceremony by the others present.

In Santería, a *casa de santos* (house of saints) known as *ilé* are founded in response to the knowledge and power of a *santero* or *santera* within their community. Individuals flock on these *santeros* or *santeras* for spiritual guidance. The *ilé* serves as a kind of house church. Most *ilés* are basements or bedrooms converted to house the believer's sacred objects. Shrines are built to the different *orishas* and a space for worship, called an *igbodu*, is created.

The head of the home church is called the *padrino* or *madrino*, the Spanish word for godfather or godmother. All individual santeras or santeros are consecrated, recognized as extensions of the supreme spiritual source Olodumare. The primary purpose in life is to serve as mediators between mortals and the *orishas*. Consequently, they officiate during ceremonies and ritual, divine individual's destinies, annul evil spells, and serve as diagnosticians and healers. They are entrusted with the responsibility of keeping ashe (innate power) active. They are recognized as *abijados* (godsons) or *abijadas* (goddaughter) of their *padrinos* or *madrinas*, and brothers and sisters of all who are in the faith. Their primary purpose in life is to serve as mediators between mortals and the *orishas*. In performing their role as priests of the religion on a day-to-day basis, the *santeros* or *santeras* are at times confronted by a particularly difficult case. In such situations they consult *babalawo* (the father of mystery). *Babalawos* are high priests who are able to perform certain duties that are beyond the ability of *santeros* or *santeras*. For example, they are the only ones who are usually responsible for animal sacrifices and are the only ones who can read the oracles of *Ifa*.

Every ceremony and ritual has a *derecho* (literally "right"), or fee, that belongs to the *orisha*, not to the *santera* or *santero*. The *derecho* is determined by the *orisha* and must be paid before the ritual is performed. It is expected that the *derecho* will be used to purchase ritual paraphernalia such as candles, offerings, or items of appeasement for the *orishas*.

There are four major entry rituals for a believer, namely: obtaining the beaded necklace (*elekes*), receiving the *eleggua*, receiving the warriors, and making saint (*asiento*).

Elekes

The first step toward entrance into the faith is the acquisition of beaded necklaces known as *elekes*; it is believed that the colors and patterns of the beads on the *elekes* will be those of the *orisha* that serves as the *iyawo's* ruling head and guardian angel, so the first ruling that must be done is to determine who that *orisha* is. This must be done by *babalawo* in a divination ritual known as *bajar a Orinla* (to bring down Orunla). Cowrie shells are consulted in the presence of at least five other *babalawo*. Once it is determined who the *iyawos* are, *orishas* necklaces are made by the madrinas. Each *orisha* owns a particular *eleke* with specific colors and shapes. The necklaces are strung with cotton string, then washed in herbal water, then "baptized" by washing them in a special mixture called an *omiero* consisting of blood from sacrifices offered during the ceremony and juices extracted from herbs that are sacred to the *orisha*. The primary purpose of the *elekes* is to protect the wearer, which they are believed to do for as long as they are worn. They are removed when bathing, participating in sexual activities, sleeping, and for women, during menstruation. Initially, the *iyawo* is given four to six *elekes*, known as *el fundamento*, representing the following orishas: Eleggua, Obatala, Oshun, Yemaya, Chargo and Oya.

Making Eleggua: the Eleggua is considered "Lord of Crossroads," who opens the doors of opportunities for people. The *babalawo* is consulted and, using seashells, he divines the *iyawo's* past, present, and future. Based on what he learns, he chooses materials that will be made to construct a garden image of Eleggua. The initiate is instructed to pick up three stones, usually in a forest or near a body of water.

Through the divination, *babalawo* then determines which of the three stones will serve as the foundation upon which the image will be constructed. The constructed figure is considered to be the *orisha*, not a representation of Eleggua. From time to time, the Eleggua should be given his favorite offering: rum, cigars, coconut, roasted corn, smoked fish, opossum meat, or candy. To neglect him can lead to closed doors and lost opportunities.

Receiving the Warriors

After Eleggua is made, the other warriors are acquired to protect the believer from danger, and to do battle with spiritual and physical enemies. These warriors attack any enemies who attempt to do harm.

Asiento

The most important, the most secret, and the most elaborate ritual in Santería is the *asiento* "ascending the throne"—the ceremony in which the *iyawo* becomes "born again" into the faith, becoming once and for all the child of the *orisha* determined to be their parent. The ritual is a process of purification and divination whereby the convert becomes like a newborn, even to the point of having to be bathed and fed like a baby. They are taught the secrets and rites of their god. They learn how to speak through the oracles, and they are "resurrected" to a new life in which they can unite their consciousness with their god. The purpose of the ritual is to condition the person's mind and body so that all of the supernatural power of their *orisha* can be inverted on the one being ordained, allowing him/her literally to become the *orisha*.

Death of a Relative

An interesting concept of voodoo belief is the ritual that takes place one year and one day after the deceased of a relative. Vodun belief states that there are two parts of the human soul. The two parts consists of *ti-bon-ange* (little good angel) and *gros-bon-ange* (great good angel). *The gros-bon-ange* is the body's life force, and after death, the *gros-bon-ange* must return to the cosmos. To make sure that the *ti-bon-ange* is guaranteed a peaceful rest, the *gros-bon-ange* must be recalled through an elaborate expensive ritual involving the sacrifice of a large animal, like an ox, to appease the *ti-bon-ange*. If the *ti-bon-ange* spirit is not satisfied and given a peaceful rest, the spirit remains earthbound forever and brings illness or disasters on others.

Blood-letting

Another ancient Vodun ritual involves blood-letting. Using metal knives, members of the ritual cut their own bodies to release their blood. In doing so, they are showing how strong their faith is.

Dance and Music

African-derived religions are dance religions. Among Santería, the *bembe* is a festival of drumming and dancing performed for the *orishas*. The *bembé* is a central public ceremony of Santería, where the spirit is most widely recognized and shown to the community. *Bembé*s might be held for a variety of reasons.[19] A *bembé* might be called to celebrate the anniversary of an initiate, to appeal to or thank an *orisha*. The link of Santería regarding drumming to the Yoruba religion is traced back to the legend that tells of a time when the Yoruba's were at war with the Congolese.[20] The rhythm of the drums invites the *orishas* to come and possess the dancers, bridging the gap between the physical and spiritual worlds.

Through a set of three sacred ritual drums known as *batás*, the messages of worshippers reach the *orishas,* and the *orishas* respond to their devotees. The drums are consecrated to the *orisha* Osain and are believed to be the home of a spirit called Ana; hence they too, must be fed through sacrifice and can be the recipient of prayers. They must always be treated with respect; dancers must never turn their back on them while dancing, and women may never play them.

Dancing and music are also major elements of the Vodun ceremony. Dancing is an expression of spirituality and of connection with divinity and the spirit world. Dance is so closely linked with the worship of *loa* that Vodun can be regarded as one of the danced religions. Dancing is a ritual act from which emanates a power that affects the supernatural world. The rhythms of drums and dances attract the spirits. *Asagwe* is a type of Haitian Vodun dancing used to honor the gods. The *manman*, the largest of the three voodoo drums, signals for a dancer to start and sets the distinctive rhythm to which it is performed. The dance is characterized by sweeping circular movements, dips, and semi-prostrations. Avalou Haitian Vodun dances are characterized by violent arm and shoulder muscle movements. The drum, on which the rhythms are beaten out for the dances, symbolizes Vodun. Beating the drum in popular speech has come to mean "celebrating the cult of the *loa*."[21] All dances, and even the main ritual acts, are accompanied by songs.

Libations

In the eyes of voodooists, libations of water performed in front of the sacred objects amount to "salutations." At the beginning of and several times during ceremonies, the *hugan* or *mambo*, equipped with a pitcher called the "cooling pitcher," carries out three libations in front of the *poteau-mitan,* or four if it is done facing the four cardinal points. The intention is to lure the spirits to come in and appear.[22]

In Haiti it is the symbolic drawings, called *veve*, which fulfill the functions elsewhere devolving upon statues and images. The *veve* reveal the presence of the god in a tangible form.[23]

Offerings

According to Haitian tradition, a servant seldom communicates with *loa* without first inviting them to eat something that he knows they like. The choice of foods and the method of preparing them are often determined by the symbolic attributes and the character of a *loa* or by the group to which he belongs. Foods—meat, tubers, vegetables—prepared for Legba, must always be *boucanes* (grilled on fire). Food prepared for the white *loa*—Damballah, Ezilli, Agwe, Grande-Bossine etc.—must be of that color. Each *loa* has his favorite drinks.[24] The way in which offerings are presented to the divinity is similarly prescribed by ritual. When a person possessed eats food prepared for the god who is lodged in him, then it is the god, and not he, who is supposed to receive the benefit.[25]

Prayer

Prayer is an elemental part of a Voodoo ritual. Prayers are sung, usually in Haitian Creole. During a ceremony, prayers are sung to *Bon Dieu*, or the "good god," and to other gods or goddesses called *loas*, or *lwas*. They usually open a ritual with a prayer first to *Bon Dieu* and their ancestors, and then continue the prayer to a specific *loa*. It is quite similar to Catholicism and their saints. In Catholicism, if you need help for your dear pet, you would offer prayer specifically to Saint Francis of Assisi, the patron saint of animals.

Adura

The Yoruba word for prayer is *adura*. Like any other religion, prayer in Santería is a way of communicating and personally unites the divine, to the human offering prayer and supplication, and receiving the power to grow and to transform spiritually—while an animal is being sacrificed, an *omiero* is being prepared, or an oracle is being read; in short, when any ritual is being conducted, a prayer is recited. Many are directed toward a particular *orisha*.

Sacrifice in African-Derived Religions

The Sacrifice

All faithful worshippers must help to provide *loa* with food, which is why Vodun ceremonies are often called *manger-loa*. From the attitude of Voodooists, and from their opinions, it may be deduced that, as in Dahomey, offerings and sacrifices "give strength to the gods" and the more numerous and magnificent the sacrifices, the more powerful the gods will become. In the course of *manger-loa*, it is not only chickens that are immolated in great numbers but also goats and bulls, and in the case of *loa* of the *petro,* family pigs. The animal is only acceptable to the god if it suits its tastes and if it embodies some of his own qualities.[26]

Animal Sacrifice

Animals are actually considered sacred in African religions and are used as offerings to the gods and ancestors. Animal sacrifice is prominent in Vodun ceremonies, but it is not such a focal point. Before any offering is made, it must be determined through divination if the animal is acceptable to the *orishas,* and if so, what parts of the animal are to be offered.

Some sacrifices, like those involved in ritual cleansings, must not be consumed. The sacrificial animals are really consecrated offerings, made sacred for communal meals by the initiate to share with their gods, ancestors, and the poor. In Vodun, animals meant for sacrifice may be a goat, sheep, chicken, or dog. They are usually humanely killed by slitting their throat; blood is collected in a vessel. The possessed dancer may drink some of the blood. The hunger of the *loa* is then believed to be satisfied.

In Santería, some animal sacrifices may be prepared and eaten following the offering, such as those offered during an ordination. Consuming a sacrifice provides members of the faith community with an opportunity to commune with one another and with their deities. A common bond develops among those who share a meal, and the sacrifice to the *orisha* ritualizes the bond, making it sacred.

Other sacrifices, like those involved in a ritual cleansing, must not be consumed. In such sacrifices, it is believed that the devotee's negative energy is transferred onto the animal. Thus, to eat the animal would be to take that energy back into the body. Spell work (*despojos*) are ritual baths meant to cleanse buildings of impurity, water for requests such as luck, fortune, and love. Devotees of Santería may also cast spells in order to achieve their desired ends. For those who face trial, for example, a special powder is made to solicit Ochosi's help. If a woman wishes to seduce a man, she can take seven earthworms, some of her menstruated blood, a dash of feces, hair from the head and pubic hair, and place them in the sun to dry. When they are dried, she can grind them into a fine powder and place the powder in the man's food or drink. Once he has ingested this concoction, followers of Santería believe, he will submit to her. In ADR spell work is another form of ritual to connect to the gods and ancestors. In Vodun, instead of dance and music, the needed materials for spell work can be herbs, oils, candles, and other talismans (dolls, *gris-gris*). Spells raise some basic questions concerning the ability of humans to determine their own fate or destiny: Do humans have free will? Are their fates determined by the gods? Or, are they in the hands of the one casting the spell? If the spell works, as *santeros* and *santeras* claim they do, do we then conclude that humans can fall under the control of any individual who has the esoteric knowledge necessary to dominate them?

Ewe

The most important impediments in any ritual, even more important than sacrificial animals, are herbs. In Santería, every plant is alive, complete with personality and temperament, and is guarded by a spiritual entity and infused with *ashe*. These herbs and trees communicate their healing properties to humanity; however, few humans know how to listen properly to the forces of nature. *Santeros* and *santeras* are able to concoct herbal remedies capable of curing illnesses. For this reason, every *santeros* or *santera* is an herbalist, a diagnostician, and a healer, knowledgeable about everything that resides in the forest.[27]

Otanes

Stones known as *otanes* are also crucial to the ritual of Santería. Without them, the *santero* or *santera* would not be important. According to legend, when the *orisha* left their community of Ile-lfe, what remained was stones resonating with their ashe. *Otanes* are most merely symbols, but are believed to contain the very real presence of the *orishas*. When a *santero* or *santera* finds one, they are required to treat it like a living entity. They must feed it with blood at least once each year, refresh it in herbal baths, and house it in a special tureen known as a *sopera*. All *santeros* and *santeras* receive *soperas* for Obatala, Chango, Yemaya, and Oshun when they are ordained; many possess more.[28] From the above discussion, we can say that Santería is an earth-based religion. Stones, plants, water, and blood are the four essential components to the ceremonies and spells that are at its core. Thus, it makes sense that believers in the faith are less concerned with orthodoxy, a set of correct beliefs and doctrines, than with orthopraxis, right actions.

Divination/Oracles

In the world view of Santería and Vodun, the physical and the spiritual worlds influence and affect each other. There is no dichotomy. A physical illness may be the result of a spiritual misalignment. The two religions attempt to reestablish the proper balance between the physical and the spiritual as well as between good and evil, thus restoring the believer to a state of wholeness. But how does one know which area in life is out of balance? This is ascertained through the process of divination. Revelation, especially divination, reveals the essence of situations and problems as well as their solutions. The purpose of divination is not merely to foretell future events. Rather, it is intended to inquire into the harmony or the lack thereof, between individuals and the spiritual world, between good and evil. The ultimate question of anyone who consults the oracle is, "Am I in balance with my destiny?" If the answer to the question is no, then divination can provide remedies, restoring good health, fortune, or love.[29] Vodun is a wonderfully ceremonial-based religion. Ceremonies and rituals play a large part in the practice of Voodoo. Some can include the following: prayer, dance and music, animal and blood sacrifice, and spell work.

Sacrifice and Offering in Santería

The food offerings, herbal baths, and animal sacrifices requested by the *orishas* through divination are known collectively as *ebbos*. The generalized term is usually translated as sacrifice. The purpose of the *ebbo* is, first, to bind the individual in a series of exchanges with the spirits and, second, to awaken the individual to the subtle presence of the spirits within herself or himself. These ceremonies are meant to resolve whatever problem the individual consulting the *orisha* faces. It is never enough simply to ask an *orisha* for a blessing; the believer must also provide their own tribute. Each *orisha* is lord of certain days, and *ebbos* performed on their days are especially helpful. There are nine basic types of *ebbos*:

Food offerings—are made routinely, and they are meant to nourish the talismans. Each *orisha* has its own favorite kinds of food, some of which are taboo to all but that *orisha*. Thanksgiving offerings—are made in response to good fortune bestowed by an *orisha* or to the successful resolution of a problem about which the *orisha* was consulted. Votive offerings—are meant to win the goodwill of an *orisha*. The *ashe* expended strengthens the *orisha* who can then, in return, grant the worshipper's desires. Propitiatory offerings—are intended to appease angry *orishas*. Most often, *orishas* become angry because of neglect. When it is determined that propitiatory offerings will require blood sacrifices, the animals are generally not to be eaten afterwards. Substitutionary offerings—are those in which sacrificial animals symbolically take the place of an endangered human life. Preventative offerings—are precautionary ones intended to ward off attack. Initiatory offerings—are those made during an ordination ceremony. As in thanksgiving offerings, numerous animals may be sacrificed with most of the blood going to the *orisha* and the carcass prepared for participants to feast on. Foundational offerings—are usually conducted at the building of homes, start of new business ventures and so on. They are meant to confer the *orisha's* blessing on the new endeavor and prevent anything from thwarting it. Sanctification offerings—are used to set apart the candles, herbs, and other paraphernalia of the faith consecrating them as holy.

Continuity and Change in African-Derived Religions

It is an understatement to say that African religious beliefs and practices, specifically Yoruba ritual practices, have had a tremendous influence on ADR in the Americas and the Caribbean. Trinidadians, who are associated with Shango worship centers (chapelles), refer to themselves as Yoruba people, the Yoruba nation, or Orisha people. Many are descended from Yoruba and were brought to Trinidad as slaves, and distinguish themselves from the Radas and other groups of Afro-Trinidadians. In Trinidad, Shango is only one of a score or more Yoruba *orisha*/powers who are honored with specific chants, drum music, food, and blood offerings and communicated with through the agency of the Yoruba system of kolanut divination. African religions in the Americas, in order to ensure their survival, have adopted the wise tactics of the chameleon and learned to take on and redefine the dress and colors of their opponents while still maintaining the distinctness, wisdom, and beauty of their own cultural identities.

Mason (1992) argues that the malleability of Yoruba ritual practice has enabled it to tolerate both Christianity and Islam. It also had the capacity to survive in the oppressive slave societies in which it landed in the New World, operating clandestinely initially and now more openly.[30] Explaining further, he suggests that this characteristic adaptability in the African mentality springs from a respect for spiritual power wherever it originates, and accounts for the openness of African religions to syncretism, parallelism, or simultaneous practice with other traditions and for the continuity of a distinctive religious consciousness.[31] The unifying themes of African systems of worship focus on the relationship of the individual to the spiritual realm populated by unseen powers, those yet to be born, and the ancestors.

Among other things, the continuity of ritual and sacrifice in ADR appear to be based on the following religious beliefs and practices. Africans believe that there is one God who created and controls the universe and all that is contained therein. Africans believe that there are selected forces of nature, which deal with the affairs of mankind on earth and govern the universe in general. Africans believe that the spirit of man lives on after death, and can reincarnate back into the world of men. Africans believe that ancestral spirits have power over those who remain on earth, and must be remembered, appeased, honored, and consulted by the living. Africans believe in divination. They believe that with the correct knowledge, investigation, implementation, and sacrifice, the means to solve all problems and cure all ills are within our grasp. Africans believe in the use of offerings and blood sacrifices to elevate their prayers to the spiritual powers and the ancestors. Africans believe in magic. They believe that magic occurs when we use our heads and our abilities to become dazzling so that we can counter or frustrate evil, thus illuminating the source of the problem. Magic is the ability to transform things—i.e., negativity into goodness. Africans believe in the magical and medicinal use of herbs. Africans believe that ritual song and dance are mandatory in the worship of God and ancestors, and Africans believe that mankind can commune with God through the vehicle of trance-possession.[32]

It can be argued that, at all times, Africans thoughtfully and actively resisted the cultural oppression of the whites. They resisted in the ways they prepared their food, in the colors they selected to wear, the style of houses they built, the way they talked, the music they made, the songs they sang, the dances they danced, and the images of God they clung to and recreated. Many followers of ADR believe it is important to shed all the vestiges of Christianity, while others are comfortable with a blend of Christianity and their traditional African religion. It is interesting that there is an increase in the number of whites in Santería among the mainland adherents, and this is reflected in the make-up of the leadership. It is also on record that in the Cuban exile communities, white *babalawos* and *santeros*, many of whom are educated and upper middle class, are much more frequent than they were in Cuba.

As a result of the continued increase in the Santería faith in the United States, changes are occurring in the structure of the religion. A case in point is a change in the leadership pattern in that the *santeros* are taking on more of the priestly responsibilities with the *babalawos*, assuming a decreasing role.[33]

In the area of beliefs, Santería is moving away from a mythological structure to a belief system that is more in line with current psychological knowledge with the ethical principles of Christianity.[34] Regarding the *orishas*, out of the sixteen recognized in Cuba, seven are singled out and given special attention in the United States. Referred to as the Seven African Powers, they are Obatala, Shango, Ogun, Orula, Yemaya, Oshun, and Elegua.

The ritualistic structure of Santería is undergoing changes as it adapts to the United States environment. In the United States, all believers are encouraged to undergo full initiation, but in Cuba only those whose heads had been claimed by an *orisha* were initiated. Also, the length of time required for initiation has been cut from a traditional period of three years to a short period of three months.[35] In addition, fewer trance possessions are taking place because consecrated *batá* drums, the playing that is essential for possession, either are not available or are not played in order to avoid negative reactions from neighbors.

Another significant change in Santería, particularly in New York and the urban areas of Northern New Jersey, is that it is becoming more and more syncretized with Puerto Rican spiritism;[36] Brandon has coined a new term, Santerismo (the elision of the words Santería and Espiritsmo) for a new syncretized form.[37]

Santería is developing forms that have a more universal appeal. Canizares points out that as more non-Cubans, both black and white and from a variety of social class, are attracted to Santería, and as the practitioners rely less on the use of Spanish, and as the belief that *babalawos* can be consecrated only on Cuban soil weakens, Santería is losing some of the "ethnocentric, cliquish character."[38]

As a result of the June 1993 Supreme Court decision that ruled in the Church's favor, the church's leaders are making plans for a unified, Western-styled church organization. The president of the Church put it succinctly that "Santeria had for years been depicted as the secretive, occult, violent, organized crime religion... to make it in this society, you have to be institutionalized. You have to be a force that protects its own interests."[39]

Interestingly, there is a push within the religion for the learning of African languages, and in interpreting the rituals in more traditional Yoruba ways. This has manifested itself in the beliefs and practices of Oyotunji Village in Sheldon, South Carolina,[40] and in the publications of the Yoruba Theological Arch ministry in Brooklyn, New York.[41]

Most adherents of ADR see their faiths as the same religion first brought to the Americas from West Africa by slaves. They believe, at its root, is the same religion that adapted over the centuries to survive the intolerance of a slaveholding society, manifesting itself as Haitian Vodun, Santería, Cuban Lucumi, Brazilian Candomblé, and many other forms. Although some practices of these faiths may be a radical departure from the Christian faiths, most American followers who were once Christians, believe the new faiths are not completely incompatible. To them, these faiths are not a conniving practice of casting spells and placing curses. Rather, they are based on the accumulated wisdom of thousands of generations of ancestors. They feel that ADR have a complicated system of rituals and folk tales, which practitioners rely on to find harmony with God, known as Olodumare to the Yoruba people and other West African Supreme Beings.

For some adherents, the moral code as inherent in the Golden Rule is not different from the beliefs and practices of devotees of Santería and Vodun. Both faiths are after the same thing but just have different ways of expressing it because of different cultures. In the Vodun religion, Olodumare is the Supreme Being, but there are other, lesser divinities known as the Orisha. Some of them, including Eshu and Ifa, have been deities since creation. Others are deified ancestors, Yoruba people who were elevated after death. Some students of Voudun compare Olodumare and the Orisha to Christianity's relationship between God and the saints. It is a comparison that many Vodun practitioners resist.

Conclusion

African-derived religions is an umbrella term used to refer to various religions transplanted to the Americas and the Caribbean following the enslavement of Africans. Likewise, Santería and Vodun emerged as a reaction of the oppressed slaves to the religious and political domination of their colonial masters. In most African myths, there is an attempt to make moral sense of lived experience, and especially to account for suffering. To the Santería and Vodun practitioners, religious mythology plays a major role in adding logic and depth to the symbolic nature of their practices. African-derived religious ceremonies are a service to the spirits. The service is provided by the religious leaders. The role of a priest in various communities is part priest, part doctor, and part counselor. In the Bembé drum dance of the Santería community and Vodun Avalon dance, the ceremonies are used to communicate with ancestors and summon spirits. Devotees serve the spirits and the ancestors with offerings or sacrifices. The *orishas* demand services such as feasts, initiations, and purifying baths. *Ebo* or offerings of animals, fruits, and vegetables are given to the *orishas*. African-derived religions continue to face difficulties because of their practice of sacrifice. African-derived religions celebrate family, community, the blessings of life, and offer ways to understand the world and to deal with adversity.

One can argue that the unifying theme and focus of all these ADR is the relationship of the individual to the spirit world, the world of their ancestors, who have not gone to a better, distant place but are all around them. Spirits may manifest and control the powers of nature, have power over disease and illness, and be patrons of different occupations. People and spirits are bound together in a communal ceremony of music and dance in which a key element is the worship of the deities through veneration and feeding. In some rituals, the spirits manifest themselves by possessing their worshippers, and sometimes giving power and healing. The practice of these religions may be for the benefit of the group or community as is seen in Vodun and Santería. Many followers in ADR believe it is important to shed all vestiges of Christianity, while others are comfortable with a judicious synthesis of

Christianity and their traditional African religion. Arguably, practitioners utilize rituals and sacrifices not only to meet the demands and challenges in their mundane matters, but also to connect and maintain an epistemological and cultural relationship with their African heritage.

Notes

1. De la Torre, Miguel A. (2004). *Santeria: The Beliefs and Rituals of a Growing Religion in America*. Grand Rapids: Erdmans, p. 102.
2. Clark, Mary Ann. (2007). *Santeria: Correcting the Myths and Uncovering the Realities of a Growing Religion*. Greenwood Publishing Group.
3. Simpson, George. (1978). *Black Religions in the New World*. New York: Columbia University Press. http://science.jrank.org/pages/8037/Religion-African-Diaspora.html
4. Ibid.
5. Isichei Elizabeth. (2004). *The Religious Traditions of Africa:A History*. Praeger Publishers:Wesport, p. 299.
6. Ibid, p. 300.
7. Sigmund, Freud. (1964). *The Future of an Illusion*, trans. W. D. Robson-Scott, rev. James Strachey. Garden City, New York: Doubleday Anchor Books.
8. Turner, Victor. (1968). *The Drums of Affliction*, Oxford University Press, pp. 21–22.
9. Ibid, p. 21.
10. Ubruhe, J. O. (1996). *Traditional Sacrifice: A Key to the Heart of the Christian Message*. Journal for Theology in Southern Africa, 95, pp. 13–22.
11. Evans-Pritchard, E. (1956, 1970). *Nuer Religion*. Oxford: Clarendon Press, p. 273.
12. Ibid, p. 273.
13. Ibid, p. 450.
14. Ubruhe, *Traditional sacrifice*, p. 16.
15. Roland De Vaux, 1961: 447.
16. Mason, John. (2002). *African Religions in the Caribbean: Continuity and Change*. An unpublished paper presented at a forum Myths and Dreams: Exploring the Cultural Legacies of Florida and the Caribbean, p. 94.
17. Clark, *Santeria: Correcting the Myths*, p. 45.
18. Lugira, Aloysius. (2009). *World Religions: African Traditional Religion* House: New York, p. 74.
19. Murphy, Joseph. (1994). *Working the Spirit*. Boston: Beacon Press, p. 104.
20. De la Torre, *Santeria: The Beliefs and Rituals*. The significance of drumming to the Yoruba religion may be traced back to a legend that tells of a time when the Yoruba people were at war with their neighbors, the Congolese. The Yoruba approached Orunla for guidance, and he instructed them to make three drums and to play them prior to battle. The Congolese, who loved to dance, had the drums from afar and could not resist the urge to throw a party. Meanwhile, they had made themselves completely drunk, making it easy for the Yoruba to vanquish their enemies, p. 119.
21. Metraux, A. (1972). *Vodoo in Haiti*. New York: Shocken Books, pp. 176–77.
22. Ibid, p. 162.
23. Ibid, p. 163.
24. Ibid, p. 176.
25. Ibid, pp. 176–77.

26. Ibid, pp. 168–69.
27. De la Torre, *Santeria: The Beliefs and Rituals*, p. 130.
28. Ibid, p. 135.
29. Murphy, *Working the Spirit*, p. 111.
30. Mason, *African Religions in the Caribbean: Continuity and Change*, p. 4.
31. Ibid, p. 5.
32. Ibid, p. 5.
33. Canizares, R. (1993). *Walking with the Night*. Rochester, VT: Destiny Books, p. 31.
34. Sandoval, M. C. (1977). *Santeria: Afro-Cuban Concepts of Disease and Its Treatment in Miami*. Journal of Operational Psychiatry, p. 61.
35. Canizares, *Walking with the Night,* p. 33.
36. Perez y Mena Perez, Mena. (1991). *Speaking with the Dead: Development of Afro-Latin Religion among Puerto Ricans in the United States*. New York: AMS Press.
37. Brandon, George. (1993). *Santeria from Africa to the New World: The Dead Sell Memories.* Bloomington: Indiana University Press, pp. 107–14.
38. Canizares, *Walking with the Night,* p. 125.
39. Miller, R. (1994). *Santeria Faction Trying to Take Religion Mainstream.* Atlanta Journal and Constitution, 20 February, p. M6.
40. Omari, M. (1991). *Completing the Circle: Notes on African Art, Society and Religion in Ototunji, South Carolina*. African Arts 24, 3(July): pp. 66–75, 96; See also Hunt, C.M. (1979). *Oyotunji Village*. Washington, DC: University Press of America.
41. Lefever, Hary. "When the Saints Go Riding In: Santeria in Cuba and the United States." *Journal for the Scientific Study of Religion* Vol. 35, Issue 3 (September 1996), pp. 313–30.

Chapter 15

Socioreligious Agencies of Santería Religion in the United States of America

Robert Y. Owusu

Introduction

Quite a lot of literature, both in hard copy and electronic forms, on Santería religion is available. Cathy Smith has compiled annotated bibliography of primary and secondary sources to assist researchers interested in this religion in an article, "Santeria: The Way of the Saints."[1] David H. Brown in his notable work, *Santeria Enthroned*, has provided copious references on Santería that interested scholars and researchers will find very useful. Quite a number of studies done on Santería and its spirituality offer diverse views on this religion and its followers. For some, Santería is "syncretistic and pagan worship";[2] others label it as worship of demons or evil spirits, as "a dark contagious 'infection' or 'sore' on the Cuban body politic." A Cuban anthropologist and ethnologist, Fernando Oritz, for example, in his work, *Los Negros Brujos* (the Negroes are Witches) had this to say about the Africans and their religion: "[T]he black race has brought its superstitions, its sensuality, its impulsivity, in general its African psyche." In his estimation, the Cuban "low life" at the time was the making of the black race and "its superstitions, its organizations, its languages, its dances, etc." He called Santería *brujería* (Witchcraft) and described it as "socially negative in relation to the improvement of our society, totally immoral, contributes to retain the consciousness of the blacks deeply rooted in African barbarism." He also emphasized the "sexual corruption" of the "witches," detailing their "practice of polygamy, prostitution and pornography." As for the actual ritual and dances, Ortiz described them as "wild, vulgar and antisocial."[3]

Others, however, praise Santería for its indigenity and sociospiritual empowerment and liberation; as an icon of Cuban national culture and in the United States as a "mental healthcare system" for Cuban exiles; as a "site for ideological struggle and antihegemonic praxis"; as a "repository of Black Atlantic artistic traditions"; and as a "hero of a great constitutional battle over the 'free exercise of religion.'"[4] Some have studied Santería from judgmental perspectives, and even though such studies offer important criticisms, they, however, reveal an undeniable bias against it and thus undermine its authenticity and transformation prowess. One study laments that it is unfortunate Santarians have not been targeted as a lost community to be converted to Christianity. That study views Santería as a non-Christian tradition. Such is the interest that the religion of Santería evokes.

It has become a postmodern religious phenomenon, and Mary Pat Fisher in her *Living Religions (8th ed.)* lists Santería as one of the new religious movements, which does not fit into the normative traditional religions.[5] How did this religion of remote origin spread across the Americas? How was it developed and has been designated a new religious movement? Who were the carriers or agencies of the spread of this tradition and why? How attractive is this religion in relation to the dominant or normative religious traditions of the Americas, particularly the United States?

Nature of Santería Religion

Origin and Development of Santería

Santería is believed to be the best-known religion among the Afro-Cuban religions. Other influential Afro-Cuban traditional religions are Regla de Palo, Mayombe, the Abakuá, and Secret Society.[6] Enslaved Africans were brought to Cuba from Haiti in the early 1600s to replace the weak and diseased natives of Cuba. The successful endurance of this labor force led the Spaniards to seek more of the Africans to work on their plantations. In the nineteenth century, hundreds of thousands of men and women of the Yoruba people, from what are now Nigeria and Benin of West Africa, were brought to Cuba to work in the island's booming sugar industry. For about 350 years—from 1511 to 1886—this enslavement and forced labor continued until it was abolished in Cuba in 1886.[7] Harry Lefever argues that it was the enslaved Africans brought to Cuba in the nineteenth century from Southwestern Nigeria and the Bantu of Congo, rather than the earlier ones of the sixteenth century from Haiti, "who were the major carriers of the religious beliefs and practices that contributed to the development of the Santeria religion."[8] Of course, the major carriers were the Yorubas. These Yoruba people brought with them their African religion, the worship of *Olodumare*—the Supreme, High God—manifested in lesser gods or spirits called *orishas*. For instance, *Obatala*—meaning "king of white cloth"—is the *orisha* that was entrusted by Olodumare with the creation of the human being; *Ogun* is god of iron, and *Shango* represents fire, thunder, and lightning. As the practice was in those days, the enslaved Africans were not allowed to assert their culture or their religion. As a result, the religion became secretive. The followers, mostly of the poor lower class were persecuted by their slave masters. The media also misrepresented the faith and embarrassed the practioners.[9] For these and other reasons, it went underground, and since religion is a spiritual experience and a social fact that cannot be eliminated, the Africans found a way of living their religion and preserving its unique identity for over 500 years. The religion became attractive to and popular among the non-Yoruba enslaved people in Cuba, too.

The name "Santería," meaning "the way of the saints," is the most common Spanish word used to describe a religious practice that venerates the ancestors or the spirits of the tribe referred to as *orisha*.[10] Santería is also referred to as *Iyalocha* and *Manalocha*, which is a reference to the priestess of the religion. This is an indication of the role that women play in Santería. The terms "santero" (masculine) and "santera" (feminine) refer to the initiated devotee. Later, initiated generations of santeros and santeras would construct elaborate systems of correspondences between *orishas* and saints. According to Harry Lefever, Santería emerged as a new form of religious tradition due to the encounter between the Yoruba religion of Orisha, Roman Catholicism, and French spiritism.[11] Thus, Santería developed from these three sources. In effect, the religion's devotion to the *orishas* was expressed through the iconography of Roman Catholic saints, leading observers to see this Yoruba religion as a model for understanding religious syncretism and cultural change.[12] Despite the numerous faces of Catholic symbols in Santería rites and the attendance of santeros and santeras at Catholic sacraments, Santería is essentially a way that worship in African traditional religions has been drawn into a symbolic relationship with Roman Catholicism. Lawrence Levy, in his doctoral research paper, argues that "[t]here is no mixing of Catholic beliefs, only a use of Catholic symbolism to mask the African [religion], as a protective camouflage. And, Santería Saints, more properly called *orisha* can be propitiated, but never controlled."[13]

The *Orishas* are spirits or divinities that assist *Oludumare*, the all-powerful supreme God of the universe. The *Orishas* act as intermediaries between the people—worshippers—and the supreme deity. *Oludumare*, unlike the Judeo-Christian and Islamic God, is far removed from the day-to-day business of the world and has entrusted these affairs to the intermediary spirits. Initially, there were as many as 400 *orishas*, and some put the number in thousands,[14] serving both the interests of *Oludumare* and the needs of the community or tribe. In the course of time, the number of *orisha* went down to sixteen and, today, it is believed to be only seven, now referred to as the Seven African spirits or powers.[15] Each *orisha* is unique from the others. Raul Canizares lists the Seven *Orishas* as (1) *Obatala*—son of *Oludumare*, creator of humankind, highest among the *orishas* and typically associated with white cloth; (2) *Shango*—Orisha of thunder, lightning, and fire and known as the warrior and healer; (3) *Ogun*—Orisha of the mountains, minerals, and tools, who paves the way for humans and is associated with the colors of green and black; (4) *Orula*—advises humans, tells fortunes, and interprets events in the community; (5) *Yemaya*—Orisha of the sea, mother of all Orishas, and the extinguisher of the fires used in the creation of the earth; (6) *Oshun*—Orisha of love and all things feminine, who protects pregnant mothers and is associated with the color of yellow and all things of beauty; and (7) *Eleggua-Eshu*—two Orishas bound together, deals with issues of humanity and how to overcome them, and is the first Orisha that people must go through to contact the others.[16]

Each *orisha* is unique from the others and are not strictly speaking hierarchical in structure, although some, like *Obatala* and *Yemaya*, appear to occupy positions of prestige. In addition, it appeared that some *orishas* were more powerful or had more authority than others; hence, the number of *orishas* has declined from thousands to only a few saints. This suggests that some *orishas* were discarded, or their roles and jurisdiction incorporated into that of the more powerful ones. What are the *orishas'* counterparts in the Roman Catholic sainthood? Cathy Smith says, Santerianism developed a system of "equating each one of their *Orisha's* to a Catholic Saint in order to 'stay true' to their [Catholic] faith: *Elegba* (also *Eleggua*) became St. Anthony; *Ogun* became St. Peter; *Ochosi* was equated with St. Norbert; *Obatala* represented Our Lady of Mercy; *Babalu Aye* became St. Lazarus; *Orula (also Orunmila)* represented St. Francis of Assisi; the ultimate supreme god *Ororon (also Oludumare)* was equated with Jesus Christ and so on."[17] As mentioned above, each *orisha* controls an aspect of nature and human life. The religion has a strong social, supportive system and what anthropologists would call "magical" aspects. In reality, Santería is a religion of life.

Adherents

Santerians can be found in many countries associated with Afro-Cuban and Afro-Asiatic cultures such as Cuba, Argentina, Brazil, Colombia, Mexico, France, the Netherlands, Caribbean countries, and the United States. Santería is growing rapidly in the United States because of the rapid growth of the Latino population. It is now seen in the urban areas of Miami, Tampa, New York City, Atlanta, Savannah (Georgia), Detroit, Chicago, Philadelphia, many cities of California, and other unnamed urban places. Santerianism has also spread among the African American population in an effort to reclaim lost ethnic identity. It is also widely practiced in Puerto Rico, and there are practitioners in other Latin American countries including Panama, Venezuela, and Mexico. In addition, many non-Cuban, non-Puerto Rican Hispanics have also embraced Santería.[18] The devotees are mostly secretive and would not easily disclose that they are in the religion. For instance, in the Cuban American population, it is not certain how many of them practice a form of Santería because many of those who might use the services of a santero as folk therapist identify themselves as Catholic and do not identify themselves as being part of the religion of Santería. In addition, there are many levels of affiliation to Santería. Someone might be initiated or might simply have undergone the ceremony to receive what are called *collares* (beads), or Warriors. Some people are merely clients who go to the santero for divination when a crisis arises in their lives and have no interest in Santería as a religion. These people do not identify as being part of Santería and are most likely to identify as being Catholic.[19] It is also not known how many people are in Santería from the black non-Hispanic population. In all, it was estimated as of 1994 that there was at least 500,000 members, but that number, it is believed, has skyrocketed by now with the boom in the Latino population, and some say they number in the millions.[20]

African Americans, who were disenchanted with the predominant white socioreligious culture of North America, saw the religion of Santería as a way to getting back to their African roots. According to H. G. Lefever, one of the first documented cases of a non-Hispanic African American initiated as a santero was Walter King. King grew up a Baptist, but in his teens turned his attention to what he called the "Gods of Africa." He became acquainted with voodoo in Haiti at the age of 26. Then, he travelled to Africa—to the Yorubaland and Ghana—and upon his return founded the Order of Damballah Hwedo Ancestor Priests of Harlem. In 1969, King travelled to Cuba where he was initiated or consecrated as a Santerian priest. A year later, he changed his name to Oba Efuntola Nana Oseijerman Adelabu Adefunmi I. King was popularly called Nana Oseijerman, perhaps a misspelling of the name of a great Asante King, Nana Osei Agyemang (Prempeh) I. He founded the Shango (fire) Temple in Harlem and later changed the name to Yoruba Temple.[21]

In the 1960s, Adefunmi became active in the black power movement. He interpreted Santería as a form of Black Nationalism and Pan-Africanism. This political interpretation of Santería put him at odds with other leaders of Santería, particularly the Cuban priests. In 1970, he founded the Yoruba Village of Oyotunji at Sheldon in South Carolina, where he and his dwindled followers lived until he died in 2005.[22]

The black population was not the only racial group to take up Santería. The Anglo Americans were also fascinated with Santería. One of the first cases of Anglo American Santera was Judith Gleason, an anthropologist, who became attracted to the religion while researching Candomblé in Brazil. Candomblé is an African-Brazilian religion that acknowledges the belief in one all-powerful God called Oludumare who is served by lesser deities.[23] The increased number of white followers of Santería is reflected in the make-up of the leadership. There are now more upper- and middle-class white santeros and santeras in the American Cuban community. For example, in Miami, Babalawo Carlos Ojeda and other two leading santeros, Ernesto Pichardo and Cecilio Perez, are white.[24] The increasing number of diverse people groups joining Santería has resulted in changes in the structure of the faith with the santeros taking more priestly functions and reducing the powers or roles of the *Babalawos*, the fathers or masters of the faith.

Beliefs and Rituals

The purpose of Santería, like other religions of Africa, is "to assist the individual regardless of their religious background or affiliation, to have harmony with their assigned destiny by ensuring they possess the necessary rituals to navigate life's difficulties."[25] The root cause of the human problem is spiritual disharmony. The physical world emerged out of the unseen spiritual world. Therefore, spiritual disharmony occurs when there is imbalance between the physical and the spiritual realms. Santerians believe that there are essentially four elements of physical existence: (1) Air (fresh air) resolves ethical dilemmas for spiritual growth; (2) Fire, which burns spiritual impurities making way for spiritual transformation; (3) Water, which cleanses or washes away dirt and bad or evil energy—fresh water symbolizes fertility, salt water as the maternal of all life, and stagnant water for spiritual death, which is prerequisite for new life; and (4) Earth, which provides resources and nourishment for survival.[26]

The religious tradition of Santería is having a hard time being understood by mainstream America. Worship in Santería is quite complex and involves incantations, spirit or trance-possession, visions, and animal sacrifice, mostly chickens. The rituals carried out in Santería are not common to the modern Western world. One such ritual is that of animal sacrifice. In sacrifice, natural and human-made items are offered to the deity as expiation (to atone for wrongdoing or appease the divine), propitiation (to be favorably inclined, to seek divine favor), or thanksgiving (for favors received). In some cases, animal sacrifice is involved. In such circumstances, specific animals are offered to each saint or *orisha*. For instance, the *orisha* called *Oshun* needs a sacrifice of a female white hen, goat, or sheep.

In spiritual cleansing or healing, it is believed that "such animals absorb the problems and negative vibrations of the person being cleansed. In such cases, the animal carcass is disposed of without being eaten." Except for spiritual cleansing, the meat of the sacrificed animal is eaten. It need not be mentioned here of the many controversies associated with the religion's ritual of animal sacrifice in the United States. One vivid example was the legal suit pursued by the Church of the Lukumi Babalu Aye of Harlea in Florida in the early 1990s to assert its constitutional right to practice its ritual of animal sacrifice. The church won the case. Much importance has been placed on the statement of Justice Anthony Kennedy who states, "Although the practice of animal sacrifice may seem abhorrent to some, religious belief need not be acceptable, logical, consistent, or comprehensible to others in order to merit First Amendment protection." The decision of the Supreme Court helped to shred the cloud of acrimony associated with the religion and bring it to the public domain.

Divination is another major ritual in Santería. What roles do mediums or diviners play in the ritualistic structure? Mediums or diviners, as they are called, are links between the living (adherents) and the spirit-world, providing the presence of the latter to the former, and mediating or interceding on behalf of the former (the follower). The process or the ritual involved is what is termed "divination." Divination involves prediction, having eyes to see and interpret physical and spiritual events to the satisfaction of the seeker. Some call the practice magic. The medium can go into trance-possession, perform incantation, do sacred dance, read objects, perform sacrifice, settle disputes (peace-broker), mete out punishment, and perform many other spiritual and social functions. As explained in French spiritism that has influenced this religion, the greatest role of the diviner is to assist the spirit of the dead to attain release (light) and to aid the living to obtain total well-being.

Santería in the United States

Let me reference Lawrence Levy who contends that "there seems to have been Santeros in the United States as early as the 1930s and 40s in various Florida cities where there were communities of Cubans." There seems also to be botanicas in New York City and Santeros from Puerto Rico (Puerto Rico had once been part of Cuba and has a similar ethnic composition to Cuba) since the 1960s, but "the great upsurge in the presence of Santería in the United States occurred after the Mariel Boatlift in the early 1980's." The Mariel boatlift was a mass exodus of Cubans who departed from Cuba's Mariel Harbor for the United States between April 15 and October 31, 1980. The previous large immigration of Cubans occurred in the early 1960s "as a result of Castro's Revolution and his subsequent embrace of Marxist policies." That group of immigrants tended to be middle class, white, and Catholic. The immigrants who left Cuba because of the Mariel boatlift tended to be poor and Afro-Cuban. Santería was more widely practiced among that population than among the middle-class immigrants of the early 1960s. According to Levy, it was because of this that there was an increase in the practice and presence of Santería in the United States. [27]

Adaption

Today, Santería has adapted to the popular culture of the United States, and the open culture of the United States has been instrumental in moving the secrecy of Santería into the open. For example, when the religion pursued court cases to assert its right to offer animal sacrifice, the court proceedings brought much attention to Santería as the mass and electronic media rolled out their cameras, chased, and quizzed Santerians for more information on the faith. In that course of action, aspects of its beliefs and practices were shared with the public. Such publicity and inquiry might have contributed to some practices that were changed, transformed, or stopped and made it to conform more to the traditional religious perspectives and practices of mainstream American religions. Catholicism's encounter with the religions and cultures of the enslaved Africans was different from that of the Protestant Christianity of the United States. In the United States, the Caribbean, Brazil, and other parts of Latin America, the culture, religion, and language of the Africans was systematically attacked. Catholicism, however, tended to allow for a greater degree of syncretism than did North American Protestantism. For that reason, African religion tended to survive, albeit in variously modified forms in Brazil as Candomblé, in Haiti as Vodou (Voodoo), Trinidad as Shango, and in Cuba as Santería.

In the United States, African religion has survived in less recognizable forms as Hoodoo and as the various spiritual churches and in New Orleans as Voodoo.[28] This is not to suggest that Santería has lost all its uniqueness as a religious entity in its own terms. In fact, Melville Herskovits has rightly asserted that African culture and African ways of thinking had survived in an influential way in the United States.[29] David Brown echoed this sentiment when he argued,

> The creative choices of self-conscious leaders and their dedicated constituencies have made possible the emergence, growth, and resilience of Afro-Cuban religions in Cuba and the United States despite relentless official efforts to coopt, control and destroy them. The Afro-Cuban religions today owe their existence to a history of gains from hard-won struggles, not passive "survival", where their resilience is owed as much to innovative transformations wrought on New World soil as to the maintenance or preservation of "pure" African traditions.[30]

Also, the exposure of Santería through such publicity drew public attention to its benefit, which convinced some people that their needs could also be met by this religion.

Moreover, in the United States, Santería has acquired a new phase in the mental healthcare system as it deals with the trauma of exilic life of the "Cuban exile community." Cubans and Latin Americans, like other immigrants from developing countries who arrive in the United States, often face a profound family crisis based on three sources of stress: first, between parents and their children, many of whom adopt the cultural behavior and values of a more open and permissive US society; second, between husbands and wives, especially when the wives enter the labor force and begin contributing to the family income, thus becoming more independent; and third, internally, for fathers who are required to make a living at low-income/low-status jobs, because they either lost their businesses and/or cannot in the short term continue to work in the prestigious professions such as law, medicine, etc. that they once practiced in their country of origin. Incidentally, many of these people do not have access to the mental healthcare system of their new "home." There are those who fall on prayers to deal with their stress, while others seek the intervention of spiritualists like Santerian priests or padrinos and madrinas. Santerian ritual of healing that treats the individual as a unified whole—mind, body, and soul—and as a person-in-community—harmony within the family—provides resources in the form of mediation, counseling, divination/oracle, and by fulfilling certain moral demands. As in the yoga system that helps to discipline the mind and bring the body and mind to conform to the natural order (dharma), so also Santerian psycho-spiritual rituals seek to align the distressed person to be in harmony with the natural order—that is, spiritual and physical balance. Chaotic situations are unbalanced situations leading to an unbalanced life that needs to be corrected. Santería charms or magical prowess are sought to avert spiritual and social mishaps. Santería is seen as an alternative source of medical treatment. It is not in competition with or against modern medicine. We need to remember that Santería pulls together polarities. In Santerianism, acquisition of spiritual energy requires the use of both the negative and positive. Even dichotomies or conflicting elements within the divine realm are all useful and need to be pulled together.

Santería as a healing religion has the means of decreasing uncertainty and stress by providing meaning to one's illness. Even though the illness might still be treated medically, Santería functions to give meaning to the causes of the illness. That is, the medical scientific reasons for illness are not denied. The question Santería seeks to answer, according to Pasquali as cited by Levy, is "why does this person succumb to this microbe at this time? If the microbe is in the environment, why should one person become ill and not another?" The spiritual explanation given sees the microbe as the means or device of a spiritual force. Once the spiritual or malignant supernatural is cleaned, or once balance is reinstated, then the medications become more effective. Santería then is "a complimentary therapy" used by practitioners alongside standard conventional medicine.[31] However, some of the techniques used by santeros resembled techniques used in psychology, such as active listening, confrontation, homework assignments, interpretation, and support giving.[32]

Creolization of Santería

Creolization is another medium of spreading and communicating Santerian worldview and rites. What is creolization? Creolization has been described as a "complex dynamic of encounters, adaptations, assimilation, and syncretism."[33] Ortiz, who coined the term "transculturation" to describe the unique process of blending and merging of cultural influences and the creation of a new cultural identity deriving from this blend, says creolization, is "a mutual transformation of two or more preexisting cultures into a new one."[34] For others, creolization is the "malleability and mutability of various beliefs and practices as they adapt to new understanding of class, race, gender, power, labor, and sexuality."[35] It blends polarities—black-white, center-periphery, civilize-primitive, rural-urban, modern-primordial, present-past. Edouard Glissant is quoted saying that in creolization, "the relationship between the center and the periphery will be completely different. Everything will be central and everything will be peripheral."[36] Critics of this understanding, however, argue that "beside the broth of synthesis, there are bones, gristle, and hard seeds that never fully dissolve, even after they have contributed their substance to the broth. These un-dissolved ingredients are the survival and recreations of [new cultural] traditions within the religiocultural complexities."[37]

Creolization of Santería is often explained as a process of "borrowing" or "conversation" between cultures. For some, it is the strategic, unauthorized appropriation of symbols of power—religious or civil—that becomes empowering against their initial purpose.[38] On one hand, creolization appears to be a neutral or friendly process. On the other, it is not, but a conspicuous and deliberate effort, a subversive and innovative way, of using symbols and representations "with respect to ends and references foreign to the system [that a suppressed people] had no choice but to accept; their use of the dominant social order deflected its power, which they lacked the means to challenge. They escaped it without leaving it."[39] In this regard, one can speak of a dual creolization in Santerianism. First, one sees the efforts of the enslaved Africans in the new world, who are forbidden to practice their religion or culture, tactically appropriating the religious culture of the new world as an empowering strategy against the intended purpose of their masters. They allowed them to be directed by the currents of the stream of the new world culture, and to learn the bits and pieces that they can contextualize. And, second, such bits and pieces became a tool used by the freed slaves and their new non-African converts—who themselves have undergone colonialism—to recapture, relive, and reinforce their homeland (African) religiocultural practices.

If creolization occurs within a context of good neighborliness, a kind of friendly conversation or friendly engagement, that's a different thing and can be described as a harmonization of its different cultures; but if the environment or context is hostile, oppressive, and repressive, creolization becomes revolutionary—a radical way to disarm the initial purpose while empowering the subjugated culture at the same time. In each of these contexts—neutral-friendly versus hostile context—creolization creates new cultures or subcultures and new religions.

Iconography

One of the popular appeals in Santerianism is its iconography, which is an innovation of modern Santería that depicts history, mythology, and royalty—the colorful dress, accessories, and attributes that include, but are not limited to, the throne, crown, regalia, and handheld staff—and serves as prototype for the modern ensemble of *orisha* royal attributes.[40] Icons are symbols. Symbols either represent something (representational symbols) or present something (presentational symbol). Representational symbols *represent* things that are distinct; people become connected to their usage because of custom or habitual practice, and they are understood by their cultural context. Presentational symbols, however, are symbols that *participate in* or are *similar to* the thing they represent. They make the thing they symbolize present. They manifest or make present the sacred or the holy. Santería icons show both dimensions. Brown argues that in an analogous but redirected form of appropriation, the contemporary Santerian priests did "a transposition of their rich costume and prestige ceramics from their class position to the matter-spirit hierarchy where they came to signify the splendor, distinction, and wealth of the orishas."[41]

The Santerian *orishas* were iconographically portrayed as status equivalents (or maybe as rivals) of revered local Catholic virgins and saints. As in Roman Catholic iconography, the crown represents excellence or distinction, royalty, and victory or success, so also these Santos (*orishas*) are elaborated in Santería. For example, the Virgin Mary from the royal house of David is portrayed as the "Queen of Heaven." In Santerianism, the Virgin Regla is the one who presides over the Bay of Havana, the prototype of Yemaya—the Queen of Virgin and the Sea, who is identified with Mary. Enthroned *orishas* in their royal colorful apparel signify: (1) spiritual dignity, (2) sacred resources for the eternal protection of their children, the priests, and (3) victory over human problems. In Santerian iconography, Obatala, Yemaya, Chango (Shango), and Ochun are designated "The Four Pillars" or "The Four Cardinal Points," who together provide the spiritual resources that are basic to religious life.[42]

As a form of institutionalization and as a way to forestall the loss of the *orishas*, every initiate has the responsibility of "learning about, tending to, and transmitting the deep knowledge of a canonical set of interrelated *orishas*—a personal pantheon—whose interrelationships embodied the rankings and protocols of the pantheon as a whole."[43]

Santería and US Popular Culture

Afro-Cuban aesthetics that reflect popular conscious consumer choices that match today's popular culture were powerful media for the upward surge of Santerianism. Religious arts and artifacts are powerful symbolic expression and, as Clifford Geertz argues, they "act to establish powerful, pervasive, and long-lasting moods and motivations in men...by formulating conceptions of a general order of existence, and clothing these conceptions with such an aura of factuality that the moods and motivations seem uniquely realistic."[44] I will return to this later.

Mythology and legend are important sacred components in Santería. Religious mythology, which always keeps some important aspects of religion as "secrets" of which initiates have to be instructed, adds new expectations and aura to the faith, making seekers want to know what is "there." The aura surrounding the religion is kept intact, not exposing it to any destructive criticism or allowing it to be explained away. This secrecy has been able to heighten the mystery dimension of religious experience. Also, religious mythology adds logic and depth to the symbolic nature of the rituals. For instance, to understand the sacred story and deeds associated with the deities will enable the worshipper to perform the right sacrifice at the right time with the right elements, to use the right colors, do the right dance and drumming, and to sing the right songs. It must be underlined that these myths and legends are real and meaningful to the adherents. Thus, religious myths and legends sustain the drama in religion and the same can be said of Santería. Santería mythology includes numerology, a significant element with which members must be conversant. This is one of the reasons why initiates are required to know all the prominent *orishas* and their interrelationships—to keep the myth and legends alive since Santería is not a religion of book. There are Santería mythology greeting cards that members and seekers and the public can buy on the website of Fine Arts America.[45] These are also steps or practices that make the religion attractive to the general public. Once they are on the information superhighway—the worldwide web—they cannot be secretive anymore.

The initiation process and the role of the instructors or sponsors are crucial in Santerianism. This initiation ritual called *asiento,* meaning "ascending the throne," is believed to be the most secret and the most elaborate ritual of Santerianism. Here, credit goes to the "padrinos" and "madrinas"—godfathers and godmothers—who not only serve as consultants of the full-fledged practitioners but also are sponsors of new initiatives and are responsible for teaching the newcomers the "secrets" of the religion. Initiation takes quite a long time to complete so that the person who goes through it will be well grounded in the tradition. It can take a year or even five years or more depending upon the need and the level that the initiate wants to reach. This may account for the endurability of the religion as it becomes almost an impossible task to dissuade an initiate to abandon the faith. The ethical and moral teachings of Santería are transcultural and timeless thus indirectly endearing the religion to the general culture. The long process of initiation aided by the one-on-one mentoring offered by the padrinos and madrinas evokes a degree of importance to both the clients and the tradition and may account for the steady growth and strength of Santería.

Through the process, the initiate, called *iyawo,* receives the "new birth"—he or she is born again—dies to the old self, and is resurrected to a new life which the *iyawo* can "unite his consciousness with his god."[46] The *initiate* then becomes the "son" or "wife" of the *orisha.* Symbolically, it means a very close spiritual bond is formed between him/her and the *orisha.* This is the beginning of a path of maturation in the new faith—a process that involves learning the secrets and rites of their gods and "how to speak through the oracles."

Oracles are forms of divination that seek to reestablish "the proper balance between the physical and the spiritual as well as between good and evil."[47] Oracles become attractive to many seekers. Like the attraction of dharmic religions of the East to Westerners, Santerian world view and concepts of an integrated whole between the physical and the spiritual, even between good and evil, elicit more studies in the Western world, particularly in America. People by nature want to know the unknown. In such a situation, questions such as how a person becomes aware of the area of imbalance in her life shift from a mere philosophical specula-tion to existential concern. Recently, I invited a guest preacher to my church. After preaching, he laid hands on people and prayed for them. The next day, an African American family of three came to him to be prayed for. After the prayers and during a counsel session, the older lady asked the preacher what the spirit had revealed to him regarding her fiancée, and she wanted to know whether it was good to marry him or not. Many worshippers do seek divine revelation and will follow those who claim to have an ear to hear spiritual voices and an eye to see spiritual things. Oracles are used to meet the needs of an individual and community, but not for national theatrical spectacle.

Another agency is Fe Lekumi, a nonprofit social movement for change. This movement embodies the social philosophies of Santería and is found in Rhode Island, but its board members hail from New York, Massachusetts, Connecticut, and Florida. The movement is expected to thrive throughout the United States. The Providence branch of the organization describes itself as an agency that seeks to empower the youth and is dedicated to social growth and advancement. Their key activities include cultural dance and art, which also attracts tourism.

Furthermore, Mercedes C. Sandoval suggests that Santería's own intrinsic value, which includes its "flexibility, eclecticism and heterogeneity," has worked to its advantage allowing "functional, dogmatic and ritual changes [enabling] it to meet the different needs of its many followers." Without denying the usefulness and effec-tiveness of modern health institutions in meeting physical health and psychological needs, Santería continues to seek in adaptive ways approaches to balance those needs by spiritual means. It sees no conflict in this. The either-or dichotomy between modern science and some religious traditions, like Western Christianity, is not a problem for Santerians since it seeks to harmonize the two. The physical/material and the spiritual must work together to produce an integrated whole.[48]

As a healing religion, Santería provides that kind of healing that engages the whole person, the person and his or her community, and with his or her natural envi-ronment. As a belief system, Santería demands complete devotion of the heart from its adherents. Seekers of spiritual and material help must demonstrate a heart com-mitment demonstrated by concrete actions or behavior in order to receive positive response from the *orishas*. Where there is such commitment, a devotee, on one hand, will be very careful not to reveal the "secrets," and, on the other, will be passion-ate, strong, persuasive, and unyielding in terms of proselytizing. Devotion implies a giving of one's substance to making more disciples for the faith. The Jehovah's Witnesses and the Mormons are examples of this kind of devotion. We know that a religion that has the majority of its followers highly committed, devoted, and moti-vated rarely perishes. Such is the attitude of most members of Santería. It is believed that there are about 60 botanicas that cater to the needs of the followers of Santería in the greater Miami area alone.[49]

Music, drumming, and aesthetic conventions have carried Santería throughout the centuries and are instrumental in transforming Santería in the United States. "The religious practices of the Yoruba," says Uzoma Miller, "revolves around music and dance." The gods are celebrated with music, drumming, and dancing during such feasts like Bembé and Guiro.[50] Music, drumming, and dancing have spiritual efficacy as well as a sociopolitical message that evoke strengths for resistance and change. They educate the mind and soul, reduce stress, and provide entertainment that solidifies their ethnolinguistic and cultural ties. For the African, music is life. Subcultures have grown out of music like the self-organized social clubs (cabildos). According to Brown, the cabildo system provided the new social structure for the "recreation of discrete neo-African social groupings" and acted as "generative bases or 'incubating cells' for the regathering of specialized bodies of knowledge and intergenerational transmission of African based religious cultures."[51] In effect, the cabildos with their royalties served as the bedrock of modern Santerian culture.

Also, music transforms culture, and by it, Santería as a religiocultural phenomenon has acquired a new outlook in its festivities. For instance, the Cuban "son"—Son cubano; "son" means sound—music and its accoutrement, believed to be one of the most influential and widespread forms of Latin American music, can be viewed as "a stylistically pivotal genre linking the culture of the Afro-Cuban underclasses with that of the mainstream society."[52] Son itself encountered other Western music genres and blended with them. Although the Son music in its traditional style is seldom heard, it has assimilated into and is present in other Latin styles of music such as the salsa. A Santerian priest and singer of spirituals, Lazaros Ros, sums it up for us: "Whether it is cha-cha-cha, rumba, son, mambo or contemporary pop, all Cuban music is an expression of the same spiritual tradition... It's something that, somehow or other, is rooted in your soul and you cannot neglect."[53]

Street festival is another form of social engagement that has popularized Santería. Some Santerian festivals like Bembé, Toque de Santo, and Guiro began to be celebrated in the street in areas with high density of Cuban, Afro-Cuban, and Latino concentration. Thus, Santería as a cultural system—its music, food, norms and manners, clothing, celebrations, spirituality and politics, icons, and progenitors—engaged in what Brown has described as "a consciously motivated process of cultural conservation, transformation and innovation that found diverse outlets in a range of expressive arts and street festivals."[54] Such festivals not only serve as tourist attractions but also empower the ordinary folks giving rise to what Brown calls "street aristocracy."[55] Jose Sueiro, a scholar of Santería, says, "Santeria is not exclusively religious, rather it's a mix of spiritual practices, culture, music, and dance.[56]

Now, a word on tourism: a Reuter report says that Santería divination and oracle rituals as well as its festivities—music, drumming, and dance—have become big business in Havana and areas in the United States where Santería is practiced. A Santerian priest in Cuba, according to the report, confirms that he sees at least, "seven or eight foreigners a week. Germans, Mexicans, Italians, Americans," and "quite a few come off the cruise ship," he added. A client could pay as much as $250.00 to $500.00 to receive an oracle, or as much as $1,000.00 as initiation fee for the foreigner. Ordinary good-luck charms like gravel-filled gourds or plastic bead bracelets that a local client will buy for a few cents or pesos, a foreigner might spend $50 on it and $20.00 to meet a priest.[57] Santería's influence on tourism is not all about money. Some people visit for spiritual help, which they believe they receive, and some also for the festivities and entertainment. The tourist industry has also contributed to the expansion and transformation, to some extent, of the religion, making it transnational and giving it economic boost.

Conclusion

Santería's ability to adapt to its new environment and the encountered religion and mysticism—Roman Catholicism and French spiritism—may account not only for its survival in the new world but also for becoming attractive and relevant to the contemporary socioreligious culture. Thus, Roman Catholic symbols and icons became religious agents of Santería. Santería did not merely rename its *orishas* after the Catholic saints, but were able to recognize the essential identity of those Catholic saints and gave them their equivalent or preferably rivals in accordance with their own indigenous tradition. Thus, transculturation or creolization became a useful tool in the process. By this process, the ancient religion have retained its core identity and, at the same time, been able to embrace modernity or the post-modern climate.

Furthermore, Santería is a religion of life. It is about action here and now—that which can make something happen for the benefit of the adherent. It deals with practical life, not focusing on polarities but mediating opposites such as good and bad, spirit and matter, material and spiritual, natural and supernatural, the past and present and future.

There is also relative egalitarianism in Santería, making it attractive to women in general, and those in the priesthood in particular. In Santería, female deities are as powerful as male deities—a reflection on the original culture of Yoruba matri-archal power and role. In *Yoruba* culture, like the Akan culture, there was an even wider space and hierarchal role to women, and it was the Spanish rulers and the Catholic Church that limited those roles and spaces within the culture and the reli-gion. Santerianism is a "religion from below" but does not stay as such permanently as it has provided upward mobility for its downtrodden rural members. Today, as discussed above, Santerians are of diverse social classes—with the majority of them coming from the urban middle-class population.

It has also been argued that music, art, and the social media have contributed immensely to the survival and transformation of Santería. Its music genius has con-tributed to the modern music such as salsa, mambo, or contemporary pop and its festivals like *Bembé* is now part of the mainstream culture. Let me end with this quote cited above, "Whether it is cha-cha-cha, rumba, *son,* mambo or contempo-rary pop, all Cuban music is an expression of the same spiritual tradition...It's something that, somehow or other, is rooted in your soul and you cannot neglect." With online Santería botanicas that many devotees and nondevotees patronize, with sacred gardens into which one is invited to walk in quiet communion with nature, with Santería in Hollywood, and with the postmodern worldview of identity shift, exchange, and intercommunication, one cannot deny the popularity and role of this sociocultural and religious tradition in the American religiocultural life.

Notes

1. Smith, Cathy. *Santeria: The Way of the Saints*, at http://home.wlu.edu/~lubint/touch-stone/Santeria-Smith.htm.
2. Ibid, p. 1.
3. Brown, David H. (2003). *Santeria Enthroned: Art, Ritual, and Innovation in an Afro-Cuban Religion*. Chicago, IL: University of Chicago Press, p. 5. Brown quoted Lauren Derby's unpublished research work on Afro-Cuban cultures (1995) and Fernando Ortiz, *Los Negros Brujos* (1973[1906]: pp. 19, 227). Ortiz later in his life denounced all kinds of racism and xenophobia and called for full integration of whites and blacks in Cuba, and for the eradication of all discrimination. He exposed Afro-Cuban music and culture to white Cubans in a time when both cultures were completely segregated and has allegedly coined the term "Afro-Cuban." Ortiz rejected the term acculturation, which indicates assimilation and a cultural "take over."
4. Ibid. *See also* Murphy, Joseph M. (1987). "Santeria." In *Encyclopedia of Religion, vol.13*, ed. Mircea Eliade. New York: McMillan, p. 66.
5. Fisher, Mary Pat. (2011). *Living Religions, 8th ed.* Upper Saddle River, NJ: Pearson, pp. 478–79.
6. Rutz, Vicki L. and Virginia Sanchez Korrol, eds. *Latina in the United States: A Historical Encyclopedia, vol. 1*. Bloomington: Indiana University Press, 2006, p. 699.
7. Lefever, Harry G. (1996, September). "When the Saints Go Ride in: Santeria in Cuba and the United States," *Journal for the Scientific Study of Religion*, vol. 35, no. 3, p. 319.
8. Ibid, p. 320.
9. Rutz and Korrol, *Latina in the United States*, p. 207.
10. Murphy, "Santeria," p. 66.
11. Lefever, "When the Saints Go Ride in," p. 319. French spiritism involves the belief that spirit beings exist in hierarchical structure and are seeking enlightenment after their bodily existence. Through the efforts of a medium, a spirit can receive light and once enlightened can ascend to the next spiritual level..
12. Murphy, "Santeria," p. 66.
13. Levy, Lawrence J. (2000). "A Study of Divination within Santería," p. 10. An Afro-Cuban Religion, as a Psychotherapeutic System," Unpublished Research Paper Submitted in Partial Satisfaction of the Requirements for the degree of Doctor of Psychology (Nova Southeastern University, Center for Psychological Studies, p. 23, 26. This author did a participant-observer study and was initiated as santero for five years.
14. Compare Mary Ann Clark's "Santeria," in Zellner, William W., ed. *Sects, Cults, and Spiritual Communities: A Sociological Analysis*, p. 119, with Lefever's "When the Saints Go Ride in," p. 319.
15. Canizares, Raul. (1993, 1999). *Cuban Santeria: Walking with the Night*. Rochester, VT: Destiny Books, pp. 31–33.
16. Ibid.
17. Smith, "Santeria," p. 3.

18. Levy, "A Study of Divination within Santería," p. 10.
19. Ibid, p. 11.
20. Lefever, "When the Saints Go Ride in," p. 319.
21. Ibid, p. 321.
22. Ibid.
23. BBC, "Religions: Candomblé" at http://www.bbc.co.uk/religion/religions/candomble/beliefs/beliefs.shtml. Accessed, May 24, 2011.
24. Canizares, *Cuban Santeria*, p. 137.
25. De La Torre, Miguel A. (2004). *Santeria: The Beliefs and Rituals of a Growing Religion in America.* Grand Rapids, MI: Erdmans, p. 4.
26. Ibid, p. 5.
27. Levy, "A Study of Divination within Santeria," p. 14.
28. Lawrence, "A Study of Divination within Santeria," p. 13.
29. Herskovits, Melville J. (1937, 1966). "African Gods and Catholic Saints in the New World Negro Belief." In *The New World Negro: Selected Papers in Afroamerican Studies*, ed. Francis S. Herskovits. Bloomington: Indiana University Press, cited in Brown, *Santeria Enthroned*, p. 45.
30. Brown, *Santeria Enthroned*, pp. 5–6.
31. Level, "A Study of Divination within Santeria," p. 19.
32. Ibid, p. 24.
33. Olmos, Margarite Fernandez and Paravisini-Gebert, Elizabeth. *Creole Religion of the Caribbean: An Introduction from Vodou and Santeria to Obeah and Espiritismo.* New York: New York University Press, 2003, p. 3.
34. Ibid, p. 4.
35. Ibid.
36. Ibid, p. 7.
37. Mosquera, Geraldo. (1992, Winter). "África in the Art of Latin America," *Art Journal* (5)4, pp. 30–38.
38. Romberg, Raquel. "Revisiting Creolization" from the School of Arts and Sciences Conference Archives, p. 1, University of Pennsylvania. (Accessed: July 2011).
39. de Certeau, Michel. (1984). *The Practice of the Everyday.* Berkeley: University of California, p. xiii, cited in "Revisiting Creolization," p. 1.
40. Brown, *Santeria Enthroned*, p. 216.
41. Ibid.
42. Ibid, p. 214.
43. Ibid, p. 132.
44. Geertz, Clifford. (1966). "Religion as a Cultural System." In Michael Banton (ed.) *Anthropological Approaches to the Study of Religion.* London: Tavistock, p. 4.
45. Fine Art America, "Santeria Mythology Greeting Cards," at fineartamerica.com/art/all/santeria/greeting+cards.
46. De La Torre, *Santeria*, p. 112.
47. Ibid, p. 139.
48. Mercedes C. Sandoval, "Santeria as a Mental Health Care System: An Historical Overview." Available online June 20, 2002.
49. Cuban Information Archives, Document 0337: *Afro-Caribbean Religions* at http://cuban-exile.com/doc_326-350/doc0338.html. This is a yearly report by the Miami-Dade police Department (March 1995). One will also find a number of photographs on Santeria.
50. "Santeria's Convergence of Music, Dance and Spirituality: Historical Note," September 23, 2002, p. 2.

51. Brown, *Santeria Enthroned*, p. 34.

52. *Son* (music): Wikipedia.org.

53. Lazaros, Ros. (1993). "Spreading the Gospel of Afro-Cuban Music: Pop music: Santerian priest, Lazaros Ros performs this weekend in LA," an article in LA Times, December 17, 1993, 1. Accessed at http://articles.latimes.com/1993-12-17/entertainment/ca-2899_1_cuban-music

54. Brown, *Santeria Enthroned*, p. 112.

55. Ibid.

56. Jose Sueiro quoted by Benjamin Koconis in "Santeria Lives on in the District," a report on a Santerian workshop held in Washington DC on June 26, 2010. See www.washingtoninformer.com/index.php?option=com_content&view=article&id=40...Accessed on March 8, 2011.

57. "Santeria lures tourist cash to Cuba," Reuters (May 7, 2007) at http://www.reuters.com/article/2007/05/07/us-cuba-santeria-idUSN2936782720070507?pageNumber=1

Chapter 16

Modern Legal Issues in the Practice of African Diaspora Religions

Danielle N. Boaz

Introduction

The legal issues faced by practitioners of African and African diaspora religions can be situated within three paradigms. First, legislators, police, and animal rights activists throughout the world have sought to limit the use of animal sacrifice, a practice that is central to many African and African diaspora religions. Second, many African and African diaspora religious practitioners believe that physical sickness and social misfortune are attributable to supernatural causes. Mental health professionals have argued that these beliefs are indicators of psychological disorders, and their testimony has been offered as evidence in various kinds of insanity proceedings to show the irrationality of such beliefs. Third, negative public perceptions of these religions have resulted in nonpractitioners claiming slander and discrimination when they are associated with the practice of African and African diaspora religion. Through a comparative look at the United States, Southern Africa, and the British Caribbean, this chapter will explore these aspects of the relationship between religion and the law.

Animal Sacrifice

Animal sacrifice refers to the ritual offering of an animal to a spirit or deity, typically to request some service in return, such as healing or protection. Animal sacrifice is a central practice in many African and African diaspora religions. For instance, in Haitian Vodou and Cuban Santería, animal sacrifices are offered to the spirits/deities known respectively as the *lwa* and the *orisha*.[1] Practitioners of these religions believe that sacrifice is a way of giving life, energy, and nourishment to the *orisha* and *lwa*. It is a critical part of the reciprocal relationship of mutual benefit between the practitioner and the spirit/deity.[2]

Although scholars have confirmed that animal sacrifice was once a feature of religious rituals in virtually every part of the world, such practices are highly contested today.[3] It is not merely the killing of animals for blood offerings, like those of Vodou, Santería, Hinduism, and African indigenous religions, that have become problematic. Religions like Judaism that require certain methods of killing and cleaning animals before consumption have also been challenged.

The twenty-first century has brought contentions over animal sacrifice and ritual slaughter to the forefront of the media and in courts across the globe. Generally, debates about these practices are a result of concerns for animal welfare weighed against religious and cultural rights of human beings and a concern for public health regarding the captivity, slaughter, and disposal of the animals. For instance, in 2000, a Jewish organization, Cha'are Shalom Ve Tsedek, brought a case to the European Court of Human Rights claiming that France had violated their right to freedom of religion because the government refused to approve them to conduct the slaughter of kosher animals.[4] The Court ruled against the Cha'are Shalom Ve Tsedek association, finding that they had options to obtain properly slaughtered animals from other organizations that met the strict requirements that this group believed in.[5]

The Netherlands has also sought to limit the kosher slaughter of animals. In June 2011, the lower house of Parliament passed a bill that would prohibit killing an animal without first stunning it.[6] Both Muslim and Jewish organizations recognized the limitations this would place on their religious practices, and they banned together to oppose the bill from becoming law.[7] Further, although legal action has not yet been taken, animal rights activists have campaigned heavily against the estimated 400,000 ritual sacrifices conducted at the festival for the goddess Gadhimai every five years in Nepal.[8]

Despite a long and widespread history of controversy surrounding animal sacrifice, African and African diaspora religions are probably most famous for the practice of animal sacrifice and prosecutions regarding ritual slaughter. The United States Supreme Court case, *Church of Lumuki Babalu Aye v. City of Hialeah*, was a pivotal ruling in First Amendment rights litigation and in determining the place of African-derived religions in the United States. This case was brought by a Santería/Lukumi church because the City of Hialeah passed a law restricting the slaughter of animals that specifically targeted the ritual sacrifices to prevent the Church from establishing a location in Hialeah.[9] The City claimed that it passed these ordinances to protect animals from unnecessary cruelty and to prevent animal carcasses from being disposed of improperly. The Supreme Court declared these aims a pretext, noting because food establishments were exempt from the ordinances, it was only religious sacrifices that were targeted.[10] Further, the law was worded so broadly that it did not merely further the goals that the City expressed of regulating the disposal of carcasses and caring for animals; it also outright prohibited the entire sacrifice.[11] In 1993, the Supreme Court held that Santería/Lukumi was a religion, and that lawmakers cannot purposely proscribe its practice.[12] However, despite this ruling, there have been efforts in many regions of the country to restrict animal sacrifice in recent years.

In 2006, Jose Merced, president of the Temple Yoruba Omo Orisha Texas Inc. and Santería priest, sued the city of Euless, Texas, because officials there informed him that the practice of animal sacrifice violated city ordinances.[13] These city ordinances made it unlawful to slaughter any animal, or to kill any bird within the city except for "domesticated fowl considered as general tableflare."[14] Like the Hialeah case, the city of Euless focused on the disposal of animal carcasses as a threat to public health, despite the fact there was no evidence that Merced had ever discarded animals in a manner that was unsanitary.[15] After two appeals, the Fifth Circuit Court ultimately held that the city ordinances placed a substantial burden on Merced's religious freedom and that the government did not have a compelling interest in prohibiting such practices.[16] Therefore, the Court found in favor of Merced.

Most recently, a New Jersey woman and two practitioners of another Afro-Cuban religion, Palo Mayombe, were arrested on charges of child endangering following a ceremony where a seven-year-old child watched the sacrifice of a chicken and was given the animal's heart to consume raw.[17] The child's mother was charged with second-degree child endangerment (maximum sentence of ten years imprisonment), and the two practitioners who were also present at the ritual were charged with third-degree child endangerment (maximum sentence of five years imprisonment).[18] The prosecutor argued that the ritual was unsanitary, as well as emotionally and physically dangerous to the child.[19] In January 2011, a judge denied the defense counsel's motion to dismiss the charges on grounds that the prosecution violated their freedom of religion.[20] Ultimately, the practitioners entered into an agreement to serve one year of probation and the mother pled guilty to charges of child cruelty and neglect, for which she was sentenced to eighteen months probation.[21]

The African diaspora is not the only place that animal sacrifice has been restricted. In recent years, there has also been considerable controversy surrounding ritual sacrifices in South Africa. One of the most infamous involved Tony Yengeni, a South African politician and anti-apartheid activist. In 2007, Yengeni was released early from a four-year prison term, and he sacrificed a bull to honor his ancestors for this blessing.[22] This incident received an incredible amount of negative media attention throughout the world. One animal rights supporter compared this ritual sacrifice to cannibalism, slavery, and infanticide, claiming that these are all degrading and exploitative practices that need to be suppressed.[23] Further, just one year later, Kevin Behrens wrote a 58-page report about Yengeni's ritual slaughter to satisfy the requirements for his Master of Arts degree at the University of Witwatersrand in Johannesburg.[24] Behrens argued that a woman's right to not be killed, maimed, or abused in the name of culture should be extended to animals, meaning that animals' rights should not be violated in the name of cultural claims.[25]

Although Yengeni was only subject to criticism in the media due to his animal sacrifice, vehement concerns about animal rights turned into legal action in 2009.

In that year, Animal Rights Africa Trust filed a case to interdict King Goodwill Zwelithini Kabhekuzulu, monarch of the Province of KwaZulu-Natal, from slaughtering any bulls at the First Fruits Festival scheduled to be held at his palaces.[26] The First Fruits Festival is an annual celebration among the Zulu people, held in December or January when the new crops become ripe, as an observance of thanksgiving for the harvest.[27] The purpose of the animal sacrifice in this ceremony is that the participants believe that the people who kill the bull receive the bull's power. They then pass that power to the king so that he can use it to protect the kingdom. This ceremony has been practiced since time immemorial by the Zulu nation.[28]

To find an authority under which they could sue the King and obtain an injunction in civil court for practices that were not against the criminal laws of South Africa, Animal Rights Trust argued that allowing the sacrifices at the First Fruits Festival contravened South Africa's international obligations as a signatory of the Terrestrial Animal Health Code of the World Organisation for Animal Health.[29] They claimed that the sacrifice of the bull violated the Code because the slaughter was conducted in a manner that caused the animal undue stress. The Trust further argued that their own right to freedom of conscience, provided by the Constitution of South Africa, was violated because they sincerely believe that animals should be protected from harm by humans.[30]

On the other hand, the King of KwaZulu-Natal and other participants in the festival claimed their right to kill the bull as a part of their tradition. They argued that the significance of the festival was much more than the single act of the sacrifice of the bull; it was a month-long process where believers observe certain practices and perform certain rituals. They further contended that the way that the slaughter of the bull was depicted by the Trust was inaccurate. The bull was not kicked, beaten, or choked to death as the animal rights groups claimed. Instead, its neck was quickly broken in a way that caused no pain to the animal. The King's version of the sacrifice was documented by a well-known historian who had actually witnessed the First Fruits ceremony and the traditional method of killing the bull. The King's representatives claimed that the Trust's version of the sacrifice, which were not based on eyewitness testimony, were probably the result of "someone else's fanaticism to end ceremonial slaughter no matter how it is performed."[31]

The court found in favor of the Zulu nation largely because they were given last minute notice of the case and did not have time to prepare a proper response. As the Festival was quickly approaching, the court believed that the prejudice to the Zulu nation would have been very great if they were prevented from performing the sacrifices that year. Animal Rights Trust, on the other hand, was not merely seeking to protect the specific bull that would be killed at that year's festival and was still free to pursue injunctions of future sacrifices.[32]

As the preceding paragraphs clearly illustrate, ritual slaughter of animals has become a controversial issue in many parts of the world. Although the subject of cases, animal rights campaigns, and legislation is not always practitioners of African and African diaspora religions, the general atmosphere of antipathy toward ritual slaughter should be of great concern. The continued litigation of animal sacrifice cases nearly 20 years after the US Supreme Court decision in the City of Hialeah case illustrates that even a seemingly unambiguous ruling in favor of the practice will not prevent further challenges. Animal sacrifice is constantly being contested in new ways, as these cases involving child endangerment and international treaty obligations clearly demonstrate. It seems likely that the only way to reduce legal challenges to animal sacrifice is to increase public dialogue about the way that sacrifices are conducted, and their significance to religious practitioners. Perhaps allowing animal rights activists to witness the sacrifice could reduce campaigns that are based on misinformation about the cruelty and brutality of the rituals and analogizing ritual slaughter to killings conducted by hunters and farmers could reduce the public backlash against animal sacrifice.[33]

Supernatural Ailments: Insanity, Fraud, and Vagrancy

African people and their New World descendants often view the world of sickness and healing in a very distinct manner from the Western world. African-based conceptions of illness tend to interpret physical and mental problems in a broad sense, believing that they can be caused by spiritual imbalance and affliction.[34] The Western world, however, treats physical and mental illnesses as if they are purely "a malfunction of the body."[35] For centuries, the Western world, particularly colonists of Africa and the Americas, have regarded African perspectives of illness as illegitimate. This belief has manifested in two ways. Historically, colonial laws have tried to suppress various medico-religious practices, including targeting the spiritual healer as a charlatan and a vagrant. Second, and more recently, judges and mental health professionals have focused on the patient's beliefs in supernatural ailments, declaring that these beliefs are evidence of insanity or claiming that these beliefs interfere with an individual's ability to obtain proper medical care.

The easiest place to begin is with statutes prohibiting the practice of African religions. In Africa, these are typically laws forbidding the practice of witchcraft. For centuries, missionaries, travelers, and colonial officials expressed concern about the fact that Africans ascribed the cause of physical ailments to spiritual imbalances; in particular, that they believed that one person could inflict harm on another person by cursing or bewitching them.[36] In fact, one virtually universal component of anti-witchcraft legislation in Britain's African colonies was a provision prohibiting witchcraft accusations and trials.[37] In part, these laws were purportedly an effort to prevent an accused witch from being beaten, tortured, or dismembered by the alleged victim or the community.[38] However, colonial officials in Africa also frequently indicated that witchcraft statutes were necessary because beliefs about supernaturally caused ailments encouraged Africans to seek the services of "witch-doctors" rather than utilizing Western medicine and doctors.[39] Some of these acts prohibiting both the practice of witchcraft and accusations or trials of witches continue to be in effect in various African nations.[40]

Although in the Americas, there were no comparative statutes aimed primarily at suppressing witchcraft trials, there too officials and plantation owners complained that Africans blamed all illnesses on spiritual causes. One of the most commonly stated goals of laws prohibiting the practice of African religions was to suppress beliefs in supernatural causes of illness. During slavery, these beliefs were of grave concern to the plantation owners, who often observed that their slaves would die from "imagined illnesses" when they believed they had been cursed by a witch—who was referred to as an Obeah practitioner in the British Caribbean.[41] After emancipation, planters and colonial officials continued to arrest and imprison people who treated bodily illnesses with spiritual or religious cures.[42] They most explicitly claimed that belief in supernatural ailments impeded the progress of Western medicine; however, they were also very concerned when healers would disrupt plantation labor with their rituals and cures.[43] In the United States, police and judges also punished black healers because they could grow very wealthy and powerful from their work.[44]

In both the United States and the Caribbean, these healers were generally treated as charlatans and vagrants. In fact, virtually all colonial statutes against African and African-derived religious practices contained some element of fraud. For instance, the current Obeah Acts of Jamaica, Antigua and Barbuda define Obeah practice as anyone who "pretends to cure injuries or diseases...by means of any charm, incantation or other pretended supernatural practice."[45] Further, every British colony in the Caribbean passed laws beginning in the middle of the nineteenth century that prohibited vagrancy. These laws contained sections proscribing the practice of Obeah and "pretending" to possess supernatural powers. Both statutes prohibiting vagrancy and Obeah have been used to arrest healers that employed unorthodox medicinal practices.[46] Although arrests for this sort of healing are not common in the Caribbean today, the statutes remain in place and the media provides constant reminders that if you practice Obeah, you could go to jail.[47]

In the United States, on the other hand, there were no widespread postemancipation efforts to directly outlaw Voodoo, Obeah, or any other African religious practices. Instead, people—particularly those of African descent—who engaged in forms of medico-religious healing were arrested for unlicensed medical practice.[48] Others were arrested for fraud or obtaining money under false pretenses.[49] Either way, the police and prosecutors sent a clear message to spiritual healers that their treatments were unacceptable, sentencing them to prison terms, or leveling hefty fines against them.[50] As in the Caribbean, such prosecutions became less common in the middle to late twentieth century. Since there are no comparable laws to Caribbean Obeah statutes, spiritual healers are theoretically free to conduct their rituals in the United States, as long as they provide the disclaimer that their treatments have not been classified as medicine and have not been proven to have any effect.

Although criminal prosecutions for medico-religious healing seems to be a thing of the past, African spiritual healing rituals were prohibited anywhere from a few decades to a few centuries in various parts of the world. In some places, particularly the British Caribbean, they technically continue to be against the law.[51] Medico-religious healing carries the stigma of this lengthy prohibition with it, but it manifests in different ways. For instance, today, instead of prosecuting the healer as a charlatan, the focus has turned to individuals who believe in supernatural afflictions. Doctors have lamented that belief in supernatural afflictions prevents their patients from seeking "proper" medical care. Some medical professionals have even testified in court that a patient's belief in supernatural afflictions is so irrational that it must represent some form of mental instability.

The practices and beliefs known in the British Caribbean as "Obeah," have been the subject of mental health investigations since at least the middle of the twentieth century. From the 1940s to the 1970s, some were outright favorable to Obeah practitioners, noting that traditional healers such as these are not "medical neophytes. They are in fact members of healing fraternities that go back to the Africa that existed in antiquities."[52] Several argued that African and African-derived religions should be incorporated into Western medical practices to provide a more comprehensive approach to healing and wellness.[53] Others accepted that Obeah can at least work as a kind of placebo, giving the patient an explanation for their illness, a plan for overcoming it, and a sense of self worth that all contribute to improvements in the person's condition.[54] These scholars acknowledged that people often seek Obeah practitioners because Western medical treatments have failed to cure their ailment.[55]

More recently, mental health professionals have taken a far different stance. For instance, Dr. Earl Wright, director of mental health services at the Ministry of Health in Jamaica believes that the attribution of mental health issues to demon possession or obeah prevents people from being "properly" treated for their illness.[56] During a speech in 2007, Wright asserted that there needs to be a public education campaign about the causes of mental illness and the myths about its relationship with Obeah practices.[57]

Further, at least as early as 2004, Dr. Wendel Abel, head of the psychiatry section of the Department of Community Health and Psychiatry at the University of the West Indies, began publishing articles in Jamaican newspapers campaigning against Obeah. Abel argued that despite a widespread belief in Obeah in Jamaica, supernatural illnesses are not real. He expressed concern that people "who believe in obeah or the supernatural fail to seek early treatment, do not comply with their treatment and as a result their condition may worsen or they might die."[58] Abel said that while health care providers "have to be sensitive to people's beliefs and cultural practices and...never devalue their beliefs or embarrass and humiliate them" they also "have a responsibility to educate people about their illnesses."[59] Abel further went on to say that although culturally people may attribute hearing voices and feeling that other people can control their thoughts to supernatural causes, these are really signs of mental illness.[60] With an unmistakable tone of condescension, Abel says, "Clearly, if these were cases of demon possession, medication could not treat or control these conditions."[61]

Although mental health professionals have written articles and books about the affects of belief in Obeah on mental health in the Caribbean, belief in supernatural afflictions has not received the same type of academic consideration in the United States. Instead, recent court cases seem to suggest that believing that physical illness can have spiritual causes is a clear sign of mental instability. For instance, in 2006, a United States District Court determined that Maharaj M. suffered from mental illnesses so substantial that they prevented him from obtaining food, shelter, and clothing and generally taking care of his own basic needs. Belief in Voodoo and in illnesses caused by witchcraft was listed among factors that the court considered in its determination.[62]

One of the most common ways that belief in supernatural afflictions is raised in US court proceedings is when the attorney for an individual who has been charged with a crime asserts belief in Voodoo, or practice of Voodoo as a defense to their criminal actions. For instance, Paul Howell was convicted of first-degree murder in Florida in 1995 and was sentenced to death.[63] His attorney appealed the sentence, stating that there were mitigating factors that were not considered before his client was given the death penalty. One of those factors was Howell's mental condition. In an effort to illustrate the decline of his mental condition, Howell's attorney listed various considerations, like the fact that Howell was hearing voices, had unexpected outbursts, and was admitted to a mental hospital. Here, the attorney also indicated that Howell "was also seeing American "voodoo" doctors, not an uncommon practice with people of Caribbean heritage." As is typical of both briefs and decisions in these cases, Howell's attorney goes no further in explaining the significance of Howell's belief in "Voodoo," but instead merely suggests that it has negative implications on his sanity, as he lists it within a group of factors showing mental instability.[64]

Similarly, when Marjorie Diehl-Armstrong was put on trial for armed bank robbery and other crimes, her attorney filed a motion to determine her competency to stand trial.[65] When sent for further psychiatric testing, a psychologist employed by the Federal Bureau of Prisons found her competent to stand trial. Her attorney appealed this finding to the United States District Court in Western Pennsylvania. He submitted the report of Dr. David Paul, who had examined Diehl-Armstrong on multiple occasions.[66] Dr. Paul opined that Diehl-Armstrong suffered from bipolar affective disorder and exhibited "the typical manic's capacity for terribly poor judgment."[67] As an illustration of her terrible judgment, Dr. Paul mentioned that Diehl-Armstrong freely admitted to the jury that she believed in Voodoo and astrology, without any understanding of the impression it might leave on them.[68]

The problem with supporting a defense of insanity based on a belief in Voodoo or witchcraft is best illustrated by contrasting how witchcraft was raised as a defense to murder in many African countries. There, instead of regarding the accused as outright insane, belief that the victim was a witch has often been considered a type of provocation for homicide.[69] Although many judges subscribe to the view that witchcraft does not exist, they do not consider a belief in witchcraft so irrational that the defendants are not culpable for their actions. Instead, witchcraft is an extenuating or mitigating factor to be considered in sentencing.[70] In fact, in a case in Swaziland, defense counsel argued and the Judge carefully considered whether the belief that the victim was a witch and had killed someone in the community using witchcraft was a complete defense of necessity provocation absolving the defendants of murder.[71] This defense ultimately failed, not because witchcraft was not perceived as a credible defense but rather because a defense of provocation requires action, not mere threats, and directed at the defendant.

Therefore, it is clear that there are a wide range of responses to African and African diaspora religions throughout the world. In the Caribbean, statutes remain in places that describe African-derived religious beliefs as fraud. In this region, mental health professionals also debate over the implications of belief in supernatural ailments, with some complaining that these beliefs interfere with Western medicine, and others asserting that cultural beliefs in spiritual healing should be respected alongside more mainstream medical treatments. Finally, in the United States, belief in African-based religions is introduced as evidence of insanity in criminal prosecutions. All of these responses to African diaspora religions are rooted in years of colonial prosecutions of spiritual healers as vagrants and charlatans.

Slander/Discrimination

The final challenge to African and African diaspora religions that this chapter will address is based on the fact that the terms that Europeans used to describe African belief systems have been steeped in ambiguity. Obviously, witchcraft is not what Africans traditionally called their own beliefs, yet this is how they were almost universally labeled in colonial laws, missionary and traveler accounts, as well as other documents written and published by Europeans. While researchers have recently debated what African words the terms "Voodoo" and "Obeah" may have derived from, the fact remains that these words were greatly influenced, if not primarily shaped, by Europeans.[72] As many African spiritual beliefs and practices were glossed as "witchcraft," the terms "Voodoo" and "Obeah" were similarly used in colonial laws and European descriptions of African religion in Haiti, New Orleans, and the British Caribbean. Laws against Voodoo and Obeah first surfaced as an attempt to prohibit religion from inspiring and protecting insurgents in slave rebellions.[73] These words have become more ambiguous through the years, as Voodoo and Obeah have been described in the newspapers, television shows, and movies, usually in a negative light and generally portrayed as sorcery and harmful rituals. This ambiguity is important to understanding the complexity of civil court cases where the plaintiff claims that the defendant has slandered or defamed him by calling him a practitioner of Voodoo, Obeah, or witchcraft. Although followers of African and African diaspora religion do not typically self-identify as "Voodoo doctors," "witches," and "Obeah men," nonpractitioners often find it impossible to separate the stereotype from the religion. Therefore, when they object to being associated with Voodoo, Obeah, or witchcraft, they are simultaneously rejecting a relationship with these actual belief systems and the mainstream misconceptions of them.

Obeah was criminalized in Jamaica in 1760, and the rest of the British Caribbean soon followed passing similar laws. Just before the turn of the twentieth century, Jamaica passed its most recent Obeah statute, a law that is still on the books today.[74] Shortly thereafter, prosecutions for Obeah increased, peaking in 1900 at 88 prosecutions for Obeah in one year.[75] Around this time, perhaps because of such a lengthy period of criminalization of Obeah and the active prosecution of Obeah practitioners, people who had been referred to as Obeah practitioners in social settings began to sue for slander. Such cases occurred at least as early as 1909, when Ellen Knight sued Mr. and Mrs. Moore for stating that "she was holding the communion cup in one hand and obeah in the other" and that Knight had used Obeah to kill Ms. Moore's mother.[76] Knight won her case and was awarded two pounds plus court costs.[77] Similarly, about ten years later, Alice Jones sued Rebecca Spenser, claiming that Spenser had referred to her as an "obeahering wretch" and that Spenser had accused her of placing an Obeah curse on Spenser's husband that caused him to drink excessively.[78] Jones was awarded ten pounds in damages for the slander.[79]

These cases were often published in one of Jamaica's oldest newspapers, *The Daily Gleaner*, until about the 1940s, when either individual stopped suing each other for slander, defamation, or libel because of Obeah references or the newspaper stopped being interested in publishing information about such cases. Interestingly, the decline of these civil cases coincides with the decline of criminal prosecutions for Obeah, which were generally less than 20 per year in the 1950s, and sometimes fell into the single digits.

Cases of defamation and slander have also been brought in African courts for referring to someone as a "witch" or claiming that someone practiced witchcraft. For instance, in 2005 in Botswana, Joseph Makati sued a newspaper for publishing statements that Makati claimed were false, malicious, and defamatory.[80] The newspaper printed a story reporting that Makati believed that a storm that interrupted his wedding was the work of witchcraft, that Makati had consulted a local healer prior to his wedding, and that Makati believed that the mother of his child was a witch. Makati claimed that these statements damaged his reputation because he is a Christian, and the story made him appear to be a hypocrite. He further claimed that some of his business associates had detached themselves from him and that the story had caused friction between Makati and his wife. The court found in favor of Makati and awarded him monetary damages, agreeing that the newspaper story made Makati, a Christian, look like a hypocrite and noting that Makati had been shunned by members of his church since the article was published.[81]

Similarly, in 2006 in Malawi, Rose Chiwanda sued defendants Mr. and Mrs. Phoso and Mrs. Amoni for slander and defamation, claiming that the defendants had damaged her reputation when they published statements that Chiwanda practiced witchcraft and taught Mr. and Mrs. Phoso's children to practice witchcraft.[82] Chiwanda claimed that people surrounded her chanting "witch" and threw stones at her after hearing the defendants' accusations. The court found in favor of the defendants on a technicality, because to make a case of slander under Malawian law, the plaintiff must prove "special damages," such as showing that the defendants had accused Chiwanda of committing a criminal act. Since the defendants had not accused her of a crime under the Malawian Witchcraft Act, she failed to make her case.

Such cases were not limited to the British Caribbean and Southern Africa. In the United States, there have been dozens, perhaps even hundreds or thousands, of cases where an individual has claimed slander, defamation, or discrimination because they were "accused" of practicing an African-derived religion. These cases are typically employment discrimination lawsuits, where a person claims that their boss or coworkers have referred to them as a Voodoo practitioner and claims that these references are evidence of racial discrimination.

For instance, Mercy Edwin, a Ghanian American sued her employer for racial discrimination and a hostile work environment.[83] Among other things, she alleged that her coworkers had referred to her using ethnic and racial slurs. Specifically, they called her "that fat Nigger," "Voodoo Nurse," and "Nigger Nurse."[84] Analogously, an African American school teacher named Linda Thompson relied on "racial comments," as evidence that racial or religious discrimination was the reason that she had been denied several positions for which she had applied.[85] These comments included claims that her coworkers referred to a Jamaican doll on her desk as a Voodoo doll, her principal accused her of placing a Voodoo curse on him, and some of her coworkers believed that she practiced Voodoo.[86]

Although the vast majority of these cases involve African Americans, there are a few exceptions to this rule. For instance, in 2007, a Native American named Beverlee Steffy filed suit against Ford Motor Company for employment discrimination based on her gender and her national origin.[87] Steffy claimed that her manager had "subjected her to comments, name calling, slurs, ridicule, belittlement, embarrassment and harassment because of her Native American heritage."[88] Among the specific instances she cited, most of them were clearly related to stereotypes about Native Americans. For example, she claimed that her manager danced around in a circle and made "whooping noises," referred to her as "squaw," and made references to tepees and smoke signals.[89] However, Steffy also complained that her manager had referred to her beliefs, rituals and customs as "voodoo and pagan,"[90] and this was one of a list of comments that she considered "derogatory to her national origin."[91] Like the claims of racial discrimination made by African Americans in the cases cited above, the court did not specifically address the references to "Voodoo" in its analysis of Steffy's claim.

Evidence of voodoo practices has appeared in criminal cases in the United States in a manner that is very similar to its introduction in civil discrimination cases. These cases are typically where someone introduced evidence about Voodoo practice at an individual's trial, and that person appealed their conviction, stating that these comments were prejudicial. For instance, Sylvain Nicholas sued Lisa Holley, chair of his parole board, and the parole board itself when Holley asked him during his parole hearing "Have you been practicing a lot of Voodoo and Black Magic?"[92] Unfortunately, the judge did not discuss whether this question could have harmed Nicholas's chances for parole, but instead focused on technical issues like Holley's immunity from being sued as an individual for actions she engaged in as a government official.

These cases are not just about religious beliefs that have been attributed to nonpractitioners; even followers of African-derived religions recognize the potential for prejudice if their religious beliefs are discussed in court proceedings. For instance, defendants Jesus Jimenez and Belkis Hernandez claimed that evidence of their religious practices was inappropriately admitted in their prosecution for drug possession and possession of a firearm.[93] At trial, the government wanted to introduce evidence about a box filled with $5,000 cash that was found in Jimenez's living room. The prosecution asked a witness about a photo where the box was next to a statue of Saint Lazarus, and the witness, Quintenilla, replied that when people went to Jimenez's home they would put money in the box to protect themselves from sickness and evil.[94] Quintenilla stated that this practice was "(r)eligious sort of like voodoo."[95] In an effort to admit the photo into evidence, the government asked another witness if he was familiar with "Santa Rea" (presumably "Santeria"). The witness replied that he was and that the practice of "Santa Rea" was connected with Saint Lazarus.[96]

Finally, a third witness testified that a customer of the defendants bought a goat to sacrifice to Saint Lazarus.[97] Defense counsel moved for a mistrial due to the "continued interjection of the voodoo and Santa Rea into the case."[98] The judge did not grant the mistrial, but gave specific instructions to the jury that the defendants were not on trial for their religious beliefs, and that the jury was not to develop an attitude toward the person's guilt or innocence based on religious beliefs.[99] On appeal, the government did not argue over whether or not these references to "Voodoo" or "Santa Rea" were prejudicial to the defendants but rather noted that the prosecution did not intend to introduce evidence of the defendants' religious practices; they were either unexpected comments by witnesses or were relevant to the prosecution.[100] The court did not discuss the issue of possible prejudice but merely affirmed the decision of the lower court to admit the evidence.[101]

Unfortunately, instead of engaging in an analysis of whether the comments or conduct of employers, coworkers, or witnesses constituted discrimination, these cases typically turned on technical issues like the legal immunity of government employees, and whether the alleged discrimination was the proven cause for the employee's demotion or termination. This means that unlike the African slander cases above that analyzed the effects of claiming that someone was a witch or believed in witchcraft on that person's reputation in his/her community, employment or church, we do not generally know how US courts view attributions of Voodoo practice. However, some conclusions can be extrapolated from the lack of discussion of this topic.

US court cases are only available in comprehensive national databases when they have reached an appellate level. Appellate courts are generally restricted to the issues that the party filing the appeal has raised. Therefore, it is likely that at least part of the reason that courts have not analyzed whether comments about Voodoo practice are evidence of discrimination is because neither party disputed that such statements are discrimination; instead they disagreed as to whether the discrimination led to the adverse action (i.e., termination). To state this a little differently, there is no reason to analyze points on which the parties agree. If an employer or prosecutor argued that calling the person a Voodoo practitioner was not discrimination, discussion of this issue would appear in the court transcript.

Cases of slander and discrimination resulting from labeling people as Voodoo and Obeah practitioners reveal the great social stigma attached to African-derived belief systems in the Western hemisphere. In fact many scholars have noted that practitioners of Vodou and Obeah do not label themselves as belonging to these religions. Instead, they say that they "serve the spirits" or that they "help people." Although this may be a more accurate description of how individuals that belong to these belief systems view themselves, one must also wonder how much of an influence the stigma attached to these terms plays in their choice not to use them.

Conclusion

Between the seventeenth century and the middle of the twentieth century, African and African diaspora religions were prohibited, and their practitioners were prosecuted in many countries across the globe. Today, in the name of freedom of religion, most countries no longer have laws that ban these religions by name. Limitations on the practice of African and African diaspora religions are now indirect restrictions and are sometimes even more of a social than legal restraint.

Laws and ordinances against animal sacrifice prohibit a central practice in African and African diaspora religions in the name of restricting animal cruelty, and regulating the disposal of organic waste. Though practitioners have typically won cases contesting laws prohibiting animal sacrifice, they have also spent untold numbers of years litigating these cases through several appeals, and even to the United States Supreme Court. Since practitioners generally lost their cases before the lower courts, they were unable to conduct their sacrifices in the years while they waited for the final appellate court ruling in their favor. Further, practitioners must keep a wary eye on new attempts to restrict animal sacrifice, like prohibiting followers of African and African diaspora religions from sharing their beliefs with their children by prosecuting them for child endangerment and cruelty if a child witnesses or participates in a sacrifice. Finally, practitioners must worry about the trend to limit the ritual slaughter of animals in Europe. Other courts may take cues from their European brethren and decide that animal rights supersede the rights of people to freedom of religion.

Followers of African and African diaspora religions must also be concerned about the damage that has been done to public perceptions of their beliefs by years of prosecutions of spiritual healers for fraud, vagrancy, and obtaining money under false pretenses. In the Anglophone Caribbean, healers can still be arrested for the practice of Obeah, which includes any "pretense" of possessing supernatural powers. Practitioners must also contend with public education campaigns by mental health professionals, who claim that belief in supernatural afflictions is a barrier to the progress of Western medicine. In the United States, the public is so unwilling to tolerate the concept of spiritually induced physical ailments that belief in such notions has been used as evidence of insanity and mental disease in various court proceedings.

Finally, practitioners of African and African diaspora religions must cope with the fact that public opinions of their beliefs are so negative that nonpractitioners claim that they have been slandered and defamed if they are associated with these religions. These cases are complicated because of the ambiguity of terms like "witchcraft" and "Voodoo," because while practitioners may not self-identify using these terms, the public continues to employ these ambiguous words to refer to African and African diaspora religion. Therefore, when Christians claim that being associated with witchcraft is damaging to their reputation, and when African Americans claim that being associated with Voodoo is evidence of racial discrimination, they are also objecting to being connected with "traditional" or indigenous African and African diaspora belief systems, because of their own prejudiced understanding of these religions.

In general, all of these problems could be considered remnants of colonial legislation and the imposition of Western culture on people of African descent. African and African diaspora religions are stereotyped, sensationalized, and misunderstood. While the world embraces Asian, European, and Middle Eastern religions as worthy of serious academic analysis, there are probably more horror movies about African and African diaspora religion than there are scholarly works. Increased education and public dialogue could drastically reduce the modern legal challenges facing African and African diaspora religions. Animal sacrifice may not be so contested if the public had more comparative information about the way sacrificial animals are raised and killed in relationship with animals that are designated for human consumption. Medico-religious healing may not be so stigmatized if it was scrutinized in relationship to other trends in holistic medicine that heal through achieving a balance between mind, body, and the surrounding world. Finally, nonpractitioners might stop making claims of discrimination for being associated with African and African diaspora religion, if they understood the role that these belief systems played in resisting colonization and slavery, and were aware of the history of racism that was intrinsic in the prohibition and demonization of these beliefs.[102]

Notes

1. Murphy, Joseph. (1993). *Santeria: African Spirits in America*. Boston: Beacon Press, pp. 135–136. Margarite Fernandez Olmos and Lizabeth Paravisini-Gebert. (2003). *Creole Religions of the Caribbean: An Introduction from Voodoo and Santeria to Obeah and Espiritismo*. New York University Press, pp. 124–125.
2. Murphy, pp. 135–136; Olmos & Paravisini-Gebert, pp. 124–125.
3. Bremmer, Jan Nicolaas. (2007). *The strange world of human sacrifice*. Leuven: Peeters, p. 1.
4. Case of Cha'are Shalom Ve Tsedek v. France, Application No. 27417/95 (June 27, 2000).
5. Ibid.
6. "Uniting against the shechita ban," *Jerusalem Post Editorial*, June 30, 2011, http://www.jpost.com/Opinion/Editorials/Article.aspx?id=227392 (accessed August 6, 2011)
7. Ibid.
8. "Campaign targets Nepali animal sacrifices," *The Taipei Times*, Oct 21, 2009.
9. Church of Lukumi Babalu Aye v. City of Hialeah, 508 U.S. 520 (1993).
10. Ibid, pp. 521–522.
11. Ibid, p. 521.
12. Ibid, pp. 523–524.
13. Merced v. Kasson, 577 F.3d 582 (2009).
14. Ibid, pp. 582–585.
15. Ibid, pp. 593–594.
16. Ibid, pp. 591, 594.
17. Petrick, John. "Is case child endangerment or religous practice?" Jan. 21, 2011, http://www.northjersey.com/news/012111_Is_case_child_endangerment_or_religous_practice.html.
18. Ibid.
19. Ibid.
20. Petrick, John. "Judge rejects religious freedom defense in Palo Mayombe trial," Jan. 22, 2011, http://www.northjersey.com/news/114408434_Mother__couple_to_face_trial_in_ritual_case.html.

21. Petrick, John. "Mother pleads guilty over Paterson bloody ritual," May 23, 2011, http://www.northjersey.com/news/crime_courts/052311_Mother_pleads_guilty_over_bloody_religious_ritual.html. State of New Jersey v. Yenitza Colichon, Case #09-003395-001, Passaic County, New Jersey (2011).
22. Amoah, Jewel & Bennett, Tom. (2008). "The Freedoms of Religion and Culture under the South African Constitution: Do Traditional African Religions Enjoy Equal Protection?" *Journal of Law and Religion*, 24, p. 1.
23. Behrens, Kevin G. (2008). "Tony Yengeni's Ritual Slaughter: Animal Anti-Cruelty vs. Culture" (M.A. Thesis, University of the Witwatersrand, Johannesburg, pp. 12–13).
24. Ibid, p. 1.
25. Ibid, p. 6.
26. Smit, et. al. v. His Majesty King Goodwill Zwelithini Kabhekuzulu, et. al., High Court of South Africa, Kwazulu-Natal, Case No: 10237/2009 (2009).
27. Ibid.
28. Ibid.
29. Ibid.
30. Ibid.
31. Ibid.
32. Ibid.
33. For instance the National African Religion Congress reports that a Haitian group allowed a Philadelphia reporter to witness an animal sacrifice and the journalist provided information to the Society for the Prevention of Cruelty to Animals, who responded that the way the sacrifice was conducted did not constitute animal cruelty. See National African Religion Congress, Animal sacrifice versus cruelty to animals, http://www.narcworld.com/btgiu.html.
34. Roslyn Roach, "Obeah in the Treatment of Psychological Disorders in Trinidad: An Empirical Study of an Indigenous Healing System" (M.S. Thesis, McGill University, 1992, p. 37).
35. Ibid, p. 36.
36. Ashforth, Adam. (2005). *Witchcraft, Violence and Democracy in South Africa.* Chicago & London: University of Chicago Press, p. 317.
37. For example see E. M. Jackson, ed., *Statutes of the Cape of Good Hope, 1652–1905* (Cape Town: Cape Times Limited, Government Printers, 1906), p. 2388; Native Affairs Department, *Laws and Regulations Specially Relating to the Native Population of Transvaal* (Pretoria: Government Printing and Stationary Office, 1907) p. 151. Edwin Arney Speed, *Laws of the Colony of Southern Nigeria: Being the Schedule to the Statute Laws Revision Ordinance, 1908* (London: Stevens and Sons, Limited, 1908), pp. 305–6.
38. Wesleyan Missionary Society, *Wesleyan Missionary Notices, Relating Principally to the Foreign Missions Under the Direction of the Methodist Conference* (London: Wesleyan Mission-House, 1868), pp. 90–91. Lieutenant John Wedderburn Dunbar Moodie, *Ten Years in South Africa Including a Particular Description of the Wild Sports of That Country* (London: Richard Bentley, 1835), p. 330.
39. Allen, W. O. B. and McClure, Edmund. *Two Hundred Years: The History of the Society for Promoting Christian Knowledge, 1698–1898* (London: Society for Promoting Christian Knowledge, 1898), pp. 477–80. Francis Schimlek, *Medicine Versus Witchcraft* (Natal: Mariannhill Mission Press, 1950), pp. 15, 42. Alexander Davis, *The Native Problem in South Africa* (London: Spottiswoode and Co., Ltd., 1903), p. 36.
40. For examples see Witchcraft Act, Zambia, Chap. 90, No. 5 of 1914; Witchcraft Act of 1957, Uganda, Chap. 124.

41. For example, William Burdett. *Life and Exploits of Mansong, commonly called Three-fingered Jack, The Terror of Jamaica in the years of 1780 & 1781: with a Particular Account of the Obi* (Sommers Town: A. Neil, 1800), p. 20; Benjamin Moseley. *Medical Tracts. Second Edition with considerable additions.* (London: Red Lion Passage, 1800), p. 194; R. Poole. *The Beneficent Bee: or Traveller's Companion.* (London: E. Duncumb, 1753) p. 301.

42. For example see Derrick Murray. "Three Worships, an Old Warlock and Many Lawless Forces: The Court Trial of an African Doctor who Practised 'Obeah to Cure', in Early Nineteenth Century Jamaica," *Journal of Southern African Studies*, 33, no. 4 (Dec. 2007), pp. 812–822 and "Trial of James Rose," St. Catherine Circuit Court Records, Jamaica National Archives, J.A. 1A/5/1 (2).

43. Schuler, Monica. (1979). "Myalism and the African Religious Tradition," In Margaret Crahan & Franklin Knight (eds.) *Africa and the Caribbean: The Legacies of a Link*, pp. 69–73. Baltimore & London: The Johns Hopkins University Press.

44. Chireau, Yvonne. (2003). *Black Magic: Religion and the African American Conjuring Tradition.* Berkeley, Los Angeles & London: University of California Press, p. 24.

45. "Obeah Act," Chap. 298, Sect.5, Laws of Antigua and Barbuda, http://www.laws.gov.ag/acts/index.html,search Obeah. (emphasis added) Interestingly, when Trinidad repealed their Obeah statutes in 2000, instead of simply deleting the statute altogether, they replaced the language prohibiting the practice of Obeah or any "occult" with prohibitions of fraud or committing certain acts by fraudulent means. See "Legal Supplement Part A" *Trinidad and Tobago Gazette*, 39. no. 224 (2000); "An Act to amend certain provisions of the Summary Courts Act, the Summary Offences Act and the Offences Against the Person Act to remove certain discriminatory religious references," Act No. 85 of 2000, Republic of Trinidad and Tobago (Nov. 2, 2000), ¶ 2.

46. For example see "Convicted on Obeah Charge. Case Heard at Chapelton Court on Tuesday. The Evidence Given. Accused Bargains to Take "Duppies" Off Child." *The Gleaner*, Oct. 3, 1913; "Obeah Charge in Portland: Case Heard Before Resident Magistrate," *The Gleaner*, Jan. 27, 1914; "Case Under the Obeah Law: Girl Dying, Declared it was due to 'Female Ghos'" *The Gleaner*, Apr. 16, 1909.

47. Dwayne McLeod, "Obeah In 'Store'," The Jamaican Star, Oct. 12, 2007, http://www.jamaica-star.com/thestar/20071012/news/news1.html

48. For example see "Voodoo Doctor is Held Authorities," *Ironwood Daily Globe*, Aug. 22, 1927. "Hold Voodoo Doctor and His High Priests," The Times Recorder, Aug. 22, 1927; "Quack Doctor Held for Court under $3000 Bail At Hearing Last Night," *Monessen Daily Independent*, Aug. 27, 1930.

49. For examples see "'A Wicked Thing' R.M. Tells Man Convicted of Obeah," *The Gleaner*, Dec. 22, 1953; Jessie Ruth Gaston, "The Case of Voodoo in New Orleans," in Joseph E. Holloway, *Africanisms in American culture* (Bloomington: Indiana University Press, 2005) pp. 139, 142–143. "Secrets of Vicious Voodoo Doctors Who Victimize Gullible Girls," Hamilton Evening Journal, Oct. 9, 1926. "Voodoo Doctor Voodoos Himself into Jail Cell," *Titusville Herald*, Sept. 15, 1930.

50. Gaston, pp. 142–143; "Voodoo man fined," *San Antonio Express*, June 5, 1930; "Obeah Charge: Alexander Robinson Convicted at Port Antonio," *The Gleaner*, Jan. 13, 1914, pp. 13, 14.

51. See infra note 46.

52. Roach, p. 10.

53. Ibid, p. 37.

54. Borofsky, Robert. "Obeah: A Description of an Occult Medical System in Trinidad," (M.A. Thesis, Brandeis Univ. 1968) pp. 16, 23–24.

55. Ibid, p. 22; Lawrence Fisher, *Colonial Madness: Mental Health in the Barbadian Social Order* (New Brunswick, N.J. : Rutgers University Press, 1985), p. 105.

56. Ingrid Brown, "Obeah beliefs hurting mental health care," *Jamaica Observer*, October 6, 2007.

57. Ibid.

58. Dr. Wendel Abel, "The Impact of Obeah on Mental Health," *The Gleaner*, July 28, 2004.

59. Dr. Wendel Abel, "Obeah, duppy and your health: Part I," *The Gleaner*, Nov. 24, 2010.

60. Dr. Wendel Abel, "Obeah, duppy and your health: Part II," *The Gleaner*, Dec. 1, 2010.

61. Ibid.

62. Conservatorship of the Person and Estate of Maharaj M. v. Maharaj M., 2006 WL 2356177 (Cal.App. 5 Dist.).

63. "Initial Brief of the Appellant," Howell v. State of Florida, 1996 WL 33416305 (Fla.), 5.

64. Ibid, p. 67.

65. U.S. v. Marjorie Diehl-Armstrong, 2008 WL 2963056 (W.D.Pa.).

66. Ibid, p. 6.

67. Ibid, p. 8.

68. Ibid, p. 8.

69. For example see, Rex v. Rankali, CRI/T/71/89, LSCA 130, High Court of Lesotho (1989).

70. Ibid.

71. Rex v Mabuyakhulu, Case No. 133/1999, High Court of Swaziland (1999).

72. For research on the etymology of Obeah, see J. S. Handler and K. M. Bilby, "On the Early Use and Origin of the Term 'Obeah' in Barbados and the Anglophone Caribbean" *Slavery & Abolition*, 22, no. 2 (2001): pp. 87–100.

73. Danielle N. Boaz, "Introducing Religious Reparations: Repairing the Perceptions of African Religions through Expansions in Education," *Journal of Law and Religion*, 26 (2010): pp. 216–220.

74. "The Obeah Law," Law 5 of 1898, Sect. 7, *The Laws of Jamaica passed in a session which began on the 15th day of March, and adjourned sine die on the 29th day of August, 1898* (Kingston: Government Printing Office, 1898), pp. 2–3.

75. "The Crusade Against Obeah," *The Gleaner*, Jan 18, 1901.

76. "A Costly Slander," *The Gleaner*, May 6, 1909.

77. Ibid.

78. Jones v. Spenser, *The Gleaner*, Nov. 21, 1919.

79. Ibid.

80. Makati v. Beama Publishing Ltd., Civil Case No. 1469 of 2005, High Court of Botswana.

81. Note that the amount of damages awarded to the Plaintiff was later reduced by an appellate court, but the finding of defamation was confirmed. Beama Publishing Ltd. v. Makati, CACLB-010–08, Court of Appeal of Botswana (2009).

82. Chiwanda v. Amoni, et. al., Civil Cause No. 547 of 2006, High Court of Malawi.

83. Edwin v. Blenwood Associates, Inc., 9 F.Supp.2d 70 (1998).

84. Ibid, p. 72.

85. Thompson v. City of New York, et.al., 2002 WL 31760219 (S.D.N.Y.) (2002).

86. Ibid., p. 4, footnote 3.

87. Steffy v. Ford Motor Co., Inc., 2007 WL 895506 (W.D.N.Y.) (2007).

88. Ibid, p. 1.

89. Ibid, pp. 1–2.

90. Ibid, p. 1.

91. Ibid, p. 2.

92. Nicolas v. State of Rhode Island, 160 F.Supp.2d 229 (July 3, 2001).

93. "Brief for the United States," U.S. v. Jesus Jimenez, et. al., 1992 WL 12135144 (C.A.11).

94. Ibid, pp. 28–29.

95. Ibid, p. 29

96. Presumably this reference to "Santa Rea" is a misspelling of "Santería." Ibid, p. 29.

97. Ibid, p. 30.

98. Ibid, p. 30.

99. Ibid, pp. 30–31.

100. Ibid, p. 32.

101. U.S. v. Jesus Jimenez, et.al., 983 F.2d 1022 (1993).

102. For more information on the history of the prosecution of African diaspora religion in the Americas, see generally Boaz, *Introducing Religious Reparations*.

Chapter 17

African Religious Systems in the Context of World Religions: Challenges for the American Scholars

Maha Marouan

Introduction

I have been teaching religions of Africa and the African diaspora at the University of Alabama for the last six years. The first question that came to my mind when I chose to write on trends in African religious beliefs and practices is to what extent have the views of my students changed about Africa and its belief systems in the last six years. The challenge that faces scholars of Africanist religions in the United States is that we are constantly facing audiences in and out of the classroom who have negative perceptions of Africa. Thus, we never have the luxury of a neutral platform from which to address and communicate with our audiences. In the Deep South, especially, the path of scholars of Africanist religions is even more difficult. One has a hard task in a place that has a problematic racial history and where even Catholicism is still considered a foreign brand. For example, Catholics were on top of the list in the KKK Manifesto.

Thus, how does one approach and write about African religious beliefs and practices against the preconceptions about Africa, its religions, and its cultures? African belief systems are often viewed as "primitive" and lacking in diversity and sophistication. Even those who are open to learning about these traditions still often believe that African belief systems have been rather inconsequential to world civilizations. This is, of course, in addition to a construction of Africa in the American imaginary that does not consider Islam and Christianity indigenous to the African continent. The fact that Christianity has been in Africa since the second century, and Islam since the seventh century, escapes many.

This lack of knowledge about Africa in the American imagination also stems from an educational system that does not teach students about Africa. In many world history textbooks, for instance, Africa begins and ends with Egypt. This is further fueled by a popular culture that continues to trivialize and sensationalize Africanist traditions. The examples are endless, but a most recent example, closely related to what we think of African religious belief systems is from the reality television show, *The Housewives of Atlanta,* where "the wives" decide to take a trip to South Africa to reconnect with their African roots and learn more about "Africa." While there, they meet a diviner (of course!) who reads their fortunes to them. When one of the women falls ill shortly afterwards, she is told that that was the wrath of the witch doctor. While one does not expect the use of such imperialistic terminology as "witch doctor" in the twenty-first century, the message conveyed by this comment is also very problematic. Here, African religious practices become associated with harm and magic, turning into the antithesis of what people who adhere to religion normally seek in religious practices: protection and healing. This construction of Africa also justifies a paternalistic discourse about an Africa that needs to be rescued from its evilness and ignorance.

In *The Invention of Africa,* V. Y. Mudimbe argues that the colonial discourse in Africa has essentially transformed Africa into a European construct leading to the emergence of a dichotomizing structure that divided the world into "the civilized" and "the uncivilized." He argues that:

> The forms and formulations of the colonial culture and its aims were somehow the means of trivializing the whole traditional mode of life and its spiritual framework. The potential and necessary transformations meant that the mere presence of this new [colonial] culture was a reason for the rejection of unadapted persons and confused minds [of the colonized.][1]

This process of marginalization of Africa, or what he calls the "ordering of its Otherness" leads to the construction of an imaginary Africa that served as a shadow image of the West, representing everything that Europe did not want to be. Mudimbe explains, "The African has become not only the Other who is everyone else except me, but rather the key which, in its abnormal differences, specifies the identity of the same."[2]

Like the European colonial enterprise, which envisioned a projected transformation of Africa and its inhabitants from "primitivism" to "progress"—that is, paganism to European Christianity—the discourse of black Nationalism in the West has also reinforced the same epistemology. While it is important to talk about Africa as an originary point for people of African descent in the New World, Afrocentric discourses over the last three centuries have also contributed to a mythologizing of Africa, placing the continent outside the realm of history, and preventing a serious engagement with Africa and the lived realities of its people. Black Nationalism, especially in the turn of the twentieth century, has shown contempt to Africa's "tribal" and "pagan" religions, and the "civilizing mission in Africa" was about the redemption of Africa from the claws of primitivism. In *Afrotopia,* Wilson Moses writes that "African American leaders who were most committed to the redemption of Africa were dedicated to the replacement of "pagan" and "primitive" cultures with a new bourgeois Christianity that was to be based on scientific and industrial progress."[3] Thus, Black Nationalism also fell victim to the evolutionary language of European enlightenment that placed Africans at the bottom of the evolutionary scale.

Additionally, while it is undeniable that Afrocentric discourses have provided the basis for a common sense of destiny between diasporic groups and the African continent, the identification with Ethiopia and Egypt has also been problematic, and belies an implicit acceptance of a colonial discourse about Africa. As these ideologies still continue to prove meaningful and relevant to many pan-Africanist movements, perhaps the most conspicuous being Rastafari who see Ethiopia as the African Zion, this construction of Africa that excludes West and Central Africa, the actual ancestral home of most people of the African Americas, and glorifies Ethiopia and Egypt, remains questionable. Thus, while African diasporic communities have indeed contributed to preserving African religious practices and symbols in the diaspora, Africa has also been misconstrued by its diaspora.

Then, to what extent does the academy still contribute to this particular construction of Africa? How do world religion textbooks and "world religion" as a discourse in US academy continue to reinforce the cultural hierarchy that insists on marginalizing Africa, and positioning its belief systems outside the realm of history? An examination of world religion textbooks—which are a standard in most religious studies curricula in the US universities and colleges—shows that these texts often either ignore African religions, or conflate them with other religious traditions. They are repeatedly classified under dubious categories such as "primal religions," "basic religions," "pre-literate religions," or simply with curiously ambiguous headings such as "New Horizons."

While African religions are indeed accommodated in world religion textbooks, there is an underlying hierarchy that still conveys the idea that they are primitive, prehistoric, or "minor" as opposed to the "great" religions of the world: Christianity, Buddhism, Islam, Hinduism, and Judaism. This classificatory system, which privileges the West/East dichotomy, preserves a Eurocentric perspective that situates European Christianity at its center, and African religions outside its orbit. Tomoko Masuzawa supports this claim in her seminal work, *The Invention of World Religions,* where she argues that world religions as a category and a concept "quickly became an effective means of differentiating, variegating, consolidating, and totalizing a large proportion of the social, cultural, and political practices observable among the inhabitants of regions elsewhere in the world."[4] It only takes one to look at the table of contents of world religion textbooks to become aware of this discrepancy in classification that separates African religions from the "major" religions of the world. For example, in his chapter entitled "New Horizons," under the category of "African religions," Willard Oxtoby introduces African religions in the following way:

> Compared to the 5,000-year span of recorded history in the Middle East, Africa's past is a mystery because its cultures were without writing until their contact with Middle Eastern and European civilizations in recent times. The line dividing Africa's "prehistory" from history is a recent one.[5]

It is clear here that Oxtoby, who subscribes to the West/East centrism, finds it necessary to locate Africa outside the realm of world civilizations dictated by the "recorded" histories of West and East. Yet, what is precarious about this symbolic inclusion of African religions in world religion textbooks is that although they position Africa outside the realm of history, they still retain the illusion that the West and Western academy commit to a discourse of plurality and egalitarianism. Masuzawa explains:

> By converting from the evolutionary, psudotemporal, hierarchical order to a geographic, psudospatial, decentralized order of representation, the emergent world religions discourse appears to have liberated itself from a Eurocentrism of certain kind, since it acknowledges the actual plurality of cultures and of civilizing processes. But how does the discourse of world religions achieve this liberation? Or does it achieve it at all?[6]

Masuzawa's question takes me to my final point about how the discourse of world religions becomes challenged considering globalization and the massive human movements across the world. In light of current migration from Africa to Europe and North America, African Christianity, Islam, and Yoruba religious beliefs have become undeniable components to Europe and America's religious landscapes. The Yoruba religious culture, for instance, has acquired today a global status spreading beyond the African- Americans. In his Introduction to *Òrìṣà Devotion as World Religion*, Jacob Olupona challenges the conceptual framework of world religions and argues for the necessary inclusion of Yoruba religious culture, that has tens of millions of devotees across the globe, as world religion. He writes:

> The term "world religion" is only salvageable (and can only move beyond its "East"/"West" centrism) through a critical rehabilitation in light of today's global religious landscape, and through an uprooting of the evolutionist premise of such Western typologies: such as "high" versus "low" religions, "scriptural" versus "primitive," "big traditions" versus "little traditions."[7]

I will also argue that the marginalization of African Christianity and Islam and the privileging of European Christianity and Middle Eastern Islam in world religions discourse need to be addressed. The way that African Christianity and Islam have, and continue to, shape these religions needs to be acknowledged, especially with the intensification of African migration to Europe and the Americas that turned African Christianity and Islam into global cultures.

The number of African migrants to Europe in the last three decades has led to the growth of African churches and African Christianity at the heart of the European Christian world. This has signified a major change from the era of European missions in Africa to an African Christian landscape in Europe that undermines the traditional association of Christianity with Europe and Europeans. It is safe to say that Christianity in the twenty-first century has become a "non-Western religion," as the largest congregations in Europe today are established and led by Africans. This contains a sharp contrast to the sixteenth's century missionary discourse in Africa, which viewed African Christianity with suspicion and condensation. The account of the Portuguese Jesuit missionary Jerome Lobo in his 1633 visit to Ethiopia in his travelogue, *A Voyage to Abyssinia*, reflects this reality. Lobo was dismayed by the "African" nature of religious worship of the Abyssinians and did not think of them as "true" Christians, referring to their religious services as "concerts" and their mode of worship as "riotous":

> They begin their concert by stamping their feet on the ground, and playing gently on their instruments; but when they have heated themselves by degrees, they leave off drumming, and fall to leaping, dancing, and clapping their hands, at the same time straining their voices to the utmost pitch, till at length they have no regard either to the tune or the pauses, and seem rather a riotous than a religious assembly.[8]

However, while African Christianity now is free of Lobo's scrutiny, becoming a major feature of Europe's Christian world, one can only wonder what the next decades will bring considering the important position that African Christianity has come to occupy in Europe and around the globe.

While Islam is also integral to Africa and its many cultures, there is a prevailing misconception that Islam never took root in Africa. While roughly half of the African continent is Muslim, most Africans, and more specifically sub-Saharan Africans, they are not thought of as Muslims, and are often considered recent converts to the faith and irrelevant to the history of Islam. The colonial division between North and sub-Saharan Africa has also contributed to this misconception and obscured the African Sufi tradition that has developed in North and West Africa and continues to tie the histories of these parts of Africa together.

The alienation of sub-Saharan Africa from Islam is also related to the discourse of Arab-centrism that associates Islam closely with Arabic language and ethnicity despite the fact that the majority of Muslims express their faith in languages other than Arabic. Like Christianity and the religion of the Orisa, African Islam has also become a global faith. The influx of postcolonial African Muslim immigrants mainly from North and West Africa to Europe in the 1960s, followed by a more recent influx in the last three decades, to both Europe and North America, has signaled an important presence of Islam in the heart of the Western world.

While the global presence of African religions does not necessarily signify that Africans have succeeded in breaking racial and cultural barriers in the West, or that African religions have become a unifying factor beyond identity politics in places like Europe and North America. In fact, African religions in the West still remain marginalized and are viewed with suspicion. Yet, what remains clear is that movements of Africans across the globe is changing the religious map of the world, and demands a reconsideration and a reorganization of the category of world religions. It is necessary that US academy commit to pluralism and diversity in a true sense, and in a way that breaks the established traditional hierarchies of "major" and "minor" religions.

Notes

1. Mudimbe, V.Y. (1988). *The Invention of Afric: Gnosis, Philosophy, and the Order of Knowledge.* Indiana University Press, p. 4.
2. Ibid, p. 12.
3. Moses, Wilson. (1998). *Afrotopia: The Roots of African American Popular History.* Cambridge University Press, p. 26.
4. Masuzawa, Tomoko. (2005). *The Invention of World Religions, Or, How European Universalism was Preserved in the Language of Pluralism.* The University of Chicago Press, p. 20.
5. Oxtoby, Willard. (2001). *World Religions: Western Traditions.* Oxford University Press, p. 463.
6. Masuzawa, *The Invention of World Religions*, p. 13.
7. Olupona, Jacob K. (2008). Introduction to Òrìṣà Devotion as World Religion: The Globalization of Yorùbá Religious Culture, *Edited by Jacob K. Olupona and Terry Rey*, p. 7. Madison, WI: The University of Wisconsin Press.
8. Lobo, Jerome. (2005). *A Voyage to Abyssinia.* Cosimo Classics.

Chapter 18

African Initiated Churches and African Immigrants in the United States: A Model in the Redeemed Christian Church of God, North America (RCCGNA)

Ibigbolade Aderibigbe

Introduction

The Redeemed Christian Church of God (RCCG), North America, constitutes a graphic model of a transnational African Initiated Christian Church organization. The Church was founded in Nigeria in 1952. Though it started out as an apocalyptic movement, in classical parishes' format, it has become an upwardly mobile functional Christian denomination in model parishes' format.[1] It is in this structure that the church has become transnational, having been transplanted to different parts of the world, including North America, where it now has well over 400 parishes.

The operating dynamics and strategies of the church in North America have clearly indicated a near "wholesale" transplantation of the "home church." This is vividly reflected in the membership, organizational structure, doctrine, programs, and other facets of the church. All of these have afforded its members a strong sense of identity, cohesion, and psychological affinity with its Nigerian roots. However, this has inadvertently become a major challenge for the church in North America with regard to its vision and mission. Whereas, the church's "catchment area" of membership has been restricted to almost exclusively the African immigrants, this chapter raises questions of transnationalizing religion in the context of sustainability.

It further examines the prospects of how the values and doctrines of this "home church" may be affected as a transnational church serving not only immigrant communities but also an expansive range of communities, including individuals who are not part of the sociocultural currents that originally produced the church. In fact, are these values and doctrines of the church already undergoing transformations in the diaspora as its followers immerse in material realities that are often different from those they left behind at home?

I consider it essential to provide a theoretical review of concepts central to this discourse. I believe such an exercise should provide an understanding of their contexts and in addition, set out the limit of the focus and objective with appropriate appreciation of arguments and conclusions conversed in the discourse.

Transnationalism and Religious Transnationalism

There is no doubt that the study of religions and immigration has had a long history. The fact that religion has always been engaged in transnational and even transcontinental movements is not at all new. The history of the spread of world religions such as Christianity and Islam definitely attest to these dynamics. However, until very recently, the two topics have been usually treated exclusive of each other. This situation arose essentially from the conception and concerns covered under studies on transnationalism.[2] On the other hand, studies on immigrant religions had focused on different religions in specific geographical settings and diaspora contents, where immigrants were involved rather than the international links which engineer transnational identities as forms of cross-border connections.[3]

The preoccupation of studies in transnationalism was greatly influenced by the origins and definitions of the term for quite a long time. The earliest usage of the term with reference to immigration is said to have been probably used in 1916, in an essay written by Rudolph Pourme, in which he described America as a "transnational nation" composed of and constantly changed through immigration from diverse origins. From this usage, various definitions have emerged for the term. Two of such should suffice here. For example in *earthfamilyalpha*, the concept of "transnationalism" is defined as:

> Concept that focuses on the heightened interconnectivity between people all around the world, and the loosening of boundaries between countries. The nature of transnationalism has social, political and economic impact that affect people around the globe.[4]

It goes on to say:

> The concept of transnationalism has facilitated the flow of people, ideas and goods between regions, it has been greatly affected by the internet, telecommunications, immigration and most importantly globalization.[5]

The second definition from Vertovec is more interesting and illuminating. It states:

> The concept of transnationalism refers to multiple ties and interactions linking people and institutions across the borders of nation-states.[6]

In describing activities within this dynamics, Portes submits that transnational activities can be defined as:

> Those that take place on recurrent basis across national borders and that require a regular and significant commitment of time by participants. Such activities may be conducted by relatively powerful actors, such as representatives of national governments and multinational corporations, or may be initiated by more modest individuals, such as immigrants and their home country kin and relations. These activities are not limited to economic enterprises but include political, cultural, and religious initiatives as well.[7]

While the first definition cited from *earthfamilyalpha* portrays the concept of transnationalism in a broader sense, that of Vertovec fortunately redeems the concept from its limitation to sociopolitical and economic coverage, which had been the preoccupation of social anthropologists for decades, and injects the factor of religion as a significant subject of transnational activities. Within this category, religious transnationalism subscribes to a process by which immigrants forge and sustain their religious practices and identities across borders.[8]

Context and Methodology

There are now about 1,000 parishes of the RCCGNA. The region designated as North America comprises North America, Canada, and the Caribbean, and membership of the church is made up of almost exclusively African immigrants, however, the majority of these are Nigerians. The origin and development of the church both in spiritual and social strategies depict an interesting model of transnational of African-initiated churches. This observation certainly deserves a closer study, which has provoked my interest.

The methodology I have adopted, apart from the literary use of secondary sources in written materials, is a phenomenological one—dwelling on participation observer status and formal and informal interviews, which were oral in nature. The adoption of this methodology and gathering of data stems from the fact that I consider myself as both an outsider and insider of the church. My outsider status covered years of distant observation of the operations of the church in Nigeria, with my spouse being a member and attending periodic church services and other engagements of the church at the parish, area, and national levels. Indeed, our home in Iba, Lagos served as one of the house fellowship points for years. My insider status materialized when I finally became a member of the church in Charlotte, North Carolina, and in fact became a board member of one of the parishes in South Carolina. The movement from being an outside observer to an insider participant definitely constitutes a complementary approach. It began with the observation of the activities of the church, first, the mother church in Nigeria and then the transnational branch in North America. In this, I quite agree with Ezra Chitando's submission that:

> Of course there are experiences that someone from outside does not share with insiders, but this also hold true the other way round. Insiders' and outsiders' views someone who looks in from the outside observes things that are not obvious to the insiders since they are too self-evident or too close to their situation and experience. On the other hand, outsiders lack this intimate knowledge and experience.[9]

Haven said that a major concern may arise as to the limitation of objectivity as a scholar (outsider) and a member (insider).[10] The approaches I adopted to resolve this dilemma are first to use deliberate (formal and informal) approaches of interviews, concentrating on the leaders and major functionaries of the church. Second, I tried to do more listening and taking notes in services, committee meetings, and even board meetings I attend as a member. I also asked questions that elicited honest answers, in that I strived to ask the questions as an insider with constructive intentions rather than an outsider critic with negative intents. Third, I tried as much as possible to focus on the areas of my study without any suggestion of undermining the church's authority or organizational structure and dynamics.

History of RCCG Home Church in Nigeria

The history and development of the RCCG represent intriguing complexities of interests and strategies which have significantly situated the church as an enigma not only in expansion in the home country Nigeria but also globally. The phenomenal successes the church has attained are traceable to the institution of enabling features, which have facilitated not only internal mobility but have also propelled its transnational engagements in transplanting the church in different parts of the globe. These features have also greatly enlarged its membership both at the home front and in various global locations.

The RCCG was founded by Josiah Akindayomi in 1952.[11] The name of the church was claimed to have been revealed to him in a vision.[12] Under Akindayomi, the church was basically limited to Lagos and its environs. Services were held in Yoruba with English translations in few parishes.[13] Also, under the founder, the church was run under strict disciplinary measures. The classical parishes' model adopted by him was apocalyptic in orientation. As Ukah points out, this apocalyptic garment of the church represented his beliefs in the coming of the end of the world, which the Parousia will herald.[14] In addition, the membership of the church at this period was made up of largely "deprived and uneducated people."[15]

The emergence of Dr. Enoch Adeboye as the general overseer of the church in 1980, after the death of the founder and leader, dramatically revolutionized the church. After the initial controversy surrounding his election to the post, he introduced far-reaching measures, which transformed the church from the "little tribal church" under Akindayomi to a fast expanding and modern-day compliant church. Indeed, the church was literarily transformed from "a world rejecting" to "a world accommodating" church. This transformation, though revolutionary, was gradual and resulted from well thought out and executed strategical features.

Perhaps the chief architect of this transformation was the introduction of model parishes, which is a departure from the classical parishes brought in people of different socioeconomic positions thus stimulating social and economic mobility of the church. The model parishes' format became structured by the introduction of strategic and doctrinal positions. Alonzah Ukah articulated these features extensively, and his position is summed up below.

The groundwork for the development and expansion of the church began with the establishment of the Redeemed Christian fellowships in May 1998. These fellowships, which essentially were students' initiative on various university campuses, soon gave impetus to the founding of other groups such as Redeemed Christian Campus Fellowship (RCCF) and then the Christ the Redeemers Friends Universal. All of these groups became effective agents of evangelization of very important personalities and bringing them into the church's fold.

With increase in membership that belong to the educated, social, and economic elites of the society, the church introduced some teaching that ensures the commitment of the members. First, the church emphasized the doctrines, which not only prepare members to labor for the church but also to give generously to the church. The principle, as articulated by Pastor Adeboye, was "if you give God your all, He will give you His all.[16] According to him, those who trade with God never lose. The doctrine of giving generously to the church, so as to receive generously from God, became an ideal pursued by the rank and file of the church members. Second, church planting became a major focus of the church. To realize this, every member of the church was designated a church-planter. Once you became a member of the church and went through the workers-in-training program, you were expected to plant a church within a time limit of six months. To give impetus to this and realize the church's philosophy of establishing a church within ten minutes walking distance of one another, any member of the church was given the charge to establish a parish of the church wherever he or she finds him or herself, without the presence of the RCCG either locally or internationally. This ideology became a formidable stimulus for the expansion of the church.

Finally, the opening up of the clerical structure of the church, unlike the limitation of clerical offices, to those of deacons and pastors with the exclusion of women in pre-1980 years gave way to a more flexible ministerial structure of ministers, deacons, and pastors and with women gaining entrance into the structure. Also, the clerical structure became more dependent on part-time pastors rather than full-time ones. With this arrangement, pastors continued to hold on to their secular careers while pasturing parishes and areas. This made the rank of the clergy to be attractive to highly placed and economically enhanced people who brought the dynamism and the visionary capabilities at their various secular organizations to the church. It also reduced tremendously the financial burden that full-time pasturing would have had on the church.

There is no doubt that these strategies greatly enhanced the development and transformation of the church and indeed situate her in a formidable position not

only to expand nationally but globally—serving as Christian missionary organization of the twentieth and twenty-first centuries to other parts of Africa, Europe,
and America.

The first parish of the RCCG outside Nigeria could be seen as a product of both
efforts of the focus on university campus and the ideal of the church that a member holds it a duty to establish a parish of the church wherever he or she is located
without the presence of the church. Thus, Kwesi Appah, a Ghanaian who schooled
in Nigeria, achieved this feat by establishing a branch in Ghana. The advent of the
RCCG in Europe could be regarded as part of the "missionary efforts" of African
movements into the continent. The "mission work" according to Agi, was particularly the preoccupation of "Pentecostal/charismatic movements such as the RCC
G, the Deeper Life Christian Ministry (DLCM), and the Church of Pentecostal
International (CPI)." Thus, in 1985, the RCCG was established in the United
Kingdom, once again by a student.[17]

RCCG Contextual Dynamics of "Home from Home" Identity in North America

When the RCCG was to be established in North America, the lot again fell upon
a student, James Fadele. He was at the tail end of his internship at the Western
Michigan University. James Fadele is today the chairman of the board of coordi-
nators for RCCG, North America. The task of establishing the church in North
America, particularly by a struggling student, who also had to work in an auto-
mobile factory in Detroit, was very daunting according to Fadele himself.[18] The
humble beginning described by Fadele has today become a formidable transnational
mission outreach of the RCCG with about 400; 320 in North America, Canada,
and the Caribbean, known as the RCCGNA.

It is of interest that in both Europe and North America, the planting of the
RCCG has followed the same tradition. University students who were members
of RCCG Nigeria in these continents have taken it upon themselves to ensure
establishment of the church in any location they live either nationally or internationally. This is significant in that it indeed represents the birth of the modern-day
transnationalism that eventually characterizes the evangelical mission orientation
of the church.

From the humble beginning by a student in Detroit, RCCG in North America
has grown to become arguably the strongest transnational outpost for the RCCG
as a religious organization.[19] The transplantation of the church in North America
has witnessed its existence in about 400 parishes located all over North America,
Canada, and the Caribbean. The structure of the church within this region consists
of 19 zones in the United States and the Caribbean, and 3 in Canada, making a total
of 22 zones, according to 2009 figures. Each of the zones is headed by a coordinator
with the headquarters in Dallas under the leadership of Pastor James Fadele, as the
chairman of the board, the highest governing body of the RCCG North America.[20]

Each zone is further divided into parishes headed by pastors, assistant pastors, or deacons depending on the available personnel.

The "home from home" transnational identity dynamics of the Church for African (Nigerian) immigrants derives essentially from the Pentecostal brand of Christianity, or theology adopted by RCCG just like all other African-initiated Christian churches. This theology forms the very foundation for the doctrines and practices of the Church, and thus merits some discussions here.

The Pentecostalism found in African-initiated Christian churches is referred to many quarters as "prosperity theology." The prosperity syndrome associated with these churches may have been derived from two levels of observation. The first is the "prosperity context messages" of the churches, which started to look "earth ward" rather than "heaven ward" in content and propagation. The second is the flamboyant lifestyles of the pastors and leaders of the churches, which to all intents and purposes portrayed the establishment of grander living in the face of acute poverty of ordinary members of the church. In addition to these negative tendencies, the proliferation of the churches has suggested a commercialization of the gospel rather than evangelism for salvation.

Unfortunately, it has become very convenient to put all the Pentecostal churches, particularly the African-initiated ones, in the same basket and dismiss all of them as agents of prosperity theology—given to materialism rather than the saving of souls. However, there is a need for a separation to be made between what is popularly known as prosperity theology and existentialist Christianity. I believe the line of demarcation emerges in advancing simple, yet nonnecessarily exclusive description of the two dynamics. In this regard, prosperity theology may be viewed to subscribe essentially to the disproportional elevation of the materialistic concerns of the leaders and members, and the engagement of components of Christianity to propagate earthly benefits—many times, dishonestly—which indeed may be the very obstacles towards eternal salvation.[21]

However, existential Christianity suggests to me the realization that even though the goal of being saved is the ultimate and the "saved Christian" is not of this world, yet he or she is in this world. Thus, as a Christian, he must find meaning for his existence and even for his faith. His life, if it is to be meaningful, has a lot to do with his well-being not only spiritually but also material in the attainment of good health, good employment, prosperity, and beneficial relationship. All of these are, however, not ends in themselves but agencies of saving one self and their employment in the saving of others, establishing and expanding the religion of God here on earth, and as a foretaste of the eternal kingdom. Within this context, existentialist Christianity becomes a paradoxical mutual symbiosis of giving meaning to one's life through religion, but at the same time providing meaning for religiousness through "physical" well-being.

The philosophy, doctrine, and strategical dynamics of the RCCG clearly suggests an "existentialist Christian" approach rather than a "prosperity theology" approach. A brief exposition of the RCCG philosophy and ideology in mission and goal with the strategies adopted to achieve them should succinctly back up this submission.

The principal and overall mission of the Church is: To make heaven by living a life of holiness, and to take as many people as possible with us.

The visionary expectancy for the mission is: To plant churches within ten-minutes drive in every developed nation, and within five-minutes walk of every developing nation.

As if to reemphasize the transnationalism of the Church in attaining the mission by pursuing the mission, it established for itself the goal of: Pursuing the vision until every nation in the world is reached for Jesus Christ our Lord.[22]

There is no doubt that these missions, visions, and goals of the church are basically "heavenward." Thus, religion as responsive service to God becomes the tool that gives meaning to man's life, in the knowledge of being saved—becoming "born again" to make heaven. However, the church in this realization that man's life should also provide meaning of being religious subscribes to the existentialist dynamics of Christianity. This can be summed up in the involvement of the church in the "here and now" to give meaning and substances to serving God.

This paradoxical balancing of the utilization of physical embellishment to quantify or qualify a sanctimonious religious life and gains of faith in God, predominates the sayings and actions of pastor Adeboye and pastors at different levels of the churches. For instance, Pastor Adeboye has been quoted to say:

> We pray for the sick, but we pray for their prosperity, for their overcoming of evil forces and so on. While we have to worry about heaven, there are some things God could do for us here and now.[23]

Welcoming members to the North America annual convention in 2007, tagged Divine Visitation, Pastor Adeboye dwelled on the visitation of the Lord to Sarah (Genesis...) and the material gains (gift of a child) that resulted. He also read the biblical passage of the invitation of God to those who labor and are heavy laden (Matthew 11:27–28). The impact of the two biblical passages is that all those present would be divinely visited, and they would have miracles that would deliver them not only from spiritual problems but their day-to-day challenges in life.

To drive this point home, he concluded:

> I rejoice with those of you who have come. You will experience uncommon miracles and the Lord will give rest to those that are heavy laden and break their yokes.[24]

Again, welcoming participants to the 2008 12th annual convention under the theme: The King of Glory, Pastor Adeboye stressed how encountering the King of Glory, as described in the book of Psalms (24:7–10), would ensure not only the salvation of souls but "victory, breakthrough, open doors, healing, promotion, deliverance, environment, favor, honor, and glory." Emphasizing further the miraculous benefits of encountering the King of Glory,[25] Pastor Fadele, chairman of the board North America, intoned in his own welcoming address:

> Whatever has caused you shame, disgrace, humiliation, weeping, suffering, pain, affliction, stagnation, barrenness, weeping, and dishonor, as the King of Glory sends down His glory here, you will be delivered in Jesus' name.[26]

However, for those who thought this state could be attained without having genuine faith, he said: "I, however, warn that the King of Glory will fight for those who are genuinely repentant and righteous."[27]

There is no doubt that this paradoxical message of salvation laced with physical well-being has found great favor with the rank and file members of the church. It has, therefore, become a norm to not only use the word Daddy for the general overseer Pastor Adeboye as a symbol of worldly father concerns for his children but also for God with the expectation of showering of love and care in this fashion, but in a perfect form of what the worldly Daddy would bestow on his worldly children.

However, there have also been situations where the real intents of the strategies have been either genuinely or fraudulently misappropriated and the person, messages, and actions of Pastor Adebayo have been reduced to materialistic beliefs. Indeed, in December 2008, Pastor Adeboye had to publicly chastise those who were using his name to perpetuate evil. He dismissed their activities as an ungodly act, and that people should not be deceived by their antics. Two incidents were cited to buttress his point. The first was that some people carved his name on stamps and sold them to people. The second was that some people were posting hand-bills, which said that those in need of miracles should pay a certain amount of money into a given account in a new generation bank. He then warned that these activities did not emanate from him, and that those who were indulging in them should desist or they would be visited by the wrath of God.[28]

These misgivings, notwithstanding, it is quite understandable that these existentialist dynamics of the RCCG would provide not only the religious cover and succor but also the initial and sometime permanent haven for immigrants in strange lands, particularly when they are faced with the challenges of settling down, getting jobs, and eventually seeking self-identity, and status mobility. These dynamics have "existentially" emerged in the operations of the R CCG as a mother church in Nigeria and in its North American "transplant."

Transnationalism Contents in RCCGNA

The transnational structure of the church in North America, depending on its mother church in Nigeria, is derivable from a number of dynamics. In terms of personnel, the clergy who pastor parishes in North America today can be divided into two broad categories. The first are those who were already pastors in Nigeria. This category is made up of those directly posted as missionaries to local parishes, and those who have travelling opportunities from Nigeria to participate in the various programs, particularly the yearly conventions of the church in Dallas. Many of these pastors have conveniently decided to remain in the United States, to, as they put it: "serve the Lord and establish parishes of the church."[29] Consequently, RCCG North America has always been engaged in organizing special letters of invitation and visas for these pastors.[30]

The second category consists of members of the church who may not necessarily be clergymen back in Nigeria, but on arriving to the United States for other purposes, received the call to serve the Lord. In this category are lawyers, engineers, accountants, top civil administrators, and other high-career professionals who abandon their secular callings back in Nigeria to become full-time pastors of RCCGNA.

Transnational transplantation is also very much obvious in the various doctrinal beliefs, practices, and programs of the RCCGNA. To begin with, services on Sunday and during the week are direct replicas of those of its mother church in terms of content, structure, and timing.

Programs such as the Holy Ghost service, and the annual convention follow the same patterns. All of these programs are presided over by the General Overseer himself—Pastor Adeboye. Of course, not only do many pastors and other officials of the mother church come from Nigeria to attend these programs, but also pastors, ministers, workers, and members of the RCCGNA are strongly encouraged to attend these programs in Nigeria. Much premium is given to attendance as agencies of spiritual blessing and physical (material) breakthrough.

The existentialist characteristics of the RCCG, which have propelled the transnational significance of the church to immigrants, and thus its dynamic expansion ironically, may not have been consequent on the missionary zeal of the church[31] but rather the materialistic exegesis beginning from the 1980s, widening in the 1990s, and now becoming endemic in the 2000s. As the collapsing economy and the search for greener pastures "forced" flocks of Africans into modern-day voluntary migration, the fortune of African-initiated churches has increased. Indeed, the RCCG has had its "fate" in transnationalism transformed. The United States has became a focal point of migration, not only because of its promise of good life and economic buoyancy but also the lottery program that has made migration to the United States a lot easier and convenient. The Church, through its doctrine, administrative structure, and organizational strategies, has become a transnational existential packaged religious organization, addressing not just the spiritual needs but even more significantly material well-being of African immigrants. It serves as an adjusting, integrating, social mobility, and self-identity agent for immigrants. This has extensively stimulated an unprecedented growth of the church among the immigrants.

The structural strategies to realize these dynamics are located in the various parishes of the RCCGNA, constituting a transnational "home community," and providing a "safe haven" for the African immigrants. Not only do the parishes create an African Christian space, it also afforded the members the opportunity to worship in a form and fashion most fulfilling, and in harmony with their experiences and practices back home. Not only do they acquire religious identity but also self-definition and self-expression in an environment that is most times not congenial to their cultural, religious, and social values. An environment sometimes is basically built on individualism in contrast to the community kinship dynamics of the African heritage.

This basic spiritual and material "home haven" is then manifested through a number of features of the parishes. At the parish levels, church activities consist of Sunday services, midweek services, such as searching the scriptures, and fellowship meetings. Apart from these, there are special prayer seasons, Friday night vigils, and fasting periods. These rather busy religious activity schedules are regarded essential to both spiritual and material well-being of members who also consider devoted attendance of them as sources of immense spiritual and material breakthroughs.[32]

A well-organized agency in the parishes is the welfare committee, which is responsible for the welcoming and integration of new immigrants to the parish. The activities of the committee includes providing transportation, accommodation and paying for them—for those who do not have families to live with—for a period of time for the new arrivals to settle down. The committee also puts into action the necessary networks to look for jobs for the new arrivals. Upon securing accommodation, members of the church donate furniture, drinks, food, and other household items to assist the new arrivals to live comfortably. Sometimes, financial assistance is given by the church and donations are encouraged from members to sustain the new arrivals until they can stand on their own feet.

In serving the economic concerns of members not just in prayers, the parishes constitute organs that promote the profession of members by advertising their businesses. They also encourage members to patronize one another's businesses. Many parishes have also established institutes where members are trained in Computer Studies such as ITT and other forms of business enterprises. [33]

For both new and old members, the church communities usually assume the role and responsibilities of family, comparable to those of the home countries. They offer and anchor spiritual, emotional, and personal needs of members. Characteristically, church officials are the first baton of support in activities involving members such as weddings, baby warming and dedications, birthday parties, and even funeral ceremonies, thus sharing the joyous and painful moments with one another. In times of need such as the above, raising of funds is quite fashionable. Members are assisted in paying hospital bills, disputes are settled among members, and interventions are made to settle marital disputes. Bailing members out of jail, particularly for immigration offenses, are quite common.[34] While some of these tasks are taken up formally by established social and welfare committees in some parishes, in others, the pastors and other well-to-do members of the parishes assume the responsibilities.

The different parishes of RCCGNA also organize educational and informative talks, seminars, and workshops for members. Professionals in different spheres of life are usually invited to conduct these activities. Major items of discussion include finance where members are tutored on how to manage their finances and instructed on the use of credit cards, acquiring properties, and how to be debt free.[35] Another area of concentration is immigration laws. Lawyers are invited to address issues such as acquiring permanent resident status, filing for family members, and rights and privileges as immigrants. One other very central preoccupation is the setting up of businesses. Members learn of the process to register small businesses, obtaining loans for such, and how to profitably administer the businesses periodically, too. The issue of marriage has become subjects of formal and informal tasks and workshops. While marriage counselors are periodically invited to organize marriage counseling clinics, different parishes integrate marriage counseling into their monthly schedule, where members come together led by the pastor or other ministers in the church. Discussions focus on different marital problems, and proffer solutions to prevent marriage breakups such as divorce and/or separation, which are seen to be endemic problems in the American society and against which members should be protected.

The belief is that if individual families are healthy, the church as the larger family will also be healthy. The church cannot progress if there are marital strifes on families constituting the church.

It can be discerned from the discourse above that far more than providing spiritual succor and saving of the souls of members, the parishes of RCCGNA engage in a wide spectrum of activities ranging from social, health, education, economic and marital to ensure that members achieve success in the worldly engagements, making meaning of them with the overall conviction that once they are "materially" comfortable, they would not only be able to serve God better but that Christianity in the form of church organizations provide existential agencies, which according to Sabar[36] serves as the "central focus of personal and community identity formation." The dynamics and strategies resulting from these phenomena vividly demonstrate the capabilities of these churches to provide a "safe haven" of personal and communal identity. Van Dijk succinctly expresses it thus:

> Religious terms, concepts and organization address the modern predicament of the stranger...and offer the individual the means and technique to create a subject identity that fits the condition of translocality—(that is) of not being part of a geographically fitted community and of belonging to a category that is perceived to threaten the "smooth evenness" of everyday life (existential meaning of life).[37]

The fallout of the combination religious and nonreligious organizations of the RCCGNA at the parish, zonal, and headquarter levels is that the church has been transformed into a very influential and popular transnational organization. Its recognition as a formidable religious and social construct is not limited to its members. While the members have come to recognize it as a baton of material "protective hedges" in "imagination" the African community, individuals, government agencies, news media, and other segments of the American society have come to feel the impact of the church because of its large membership. For example, *Newsweek*, an American international news magazine in its January 2009 edition listed the General Overseer of the RCCG, Pastor E. A. Adeboye, as the forty-fifth most powerful person in the world.[38] He was recognized not only for the mega-population of his church[39] but also for "remaining above the fray in faking supernatural powers and honesty." A number of Christian leaders in the United States have voiced their support for *Newsweek's* position. For Yinson Syneu, his visits to the church both in Nigeria and other places in the world have convinced him of not only the "mass" followership of the church, but also that Pastor Adebayo is a person with tremendous power. Peter Wagner, the president of Global Evangelical Ministry spoke of Pastor Adeboye: "[I]f I have to name the top 10 apostles in the world, Adeboye would have to be the top on the list.[40] He goes on to say that Adeboye "represents a new center of gravity for Christianity."

The annual convention of the RCCGNA, which had in the past been rotated among cities in North America, has now found a permanent home in the Redemption Camp, Floyd, Texas, since 2007. The predominant influence and the large number of people who attend these conventions have gained the recognition of the state government, city mayors, judges, and county commissioners. These various governmental officials send messages of solidarity to the convention. In 2008, for example, Rick Perry (then Governor of Texas), John L. Horn (Hunt County Judge), and Kenneth D. Thornton (Hunt County Commissioner), all sent messages of welcome, solidarity, and goodwill to the convention.

The RCCGNA headquarters has also begun to have significant impact on the American society. With the acquiring of expansive property as its headquarters in Floyd, Texas, the church has not only stimulated economic growth in terms of employment and a business conducive environment in the area, it has also inaugurated a process of giving out land freely to its members to build houses. Soon, the camp, just like its mother location in Nigeria, will become a flourishing city community with all the compliments of social, educational, health, business, and other facilities that should stimulate the American economic growth at least in that region. In addition, RCCGNA has commenced the process of establishing a University at the camp, again just like the mother church in Nigeria.

RCCGNA and the Challenges of Transnationalism

With all the growth and influence of the church in North America, the leadership, and membership of the church have been largely restricted to immigrants from Africa, particularly from Nigeria, with the Yoruba from the western part of the country dominating the two categories. This scenario is vividly demonstrated in the statistics of its officials and congregation. An estimated 95 percent of pastors heading the different parishes in RCCG North America, comprising the Caribbean and Canada are made up of immigrants from Nigeria with the overwhelming majority of them being Yoruba.[41]

A number of factors could be identified for this situation. Without a doubt, these factors cannot be isolated from the general American religious configuration of racial "demarcating lines" of Christian affiliations and attendance of places of worship.[42] However, in the case of RCCG North America, this challenge is complicated by the very structure and operation of the church as well as the perceptions of members who largely regard the church as their "home church" in a "foreign land" providing the necessary "haven" of all-round "homeness" not just for spiritual convenience but cultural, social, economic, and so on. Thus, inadvertently, an "exclusivity" of our "church" sustaining "our" vital links to the home land, spiritually and materially, generally prevails.

The relatively "guaranteed" assistance of generating and sustaining an enabling environment for self-identity, confidence, communal acceptability—all needed "tranquilizers" to grapple with intimidating exegeses of "migration" challenges particularly with the American culture of "individualism,"—have become essential stimuli which have greatly enlarged the coast of RCCGNA. Indeed, it has become the fastest and most populous African-initiated church in North America with a membership estimated to be 25,000 according to 2005 figures.[43]

However, these stimuli, which have led to the expansion of the church in North America, have paradoxically become a limiting factor for non-African immigrants to embracing the church. This challenge for the RCCG is aptly captured by Hunt when he points out that the church outside Africa, particularly in Europe and America, has failed to attract non-Africans because it is locally grounded in religious ideology.[44] This situation necessarily raises some fundamental questions for the mission and vision of the church. Should its mission be limited to serving the religious and material needs of just African immigrants, or should it be a mission to all people and races, fulfilling the injunction of Jesus and the expressed desire of the church when it says its goal is to pursue the vision of reaching every nation in the world and making them ready for Jesus Christ. Is it, therefore, necessary for the RCCGNA to reexamine the values and doctrines of the RCCG in the context of the realities of the dynamics of a transnational religion? This becomes an essential engagement for the church if it must address the questions of its sustainability and prospects of not only becoming attractive to an expansive range of communities of individuals with different sociocultural currents of the home origin of RCCG, and in addition providing the African immigrants with the necessary spiritual capabilities to cope with material realities different from their original homeland.

It is instructive that both the leadership and rank and file of the RCCGNA are aware of these challenges and have strived to introduce policies and practices to attempt some transformations that are diaspora friendly. For example, the church discourages the use of native languages, particularly Yoruba, during it services, even for songs. This is to ensure that all members of the congregation are able to follow and understand the language of service and not feel alienated. Consequently, the English language is the official service language. Also, the mode of dressing, particularly of the ministers and workers, has been Westernized. Though this is usually justified on the basis of smartness and avoidance of clumsiness of putting on native attires, it also portends uniformity and conformity with climatic and dressing realities on the ground.

Another area where there has been transformation is the number, days, and duration of services. Unlike the situation in the mother church in Nigeria, where there are one form of services or the other every day of the week, these have been reduced to about two times—Wednesdays and Fridays—in a week. The duration of service has been reduced, ensuring that services do not last more than two hours at most. All of these are forms of responses to work ethics, as people work even on Sundays and in shifts, and the prevailing time consciousness in the United States, which are culturally different from the original home church.

Perhaps the most obvious and significant area where RCCGNA has attempted to transform the values and doctrines of RCCG has been its accommodation of people who ordinarily would have been excluded from its membership. There is now a policy of allowing people to "come as they are" to the church. This entails modes of dressing, conducts, and some habits that in the mother church would have been considered "ungodly" and unacceptable from a "child of God." For instance, women are allowed to attend services without covering their heads and men with dreadlock hairdo, earrings, and chains on their necks are not prevented from attending services, etc. The justification for this is not only a response to cultural realities but also a perception that these people are first and foremost children of God and that they will eventually change to conform to the "original standard" of the church.

While these attempted efforts to transform the values and identity of the "Home RCCG" to conform to the realities of North America and therefore open up the Church to people of diverse races and backgrounds are quite laudable and have been pursued vigorously, their impacts have been at best marginal. This is because there seems to be a difference of perceptions, particularly by people outside RCCGNA, with regard to the factors actually responsible for the apathy of non-Africans for the church. For example, I carried out a survey with students, offering Religions of Africa and African Diaspora in the African Department at the University of North Carolina–Charlotte in 2008. The survey was to examine the membership compositions of different Christian denominations in Charlotte and find out why they belonged to these denominations and why they would want or not want to belong to other denominations. With regard to the RCCG, the findings were quite interesting and illuminating. Only 10 percent of the respondents would not want to be members of the church because of the possibility of conducting part of the service or singing in "original home language(s)" of the church. Indeed, 85 percent of respondents who have at one time or another had cause to attend one or two services of the church found RCCG services not only easy to follow but actually enjoyed the services and adjudged them very interesting and highly spiritual. However, when it came to the doctrines and moral/ habit expectations, 90 percent African-American respondents and 65 percent whites who belong to other Christian denominations find the RCCG doctrines too rigid. Some of the rigid rules cited have to do with habits of smoking and drinking. Others are associated with marital and sexual relationships.

Interestingly, the survey results indicated that in spite of the Pentecostal grounding of RCCG coupled with its African origin, which expectedly should have made it attractive to African-Americans, the reverse seems to be the case. Indeed, African-American respondents were extremely not favorably disposed to becoming members of the church. This situation is empirically demonstrated in the insignificant number of African Americans found in the church as both officials and rank and file.

Based on the above findings, it was the conclusion of the survey that what determines affiliations to a church may be more than just its structure, basic doctrines, and practices. There seems to be a vital and fundamental connection between what religion as a phenomenon ultimately represents for individuals, and their functional expectations from it. Such dynamics are then concretized in a process or processes of choice(s) based on cultural attitudinal fixations that are very difficult to change. In relation to RCCG North America as a transnational church, its determination to incorporate non-African immigrant populations of America, in fulfilling its global mission, will have to contend with these realities, which are endemically linked to what James Spickard refers to as the American sociology of religion.[45]

Conclusion

Our preoccupation in this chapter was to present an exposition of the RCCG North America as a model of transnational church with all attendant sustenance of "home" values and identity in providing both the spiritual and material "instruments" as a "home away from home" congregation for African immigrants to adjust, and be part of the American society, and at the same time fulfill its universal mission of incorporating the non-immigrant population as members of the Church. The challenges faced by the church in its attempt to successfully grapple with these two seemingly exclusive and paradoxical engagements, form the central discourse.

There is no doubt that the church has successfully "transplanted" its leadership, clerical, and administrative structures along with its doctrines and practices. These have essentially preserved the identity and values of the "home church" in Nigeria. The church has significantly fulfilled its functional role of providing spiritual and material needs for African immigrants who have come to view the various congregations of the church all over North America as "bastions" hope and supportive family frontiers in adjusting and settling into the unfamiliar and sometimes intimidating new environment of a different cultural and social dynamic. Even if a total assimilation of the immigrants may not be intended or even achievable, the necessary tools of attaining self integrity and upward social mobility are placed at the disposal of the immigrants. The various church organizations and programs offered have made tremendous strides to provide, temporarily and hopefully permanently, the spiritual and material "covers" to make the African immigrants contented and productive individuals and communities of their "new home."

RCCG North America has expanded tremendously, and has become very visible as a religious organization with a large membership. Unfortunately, its membership has been limited in quantity and quality to African immigrants, particularly from the Nigerian extraction. While the church is quite aware of this challenge and has introduced a number of changes to transform the identity and values of the church to make it universally, and particularly American, friendly, it appears it must further identify the real problems associated with these challenges, and design realistic antidotes to the American sociology of religion, which has kept non-African immigrants at bay.

Notes

1. Ukah, Asonzeh. (2005)."Mobilities, Migration and Multiplication: The Expansion of the Religious Field of the Redeemed Christian Church of God (RCCG) Nigeria" In Adogame, A. & Weissicoppel, C. (eds.) *Religion in the Context of African Migration*, p. 320. Berlin: Bayreuth African Studies.
2. Mensah, Joseph. (2008). *Religious Transnationalism among Ghanaian Immigrants in Toronto: A Binary Logistic Regression Analysis* In Canadian Geographer, vol. 52. Issue 3, p. 309.
3. Ibid, p. 309.
4. See Earthfamilyalpha, *Transnationalism,* Saturday October 21, 2006, p. 1. http://earthfamilyalpha.blogspot.com/2006/10/transnationalism.html
5. Ibid.
6. Vertovec, S. (1999). "Conceiving and Researching Transnationalism." *Ethnic and Racial Studies,* vol. 22, no. 2, p. 452.

7. Portes, A. (2001). "Introduction: The Debates and Significance of Immigrants Transnationalism." *Global Networks,* vol.1 no. 3, p. 183.

8. Vertovec, *Conceiving and Researching Transnationalism,* p. 453.

9. Schipper, M. (2005). Taken from Ezra Chitando, "The Insider/Outsider Problem in Research on Religion and Migration" In Adogame, A. & Weissicoppel, C. (eds.) *Religion in the Context of African Migration,* p. 83.

10. My experiences in association with RCCG comprise of periods of being a nonmember and then a member and official of the church.

11. Ukah, Asonzeh. (2005). "Mobilities, Migration and Multiplication: The Expansion of the Religious Field of the Redeemed Christian Church of God (RCCG) Nigeria" In Adogame, A. & Weissicoppel, C. (eds.) *Religion in the Context of African Migration,* p. 320.

12. Ibid, p. 321.

13. Ibid.

14. Ibid.

15. Ibid.

16. Ibid, p. 327.

17. Ibid, p. 336.

18. See *Redemption Light* (2002), Vol. 7, No.5, p. 25.

19. Ibid, p. 24.

20. Ibid.

21. A commitment to this facet of Christianity has been identified as the major reason for the proliferation of Independent (Pentecostal) African Christian Churches.

22. The 11th Annual RCCG North America Convention (Divine Visitation) Program June 20–22, 2007, p. 7.

23. Adeboye, E.O. (1989). *How to Turn your Austerity into Posterity.* Lagos: CRM Publishers, p. 29.

24. The 11th Annual RCCG North America Convention (Divine Visitation) Program June 20–22, 2007, p. 1.

25. The 12th Annual RCCG North America Convention (The King of Glory) Program June 18–20, 2008, p. 1.

26. Ibid, p. 2.

27. Ibid.

28. See *Nigerian Tribune* Monday December 2008, p. 3.

29. Ukah, *Mobilities, Migration and Multiplication.*

30. Ibid.

31. Ibid.

32. An Interview with the Pastor in charge of RCCG Charlotte North America, Pastor Isaac Aladeniyi.

33. Interview with the Minister in charge of Welfare committee RCCG All Nations, South Carolina.

34. Interview with the Minister in charge of Welfare committee RCCG Victory Temple Charlotte, North Carolina.

35. Interview with the Pastor in charge of RCCG All Nations, South Carolina.

36. Sabar, Gelia. (2005). "The African Christian Diaspora in the Holy Land: Preliminary Notes and Observations" In Adogame, A. & Weissicoppel, C. (eds.) *Religion in the Context of African Migration,* p. 176.

37. Van Dijk, (1997). "From Camp to Encompassment: Discourses of Transsubjectivity in Ghanaian Pentecostal Diaspora" In: *Journal of Religion in Africa,* vol. 27, no. 2, p. 138.

38. See *Newsweek,* December 20 2009.

39. See *Nigerian Tribune Newspapers*, Monday December 28 2008.

40. *Newsweek,* December 20, 2009.

41. Statistics compiled from the 2009 convention program of RCCG North America.

42. Spickard, James. (2005). "Networks, Homes, or Congregations? Exploring the Locus of Immigrant Religiosity" In Adogame, A. & Weissicoppel, C. (eds.) *Religion in the Context of African Migration,* p. 34.

43. *Dallas Morning News*, July 20, 2005.

44. Ukah, *Mobilities, Migration and Multiplication*, p. 338.

45. Spickard, *Networks, Homes, or Congregations? Exploring the Locus of Immigrant Religiosity*, p. 36.

Chapter 19

Islamic Communities in the United States: Issues of Religion and Political Identity

Yushau Sodiq

Introduction

This chapter addresses the issues of religion and political identity among three Islamic groups in the United States—the African American Muslims, African Immigrant Muslims, and the Arab community. Who are these groups, and how do they define themselves? Are they Americans or Muslims, and to what extent do they engage in the civil society of America? Can Muslims retain their Islamic identities, and participate effectively in American politics? Would their loyalty be questioned? Identity here refers to how an individual and the community are shaped and reshaped by each other. That is, what makes a person a Muslim, what differentiates a Muslim community from a non-Muslim community, and how does a Muslim relate to his/her community?[1]

Muslim communities in the United States are diverse. They come from all over the world; they speak different languages and hold different nationalities. Muslims do not come to America to spread Islam or convert Christians and others to Islam, nor to establish an Islamic state as alleged by ill-informed media. It was America, in the seventeenth century, which actually imported Muslim slaves from West Africa to the United States to work on the plantations. They were brought here by force. Ignorantly, the slaveholders thought that all slaves were illiterate and uncivilized. Thus, they maltreated them and deprived them of their liberty as human beings. Little did the slaveholders know that some of their slaves were Muslims, literate and religious leaders before they were enslaved. It did not take a long time before a few strong Muslim slaves asserted their identity by not eating pork or drinking wine.[2]

Some slaves actually prayed on the plantation, started fasting during the month of *Ramadan* and reading their *Qur'an,* the Muslim scripture, from their memory. Some slaveholders were shocked because they did not know what those slaves were doing and what languages they were speaking. A few slaves began to document their experiences in Arabic language as alluded to by Austin Allen in his celebrated work, *African American in the Antebellum America.*[3]

The slaveholders labored relentlessly to rid Muslim slaves of their religious identity. While many slaves succumbed to such brutal and immoral pressure, a few Muslims renounced such pressure and courageously held on to their beliefs. Eventually some of them worked hard and bought their freedom, and returned to Africa like Job ben Solomon (Ayub bin Sulayman).[4] Those who remained in the United States kept their religious beliefs as much as they could. As time went on, African Muslims practiced less and less of Islam because of the unconducive environment, which surrounded their daily lives. Many converted to Christianity[5] for practical purposes to win favorable treatment from their masters. The social attitudes toward Muslim slaves remained very hostile until the beginning of the twentieth century when Islam resurfaced. It was a "recovery" of practices thought to be long buried. It was revived by a few American Muslim pioneers like Alexander Webb, Mr. Wallace Fard, Timothy Noble Drew Ali, Elijah Muhammad, and Malcolm X between 1890 and the 1940s.

Alexander Russell Webb was a Caucasian working at the American Cultural attaché in the Philippines where he became a Muslim in Manila. On his return to America, he continued to practice Islam and represented Muslims in the World Parliament of Religion in Chicago in 1893, which was chaired by Rev. Dr. John Henry Barrows. Timothy Noble Drew Ali and Elijah Poole (Muhammad) were African American Muslims, who helped African Americans regain their identity as humans and as Muslims.[6] These pioneers believed that they had significant roles to play in reforming and reshaping American attitudes toward blacks.[7] Drew Ali was one of the early pioneers who emphasized the importance of having self-identity. He established a Moorish Temple for his community and made great contributions to many Americans of African descents—as he used to label them. His contributions to Islam in the United States cannot be underrated as pointed out by Richard Turner. He enhanced their self-esteem.

> No matter how bizarre his (Drew Ali's) ideas may appear in retrospect, he introduced thousands of Black people to Islam early in the twentieth century. Because of his ideas, Black Americans developed a global perspective on race and politics in the context of his version of Islam. Drew Ali's religious imagination was boundless and his esoteric vision of Islam brought the religion from the elite international circles of Mohammed Alexander Russell Webb into American popular culture, where it would eventually thrive in spite of harassment by the federal government.[8]

Black's appeal for equal and fair treatment as human beings did not resonate in the beginning, but it gained huge momentum when Malcolm X joined the Nation of Islam (NOI) in 1952 after his release from prison. He carried his Islamic message to the American public on a large scale for the first time. Both Elijah Muhammad and Malcolm X emphasized the importance of self-identity as a group. It was also in 1952 that the Muslims in the Armed Service sued the Federal government to be recognized as Muslims.

When Malcolm X became a minister in the NOI, anyone who converted to Islam and joined the Nation of Islam was given a new name, and the letter "X" as a surname to replace whatever name that was given to him by the slaveholders.[9] The issue of identity characterized the whole nature of the NOI at that time. With this new identity, Muslims were assured that they were full human beings like others, that they had a remarkable great history and origin, that they possessed great intelligence, and that the blacks had contributed tremendously to human civilizations and built enormous empires and a great culture in Egypt just like any other human race. Elijah and Malcolm X preached that blacks should assume their leadership roles of humanity as they did in the past before it was usurped by the white people. Wallace Fard,[10] the real founder of the Nation of Islam, preached that blacks were superior to the whites to boost the morale of African Americans.[11] He assured them that they were unique human beings with their distinctive qualities. When Elijah Muhammad became the leader of the NOI in 1934, after the disappearance of Wallace Fard, he reiterated the same idea that white people were devils and that black men were the cream of and origin of humanity. Elijah Muhammad stated:

> The origin man, Allah has declared, is none other than the black man. The black man is the first and last, maker and owner of the universe. From him came brown, yellow, red and white people. By using a special method of birth control law, the black man was able to produce the white race... The White race is not, and never will be, the chosen people of Allah (God). They are the chosen people of their father Yakub, the devil.[12]

This approach is termed as "reversed psychology" among the Nation of Islam. It was an attempt to ascertain the identity of blacks that he is the origin of human beings and is superior to a white man. Elijah believed that this would enable a black man to recover his true faith and authentic sense of himself. The members of the NOI held on to this identity of their superiority over the white man for more than 40 years. It was Imam Warithu Deen Mohammed who changed this racist ideology and asserted that there is no superiority of one race over another in Islam.

Elijah and Malcolm X reconstructed the worldviews of the African Americans and taught them self-respect for themselves, respect for their family, and work ethics of hard work in order to be self-independent economically. They expressed what they wanted as follows:

a) We want freedom, equal justice under the law, and equal opportunity;
b) We want our own people in America whose parents or grandparents were descendants from slaves, to be allowed to establish a separate territory of their own—either on this continent or elsewhere;
c) We want freedom for all believers of Islam now held in federal prisons;

d) We want an immediate end to the police brutality and mob attacks against
the so-called Negro throughout the United States;

e) We want equal education—but separate schools up to 16 for boys and 18
for girls on the condition that the girls be sent to women's colleges and
universities.[13]

The above shows how self-identity was crucial for the survival of the African
American Muslims in the 1950s and 1960s. Despite this orientation by these pioneers, many African Americans perceived themselves as different from all others and
considered America as very hostile to them.[14] Hence, they withdrew from engaging
in politics by choice. They became alienated in their own country. This hostile
situation lasted until the death of Malcolm X in 1965 and Elijah Muhammad in
1975. Neither pioneer wanted to do anything with American politics because they
believed that the government was against them and wanted to keep them as uneducated and uninformed people for as long as possible.

When Imam Warithu-deen Mohammed, the son of Elijah Muhammad, took
over the leadership of the NOI after his father's death in 1975, he breathed new
hope into the NOI, changing nearly everything that his father had taught and
strongly encouraged his followers to embrace America as their great country. He
appealed to them to engage in politics for their own good. Eventually, he himself
held the American flag in 1978, pledging allegiance to America, and asked all of
his followers to do the same. He emphasized that African Americans are pure and
fully Americans.[15]

That drastic change in ideology and complete assimilation toward America
embarrassed those who were still clinging to the rhetoric of the NOI of separatism.
It was at that point that Minister Louis Farrakhan,[16] the present leader of the NOI,
broke away from Imam W. D. Mohammed in 1978 because he could not believe that
Imam W. D. Mohammed would disapprove his father's teachings[17] and embrace the
American flag. Farrakhan resorted back to the rhetoric of Elijah Muhammad of
depicting the white man as an evil person.[18] Farrakhan in those days preached that
the Black Muslims should not participate in American politics, which is a racist
government. This was a card, which Malcolm X played for many years before he
changed to a mainstream Islam when he went to Mecca for pilgrimage in 1964.[19]

However, from 1978 on, many followers of Imam W. D. Mohammed engaged
in politics and some became mayors, like Mr. Charles Mustafa Bilal,[20] the mayor
of Kountze, Texas; some became councilmen, while a few others served in high
political positions in the state[21] and at the national level. With such participation,
they once again proved themselves to be fully Americans. They dropped the idea
of going back to Africa, the origin homeland, as preached by Marcus Garvey, or
seeking a separate state exclusively for African Americans as advocated by Elijah
Muhammad.[22] The leaders of the NOI in the 1960s thought that they would be able
to practice their religion peacefully if they had their own state.

The followers of Imam W. D. Mohammed were able to practice their religion
of Islam publicly without any persecution or restriction as they resided everywhere
in the country. The only place where they had their freedom curtailed to some
extent is in the correctional institutions for security purposes. The department of

transportation also insists that Muslim women who are taking photo IDs must not cover their face with a headscarf (*Hijab*) because the main purpose of having a photo ID is to identify who a person is. If a female Muslim covers her face, it will be difficult to identify her. On most other issues, Muslim practices are accommodated and tolerated. Where there arises a dispute between a Muslim and local authority or employer on the issue of practicing a specific aspect of Islam, if they could not solve the problem, they go to the court of law for clarification and jurisdiction, like the issue of recognizing Islam in the prison as a religion on the same level with Christianity and Judaism.[23]

> It is sufficient here to say that one concept of religion calls for a belief in the existence of a supreme being controlling the destiny of man. That concept of religion is met by the Muslims in that they believe in Allah, as a supreme being and as the one true god. It follows, therefore, that *the Muslim faith is a religion*.[24]

In addition, after a long controversy, the employers are encouraged in the United States to permit their Muslim employees to observe their religious practices like Friday prayer. Such decision was based on the freedom of religion as stipulated in the United States Constitution. However, if any particular employer does not allow his employees to pray, for one reason or another, the employees are free to find other jobs.

Today, there are many African American mayors around the country and some of them are Muslims. They engage in politics; they hold strategic positions in the government on local, state, and national levels.[25] The fear of losing their Islamic identity by engaging in politics is fading away rapidly. They learn how to preserve their identities from their new experiences through their interacting with the society at large. They become aware that engaging in American politics amounts to serving all Americans including Muslims. With such interactions, they are better situated to promote the common agenda of their people not on the premise of Islam, but on the grounds that whatever is good for America is good for Muslims also.[26] A few Muslims who are holding political positions today continuously and consciously assert that they are proud of serving their country and to be Americans first before being Muslim Americans.

On voting, a majority of African American Muslims voted for President Obama in 2008. Of course, their votes could not be separated from the votes of the African Americans in general. The Gallop poll affirmed that 93 percent of African Americans voted for Obama in 2008. They show more inclination toward the Democratic Party than to the Republican Party. Whatever the situation, since the 1980s, African American Muslims did vote because their leaders encouraged them to do so for their own benefit. However, the immigrant Muslims might keep their presidential election secret so as not to be vilified by the Islamophobia trend in the country.[27] African American Muslims keep their preference open, and even advocate it publicly because they have a greater stake in elections and in politics.

Indeed, the African American Muslims assert their unique identity as Muslim, and they portray it in their involvement in politics. While they are not running/contesting for many political positions on the platform of Islam, they believe very strongly that their progressive agenda for the minority is inclusive. American Muslims would never be left out, for they will all benefit from it because of the freedom of expression and religion, which the Constitution guarantees them in terms of protection, and the exercise of their legal rights as citizens of the United States. With this analysis, one can say that the African American Muslim community represents a unique marriage between its personal identity and engagement in politics. It perceives no contradiction between being a good Muslim and a good politician. The only distinctive quality of African Americans is that they are Americans first and Muslim second,[28] whereas, many immigrants claim to be Muslims first and Americans second. Which of these two identities is preferred should be left to each individual to decide. Those who embrace this unique marriage between politics and their identity continuously find themselves involved and engaged in the community. Those who think that politics is incompatible with their religious identity remain isolated and noninvolved. Alas, they bring little benefit to their community.

The Case of the African Immigrant Muslims in the United States

African immigrants refer to the people who migrated to the United States from Africa toward the end of the twentieth century, and not the African Americans whose ancestors were imported to the United States as slaves. There exists no reliable census on the population of the Muslim immigrants from Africa. Perhaps, some countries have more immigrants in the United States than others. There are thousands of Nigerians who came to the United States after the Biafra Civil War of 1967–1970, with the majority of them being Christians. However, there are many Somali people in the United States; they are all Muslims. They come to the Americas for economic, political, and religious reasons. Some come as refugees and are not educated and hardly speak English. The immigrants from Francophone West Africa are Muslims but many of them are not skilled persons like Nigerians and Ghanaians, and English is their third language. Their life in the United States is extremely tough. Yet, they too are trying to assert their African and Islamic identity as pointed out by Zain in his work on Senegalese Murid group in New York.[29] The majority of Francophone West African immigrants are Sufis, and they often reside on their arrival to the United States in cities where many others are living like New York and Michigan.

Some Muslim immigrants do convert to Christianity[30] in the United States in order to improve their social and economic status. Quite often, their hosts upon arrival to the United States are Christians: either their immediate relatives or Christian volunteers or missionaries.[31] These hosts primarily render needed support on the condition that their guests become Christians as we have been told by some informants. They offer them financial support and educational scholarship to entice them into Christianity. Therefore, many "weak" Muslims from Nigeria or Ghana, Sierra Leone, and even from North Africa convert to Christianity just to fit in and earn what they want, especially after the September 11 incident. Immigrants from North Africa have different stories, which we will address later. They are not as vulnerable as Muslims are from West or East Africa.

The African Muslim immigrants struggle to maintain their religious identity in the United States. They believe that America is a Christian country, even though America never declares itself to be a religious state. Some Muslim immigrants think that they would not be able to achieve their dreams or attain their goals if they practice Islam in public. As such, they have an identity crisis and want to be accepted socially by attending church services and drinking publicly. A few would change their names from Jibril to Gabriel, from Yusuf to Joseph, from Maryam to Mary, and from Muhammad to Moe. Occasionally, a few others would deny their affiliation to Islam in which secure a job, or to be recognized as a loyal American. There is a story where a Caucasian Muslim professor was returning home from a visit abroad. He landed at John F. Kennedy Airport in New York and took a taxi. The cab driver from Africa welcomed him and proudly said to his passenger without being asked, that his name was Moe and that he was not a Muslim, so as to impress upon his passenger that he was not a terrorist. The passenger (the professor) responded that his name was Ahmad (not real name), that he was a Muslim, and that he taught Islam at one of the universities in California. The cab driver, who unconsciously showed his inferiority complex, was shocked and remained silent until he dropped his passenger at the hotel. In other words, some immigrant Muslims are afraid of being identified as Muslims especially after September 11. They hide their religious identity as much as they can for their own personal well-being.

Many African immigrant Muslims from the Anglo-Saxon area of West Africa come to America for a higher education. Most of those from Francophone West Africa come to work. However, the majority of them have to learn English anew, whereas those from Nigeria or Ghana or Sierra Leone or Liberia already speak fluent English and have no problem in pursuing their goals immediately after their arrival. It should be pointed out that less that 10 percent of all immigrants from Anglo-Saxon West Africa are Muslims; the remaining are Christians. Many Muslims from West Africa are not encouraged to come to the United States but to travel to Arab countries for their higher education and advanced study of Islam or Arabic language.

Muslim immigrants face the dilemma of assimilation.[32] Their ways of life are very different from the Christian ways, especially for those who are determined to practice Islam on a daily basis. In their early years in America, they have to struggle for survival. After finishing their education, they marry or bring their wives from Africa. Then they have children and begin to plan for their children's education. A few Muslims may show some interest in politics, but this interest is restricted to American foreign policy regarding their home countries and not about the internal issues of their places of residence in the United States. As such, they do not participate in local, state, or national politics of America whatsoever. Only on rare occasion can one find a Muslim immigrant or African immigrant who truly participates in school boards or PTAs, becomes a member of City Council, or competes for chairmanship at his job despite the fact that s/he may be well qualified and capable of doing the job extremely well. African immigrant Muslims do not contribute in the decision-making on how the schools their children are attending are run or who wins what in local government races and elections. "Even if we're members, nobody would listen to us," they mockingly argue during my interviews with some of them. Therefore, it can be concluded that African immigrant Muslims are passive members of the society in America, and they do not easily assimilate. They often see something "wrong" with American values. They embrace the "myth" that they are living temporarily in the United States, and that one day they will return to their country of origin. This is a dream, which 90 percent of them have never achieved. Nevertheless, they opt out of politics just as the Amish and Mennonites did in the United States. And by opting out, such nonparticipation subjects them to the vagaries resulting from the political and social choices of the larger communities. That is, they are vulnerable to accept any decision made by the larger society on their behalf on what they like or dislike.[33]

The children of the African immigrants receive their education in the United States and become affluent, socially and economically. However, many lose their Islamic identity during their educational training, and some do change their names or adopt new nicknames to fit in. They often do not practice Islam on a daily basis, and only a few of them retain their Islamic identity. They too show no interest in politics or in rendering any services to the civil community where they grow up or reside because they observe that their parents do not participate in politics. Mostly, they are interested in jobs, games, music, and entertainment. Ironically, African Muslim immigrants associate less with one another from Africa. Each country has its own organization representing different ethnic groups, and they hardly collaborate with one another on any major social or political issue. For instance, there are Nigerian Muslim organizations, Sudanese associations, Senegalese associations, Gambia associations, and others. But there are no genuine interactions among them except on celebrating national, cultural festivals, or independent days. They attend such cultural events to socialize. On any other important issues regarding promotion of democracy, public good, or prevention of HIV/AIDS, they lag behind and lack team work. They do not have any collective common project or specific goals, which they collaborate to achieve.

In regards to voting during the elections, there exists no statistics on how many African immigrant Muslims voted in the 1996, 2000, 2004, and 2008 elections. In my interviews with a few of them in the Dallas/Fort Worth areas, the majority did not vote in 2000 nor in 2004. The minority who did vote cast their ballots for Bush in 2004, and for Obama in 2008. They have mixed feelings for the upcoming elections. As they show no keen interest in politics, they form no political group, contribute no financial support to any candidate, and hence affiliate not to any specific political party. Yet, they can debate about politics from morning to evening. No political party seeks out their votes despite the fact that they are well educated; some are professionals, educators, businessmen, and women. Interestingly, many African immigrant Muslim women are not voting either. They are busy working and attending to their livelihood. The failure of many African immigrant Muslims to vote may be due to the fact that they and their family had never voted before in their country of origin, and hence do not know the value and importance of voting in a civil society. Another reason for not voting may be their lack of concern for American policies, especially when those policies relate not to their countries of origin. They also express less interest in domestic issues that they think do not affect them directly. As a result, many are not registered voters even though they are citizens and eligible voters.

It is pertinent to point out that self-identity and recognition cannot only be attained through political processes, but also through establishing private institutions of learning whereby a person learns about his community's values, morals, history, and identity. After learning these distinctive qualities, they can be projected to the larger community through interaction with them and participation in the public sphere. For instance, African American Muslims focus on these efforts by helping reshape America from the bottom up. They seek the redemption of African American society through the teaching of responsibility, family values, respect for the law and accountability. Through this process, Imam Warithu Deen Mohammed asserts that African American Muslims are able to save their children and their community from a future of violence and the drug-infested ghettos of America.[34] The role of the NOI in "cleaning up" some American ghettos where African Americans live cannot be underrated as pointed out by Turner in his work.[35]

African immigrant Muslims have had no specific institution of learning or training center, which cater to their social and economic needs. The Jews who are minorities in the United States have many institutions of learning, colleges, universities, training centers, seminaries, and other facilities where they train their own people, and teach them on what they want them to uphold in the future, and the roles they like them to play in American politics and economy. The Native Americans, Asians, Japanese, and the Chinese build institutions and establish different social centers, which attend to the specific needs of their own people in America. Through these institutions, they determine and define their own identity, what exactly they wish to accomplish in their American communities, and how they want to be perceived.

As pointed out earlier, African immigrant Muslims, so far, have no specific institutions of learning or businesses[36] that cater to their specific or cultural needs. Therefore, they have no influence on American politics, and no political group consults them or even asks them for their votes because they are not organized under any umbrella. The negative results of the lack of participation in politics can be seen in the following. African immigrants receive no recognition from the larger community for anything they contribute to America, economically or scientifically. Often, since they are blacks, the white people see them as free riders. The African- Americans, on their part, perceive them as usurpers of their "rightful jobs." They even hold them responsible for the plight of their precarious lives in America. They allege that the grandfathers of the present African immigrants sold them into slavery in Africa. Therefore, they were the cause of their predicaments. The African immigrants reject this accusation.

The African immigrants, on their part, hold negative attitudes toward African Americans in general, and perceive them as nonambitious people because they hold back on pursuing education or receiving training in modern sciences despite all the numerous opportunities and resources available to them through the US Government. Hence, many African immigrants establish fewer relationships with

African Americans and do not wish to identify with them, except perhaps when they solicit their help through marriage to obtain legal status in America.

African immigrants allege that the identity of African Americans has been strained, and therefore they do not want to associate with them. They assume that they are better off than the African Americans who in turn assume that the immigrants in general have no experience in how America functions and operates. But in reality, Africans are Africans, and they are all black in the eyes of the white Americans. Indeed, many white people think that African immigrants are lower in quality than the African Americans. Africa and Africans are portrayed in American media today as poor, illiterate, and carriers of diseases like HIV/AIDS. They feel that the Africans and the African continent needs assistance and urgent rescue from many social and economic problems, which destabilize their lives.

Fortunately, many African immigrant Muslims are aware of this negative attitude, and thus work hard to be very independent financially from the tutelage of the whites, and the disdain and contempt of the blacks toward them. Nonetheless, they remain isolated politically for lack of involvement in American politics, and hence lose their identity gradually as loyal Americans.

The Case of the Immigrant Muslim Communities from North Africa

There is no strong evidence that immigrant Muslims from North Africa came to the United States as slaves, nor were they seeking asylum in the United States as did many other migrants. Immigrant Muslims from North Africa come here voluntarily searching for a better life just like Europeans and Russians. From the diplomatic point of view, Morocco was the first Muslim country to recognize the independence of the United States—as a sovereign state—from British colonial rule. Since that recognition, the political relationship between North Africa and the United States has been cordial. Nevertheless, the early Muslims from North Africa to arrive in the United States did not come to propagate Islam but to seek a better livelihood. They actually assimilated completely into the American society and identified themselves as Americans. The number of Muslim immigrants from North Africa was very small. It was after the French colonial rule over North Africa that we began to see a flood of Muslims from that area coming to the United States after the 1960s. The first and second generations of these immigrants did not pay attention to religious identity at all. But as they became older, they wanted to leave an Islamic legacy and culture for their children. This prompted them to search and embrace their Islamic identity and start affiliating themselves more to Islam. Hence, they embarked on the building of mosques and Islamic centers. Yet, they did not participate in the civil society or engage in politics, which they perceived as unimportant and irrelevant to their economic survival.

However, after September 11, they witnessed relentless efforts by the government to vilify them and tarnish their image. Some Christian evangelicals joined the bandwagon of Islamophobia and began to suspect Muslims from the Arab world as terrorists. The Arab Muslims have no choice but to defend their identity as non-violent people and nonterrorists. They began to participate in social activities of their community, engage in religious dialogues and interfaith discussions, and reach out to compete for political positions to defend their identity and participate in decision-making on issues relating to them in America. They form their own organizations on civil rights and advocate groups and encourage their people to register and vote in local, state, and national elections. They realize that in order for them to effect change, they must participate and interact with American people and engage in politics, which they do.

Unfortunately, they do not collaborate with other minority civil rights groups like African Americans or Latinos. Thus, their achievements in politics remain very limited. They would have achieved a lot more and accomplished most of their goals if they had interacted and learned from the experiences of others.

Muslims in the United States have never witnessed so much hostility against them and Islam as they experienced after September 11. Indeed, all American Muslims became suspects and potential terrorists, particularly the immigrants. They have to prove their identity as good and loyal "citizens" wherever they go. Their activities, social gatherings, traveling within and outside the country, and even their assembly at the houses of worship, in the mosques and Islamic centers, are put under constant surveillance to know exactly what they are doing and who they relate to.[37] All of these suspicions and intrusions upon their rights and identity were carried out under the pretext of the War on Terrorism by the Bush Administration. The government agencies who are working for the Homeland Security encroach upon the religious and civil rights of Muslim citizens to root out terrorism alleged. However, they do more damage than they repair.

As a result of this surveillance, Muslims receive negative portrayal in the media as well as relentless propaganda of some Christian evangelicals against Islam and Muslims. Suffer under the members of the Muslim communities were abused by the government and some were deported; some were wrongly imprisoned, tortured, harassed, and vilified. Some are constantly monitored and prevented from traveling abroad, and a few who had traveled abroad were not allowed to reenter the United States under the allegation that they are threat to the security of the United States. Even a scholars like Tariq Ramadan was prevented from attending an international conference of the American Academy of Religion in America due to a suspicion that he had assisted a terrorist group in Palestine some years back. With such attitudes from the American government, many Muslims lose their identity to the extent that some are afraid to be known as Muslims. September 11 has been a terrible experience for many Muslim communities all over the United States as their identities as loyal citizens are questioned. Some Americans wonder how a person can be a Muslim and an American simultaneously. They forget that the African American Muslims who are the majority of the Muslims in the United States are Americans, not immigrants. They and their parents and grandparents were born and raised in America, and they serve in all spheres of life, including in the military.

Occasionally, some neighbors of Muslims prevent them from expanding their mosques or centers, or even starting a new building as in the case of the Ground

Zero Center in New York. At times, they are not allowed to use neighborhood burial grounds to bury their deceased. At other times, neighbors protest against the building of Islamic schools or mosques in their areas thinking that such institutions are breeding facilities for terrorism, and thus a threat to the security of the United States. The media projects the fear of Muslims and Islam in the hearts of the American people and nurtures it with horrible bad news from national and international events abroad. Since the majority of Americans believe whatever is reported by the media, their perception of Islam and Muslims reflect what they have been fed, which is negative, biased, and unfair indictment of Muslims.

However, Muslim immigrants were passive citizens. In the past, they engaged not in politics believing that they would not be affected by political decisions. They believe that they came to the United States to improve their economic status and then return home. They have a strong feeling that as long as they have enough educational credentials, they will make it in America. Hence, they concentrated on the accumulation of wealth, and neglected involvement in politics at all levels. They felt no need to collaborate with one another until the 1980s after the bombing of American embassies abroad, and they became suspected of terrorism acts. It was then that they formed different Muslim organizations, which aim at defending the rights of the Muslims in the United States. The Council of American Islamic Relations (CAIR) champions this struggle and establishes it branches all over the United States, and monitors how Muslims are being treated or persecuted or abused in all spheres of life in the United States. Another organization, which helps Muslims organize themselves politically, is the American Muslim Alliance (AMA). This is an umbrella political group that assists and encourages Muslims to register for voting in order to effect change on issues relating to them like the case of terrorism and the Patriotic Act I and II.

One of the reasons why Muslim immigrants have not achieved substantial progress or created a big challenge to the US government is their failure to collaborate with one another and with other minorities like Latinos or the African American Muslims. There is no alliance with other racial minority groups. Such alliances would have enabled them to advocate collectively on issues of their interest like the abolition of the Patriotic Acts, which criminalize Muslims as suspects of terrorism before they are proven guilty in the court of law or profiling them after September 11. The African American Muslims did not come to the rescue of these Arabs because the Arab Muslims never sought their support and also on the grounds that the Arabs in America never supported the African American Muslims on any social issues.

Indeed, many Muslim immigrants feel that they have nothing at stake in the United States. But experience has shown that they do have some moral problem that is at stake in this melting pot of America. The second and third generations of the immigrants from Africa embrace not the moral values that their parents subscribe to, especially the respect for others and the art of kindness and generosity. As they receive education in the United States, they lose some traditional values, which were taught them at home. And since they do not teach ethics at elementary and high school in the public schools, the children grow up without knowing what is actually right or wrong. They also lose their distinctive aspect of their culture as

Africans. The result being that when they grow up, they are neither fully accepted as Americans, and the African identity they could fall back upon has been lost. Hence, they live in two worlds: the dreamed American world and the lost African past.

We believe very strongly that African Muslim immigrants should work hard to be financially independent, socialize, interact, and participate in American politics to effect change especially on moral issues, equal opportunity, fair treatment, and discrimination. By joining hands with other minorities, they can achieve their collective goals and become recognized in America just like the Europeans and the Jewish people. From the above analysis, it should be concluded that African immigrant Muslims hardly engage in politics. What we are asserting is that even when they participate, they do so on an individual basis, and not in the name of an organization. Nevertheless, African American Muslims are not foreigners in this country; they are fully American citizens regardless of whatever labels are given to them.

Conclusion

Despite all of the social discrimination or prejudices that Muslims encounter in the United States, Muslims are safer and freer to practice Islam in America than they are in most Muslim countries.[38] They also have the opportunity to participate in politics if they choose to. Muslims are better off economically in the United States than in their country of origin. They consider America as a country of opportunities and safe haven.

> Many American Muslims, particularly African-American Muslims, are proud to be American citizens. They are native to America, and Islam has given them the dignity and self esteem to make their lives meaningful even as they struggle against racial discrimination. Immigrant Muslims share sentiments to the extent that they are grateful for the opportunity that America has given them to prosper and practice their faith. They believe that America is *Dar al-Sulh* (the abode of peace) and in many of its practices much more Islamic than are many contemporary Muslim states.[39]

African American Muslims are proud of their Islamic identity. They choose to be Muslims despite all the odds they encounter in their communities. They are fully Americans and some participate in American politics, locally and nationally, and they reap the great benefit of their participations by seeing some of their leaders holding high political positions and advocating for the interests and needs of the Black population. On the contrary, the immigrant Muslims are proud of residing in America but occasionally shy away from identifying themselves as Muslims for the fear of being persecuted or profiled. Many of the immigrants are Muslims by nationality; they do not choose Islam; they are born into it. They participate less in American politics believing that they have little at stake in America. Nevertheless, they believe very strongly that America remains the best place to live. The American government and American people should recognize Islam as one of the Abrahamic religions and Muslims as indispensable members of our community.

Muslim immigrants themselves should venture out of their confinement, reach out to the community, and contribute to the betterment of their own people and of all Americans. They should recognize that there is no one to scratch their back for them better than themselves. The religion of Islam, which they profess, differentiates not between religion and politics since its inception. It is very ironic that African Muslim immigrants refrain from engagement in politics, an attitude that their religion discourages. Islam has a lot to offer to this country in terms of morals and values. Muslims should be the engine of change to a better life for all Americans. That cannot happen if Muslims are not proud of their religious identity or withdraw from positive engagement in our civil society. And as long as they lag behind economically and politically, they will always be marginalized by the majority public, and their condition will not improve until they participate and contribute their best to this community of ours. It is through these participations, unwavering love, and strong commitment that they will attain success and prosperity in America, the land they are destined to spend their lives.[40]

Notes

1. For more meanings of what constitutes an Islamic or Muslim identity, see Mohommed A. Muqtedar Khan, "Muslims and Identity Politics in America," In *Muslims on the Americanization Path*, edited by Haddad and John Esposito (Oxford: Oxford University Press, 2000), pp. 87–101.
2. Sodiq, Yushau. (2011). *An Insider's Guide to Islam*. (Indianapolis: IN, Trafford Publishing, pp. 432–4.
3. Austin, Allan. (1995). *African Muslims in the Antebellum America: A Sourcebook*. New York: Garland Publishing Company.
4. For more information about African Muslim slaves in the United States, see Sylviane A. Diof, *Servants of Allah: African Muslims Enslaved in the Americas* (New York State University Press, 1998).
5. See Jeffrey Sheller, "Black Muslims: From Fringe to Bedrock," *U.S News & World Report*, 8 October, 1990: p. 70; Asma Gull Hasan, *American Muslims: The New Generation* (New York: Continuum, 2002, p. 17).
6. Haddad, Y. & Smith, Jane. (1993). *Mission to America: Five Islamic Sectarian Communities in North America*. Gainesville: University Press of Florida, pp. 79–80.
7. McCloud, Amina. (1995). *African American Islam* (New York: Routledge, pp. 30–31). McCloud explains the agenda which the Nation of Islam attempts to achieve for the African American Muslims.
8. Turner, Richard B. (1997). *Islam in the African American Experience*. (Indianapolis: Indiana University Press, pp. 107–8.
9. Haddad & Smith, *Mission to America*, p. 82.
10. For more information on Wallace Fard, see Sodiq's *An Insider's Guide*, pp. 439–41.
11. Ibid, pp. 439–41.
12. Elijah Muhammad, *Message to the Blackman in America* (Chicago: Muhammad's Temple No. 2, 1965), pp. 53, 134.
13. McCloud, *African American Islam*, pp. 30–31.

14. Turner, *Islam in the African American Experience*, p. 208. See also Sodiq's *An Insider's Guide to Islam,* p. 453.

15. Sodiq, *An Insider's Guide to Islam,* p. 465. See also Larry Poston, *The Changing Face of Islam in America* (Penn, Camp Hill: Horizon Books, 2000, pp. 140–2).

16. For more information about Minister Louis Farrakhan and his role in the Nation of Islam, see Yushau Sodiq's article "Nation of Islam" in *Religion and Violence: An Encyclopedia of Faith and Conflict from Antiquity to the Present.* Edited by Jeffrey Ian Ross. (New York: M.E. Sharpe, Inc. 2011), pp. 488–493.

17. Barboza, Steven. (1993). *American Jihad: Islam after Malcolm X.* New York: Doubleday, p. 143.

18. McCloud, *African American Islam,* pp. 80–1.

19. For more information about the life and contributions of Malcolm X to African American's identity and to Islam in the United States, see Alex Haley, *The Autobiography of Malcolm X as told to by Alex Haley* (New York: The Random House Publishing Group, 1965). Many other books have been written on Malcolm X and his impact on African Americans.

20. Charles Mustafa Bilal is the first African American Muslim mayor in Kountze, Texas in 1991 in a city which is predominantly 70 percent white, and blacks only 22 percent.

21. Larry Shaw, an African American Muslim, became a Democratic State Senator in North Carolina in 2006. He did not change his name to a Muslim name.

22. Ibid, pp. 30–1.

23. Moore, Kathleen. (1991). "Muslims in Prison: Claims to Constitutional Protection of Religious Liberty," in *The Muslims of America,* ed., Yvonne Y. Haddad (New York: Oxford University Press, p. 138).

24. Ibid. p. 138. That Islam is a religion is expressed in the case of *Falwood v. Clemmer* as determined by the US District Court for the District of Columbia, 206 F. Sup. 370 (1962) at 373.

25. Keneth Ellison was elected as a US congressman from Minneapolis on November 7, 2006. He took the oath of office by using the Qur'an to prove his Islamic identity.

26. Johnson, Steve A. (1991). "Political Activity of Muslims in America," in *The Muslims of America,* edited by Yvonne Haddad (New York: Oxford University Press, pp. 111–24).

27. For more information on how Muslim organizations began to plan for participation in politics, see Steve A. Johnson's article above in *The Muslims of America,* pp. 111–24.

28. For more articulation on this topic, see Ali Mazrui's article, "On Being American and a Muslim: Dilemmas of Politics and Culture," as accessed on www.ispi-usa.org on May 29, 2012. In this article, Mazrui argues that Muslims in America face three crises: the crisis of identity, the crisis of participation and the crisis of values and code of conducts. He believes that these crises are interrelated in the real lives of the Muslims. He suggests how those crises can be addressed and possibly overcome.

29. For more information about this African group and their life in the United States, see Abdullah Zain, *Black Mecca: The African Muslims of Harlem* (Oxford: Oxford University Press, 2010).

30. The issue of Muslims converting to Christianity was not something new in Islam. In the early days of Islam when Muhammad sought refuge with King Negus of Ethiopia in 615 CE, one of the Muslims who left Mecca to Abyssinia became Christian in Ethiopia. His name is Ubaydullah bin Jahsh. The Prophet Muhammad did not issue any verdict against him and he remained Christian until he died. Other Muslims who were with him in Ethiopia also left him alone to follow his path. It is natural that wherever there is a freedom of religion, people convert from one tradition to another without persecution or humiliation.

31. Many Churches help African immigrants win their green-card and assist them in getting jobs and cheap accommodation through the church. Often, they provide assistance and scholarship for newcomers.

32. By assimilation, we mean acquisition of good English, adoption of US Citizen or Green Card, social interaction, intermarriage, and home ownership. These are things which will allow people to accept them as Americans.

33. For more information of this, see Amina McCloud on "Muslim in America: Identity and Participation." www.ispi-usa.org. Accessed on June 1, 2012.

34. Haddad & Esposito, *Muslims on the Americanization Path*, p. 21. See also, Imam Warithu Deen Muhammad, *Challenges that Face Man Today* (Chicago: W. D. Muhammad Publication, 1985).

35. Turner, Richard. *Islam in the African American Experience*, p. 231, quoting Farrakhan Interview, "Cliff Kelley Show," WGCI Radio Station, Chicago, IL, 1990.

36. It is very unfortunate that the biggest chains of West African foods are run by non-West African business men in the big cities of America: New York, Philadelphia, Dallas, Michigan, and other places.

37. See Jeff Strickler's article, "Smile, you're on security cameras like never before," in *Minneapolis Star Tribune*, June 19, 2012. (Scrippsnews). Strickler asserts that the government agents, the FBI, put cameras in nearly all the mosques in the USA to monitor who attends the mosques and who do not.

38. Lo, Mbaye. (2004). *Muslims in America: Race Politics, and Community Building.* Maryland: Amana Publication, p. 135.

39. Mohammad Muqtadar Khan in *Muslims on the Americanization Path*, pp. 96–7. See also Steven Barboza, *American Jihad: Islam after Malcolm X* (New York: Doubleday, 1993, pp. 19–24).

40. Barreto, Matt A. & and Dana, Karam. (2008). "Muslim and American: Transnational Ties and Participation in American Politics." Paper presented at MPSA Conference, Chicago, IL. in April 2008. This article discusses how Muslims from Arab and Asian countries participate more in American politics than any other Muslim immigrant group.

Contributors

Adeoluwa Okunade, PhD, is a senior lecturer at the Department of Music, University of Port Harcourt, Nigeria. He holds a PhD in African Studies with emphasis on African Music from the University of Ibadan. He has over 20 years of experience in the classroom across tertiary institutions in Nigeria and has read academic papers both locally and internationally.

Carolyn M. Jones Medine, PhD, is a professor in Religion and the Institute for African American Studies at the University of Georgia. Her research interests are in Arts and Literature, particularly in Southern and African American women's religious experience. She has written extensively on Toni Morrison, Harper Lee, and others. She is the coauthor, with John Randolph LeBlanc, of *Ancient and Modern Religion and Politics: Negotiating Transitive Spaces and Hybrid Identities* (2012) and the co-editor, with Theodore Trost, of *Teaching African American Religions* (2005).

Danielle N. Boaz, PhD, is an assistant professor in the Law, Politics, and Society Department at Drake University. Dr. Boaz received her PhD in African and African diaspora history from the University of Miami and her Juris Doctor with a concentration in International Law from the University of Toledo. She obtained her Master of Laws in Intercultural Human Rights from St. Thomas University School of Law. Dr. Boaz is also licensed to practice law in the state of Florida. She has published several articles and book chapters regarding cultural, religious, and linguistic rights in Africa and the African diaspora.

Francis Adewale Olajide, PhD, is professor of Philosophy with over three decades of teaching experience of postgraduate and undergraduate students in Nigeria and overseas universities. His readiness to establish the vitality and relevance of Philosophy on every aspect of human endeavor underscores his extensive and rewarding engagement with the banking, media, and publishing industries. A widely travelled motivational speaker; he is an adjunct faculty member of Liberty Kingdom Academy, Northampton, United Kingdom. Professor Wale Olajide presently teaches philosophy at the Ekiti State University, Ado-Ekiti, Nigeria.

Ibigbolade Simon Aderibigbe, PhD, is currently an associate professor of Religion and African Studies at the University of Georgia, Athens. He earned his BA in Philosophy and Religious Studies, MA and PhD in Religious Studies from the University of Ibadan, Ibadan, Nigeria. He also earned a diploma in Religious Studies at the SS Peter and Paul Catholic Major Seminary, Bodija, Ibadan, Nigeria.

Dr. Aderibigbe taught for many years at the Lagos State University, Ojo, Lagos, Nigeria. His main fields of instruction and research were Philosophy of Religion, African Religion, Phenomenology of Religion, Comparative Study of Religion, and Sociology of Religion. Currently, Aderibigbe's area of research interest is African Religion in Africa and African diaspora.

Kelvin Onongha, PhD, is an adjunct professor in the Seventh-day Adventist Theological Seminary, Andrews University, Michigan.

Martina Iyabo Oguntoyinbo-Atere, PhD, studied at the University of Ilorin, Kwara State, and University of Ibadan, Ibadan, Oyo State, Nigeria. She started her career at the University of Ibadan, where she taught for 11 years before she moved to Lagos State University, Lagos, Nigeria in 2006. She is a professor of New Testament Studies and the current Dean of the Faculty of Arts at Adeleke University, Ede, Osun State, Nigeria.

Maha Marouan, PhD, is Associate Professor of African Diaspora Studies in the departments of African American Studies and Women Studies Race Studies at Pennsylvania State University. Her research focuses on the intersection of race, gender, and religion in the construction of diaspora female subjectivities. She is the author of *Witches, Goddesses, and Angry Spirits: The Politics of Spiritual Liberation in African Diaspora Women's Fiction* (Ohio State University Press, 2013) and the co-editor of *Race and Displacement: Nation, Migration and Identity in the Twenty-First Century* (University of Alabama Press, 2013). Dr. Marouan is also the founder and chair of the African Diaspora Religions Group at the American Academy of Religion.

Melanie L. Harris, PhD, is associate professor of Religion and Ethics at Texas Christian University where she teaches in the areas of Womanist Ethics, Black Liberation Theology, Eco-Justice, Interfaith Dialogue, and African American Religious History. She is also a Black Church Studies and Environmental Justice Scholar in Residence with Green Faith, an interfaith collective of scholars and activist working for the environment Dr. Harris has authored numerous articles and books including "Gifts of Virtue: Alice Walker and Womanist Ethics" and is co-editor of the volume *Faith, Feminism, and Scholarship: The Next Generation*. Her research foregrounds the methods, and approaches that women of color, and especially African American women scholars, have contributed to the environmental justice movement

Oguntola Oye-Laguda, PhD, is a scholar of philosophy of religions. Dr. Oye-Laguda works as faculty at the Department of Religions and Peace Studies Lagos State University Lagos Nigeria. He is a member of American Academy of Religion (AAR). He has a particular interest in Yoruba philosophical thoughts and religion. He has published research works in reputable journals in Nigeria. Currently, he works at Lagos State University in the Department of Religions. He is putting the finishing touches to his thesis on Determinism and the activities of Esu in Yoruba Religion and Philosophy. Mr. Oye-Laguda is the secretary general of Nigerian Association for the Study of Religions.

Osei A. Menash, PhD, is currently interrelated Special Education teacher with Clarke County School District, Athens, Georgia. He received his doctoral degree in Religious Studies from University of South Africa in Pretoria. He also is Oracle Certified Database Administrator and Associate of Chartered Institute of Marketing, England. He has taught in secondary and tertiary institutions in Ghana, Nigeria, and South Africa. Before relocating to the United States, Dr. Menash taught Religious Studies and Social Studies Education at the University of Transkei (now Walter Sisulu University) in Umtata, South Africa. He is coauthor of *Digging Up Our Foremothers: Stories of Women in Africa* (Unisa Press: Pretoria) and *African Traditional and Oral Literature as Pedagogical Tools in Content Area Classrooms K-12* (Information Age Publishing: Charlotte, NC).

Pius Oyeniran Abioje, PhD, studied dogmatic/systematic theology in Rome and Calabar, respectively. He lectured in SS Peter and Paul Catholic Major Seminary, Ibadan, before joining University of Ilorin, where he is currently a senior lecturer in Afro-Christian theology.

Robert Yaw Owusu, PhD, is a member of the faculty at Southern Polytechnic State University, Marietta and Morehouse College in Atlanta, Georgia. Robert received his Master of Divinity from Boston University School of Theology, Master of Theology from Candler School of Theology of Emory University, and PhD in Church-State Studies from Baylor University, Waco, Texas, in 2003. Dr. Owusu, an ordained minister of the Ghana Baptist Convention, is also the church planter and senior pastor of Amazing Grace Baptist Church of Atlanta. He is the author of Kwame Nkrumah's *Liberation Thought: A Paradigm for Religious Advocate in Contemporary Ghana* (2006), co-author of *Exploration of World Religions* (January 2015), and has published some articles and book reviews.

Rotimi Williams Omotoye, PhD, is a professor in the Department of Religions at the University of Ilorin in Ilorin, Nigeria. He is the author of "The Study of African Traditional Religion and Its Challenges in Contemporary Times," in the *Ilorin Journal of Religious Studies* (2011); "The Use of African Traditional Medicine, Orthodox Medicine, and Christian Faith Healing in Yorubland, South Western Nigeria" in the *Ilorin Journal of Linguistics* (2103). He an editor for Science and Religion in the Service of Humanity.

R. Ibrahim Adebayo, PhD, teaches in the Department of Religions at the University of Ilorin in Nigeria. He is the author of "Ethno-Religious Crises and the Challenges of Sustainable Development" in the *Journal of Sustainable Development in Africa* (2010); "Ethical Principles of Islamic Financial Institutions," with Dr. M. Kabir Hassan (2013) and "Zakat and Poverty Alleviation: A Lesson for the Fiscal Policy Makers in Nigeria" (2011), both in the *Journal of Economic Cooperation and Development*.

Umesh Patel, MA, has completed degrees in Religion and Literature at the University of Georgia, Athens, and is currently working towards his PhD in American Studies through the Transnational Studies Department at the State University of New York in Buffalo.

Yushau Sodiq, PhD, is an associate professor of Religion and Islamic Studies at Texas Christian University, Fort Worth, since 1992. He specializes on Islamic Studies, Islamic Law, African religions and Islam in America. He taught at Virginia Commonwealth University, Richmond from 1990–1992 and was a lecturer at the Faculty of Law, University of Sokoto, Nigeria from 1980–1983. Dr. Sodiq has presented papers and participated in panels at numerous scholarly meetings and has provided Islamic legal and professional advice to Muslim communities in Philadelphia, Richmond, Fort Worth, Houston, and Dallas. He has also published articles in reputable journals and scholarly volumes. His latest book is *An Insider's Guide to Islam* (Indianapolis: Trafford Publishing Co., 2011).

Index